Health for Life

Karen E. McConnell
Pacific Lutheran University

Charles B. Corbin
Arizona State University

David E. Corbin
University of Nebraska at Omaha

Terri D. Farrar
Pacific Lutheran University

Human Kinetics

Library of Congress Cataloging-in-Publication Data

McConnell, Karen E., 1969-
    Health for life / Karen E. McConnell, Pacific Lutheran University, Charles B. Corbin, Arizona State University, David E. Corbin, University of Nebraska Omaha, Terri D. Farrar, Pacific Lutheran.
        pages cm.
    Includes index.
    1. High school students--Health and hygiene--United States--Textbooks. 2. Health education (Secondary)--United States--Textbooks. I. Title.
    LB3409.U5M38 2014
    373.18--dc23
                                2013043035

ISBN: 978-1-4925-0052-0 (soft cover)
ISBN: 978-1-4504-3493-5 (hard cover)

The web addresses cited in this text were current as of November 2013, unless otherwise noted.

Acquisitions Editor: Scott Wikgren; **Developmental Editor:** Melissa Feld; **Assistant Editor:** Rachel Fowler; **Copyeditor:** Tom Tiller; **Indexer:** Nancy Ball; **Permissions Manager:** Dalene Reeder; **Graphic Designer:** Nancy Rasmus; **Graphic Artist:** Nancy Rasmus; **Cover Designer:** Keith Blomberg; **Photographs (front and back covers):** © Human Kinetics, © Richard Levine/age fotostock; **Photographs (interior):** ©; Human Kinetics, unless otherwise noted; **Photographs in Illustrations:** Upper left photo in figure 6.2 and photo on right in figure 14.2: PhotoDisc/Barbara Penoyar; lower right photo in figure 6.2 and photo on left in figure 14.2: PhotoDisc/Kevin Peterson; first and second photos in figure 13.1: Photodisc; third photo in figure 13.1: © Shannon Fagan | Dreamstime.com; fourth photo in figure 13.1: Photodisc/Getty Images; photo in figure 14.3: Suprijono Suharjoto/fotolia.com; photo on right in figure 14.4: iStockphoto/Eduardo Jose Bernardino; photo on right in figure 14.5: Monkey Business/fotolia.com; photo on right in figure 20.2: PhotoDisc; **Photo Asset Manager:** Laura Fitch; **Visual Production Assistant:** Joyce Brumfield; **Photo Production Manager:** Jason Allen; **Art Manager:** Kelly Hendren; **Associate Art Manager:** Alan L. Wilborn; **Art Style Development:** Joanne Brummett; **Illustrations:** © Human Kinetics, unless otherwise noted; **Printer:** Courier Companies, Inc.

We wish to thank the *Health for Life* editorial board: Kathryn Coffey, Lonnie Halusic, and Georgi Roberts (reviewers).

Printed in the United States of America

10 9 8 7 6 5 4 3 2 1

The paper in this book was manufactured using responsible forestry methods.

Human Kinetics
Website: www.HumanKinetics.com
United States: Human Kinetics
P.O. Box 5076
Champaign, IL 61825-5076
800-747-4457
e-mail: humank@hkusa.com

Canada: Human Kinetics
475 Devonshire Road Unit 100
Windsor, ON N8Y 2L5
800-465-7301 (in Canada only)
e-mail: info@hkcanada.com

Europe: Human Kinetics
107 Bradford Road
Stanningley
Leeds LS28 6AT, United Kingdom
+44 (0) 113 255 5665
e-mail: hk@hkeurope.com

Australia: Human Kinetics
57A Price Avenue
Lower Mitcham, South Australia 5062
08 8372 0999
e-mail: info@hkaustralia.com

New Zealand: Human Kinetics
P.O. Box 80
Torrens Park, South Australia 5062
0800 222 062
e-mail: info@hknewzealand.com

E5792

Contents

UNIT III   Embracing Priority Lifestyles

UNIT VI Creating Healthy and Safe Communities

Touring *Health for Life*

Do you want to be healthy and well? Do you want to look your best and feel good? In this book, you'll study all aspects of health, including wellness. You'll see that, although your health and wellness are not totally under your control, the choices you make and the way you live can make a big difference in both your health and your wellness. By learning about the skills for healthy living and assessing your current health status you'll be able to develop a plan for healthy living to either maintain or improve your healthy behaviors. Two lessons are included in each chapter to help you learn key concepts relating to health and wellness. *Health for Life* will help you meet your fitness and physical activity goals. Take this guided tour to learn about all of the features of this textbook.

In addition to the following features, the Health for Life program includes several other components:

- **Student Web Resource.** You have access to a wide variety of resources at www.healthforlifetextbook.org/student. These resources will aid your understanding of the textbook content and include worksheets, interactive review questions, vocabulary pop-ups, and expanded discussions of topics that are marked by web icons throughout this book.

- **Teacher Web Resource.** Your teacher has access to a special web resource with lessons and activities that you can do to better learn and understand the information in this textbook.

Monkey Business

Monkey Business

UNIT OPENER: Provides a brief overview of the content in each unit.

UNIT I

Understanding Health and Wellness

HEALTHY PEOPLE 2020 GOALS: Lists national health goals covered in each unit.

Healthy People 2020 Goals
- Help people live high-quality, longer lives.
- Reduce preventable disease, injury, and early death.
- Increase awareness and understanding of what determines good health.
- Help people adopt a healthy lifestyle in order to achieve lifetime health, fitness, and wellness.
- Create environments that promote health, fitness, and wellness for all.
- Increase health literacy.
- Live high-quality, longer lives free of preventable diseases, injury, and early death.
- Increase the percentage of people who receive risk factor information.

Self-Assessment Features in This Unit
- The Wellness Questionnaire
- Stages of Health Behavior
- Healthy Living Skills

Making Healthy Decis[...]
- Self-Assessment
- Goal Setting
- Self-Planning

Special Features in Th[...]
- Diverse Perspectives:
- Consumer Corner: D[...]
- Advocacy in Action:

Living Well News Fea[...]
- The State of Youth H[...]
- Do the Rich Get to [...]
- Can You Make a Co[...]

STUDENT WEB RESOURCES: Provides the web addresses for finding additional information in each lesson.

FEATURES: Lists the Self-Assessment, Making Healthy Decisions, Skills for Healthy Living, Living Well News, and special features in each unit.

2

Health Behavior Change and Personal Health

In This Chapter

LESSON 2.1
Personal Health and Wellness

SELF-ASSESSMENT
Stages of Health Behavior

LESSON 2.2
Changing Health Behaviors

MAKING HEALTHY DECISIONS
Goal Setting

SKILLS FOR HEALTHY LIVING
Goal Setting

(www) **Student Web Resources**
www.healthforlifetextbook.org/student

CHAPTER OPENER: Provides a brief overview of the content of the chapter.

IN THIS CHAPTER: Lists the main elements of each chapter.

WEB ICONS: Indicate that additional information is available on the student website.

LESSON VOCABULARY: Lists key terms in each lesson, which are defined in the glossary and on the student website.

DIVERSE PERSPECTIVES: Helps you understand another's point of view.

CONNECT: Asks you to reflect on family, peer, media, or technology influences related to a specific topic in a chapter.

CONSUMER CORNER: Helps you to become a good consumer of health and wellness information and to avoid quackery.

Lesson 14.2
Aging Well

Lesson Objectives

After reading this lesson, you should be able to
1. identify the benefits of regular physical activity during the aging process,
2. understand how aging affects dietary needs and preferences, and
3. identify common sources of stress for aging individuals.

Lesson Vocabulary

activities of daily living, chronological age, physiological age

We're all growing older every day, but aging is a slow process that affects each of us differently. As a result, it is somewhat subjective. Most young people consider anyone who is 10 to 20 years older than themselves to be old, and many people over 60 still think of themselves as young and vital. In reality, decisions you make now can affect the aging process that you'll experience decades from now. For example, eating a balanced diet and doing weight-bearing exercises can help you develop strong bones that protect you from osteoporosis later in life and keep you safe if you fall or have a traumatic accident.

Conversely, if you choose, for example, to start smoking at a young age, you can accelerate the aging process of your skin and organs, making you look and feel older. You can also begin a slow process of damaging your lungs in a way that results in cancer 20 years down the road.

This lesson explores some of the ways in which aging is affected by healthy lifestyles choices and how the aging process affects healthy lifestyle recommendations.

Middle and Older Adulthood

The fifth and sixth stages of the life span are middle and older adulthood. At these stages, it is important to maintain emotional and physical health. Managing stress is also an important factor at this age, too. Adults have more care and support responsibilities for themselves, children not quite on their own, or parents in older generations. There can be changes in oneself with new career and personal goals or in a relationship with children moving out of the

DIVERSE PERSPECTIVES: Being an Older Parent

Our names are Madeline and Steve. We are both almost 60, and we have a son in high school and a daughter in junior high school. We met at work when we were both in our 30s and got married at almost age 40. Both of us wanted children earlier in life but had been committed to our careers; we also wanted to spend the first few years of our marriage traveling.

Having children in our mid-40s was difficult physically—we didn't have as much energy as

we'd once had. But we've both noticed that we don't seem to get as stressed out about parenting as younger

---

LESSON OBJECTIVES: Describes what you will learn in each lesson.

HEALTH TECHNOLOGY: Helps you become aware of new technological information related to health and wellness.

Nongovernmental Organizations

Many private organizations are also invested in public health. They include charitable and religious organizations and private for-profit organizations. Well-known examples are the American Heart Association, the American Cancer Society, and the American Diabetes Association. Smaller organizations—such as community centers, churches, and local nonprofit agencies—are also involved in public health efforts. For example, they operate food banks

CONNECT

Is there a food bank in your community? Is there a homeless shelter? What are two ways that a food bank or homeless shelter can help the community it serves? What is one thing you could do to support a food bank or shelter this year?

CONSUMER CORNER: Donating to Ch

One great way to support a community and develop an altruistic (giving) attitude is to make a financial donation to a charity that supports a cause you find meaningful. Unfortunately, we live in a world where some people take advantage of others' generous hearts by organizing scams and committing fraud. Use the following guidelines to help you determine whether a charity is legitimate and worthy of your donation. Be suspicious of any charity that

- fails to provide detailed information about its identity, mission, costs, and planned use of your donation;
- refuses to provide proof that a contribution is tax deductible;
- uses a name closely resembling the name of a better-known, reputable organization (this could be a sign that someone is trying to trick you);
- thanks you for a pledge you don't recall making, then asks you to consider giving more;

- uses high
  to get you
- asks for do
  wire money
  multiple for
  credit card,
- offers to com
  diately; or
- guarantees
  exchange for a contribution (by law, you never have to give a donation to be eligible to win a sweepstakes).

Consumer Challenge

Identify three charities of your choosing and visit their websites. Look for information about mission, costs, planned uses of the donations, tax status, and donation methods. Evaluate the charities using the information you gather and determine your willingness to contribute to each cause based on what you learn.

and
hon
by p
tion

Public
on the
ondary,
preventi
risk and
efforts to
Secondary
for (or beg
before serio
is an educati
who engage
young people
avoid becomi

❤ HEALTH TECHNOLOGY

An application, or app, is a computer program that allows you to perform tasks on a smartphone or other device. Some apps are designed to help you use skills for healthy living—for example, by self-assessing your food content, self-monitoring your physical activity, or planning healthy meals. If well designed, apps can help you change your health behaviors, but not all apps are based on good health information. Before using an app, determine whether the people who developed it are health experts; ask people you know and trust about the app, and test it out for yourself. For more information about health-related apps, see the student section of the Health for Life website.

CONNECT

Do you currently use any apps to help you live a healthier life? If so, what features do you think make a good health application? If not, what type of app might appeal to you? Can you imagine using a health app in the future?

Self-help skills such as practicing good personal health habits like flossing and tooth brushing help you to be healthy and well.

Comprehension Check

1. What is the meaning of the term skills for healthy living?
2. List each of the skills for healthy living and explain one of them in more detail.
3. Explain how the skills for healthy living can help you be healthy and well.

44

COMPREHENSION CHECK: Helps you review and remember the information you learned in the lesson.

ADVOCACY IN ACTION: Provides you with personal, school, or community advocacy challenges.

SELF-ASSESSMENT: Helps you evaluate and reflect on your personal health habits related to a wide variety of behaviors, which can help you to prepare a plan for healthy living.

HEALTH SCIENCE: Focuses on the role of science in health and allows for cross-disciplinary learning and exploration.

HEALTHY COMMUNICATION: Uses your interpersonal communication skills in order to share your health knowledge, debate controversial topics, or promote healthy living among your peers.

HEALTH QUOTES: Provide quotes from famous people about health and wellness.

ADVOCACY IN ACTION: Promoting Recycling

Not surprisingly, people are more likely to recycle when appropriate recycling bins are readily available. Evaluate your school to determine whether an *effective* recycling program is in place.

If your school doesn't provide recycling bins or lacks some needed options (e.g., paper, plastic, refuse, glass), determine what bins the school should add and what company or community organization will recycle the materials. You can even create a map showing where recycling bins

should be located. Then write a one-page letter to the school board advocating for the purchase and appropriate placement of the needed recycling bins. Include information about the four Rs and explain why recycling is important for both environmental and personal health.

If your school already has adequate recycling bins, create posters to place above the bins that explain their importance and encourage students, teachers, and staff members to use them regularly.

SELF-ASSESSMENT: How Healthy Is My School Community?

Your school is an important community to which you belong. This assessment asks you to think about aspects of a healthy school community and consider your connection to your school. Answer each question by circling the proper

response, then add up the total number of points as directed in the assessment. You may need to ask a teacher or school staff member for help in answering some of the questions in parts 1 and 2.

	Yes (2 points)	No (0 points)
Part 1: Health and safety		
My school . . .		
has a no tolerance policy for harassment or bullying.	2	0
has emergency plans, like evacuation routes, in place.	2	0
has active supervision in place to ensure safety and reduce violence.	2	0
is a safe physical environment.	2	0
does not allow smoking on campus.	2	0
is kept clean and bright.	2	0
provides help to those who want to quit smoking.	2	0
has at least one full-time nurse on campus.	2	0
provides counseling and mental health services.	2	0
Part 2: Nutrition and physical activity		
My school . . .		
requires students to take physical education.	2	0
provides physical activities after school.	2	0
requires students to take health education.	2	0
promotes healthy food and beverage choices.	2	0
provides healthy and low-fat food.	2	0
has a clean and pleasant cafeteria.		
Total points from parts 1 and 2: _____		

The higher the score, the healthier and safer the school community.

Part 3: My school engagement

| As a member of my school, I . . . | 2 | 0 |
| am involved in at least one club or organization at school. | 2 | 0 |

HEALTH SCIENCE

Malaria was eliminated in the United States by a concerted effort made from 1947 to 1951, yet somewhere in the world a child dies from malaria every 30 seconds. In Africa, one in every five childhood deaths is attributed to malaria. Poorer individuals are at highest risk because their homes and dwellings provide little protection from infected mosquitoes. They can't afford preventive medication or, if symptoms arise, medical care. The elimination of malaria in the United States was aided by spraying homes with mosquito-killing insecticides, spraying insecticides over large land areas, and removing mosquito nesting sites. In addition, U.S. residents have access to medicine that helps prevent and treat malaria.

The advances in chemical and medical science that contributed to effective insecticides and medications are certainly not new, yet malaria remains a global threat. This disparity illustrates

the fact that even when science can solve a particular health problem, challenges may still exist in distributing the solution to those most in need. In addition, many developing countries have little in the way of organized public health services, and citizens often have no education or awareness of options that might exist. Therefore, humanitarians and scientists must often work together to make the greatest gains in global public health.

of exercise, much of the world faces very different public health issues, and the biggest challenge in global public health is poverty.

Countries with a poor economy and low standards of living are sometimes referred to as **developing nations**, and these are the places where the majority of the world's people live. These countries often face particularly intense public health problems, including malnutrition and widespread disease (e.g., malaria, AIDS). As a result, major global health initiatives are focused on bringing vaccinations, antibiotics, safe water, and sustainable farming techniques to developing countries.

Another key effort focuses on creating educational opportunities for more children around the world. Access to education is considered a primary way to end the cycle of poverty and improve global public health. It opens doors for employment, which can bring individual freedom as well as

opportunities for acquiring healthier food, safer living conditions, and higher-quality health care.

HEALTHY COMMUNICATION

If you had US$1,000 to donate to a group addressing a serious health problem, what would it be? Why? Would you choose to support a cause in the United States or donate to a group addressing a global health issue? Why? Share your response with a group of classmates or peers.

> Of all the forms of inequality, injustice in health care is the most shocking and inhumane. ">"
>
> —Martin Luther King, Jr.

Comprehension Check

1. What types of organization serve the public health in the United States? Provide three specific examples.
2. What are the three levels of prevention addressed by public health services? Which are the most effective in improving public health?
3. What is the difference between the prevalence and the incidence of a disease?

MAKING HEALTHY DECISIONS:
Asks you to apply the identified skill to evaluate potential solutions to the problems posed in the scenario.

 MAKING HEALTHY DECISIONS: Time Management

Alexis was one of those people who was always going from one commitment to the next. Her friends rarely saw her sitting still, and she often complained about having too much to do. Alexis played on the softball team and volunteered at her church on the weekends. She also helped out around the house with cleaning and cooking. When her friend Deborah asked her to go to yoga class together as a way to manage stress, she said, "I totally want to—it would be really great—but I just don't have any free time." Later in the conversation, Deborah noticed Alexis talking about TV shows she'd been watching and showing off a new video

game she'd been playing. Deborah wondered if Alexis was as busy as she seemed to be. Deborah herself worked two jobs, was an honor student, ran cross country, and played in the school orchestra.

For Discussion

What could Deborah suggest that Alexis do to make time for yoga class? What could Deborah say to Alexis that might help her better understand her time management needs? To help you answer these questions, review this chapter's Skills for Healthy Living feature.

SKILLS FOR HEALTHY LIVING:
Provides guidelines for learning skills for healthy living that help you adopt healthy behaviors.

 SKILLS FOR HEALTHY LIVING: Time Management

How you manage your time is an important part of your overall health. If you struggle with time management, you may have higher levels of stress and you may end up coping with your stress by engaging in destructive habits that seem to provide quick fixes, such as smoking or drinking alcohol. Poor time management can also interfere with your ability to create time for healthy pursuits, such as exercise.

Young people, like adults, often tend to book their schedules solid with work, school, errands, and other tasks they deem important. For example, you may be involved in a community organization, spend time tending to a school garden, play a sport, or care for an aging relative. The time you spend doing all of these activities is referred to as your committed time. What's left over is your free time. Learning to manage your free time can help you manage stress, avoid destructive habits, and make time for healthy habits. The following tips can help you with your time management:

- **Monitor your time.** Write down what you do during the course of each day. Record when you sleep, when you eat, when you're at school, when you're at work, and when you do all of the other things you do. Most people who track their use of time are surprised by the findings.
- **Evaluate your use of time.** Once you've tracked your time for several days, review

your records to see how many hours you spend in various types of activities. For example, you can arrange all your activities into three categories: school and work, committed time, and free time. Then you can evaluate whether there is a good balance between the categories. Alternatively, you can think of all of your activities as fitting into three drawers: the lower drawer (not important or urgent), the middle drawer (important but not urgent), and the top drawer (urgent and important). If any drawer is overflowing, you may need to re-evaluate your commitments and priorities. Evaluating your time can help you decide whether you're using your time the way you want and need to use it. Having a lot of important and urgent things to do can add to your stress levels significantly.

- **Plan a schedule.** After you determine how much time you spend on various activities, work on creating a time management plan for yourself. Efficient time management means you get to do all the things you think are important so that you don't feel rushed or anxious, and it also allows you to make time for those things that you value, such as relaxation and recreational activities. Begin by blocking out your committed time (school, work, practice time). Then, make decisions about your free time.

that are important to you but may not be as urgent. Plan ahead and schedule in the time you need along the way. Most important, follow through with your plan so that you don't end up in a bind.
  ○ Third, schedule in and plan time for yourself to do the things that you value (even when they don't seem

important or urgent), such as exercising, reading a novel, or playing a musical instrument. Ensuring you are balanced and have the opportunities to relax and recover from the demands of life is critical to overall health. Often people do not take the time for these important activities unless they plan for them. It is also important to ensure that these activities do not interfere with obligations such as schoolwork.
  ○ Finally, schedule some time every day for the unexpected. Meetings, appointments, and practices can run late, unexpected opportunities can arise, or other scheduled tasks can take longer than expected. Allowing some flexibility in each day can help you adjust your schedule to adapt to changing demands.

ACADEMIC CONNECTION:
Relates concepts from other academic subject areas to health and wellness.

ACADEMIC CONNECTION: College and Career Skills

Being able to respond to precise instructions is an important skill for college and career readiness. For example, if you were asked to *analyze* how physical activity contributes to overall health, would you know how to respond? Would you be confident in your ability to *compare* carbohydrate and protein? What about your ability to *contrast* them? Each of these is different, and you must first understand what is being asked before you can accurately respond. The following are some of the most valuable skills for successful college admissions (performance on standardized tests like the SAT or ACT as well as for writing college admissions essays) and job performance.

- *Analyze:* Explain how each part functions or fits into the whole. For example, how does each type of physical activity (see the Physical Activity Pyramid) affect each component of health?
- *Persuade:* Take a stand on one side of an issue and convince others of the validity of that stance. Use facts, statistics, beliefs,

opinions, and your personal view. Showing passion for your point of view can help you be persuasive.

- *Compare:* Find the common characteristics between two things. For example, carbohydrate and protein are both energy-yielding nutrients, and both contain 4 calories per gram.
- *Contrast:* Identify how people, events, or objects are different from one another. For example, carbohydrate is primarily used as fuel for the body, whereas protein is primarily used to build and repair tissues in the body.
- *Describe:* Present a clear picture of a person, place, thing, or idea. Try to write or speak so that the reader or listener could accurately visualize what you are saying.
- *Summarize:* State the meaning in a concise way (e.g., describe each of the factors that lead to teen stress and explain the relative importance of each).

LIVING WELL NEWS: Provides an article to test your health-literacy skills.

LIVING WELL NEWS, ISSUE 14

Does a High-Carbohydrate Diet Contribute to Mild Cognitive Impairment?

Most adults have considered the possibility of dying from heart disease or cancer. We're all familiar with the fact that these diseases are among the most common causes of death. At the same time, Alzheimer's disease is contributing to more deaths each year (see figure 14.6). In fact, Alzheimer's affects 5.2 million adults in the United States, and that number is expected to triple by 2050. While we know that eating a diet lower in saturated fat may help us hold off heart disease or cancer, what do we know about how diet affects the risk of Alzheimer's?

Seeking to answer this question, Mayo Clinic researchers tracked the eating habits of 1,230 people between the ages of 70 and 89 for one year. Next, the 940 people who showed no sign of cognitive impairment were asked to return for a 15-month follow-up. By the study's fourth year, 200 of those 940 people were beginning to show mild cognitive impairment (MCI), which can include problems with memory, language, thinking, and judgment.

People with the highest carbohydrate intake were nearly twice as likely to develop MCI as people who ate a balanced diet.

"Not everyone with MCI goes on to develop Alzheimer's disease, but many do," says Professor Rosebud Roberts, a researcher in Mayo's epidemiology division in Rochester, Minnesota. "A high-carbohydrate intake could be bad for you because carbohydrates impact your glucose and insulin metabolism."

Since sugar fuels the brain, a moderate amount is essential. However, high levels of sugar may actually interfere with the brain's ability to use the sugar for fuel. Roberts says high glucose levels might affect the brain's blood vessels and also play a role in the development of plaques in the brain that interfere with normal neural functioning. "Those proteins are toxic to brain health and are found in the brains of people with Alzheimer's," states Roberts.

The study found that people whose diets had the highest intake of protein (e.g., from chicken, meat, or fish) reduced their risk of cognitive impairment by 21 percent. Those whose diets were highest in fat (e.g., from nuts or health[...] less likely to have cog[...] DeMarzo[...] Cancer S[...] show th[...] preventi[...] diet pro[...] heart di[...]

Do you[...] diseas[...] reduce[...] increa[...] diseas[...]

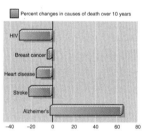

☐ Percent changes in causes of death over 10 years

HIV
Breast cancer
Heart disease
Stroke
Alzheimer's

-40 -20   0   20   40   60   80

Figure 14.6 Recent changes in death rates. Alzheimer's has greatly increased while the others have decreased.

CHAPTER REVIEW: Helps you reinforce what you've learned in the chapter's two lessons.

CHAPTER REVIEW

Reviewing Concepts and Vocabulary

As directed by your teacher, answer items 1 through 5 by correctly completing each sentence with a word or phrase.

1. Changes in motor skills, perception, and hearing are a normal part of _____ development.
2. The acquisition and development of skills such as language, problem solving, and reasoning are part of _____ development.
3. Periods of relatively rapid growth called _____ _____ can cause aches and pains as well as muscle cramps.
4. Bathing, preparing food, eating, and dressing are examples of _____.
5. Regular exercise has been shown to play a role in reducing the risk of _____, which is the leading cause of disability among people over the age of 80.

For items 6 through 10, as directed by your teacher, match each term in column 1 with the appropriate phrase in column 2.

6. abstract thinking
7. reasoning skills
8. socioemotional development
9. chronological age
10. physiological age

a. the way you solve problems and make decisions
b. the number of years you have been alive
c. includes self-esteem, empathy, and friendships
d. how well your body systems are aging
e. the ability to consider things that are not visible, immediate, or concrete

For items 11 through 15, as directed by your teacher, respond to each statement or question.

11. What is socioemotional development?
12. What are two things you should never do when caring for an infant?
13. Describe two health careers that might interest you.
14. Why might young adulthood be a stressful time? Provide two reasons.
15. Define *intrinsic motivation* and give an example.

THINKING CRITICALLY: Requires the use of critical-thinking skills to apply chapter information.

Thinking Critically

Write a response to the following prompt.

List and discuss the major physical and mental changes that occur with aging. Which ones can you affect through your own choices? What changes can you begin to make now to help you age well? Write a letter to yourself as you are now, and another letter to yourself at age 65, to remind yourself of these changes and motivate yourself to make healthy choices.

TAKE IT HOME: Provides an enrichment activity for use outside the classroom.

Take It Home

Think of a person you know and respect who is older than 65—for example, a parent, grandparent, neighbor, or family friend. Interview the person about his or her life. Find out what challenges the person faces and what steps he or she takes to try to overcome them. Ask the person what advice he or she has for you about staying healthy as you age. Write a brief report about what you learn.

282

UNIT I

Understanding Health and Wellness

● ● ● ● ● ● ● ● ● ● ●

Healthy People 2020 Goals
- Help people live high-quality, longer lives.
- Reduce preventable disease, injury, and early death.
- Increase awareness and understanding of what determines good health.
- Help people adopt a healthy lifestyle in order to achieve lifetime health, fitness, and wellness.
- Create environments that promote health, fitness, and wellness for all.
- Increase health literacy.
- Live high-quality, longer lives free of preventable diseases, injury, and early death.
- Increase the percentage of people who receive risk factor information.

Self-Assessment Features in This Unit
- The Wellness Questionnaire
- Stages of Health Behavior
- Healthy Living Skills

Making Healthy Decisions and Skills for Healthy Living Features in This Unit
- Self-Assessment
- Goal Setting
- Self-Planning

Special Features in This Unit
- Diverse Perspectives: Living With a Disability
- Consumer Corner: Don't Be Outsmarted! Finding High-Quality Health Information
- Advocacy in Action: Positive Attitudes

Living Well News Features in This Unit
- The State of Youth Health
- Do the Rich Get to Be Healthier?
- Can You Make a Contract for Good Health?

1

Introduction to Health and Wellness

In This Chapter

 Student Web Resources
www.healthforlifetextbook.org/student

Franz Pfluegl/fotolia.com

Lesson 1.1
• • • • • • • •
Health and Wellness

Lesson Objectives

After reading this lesson, you should be able to

1. define health and wellness and explain how they are related,
2. describe the five components of health and wellness and how they are related, and
3. answer common questions about health and wellness.

Lesson Vocabulary

health, *Healthy People 2020*, public health scientist, wellness, World Health Organization (WHO)

A large crowd was assembled to hear Dr. Lazarus, a **public health scientist**, discuss national health objectives. The title of her talk was "Health Is More Than Not Being Sick." She indicated that one major health objective "is to help all people live high-quality, longer lives." As the title of her talk suggests, Dr. Lazarus pointed out that **health** is more than freedom from disease; it also includes being *well* and enjoying a high quality of life. She emphasized that how you live your life can help you achieve both longer life and a higher quality of life.

Maggie, a first-year high school student, attended the talk with some of her friends because her mother was one of the organizers. Her grandfather and some of his friends also attended. After the talk, one of Maggie's friends said, "That was interesting, but why tell me about it? I don't have any health problems!" At the same time, Maggie's grandfather was

saying half-jokingly to some of his friends, "That's good information, but why tell it to us old-timers? They need to talk to those kids while they still have a chance to prevent health problems!"

In this book, you'll study all aspects of health, including **wellness**. You'll see that, although your health and wellness are not totally under your control, the choices you make and the way you live can make a big difference in both your health and your wellness—no matter what your age. In fact, it's never too soon or too late to learn more. This particular lesson defines health and wellness and describes their various components.

Moving From Illness to Wellness

On the way home from Dr. Lazarus' talk, Maggie, her mother, and her grandfather talked about health and wellness. "When I was a kid," said her grandfather, "we worried about polio and measles. We were more concerned about not getting sick than being well. But I can see that things have changed since then."

He's right. Prior to the 1940s, the leading causes of death in the U.S. were infectious diseases such as pneumonia, smallpox, and, as Maggie's grandfather recalled, polio. People also often died at younger ages than they do today. For example, a person born in 1900 had an average life expectancy of 47 years. Since the 1940s, however, life expectancy has been greatly increased by advancements in medical science (such as antibiotics, vaccines, and improved surgical techniques), improved public health practices

Health and wellness are important to people of all ages.

HEALTH SCIENCE

Every 10 years, scientists from more than 400 organizations work together to develop national health objectives for the United States. The most recent goals are included in a document called *Healthy People 2020*, which, as its name suggests, identifies health goals to be accomplished by the year 2020. Public health scientists and other experts from all U.S. states, federal agencies such as the Centers for Disease Control and Prevention (CDC), and other public and private agencies developed the goals. They identify health objectives for all age groups, including teens.

The *Healthy People 2020* goals help health agencies and organizations prioritize their work. They also help teachers and schools plan what is taught in health classes and what types of health-related services to provide. In this book, key *Healthy People 2020* objectives are included on the opening page of each unit. Review these objectives to help you understand how the material you learn in this class relates to U.S. health goals. You can find more information about *Healthy People 2020* and various health organizations in the student section of the Health for Life website.

(such as improved water and disposal of waste), and lifestyle changes (such as reduced tobacco use). As a result, a baby born today has an average life expectancy of about 80 years.

In 1947, the **World Health Organization (WHO)** issued a statement proclaiming that good health is not merely the absence of disease or illness; rather, it is a more complete state of being that includes wellness. Wellness is the *positive* aspect of health that includes having a good quality of life and a good sense of well-being as exhibited by a positive outlook on life.

The fact that good health includes wellness is illustrated in figure 1.1. The blue in the circle represents freedom from disease and illness, and the green in the circle represents wellness (quality of life). Illness is the negative aspect of health that we want to treat or prevent, and wellness is the positive aspect of health that we want to promote.

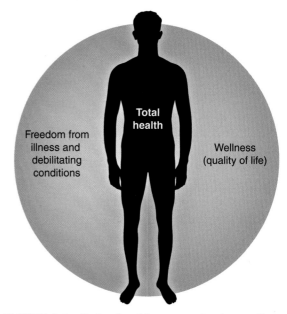

FIGURE 1.1 Being healthy means having wellness in addition to not being ill.

The Components of Health and Wellness

There are five components of health and wellness: intellectual, social, physical, emotional, and spiritual. The goal for each component of good health and wellness is to promote the positive while avoiding the negative (see figure 1.2). Look at the positive aspects at the top of the figure and negative aspects at the bottom. If you're informed, involved, fit, happy, and fulfilled, you've incorporated the positive aspects of the health components into your life. Thus you possess wellness, and your risk of illness is decreased.

 The part can never be well unless the whole is well.

—Plato, Greek philosopher

Each of the five components of health and wellness is associated with all of the others. This interrelationship is often illustrated in the form of a chain (see figure 1.2). The chain can be no stronger than its weakest link. In addition, each link, or component, interacts with the others; in other words, if you change one component in a positive way, it strengthens all of the others. On the other hand, if one deteriorates, it weakens all of the others. Therefore, for your health and wellness chain to be strong, you must focus not just on one component but on all of them.

Answering Health and Wellness Questions

During Dr. Lazarus' talk, she defined health and wellness as described in the preceding pages. Still, after the talk, many people had questions. Each question is included here, along with Dr. Lazarus' answers.

Question: Are there degrees of health and wellness?
Answer: Yes. There are different levels of health and wellness. A person who has a serious illness is different from a person who has a minor illness or who has risks for illness such as high blood pressure or high blood fat. In the same way, a person who has a high level of wellness has more positive components than a person who possesses less wellness.

Question: Can you be sick and still have wellness?
Answer: Yes. A person who has wellness is happy, fit, fulfilled, informed, and involved. A person can have a treatable disease, such as diabetes or cancer, and possess all of the components of wellness. In fact, research has shown that healthy lifestyle choices—such as eating well and doing regular physical activity—can help you reduce disease symptoms and risks while also contributing to a high quality of life.

Question: Can you be free of illness and not have good wellness?
Answer: Yes. Some people are not sick, meaning that they do not have a specific disease or illness, but also are not happy, fit, fulfilled, involved, and informed. Thus they are not well. Of course, optimal health includes wellness, so people who do not have good wellness do not have optimal health.

Question: Can you have good health and wellness if you have a disability?
Answer: Yes. Having a disability is an impairment that affects one's ability to perform certain typical functions. Most experts are quick to point out that having a disability does not necessarily mean that a person is handicapped. A disability can be associated with any health or wellness component. It may limit a person's ability to perform some of life's tasks, but good health— including wellness—can be present in people with a disability who also have a positive outlook on life.

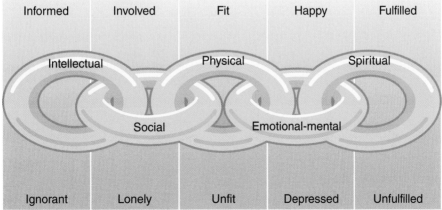

FIGURE 1.2 The total health and wellness chain.

Question: How do personal health and wellness goals differ from the national health goals described in *Healthy People 2020*?

Answer: The *Healthy People 2020* objectives are commonly referred to as goals for the community or for society. Personal health and wellness objectives are goals that each person sets to help his or her own health and wellness. National objectives help individuals set personal goals and are achieved when many individuals improve their health and wellness. For example, over the years, one national objective in the United States has been to reduce tobacco use. This national priority led to changes in public policy that encouraged people to change their personal behavior. Changes by many people over the past 20 years have resulted in better health for many individuals and improved national health.

Question: What about vocational (job-related) and environmental health and wellness? Why are they not included as components of health and wellness?

Answer: Health and wellness are personal states of being. Vocational and environment factors are very important to health and wellness, but they are not personal characteristics. Your job (vocation) and the environment (your surroundings) affect your health and wellness, so they are considered to be *determinants* of personal health and wellness rather than personal *chara cteristics* (health and wellness components).

In this lesson, you've learned about health and wellness and how they are defined. In the next lesson, you'll learn more about factors that determine health and wellness.

bilderbox/fotolia.com

DIVERSE PERSPECTIVES: Living With a Disability

Hi, my name is Travis. When I was 18, I was severely injured playing competitive ice hockey. My injury was to my spine. I have no sensation below my waist. I depend a lot on the care of others when it comes to meeting my basic daily needs. Sometimes I feel like I am a real burden on others. I think that is one of the hardest parts about having a disability like mine. But I am grateful that I still have my mind, that I'm not on a ventilator, that I have family around to support me. Sometimes I wish I could drive, that my level of injury was lower and that I had more physical movement, but I rarely ever think of those things. As the saying goes, my glass is always half-full . . . and I mostly try to think my glass is full. I know this sounds funny, but my life is full and busy. I started a foundation that raises money for spinal cord research and provides help to others in need. It isn't the life I imagined for myself when I was young, but I am proud of who I am now and what I've become.

Comprehension Check

1. Describe a hypothetical person who has good health, including good wellness.
2. List and describe the five components of health and wellness.
3. Identify and answer some often-asked questions about health and wellness.

SELF-ASSESSMENT: The Wellness Questionnaire

You've now learned about wellness and its several components. The Wellness Questionnaire will help you self-assess *your* current wellness. Use the following instructions.

1. Read each statement about wellness. Select one response for each statement. You can strongly agree, agree, disagree, or strongly disagree with each statement.
2. Record your responses as directed by your teacher. A worksheet may be provided.
3. Calculate your score for each of the five wellness components by adding the numbers associated with your responses to the three questions related to that component.
4. Add all five of your wellness component scores to get your overall wellness score.
5. Use table 1.1 to get your wellness rating for each wellness component and for your overall wellness. Record your ratings.

WELLNESS QUESTIONNAIRE

Wellness statement	Strongly agree	Agree	Disagree	Strongly disagree	Item score
1. I am physically fit.	4	3	2	1	
2. I can do the physical tasks needed in my work.	4	3	2	1	
3. I have the energy to be active in my free time.	4	3	2	1	
Physical wellness score (sum of the scores for items 1–3) =					
4. I am happy most of the time.	4	3	2	1	
5. I do not get stressed often.	4	3	2	1	
6. I like myself the way I am.	4	3	2	1	
Emotional wellness score (sum of the scores for items 4–6) =					
7. I have many friends.	4	3	2	1	
8. I am confident in social situations.	4	3	2	1	
9. I am close to my family.	4	3	2	1	
Social wellness score (sum of the scores for items 7–9) =					
10. I am an informed consumer.	4	3	2	1	
11. I check facts before making health decisions.	4	3	2	1	
12. I consult experts when I'm unsure of health facts.	4	3	2	1	
Intellectual wellness score (sum of the scores for items 10–12) =					
13. I feel a sense of purpose in my life.	4	3	2	1	
14. I feel spiritually fulfilled.	4	3	2	1	
15. I feel strong connections to the world around me.	4	3	2	1	
Spiritual wellness score (sum of the scores for items 13–15) =					

Total wellness score (sum of the five wellness scores) = *29*

Adapted, by permission, from C. Corbin et al., 2011, *Concepts of fitness and wellness*, 9th ed. (St. Louis, MO: McGraw-Hill). © The McGraw-Hill Companies.

TABLE 1.1   Rating Wellness

Wellness rating	Three-item score	Total wellness score
Good	10–12	>50
Marginal	8–9	40–49
Low	<7	<39

Lesson 1.2

Determinants of Health and Wellness

Lesson Objectives

After reading this lesson, you should be able to

1. describe the five types of determinants that influence health and wellness,
2. explain how each type of determinant is either in or out of your control, and
3. describe the five benefits of a healthy lifestyle.

 Lesson Vocabulary

determinant, medical scientist, priority healthy lifestyle choice, self-assessment, self-management skill, state of being

In this chapter's first lesson, you learned about health and wellness, each of which is a **state of being**—something that an individual person possesses. Your health and wellness are affected by many factors, which are referred to by public health and **medical scientists** as **determinants**. As the *Healthy People 2020* report indicates, you need to learn about these determinants in order to stay fit, healthy, and well.

> One who has health has hope; and one who has hope has everything.
>
> —Ancient proverb

Determinants of Health and Wellness

In her talk about health, Dr. Lazarus described determinants of good health and wellness. She also noted that some determinants are more in your control than others. As shown in figure 1.3, five types of determinants affect your health and wellness (including two on the left of figure 1.3); lighter shades of orange indicate determinants over which you have less control, and darker shades indicate those over which you have more control.

Personal Determinants

Personal factors are determinants over which you have little or no control—for example, your heredity, your age, your sex, or a disability. They are shaded in a very light shade of orange. Even though you have little control over personal factors, they still affect your health and wellness. For example, some people inherit genes that put them at risk for certain diseases. As you grow older, risk increases for such diseases. Sex is also a factor. For example, males are more prone to storing abdominal fat than females, which places them at a higher risk for some diseases. We also know that women have a longer life expectancy than men. Of course, a personal disability can also affect your health and quality of life.

You'll learn more in other chapters about personal factors and their effect on your fitness, health, and wellness. Although you cannot control personal factors, you can be aware of them and prevent them from having an undue effect on your health and wellness. Being aware can also help you alter other determinants over which you do have control. For example, if you have a family history of heart disease, you can take special care to attend to risk factors for heart disease that you can control.

Environmental and Health Care Determinants

Your health and wellness are also affected by environmental factors. They are shown in a darker shade of orange than the personal factors because you do have some control over them. For example, as an adult, you can choose to live or work in a healthy environment, and you can recycle to help protect the environment. But you cannot personally control the quality of the air in your neighborhood, and you are limited in your control of other environmental factors (e.g., pollution in local rivers and streams).

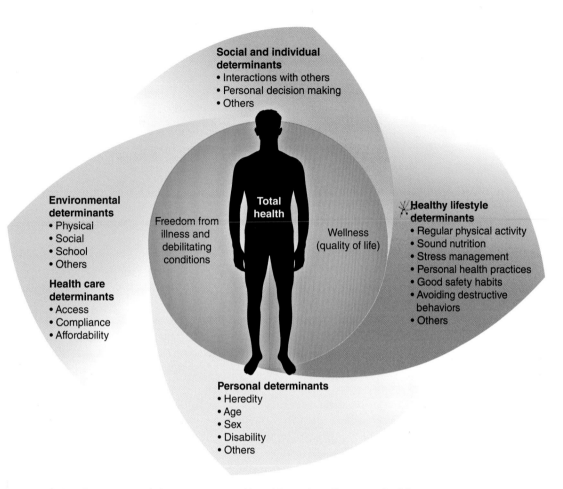

Social and individual determinants
- Interactions with others
- Personal decision making
- Others

Environmental determinants
- Physical
- Social
- School
- Others

Health care determinants
- Access
- Compliance
- Affordability

Freedom from illness and debilitating conditions

Total health

Wellness (quality of life)

Healthy lifestyle determinants
- Regular physical activity
- Sound nutrition
- Stress management
- Personal health practices
- Good safety habits
- Avoiding destructive behaviors
- Others

Personal determinants
- Heredity
- Age
- Sex
- Disability
- Others

FIGURE 1.3 The five types of determinants of health and wellness (in bold).

Adapted, by permission, from C.B. Corbin et al., 2013, *Concepts of fitness and wellness*, 10th ed. (St. Louis, MO: McGraw-Hill Education). © The McGraw-Hill Companies.

Environmental determinants can be subdivided into several groups. Physical environmental factors include, for example, air quality, water quality, and physical characteristics of your home, your school, and other human-made spaces you use. Social factors include the quality of the social environment in your home and community. To some extent, you cannot control your social environment because you may have to go to the school you are assigned to and live where your family lives. But you do have some control over your relationships and interactions with others. More information about these aspects is included in the next section of this lesson.

Health care refers to being able to see a doctor or other health care professional as needed and having access to health care facilities and medicine. Health care also includes opportunities to learn about prevention of illness and promotion of wellness. People who receive good health care live longer and have higher-quality lives compared to those who don't. This factor is shown in a darker shade of orange because you have some control over it. But health care is not equal for all people. For some, access is limited due to lack of money or insurance. Others simply do not take advantage of health care that is available to them. Still others seek care but do not comply with the recommendations given by their physicians or other health care providers. All three of these aspects—having access to good health care, seeking it when needed, and complying with health care recommendations—are important to your health and wellness.

Social and Individual Determinants

The people around you are part of your social environment. And of course the friends you choose, and the people you spend the most time with, affect

CONNECT

On a scale of 1 to 10, with 1 being the least and 10 being the most, how much does your closest friend (or group of friends) influence your health choices and behaviors? Is this influence more positive or more negative overall? How do you think *you* influence *their* behaviors and choices? Provide at least one example.

Lifestyle Determinants

By far the most important determinants of personal health and wellness are your lifestyle choices—personal behaviors that you can adopt to improve your health and wellness. In most cases, they are factors over which you have a lot of control; therefore, they're shown in dark orange in figure 1.3.

Adopting a healthy lifestyle offers you many benefits. First, it reduces your risk of disease and early death. Nearly 60 percent of early deaths in the U.S. result from unhealthy lifestyle choices. In contrast, healthy lifestyle choices—such as getting regular physical activity, eating a well-balanced diet, avoiding smoking, and managing stress—are effective in preventing and treating various illnesses. For example, eating well and being active can help you prevent diseases such as heart disease and help manage conditions such as diabetes.

Like Maggie's grandfather in this chapter's first lesson, you might assume that because illness and disease are most common later in life, older people can't do anything about them. Or, like Maggie herself, you might share a common attitude among many teenagers: "I'm young and healthy. Why should I change what I do?" But evidence indicates that the disease process begins early in life. Therefore, making healthy lifestyle choices early in your life

you more than people who play smaller roles in your social environment. The people closest to you and your interactions with them, including the decisions that you make with them, affect your health and wellness. Teens who hang out with friends who avoid destructive habits and practice healthy habits are more likely to be healthy and well than those who don't.

Individual factors are also important—for example, being a wise consumer by getting informed and making good decisions. In figure 1.3, social and individual factors are colored in a relatively dark shade of orange because you have considerable control over the choices that you make, both individually and with your family and friends.

HEALTH TECHNOLOGY

The World Wide Web allows many people to get immediate access to all kinds of health and fitness information. Some of this information is good, but much of it is inaccurate. In each chapter of this book, you'll find a web address that leads you to sound information about health and wellness.

Look for special web symbols included throughout the book; just type in the appropriate address from the first page of the chapter, and you'll find good, reliable information. For more information about health-related websites, see the student section of the Health for Life website.

CONNECT

Visit the student section of the Health for Life website. Select one or two of the web topics at this site and spend some time exploring them. How do you think accessing reliable health information online can affect a person's health behaviors? Briefly describe what you found at the websites and discuss your assessment of the information.

can do much to prevent disease and illness later on. The evidence also indicates that no matter how old you are, improving your lifestyle enhances your health and wellness.

As you work your way through this book, you'll learn about each of the lifestyle choices listed in figure 1.3. Three of the most important ones are being active, eating well, and managing stress. As a result, they're sometimes called **priority healthy lifestyle choices** because, if adopted, they can make a huge difference in your personal health and wellness. However, many other lifestyle choices also influence your health and wellness—for example, simple personal health practices learned in elementary school (such as washing your hands, brushing your teeth, and getting adequate sleep), practicing good safety habits (such as wearing a seat belt and driving safely without being preoccupied), and avoiding destructive habits (such as tobacco and alcohol use).

Benefits of a Healthy Lifestyle for Teens

Living a healthy lifestyle helps you not only later in life—you can also enjoy many benefits now. They include looking and feeling good, learning better, enjoying daily life activities, and handling emergencies.

Looking Good

Do you care about how you look? Most people do. In fact, one study showed that 94 percent of all men and 99 percent of all women would change some part of their appearance if they could. People are most often concerned with their weight (weighing too much or too little), the size of their waist or thighs, their muscles, and their teeth and hair. Experts agree that regular physical activity and eating well are healthy lifestyle choices that help you look your best. You don't have to take drastic measures to feel good about your appearance.

Feeling Good

Besides looking better, people who practice a healthy lifestyle feel better. If you're active, and therefore more physically fit, you can resist fatigue, you're less likely to be injured, and you're capable of working more efficiently. National surveys indicate that active people who eat well also sleep well and are less likely to be depressed.

Learning Better

In recent years, health scientists have found that being active and eating well help you learn better. Studies show that teens who are active and fit score better on tests and are less likely to be absent from school; thus they learn more. In addition, teens who are active and eat regular healthy meals, especially breakfast, are less tired and more alert at school. Recent studies also show that regular exercise and good fitness are associated with high function in the parts of the brain that promote learning. Your learning is also helped by getting enough sleep and learning to manage stress.

Enjoying Life

Enjoying life is important for your personal wellness. But what if you're too tired on most days to

Healthy lifestyles can help you feel good and enjoy life.

Teens who are active and eat regular healthy meals, especially breakfast, are more alert at school.

Laurence Gough - Fotolia

Good health helps you respond effectively in day-to-day demanding situations.

participate in the activities you really enjoy? Regular physical activity results in physical fitness, which is the key to being able to do more of the things you want to do. In addition, people who eat a good breakfast do not experience low energy during the day and are therefore better able to enjoy life to the fullest.

Meeting Emergencies

People who are fit, healthy, and well have the ability to handle emergencies and day-to-day demanding situations. For example, they are able to run for help, change a flat tire, and offer needed assistance to others.

Comprehension Check

1. Explain how each of the five types of determinants affects health and wellness.
2. Describe the amount of control you have over each of the five types of determinants.
3. Describe the five health benefits of a healthy lifestyle. How are they important both to teens and adults?

When you take a trip, you typically plan ahead. After you choose a destination, you use a map to help you get where you want to go. Like a map, a **self-assessment** (or self-test) helps you know where you are (your current health status) and decide where you want to go (set goals for good health). Self-assessment is one type of healthy living skill (also called **self-management skill**), and many kinds of self-assessments exist. For example, you can assess your eating patterns, your stress level, your health risks, your knowledge, your current personal health habits, your physical fitness, and, as you did earlier in this chapter, your wellness status. You'll do self-assessments throughout this book.

After attending Dr. Lazarus' lecture about health, Maggie and her grandfather talked about what they had heard. They recalled Dr. Lazarus mentioning that most Americans do not have a realistic view of their own health. For example, as many as seven million people have type 2 diabetes but don't know it, and one in three adults has high blood pressure but doesn't know it.

For this reason, Dr. Lazarus urged her audience to get periodic medical checkups. But she also pointed out that people can use self-assessments to help track their health status.

For example, she noted that many people use a home scale to self-assess their weight and that some count calories to assess their energy intake. Maggie's grandfather mentioned a friend with diabetes who did self-assessments of his blood sugar. And Maggie realized that she did self-assessments in physical education class to determine her cardiorespiratory endurance.

For Discussion

Dr. Lazarus suggested that people can learn to do self-assessments to help them plan for healthy living and set good health goals. But she also urged people to get regular medical exams to make sure that they are healthy and well. Discuss some ways in which Maggie's family could use self-assessments related to health. What kinds of self-assessment might different family members use? Might the self-assessments that Maggie and her younger brother perform be different from those done by her grandfather or her mother and father? What steps can Maggie and her family members take to make sure that their self-assessments are reliable and accurate? When answering these discussion questions, consider the guidelines in this chapter's Skills for Healthy Living feature.

As mentioned earlier, assessing your health and wellness is much like using a map; it helps you know where to go from here. You can assess your current health status to help you learn where you need to improve and make plans for doing so. Use the following guidelines as you learn to do personal health and wellness self-assessments.

- **Consider self-assessments of both health and wellness.** Tests of health and wellness assess your state of being. Examples include blood pressure tests, skin cancer screenings, dental exams for cavities, and wellness questionnaires.

- **Consider self-assessments of health and wellness determinants.** Examples include assessments of your dietary intake, activity level, use of time, personal health habits, social interactions, and personal actions, as well as environmental factors that affect your health and wellness.

- **Use a variety of self-assessments.** Using a variety of self-assessments helps you get a comprehensive profile of your health and wellness and the factors that determine them.

- **Use self-assessments for personal improvement.** Once you've learned to use self-assessments, repeat them from time to time to monitor your progress. Avoid doing assessments too often, but check yourself periodically to see how you're doing. Change takes time, so assessing before changes have time to take place may cause you to be discouraged in meeting your goals.

- **Use recommended health standards rather than comparing yourself with others.** Sometimes people feel discouraged by their self-assessment results—often because they are comparing themselves with others. Doing so can lead to unrealistic expectations or self-criticism. A better approach is to use health standards, and you'll learn more about them throughout this book.

- **Keep self-assessment results confidential.** Self-assessments are personal and confidential. The decision to share—or not share—health information is up to each person. In some cases, you're asked to share information with your teacher so that you can get feedback and advice. This is done with the understanding that the information is not to be shared with others. In other cases, you may work with a partner to perform a self-assessment. Prior to the self-assessment, you should reach an agreement about confidentiality with your partner, and you should both take the agreement seriously.

- **Learn from and periodically check with an expert.** Some self-assessments require more skill than others. For example, weighing yourself on a scale is easy, but checking your blood pressure is more difficult. Before performing a self-assessment, learn from an expert whenever possible. Your health or physical education teacher can help you with many self-assessments related to health and fitness.

Doctors establish health standards for assessments such as blood pressure. Avoid comparisons to others and focus on standards for good health.

Rob/fotolia.com

- **Take advantage of health screenings.** Health agencies frequently offer free health screenings to help people detect problems. When performed by health experts, these screenings can provide you with good information and help you evaluate the accuracy of your self-assessments.
- **If you have concerns, seek advice from a professional, a parent or guardian, or a teacher.** Self-assessments are useful in assessing your current status and helping you plan programs to improve your health and wellness. They help you set goals and monitor your progress in meeting your goals. But even the people most skilled in self-assessment do not have the professional skills to interpret some health information. And incorrect interpretations of information gained from self-assessments can lead to anxiety and unnecessary concerns. If you have questions about self-assessment results, seek help from a qualified person.

 ACADEMIC CONNECTION: Percent and Percentages

Statistics is a branch of mathematics that helps us learn from data and make comparisons of measurements. In the health sciences, percentages are used to help us determine health behavior changes over time. A percentage is a portion, or share, of the whole. The whole (total) is expressed as 100 or 100 percent. Half of the whole is 50 percent of the whole. For example, a dollar is 100 cents, so a dime (10 cents) is 10 percent of a whole dollar. A quarter (25 cents) is 25 percent of a dollar. The Living Well News feature uses percents and percentages to help us understand tobacco use in the United States. In 2011, 45 percent of teens (45 of every 100) tried smoking. As shown in table 1.2, the percentage of teens who smoke has decreased in recent years.

The State of Youth Health

The Centers for Disease Control and Prevention (CDC), a U.S. government agency, has been keeping tabs on the health of the nation's youth for years. Specifically, the Youth Risk Behavior Surveillance System (YRBSS) tracks six categories of health-risk behavior among youth and young adults: (1) behaviors that contribute to violence and unintentional injury; (2) sexual behaviors that contribute to unintended pregnancy and sexually transmitted disease; (3) alcohol and other drug use; (4) tobacco use; (5) unhealthy dietary behaviors; and (6) inadequate physical activity. In addition, the YRBSS monitors the rates of obesity and asthma in the youth population. The most recent survey gathered data from 15,000 youth in grades 9 through 12.

All YRBSS data is reported and compared by sex, age, ethnicity, and state. For example, one item addresses the percentage of youth who have ever smoked a cigarette. Nationwide, 45 percent of students reported having tried a cigarette. White (44 percent) and Hispanic (49 percent) teens were more likely to have tried a cigarette than black (39 percent) teens. Males (46 percent) were more likely to have tried a cigarette than females (43 percent). Youth were most likely to smoke regularly in Kentucky (12 percent) and Wyoming (10 percent) and least likely to do so in Utah (2 percent) and Hawaii (4 percent). Smoking has declined significantly in teens over the last two decades. See table 1.2 for a sample of student smoking data that demonstrates this trend.

Information from the YRBSS helps health professionals and educators better understand youths' health behaviors and track those behaviors over time. "We are encouraged that more of today's high school students are choosing healthier, safer behaviors, such as wearing seat belts, and are avoiding behaviors that we know can cause them harm, such as binge drinking or riding with impaired drivers," said Howell Wechsler, director of CDC's Division of Adolescent and School Health. "However, these findings also show that despite improvements, there is a continued need for government agencies, community organizations, schools, parents, and other community members to work together to address the range of risk behaviors prevalent among our youth."

For Discussion

How honest do you think teens are when they fill out a survey about their health behaviors? Do you think they're more likely to be honest if the survey is anonymous (no name attached) and confidential (used only for the research study)? Why or why not? Why is it important for people to be honest when reporting their health information on a self-assessment? What about when reporting their information on a medical history form that will only be seen by a medical professional?

TABLE 1.2 Percentage of Students Who Have Ever Tried a Cigarette

2001	2003	2005	2007	2009	2011
64	58	54	50	46	45

From Youth Risk Behavior Surveillance System (YRBSS) 2011.

Reviewing Concepts and Vocabulary

As directed by your teacher, answer items 1 through 5 by correctly completing each sentence with a word or phrase.

1. _____ is more than just freedom from disease; it also involves optimal well-being.
2. _____ is the positive component of good health and is exemplified by a positive sense of well-being and a good quality of life.
3. Factors such as your heredity, your age, your sex, and a disability are examples of _____ determinants over which you have little or no control.
4. Air quality is an example of a(n) _____ determinant.
5. The friends you choose are all part of your _____ environment.

For items 6 through 10, as directed by your teacher, match each term in column 1 with the appropriate phrase in column 2.

6. physical component
7. emotional component
8. spiritual component
9. intellectual component
10. social component

a. a sharp and engaged mind
b. having healthy interactions with others
c. happiness
d. a sense of connection to the world and others and having a strong purpose in life
e. being physically fit

For items 11 through 15, as directed by your teacher, respond to each statement or question.

11. What are the components of wellness?
12. How do health and wellness differ?
13. Why are environmental factors not listed as components of personal wellness?
14. Why is it important to learn how to conduct self-assessments?
15. What are the priority healthy lifestyle choices?

Thinking Critically

Write a paragraph in response to the following prompt.

A person with a physical disability or disease may still have wellness. Use a specific example to explain how this is possible.

Take It Home

Research some of the self-assessments related to health that are available online. Select one that you think would be of interest to a family member. Encourage that person to complete the self-assessment. You can find links to self-assessments in the student section of the Health for Life website.

anz.Pfluegl/fotolia.com

2

Health Behavior Change and Personal Health

Bananastock

Lesson 2.1
Personal Health and Wellness

Lesson Objectives

After reading this lesson, you should be able to

1. explain the difference between controllable and uncontrollable risk factors,
2. describe several healthy lifestyle choices, and
3. identify and explain some environmental and social factors that affect health and wellness.

Lesson Vocabulary

accelerometer, controllable risk factor, healthy lifestyle, risk factor, sleep apnea, uncontrollable risk factor

---

If you asked every person you know, you'd probably find that most of them want to have good personal health and wellness. But how many are aware of all the things they can do to achieve those goals? In this lesson, you'll learn about healthy lifestyle choices and how they can help you achieve good personal health and wellness. You'll also learn about other factors that can influence your health and wellness.

Determinants and Other Risk Factors

A **risk factor**, as it relates to disease, is anything that increases your chance of getting sick (having a disease). Some determinants of health and wellness are associated with disease risk and are therefore considered to be risk factors; examples include age, sex, and heredity. These particular factors are called **uncontrollable risk factors**. For example, older people are more at risk of diseases that are the leading causes of death (such as heart disease, cancer, and diabetes) than are younger people (see figure 2.1). Similarly, men have a greater risk of heart disease than women. And people with a family history of a certain disease are typically more at risk for it than people who do not have such a history.

Determinants such as health care and environment are also related to risk. For example, people have lower risk if they have health insurance, regularly see medical professionals for health screening and treatment, and follow the advice given by medical professionals. These factors may be somewhat

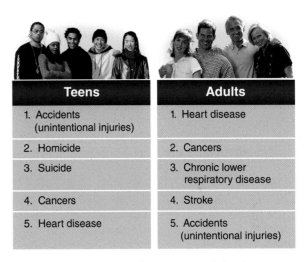

Teens	Adults
1. Accidents (unintentional injuries)	1. Heart disease
2. Homicide	2. Cancers
3. Suicide	3. Chronic lower respiratory disease
4. Cancers	4. Stroke
5. Heart disease	5. Accidents (unintentional injuries)

FIGURE 2.1 The top five causes of death in teens versus adults.

controllable by teens, but they are often controlled by other people in your life. Still, as you'll see later in this lesson, there are things that you can do as a teen to reduce your risks related to health care.

Your disease risk is also affected by where you live and work. For example, if you live or work in a highly polluted area, your risk is greater. Nor are environmental risk factors totally in your control. Teens usually cannot, for example, control where they live or go to school, though working teens may have some control over their working environment.

Factors where you can exert more control include the friends you associate with and the decisions you make. The factors over which you have the most control are your lifestyle choices. They are also among the most important factors in reducing your risk of disease.

> " It is health that is real wealth and not pieces of gold and silver. "
>
> —Mahatma Gandhi, human rights leader

Health and Wellness Promotion

The focus of early health professionals was on diagnosis and treatment of illness. Treating disease is still a high-priority health goal in the United States, but it is equally important to help people prevent illness and improve their quality of life and sense of well-being throughout their lives (health promotion). As illustrated in figure 2.2, all three factors (treatment, prevention, and promotion) are important. Treatment helps you to avoid illness. Prevention involves taking steps to avoid future illness including minimizing your controllable risk factors. Promotion involves taking action to build good health and wellness for yourself and other members of society. The remainder of this lesson describes steps that you can take to reduce your risk of disease and promote your personal wellness. The focus here is on changing personal behaviors (making good lifestyle choices), but other determinants are also discussed—especially when they relate to risk factors that are in your personal control.

Healthy Lifestyle Choices

A **healthy lifestyle** is a way of living that helps you prevent illness and enhance your wellness. Healthy lifestyle choices make up one kind of determinant of your health and wellness; more specifically, they are often considered to be **controllable risk factors**. As you can see in figure 2.3, four major factors contribute to early death. The largest number of early deaths results from unhealthy lifestyle choices. These deaths could be prevented if people changed the way they live. Remember, too, that healthy lifestyle choices not only reduce your risk of disease and disease-related death but also enhance your wellness. For example, not smoking greatly reduces your risk of heart disease and cancer; it also increases the quality of your life, because you can breathe better, have a keener sense of smell, and spend less money on tobacco and medical care.

The following lifestyle choices are ones that you can adopt to promote good fitness, health, and wellness. Of course, these options benefit you only if you choose to do them. The choices you make have much to do with your personal fitness, health, and wellness. Each choice is discussed only briefly here, but most are discussed in greater detail in other sections of this book.

Many aspects of a person's lifestyle can be changed to improve his or her health and wellness. Ten are discussed here. Three of these—being physically active, eating well, and managing stress—are sometimes called priority healthy lifestyle choices because they can help so many people. Statistics

FIGURE 2.2 Health and wellness: from treatment to promotion.

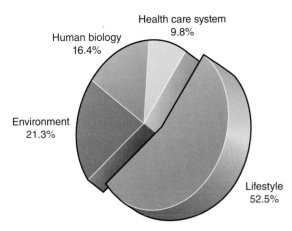

FIGURE 2.3 Four main factors contribute to early death.

Reprinted, by permission, from C. Corbin, G. Le Masurier, and K. McConnell, 2014, *Fitness for life*, 6th ed. (Champaign, IL: Human Kinetics), 407.

indicate that the majority of teens do *not* do regular physical activity, do *not* follow important dietary guidelines, and *do* report being stressed on a regular basis.

Be Physically Active

Among the health goals set forth in the U.S. government's *Healthy People 2020* report, being physically active is one of the most important. Changing your lifestyle from inactive to active can do more for your health and wellness than most other changes. In fact, being physically active can also help you manage stress, so its benefits are doubled. In addition, physical activity helps you reduce many risk factors, such as high blood pressure and high blood fat. Physical activity also builds good health-related physical fitness, including cardiorespiratory endurance, strength, muscular endurance, power, flexibility, and healthy body composition. Fitness is associated with reduced disease risk and with wellness factors such as having the energy to enjoy leisure activities without fatigue, being able to work without fatigue, and looking and feeling good.

Eat Properly

What kinds of food do you typically eat? Are your meals generally high in fat? Do you eat plenty of fruits, vegetables, and grains? Do you limit unhealthy fats and get adequate protein in your diet? Many children, teens, and adults do not eat a balanced diet—a diet that includes healthy amounts of important food groups. Some also don't eat breakfast—a very important meal. Skipping breakfast

 HEALTH TECHNOLOGY

Considerable evidence shows that getting too little sleep can lead to health problems. Teens need about nine hours of sleep per night, but 90 percent of teens report getting less than that, and 25 percent report getting less than 6.5 hours per night. However, your number of sleep hours per night isn't the only thing that's important. Your sleep patterns also matter. People who wake up numerous times, or toss and turn frequently during the night, are not getting restful sleep. In fact, for years, scientists have used sophisticated machines to detect **sleep apnea** and other serious sleep disturbances. Now, an **accelerometer**, such as one worn to count steps, can also be used to determine movement patterns during the night.

Experts do caution against overgeneralizing conclusions based on sleep reports from sleep-tracking devices. They point out that a person can sleep well most of the time but still have periodic restless nights. In addition, sleep trackers do not sense levels of sleep (e.g., light versus deep sleep) and cannot directly determine the amount of sleep you get. As a result, experts acknowledge that use of a sleep tracker could result in the cost of an unnecessary medical visit if the tracker suggests a problem where none exists. Even so, sleep trackers can be useful in screening for sleep problems in people who frequently feel tired or suspect that they have a sleep problem. If a sleep tracker indicates that your sleep is interrupted frequently, consult an expert for more analysis. For more information about sleep-tracking devices, see the student section of the Health for Life website.

 CONNECT

Investigate sleep-tracking devices. Evaluate the pros and cons of using such a device. Check to see if activity-tracking devices cost more when they also include sleep-tracking capability.

(and other meals) can burden you with fatigue, lack of attention, and poor school performance.

With all this in mind, one major U.S. health goal is to improve the nutrition of all citizens. The goals set forth in *Healthy People 2020* outline ways to improve your health and wellness by changing your eating habits. Together, regular physical activity and sound nutrition do more to reduce your disease risk than all other factors except tobacco avoidance. Eating well gives you the energy for work and play, whereas overeating contributes to overweight and obesity—problems that are all too common among Americans today.

Manage Stress

You've probably had periods of stress and know how it can affect you in the short term. But did you know that stress can also cause health problems and detract from your personal well-being and quality of life? Most people are well aware of the stress experienced by business people, elected officials, and other people in high-stress jobs, but many of us sometimes forget that stress affects everyone—including teens. You can help yourself by learning stress management techniques to use before tests and in other times of high stress. You can also reduce stress by learning to manage your time effectively. See the book's chapter on stress management.

Adopt Good Personal Health Habits

In kindergarten or first grade, you most likely learned about personal health habits, such as regularly brushing and flossing your teeth, washing your hands before meals and after using the bathroom, and getting enough sleep. Because these habits are often taught in elementary school, many teens feel that they're not still important—but they are! Table 2.1 summarizes key personal health habits and provides some related information you may not know.

Avoid Destructive Habits

Just as adopting healthy habits contributes to good health, practicing destructive habits detracts from your health and wellness. Examples include smoking, other tobacco use, legal or illegal drug abuse, and alcohol abuse. These destructive habits can impair your fitness, detract from your performance of physical activities, and result in various diseases, lowered feelings of well-being, and reduced quality of life. Another destructive practice is risky sexual behavior.

Young people sometimes claim, "I can do these things and they don't hurt me." This attitude results in part from the fact that, although many destructive behaviors do cause immediate harmful effects, other negative effects can take years to develop. As a result, it's not uncommon for older people to say, "I wish I'd listened when I was younger." If you really want to see the effects of a destructive behavior, interview a person who has done the behavior for years. If you select a person you know and care about, you may even be able to help that person.

Adopt Safety Practices

Daily news reports are filled with accounts of injury and death caused by motor vehicle crashes. Other common causes of death and injury include falling, poisoning, drowning, fire, bicycle accidents, and accidents in and around the home. Many of these outcomes could have been prevented if simple safety rules had been followed. As a result, one U.S. health goal is to reduce the number of deaths and injuries caused by accidents.

Adopting good personal health habits like applying sunscreen before sun exposure is part of a healthy lifestyle.

TABLE 2.1 Personal Health Habits

Health habit	Healthy action	Health information
Oral care	• Regular brushing • Regular flossing • Regular cleaning and screening	It's well known that oral care helps you look your best and prevents erosion of teeth, bones, and mouth tissues (periodontitis). You may not know that the bacteria that cause periodontitis have also been found in plaque in the arteries, which can lead to heart disease.
Sleep	• Getting nine hours of sleep each night • Avoiding sleep during the day	Many people think that the need for sleep dramatically decreases during the teen years. However, studies show that teens need nine hours of sleep per night. Unfortunately, teens get an average of only 7.5 hours, and one in four teens gets 6.5 hours or less. Why does this matter? Lack of adequate sleep is associated with poor grades, depression, and sleepiness during school. It's also important to get good-quality sleep. Teens who snooze during the day often do not sleep well at night.
Hand washing	• Washing your hands regularly, especially before eating and after using the bathroom, working, playing sports, or coming into contact with a sick person • Washing properly with soap • Using hand sanitizer when hand washing is not possible	Hand washing is a basic practice learned in elementary school, but it's no less important at any other age, including your teen years. Washing your hands regularly—and well—is your first line of defense against the spread of many illnesses, including flu, colds, gastrointestinal infections (e.g., diarrhea), skin infections, and some more serious diseases, such as bronchitis, hepatitis A, and meningitis. Students lose millions of days of school attendance each year due to illnesses that might have been prevented by hand washing.
Careful coughing and sneezing	• Covering your mouth and nose with a tissue • Disposing of tissues in a wastebasket • Coughing or sneezing into your upper sleeve (not your hands) when you don't have a tissue	The healthy actions listed here are part of what the U.S. Centers for Disease Control and Prevention has described as proper etiquette for coughing and sneezing. Etiquette refers to social rules that benefit people. Using good etiquette when coughing or sneezing reduces the risk of infectious illness in all settings. It's especially important in crowded places and in medical settings such as hospitals and doctors' offices.
Posture	• Sitting with good posture • Standing with good posture • Lifting with good posture • Using good body mechanics during daily activities • Using backpacks safely and with good posture	Poor posture is associated with many health problems and is also important to wellness. For example, it is associated with back and neck pain (and 80 percent of people in the U.S. experience back pain at some point). Poor posture can also lead to unnecessary fatigue. In addition, many school-age people carry backpacks, and you should learn how to use your backpack properly—with good posture. Here are some guidelines provided by the National Safety Council (a U.S. nonprofit group): • Limit the weight of your backpack to no more than 15 to 20 percent of your body weight. • Use both straps (not just one on one shoulder). • Wear your pack over your midback, where your muscles are the strongest. • If you have to lean forward to carry the pack, it's too heavy—lighten the load. • Don't bend at the waist when carrying a backpack (instead, bend your legs to squat with your back straight). Other guidelines are available at the safety council's website (www.nsc.org).

> continued

TABLE 2.1 > continued

Health habit	Healthy action	Health information
Skin care	• Using sunscreen that blocks UVA and UVB light • Avoiding lengthy exposure to the sun, especially at high altitude and in the late spring, summer, and early fall • Avoiding sun lamps, tanning beds, and tanning salons • Getting screened for abnormal skin growths and seeking medical help if in doubt	Tanning is a common practice among teens—but one that has resulted in an ever-increasing rate of skin cancer. The most dangerous kind of skin cancer is melanoma because it can spread to other parts of the body. Use the ABCDE rule when checking for skin cancer symptoms. A = Is one half of the skin growth (mole or other skin irregularity) different from the other half (**asymmetry**)? B = Are the **borders** of the growth irregular? C = Does the **color** of the growth vary (e.g., tan, brown, black, or another color)? D = Is the **diameter** of the spot larger than 6 mm (larger than a standard pencil eraser)? E = Has the mole or spot changed in appearance (**evolution**)? Research indicates that the use of tanning booths increases a person's risk of skin cancer. Some states prohibit their use by teens without a parent's permission.
Other	• Learning first aid so that you can help yourself and others if an accident occurs • Working with others to improve school and community environments so that they are safe and promote health	Health problems can be associated with the availability of health care (or lack thereof). You may not be in control of all aspects of the health care system, but there are some things you can do, such as those listed here, to help prevent disease and promote wellness.

You can do your part by making healthy lifestyle choices such as the following: wearing a seat belt, wearing a helmet when cycling or in-line skating, making sure that poisonous substances are properly labeled, installing and maintaining smoke detectors, practicing water safety, and keeping your home in good repair. And don't forget—being physically fit can help prevent accidents, too.

CONNECT

In what ways does your family influence your adoption of healthy behaviors? In what ways do your peers influence your adoption of healthy behaviors? Provide specific examples. Which has a greater influence on your behaviors—family or peers? Explain your answer.

Learn About First Aid and CPR

Even people who make healthy lifestyle choices and adopt good safety practices can have accidents.

Because accidents can happen to anyone, everyone should have a first aid kit handy and know how to administer first aid. Other important first aid skills include bleeding control, the Heimlich maneuver to relieve choking, cardiopulmonary resuscitation (CPR), and use of an automated external defibrillator (AED) to restore effective cardiac rhythm. The National Heart, Lung, and Blood Institute defines an AED as a portable device that checks the heart rhythm. If needed, it can send an electric shock to the heart to try to restore a normal heart rhythm. AEDs are used to treat heart attacks.

Medical and health scientists have been doing research for many years to find the best ways of giving first aid to people whose heart or breathing has stopped. As a result, over the past 50 years, new methods of CPR have been developed, thus saving thousands of lives. Mouth-to-mouth resuscitation was first used in France in the 1700s, and medical doctors in the late 1800s used chest compression to revive people. Doctors used these procedures for a long time before they were finally recommended to the general public in the 1960s. Since then, the

Seek and Follow Appropriate Medical Advice

Even if you make healthy lifestyle choices and stick with them, you may occasionally become ill. In those cases, seek and follow appropriate medical advice. In fact, for best results, get regular medical and dental checkups to help prevent problems before they start. Consult your own physician and dentist to determine how often you should have a checkup. Some people avoid seeking medical help because they fear they may be ill. However, this practice is dangerous, because early detection can be crucial to an ultimate cure. As noted earlier, getting the best medical help is not always under your control. If this is the case for you, seek help through your school nurse or guidance counselor.

During your school years, many decisions about your health care are made for you by others. For example, you may receive inoculations (vaccinations) for various diseases, such as polio, flu, measles, and mumps. The U.S. Centers for Disease Control and Prevention (CDC) provides a vaccination schedule for children and teens (for details, see the student section of the Health for Life website). After your school years, you become responsible for your own inoculation schedule—and for various health checks, such as annual health screenings with a physician and screenings for heart disease, diabetes, various forms of cancer, and other conditions. Many diseases can be prevented or minimized by early detection through screening. See the book's chapter on health care consumerism.

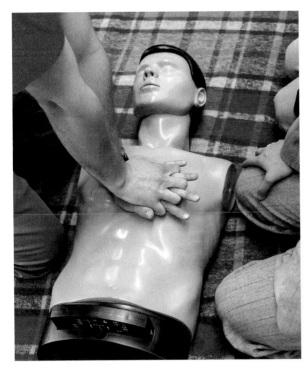

Knowing how to perform CPR is an important first aid skill.

Roman Milert/fotolia.com

guidelines for using mouth-to-mouth breathing and chest compressions have changed dramatically. In addition, the proper use of AEDs by the general public has become an essential part of CPR training and implementation. Training and certification are now offered by many schools and several national organizations. See the book's chapter on safety and first aid.

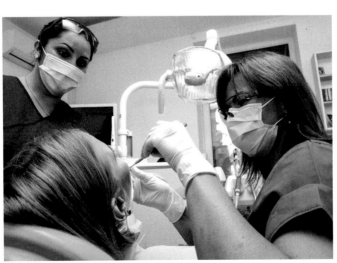

Getting regular dental checkups will help prevent problems before they start.

© Grecu Mihail Alin/Dreamstime

Make Efforts to Improve the Environment

As noted earlier, the environment is something over which you have limited control. Still, there are things you can do to change your immediate environment; in other words, even here your behavior can make a difference. Your physical environment includes the air, land, water, plants, and other physical things that exist around you. We know that certain physical environments can be very harmful to a person's health. You may be unable to change some aspects of your physical environment, such as where you live. You can, however, take action to improve your environment by, for example, not exposing yourself unnecessarily to smoke-filled places, avoiding exces-

sive exposure to the sun, and being careful about using pollutants, such as weed killers. You can also reduce your exposure to air pollution by exercising away from heavily traveled streets.

Other steps that you can take include recycling many items (such as cans, plastic bottles, and plastic bags) and conserving water and electricity. You can also help people in your community who are working to improve the "built environment," which refers to the physical characteristics of your neighborhood. Doing so—for example, by adding sidewalks and bike paths and improving street lighting and crossings—increases residents' participation in physical activity, such as walking and biking in neighborhoods. See the book's chapter on a healthy environment.

CONSUMER CORNER: Don't Be Outsmarted! Finding High-Quality Health Information

Living a healthy lifestyle requires you to seek out and use appropriate health information. Not all information about health is truthful or reliable. In fact, many health-related websites are really trying to sell you products or services, and they may not be committed to accuracy. Medline, an online database compiled by the U.S. National Library of Medicine, recommends that you take the following steps when seeking health information online.

- **Consider the source.** Know who is responsible for the site. Use sites created by recognized authorities and organizations.
- **Focus on quality.** Rely on sites with a clear and qualified editorial board and expert contributors.
- **Be a cyberskeptic.** Avoid claims that seem too good to be true—they usually are. Also, confirm information by using more than one source.
- **Look for the evidence.** Rely on medical research, not opinion.
- **Check for currency.** Look for the latest information.

- **Beware of bias.** Check to see if the site is supported by public funds, private donations, or commercial advertising. Nonprofit and government websites are less likely to include bias information compared to commercial sites that use advertisements.
- **Protect your privacy.** Health information should be confidential. Check to see if the site has a privacy policy and be careful with any information you share.
- **Consult with your health professional.** Good websites can help you become informed, but health care professionals provide the best medical information.

Consumer Challenge

Visit a government website (typically with the web extension .gov) to review a health topic (e.g., www.cdc.gov or www.fitness.gov). Compare information from this website with a commercial website that contains information on the same topic.

Seek Friends Who Support You and Who Practice Healthy Behaviors

Talking to others is a form of social interaction. So is doing things with others. Research shows that your social interactions (behaviors) have much to do with your health and wellness. For example, studies show that people with a large number of friends throughout life live longer. Regular interactions with friends can promote better brain function, thus leading to a better quality of life. Positive social interactions also contribute to happiness, which is one indicator of wellness. A recent study indicates that friends can even help each other prevent weight gain. More generally, having friends who make healthy decisions helps you make good decisions. On the other hand, having friends who practice destructive habits and make negative health decisions can lead you to make unhealthy decisions. Which scenario do you choose?

Supportive friends are important to good health and wellness.

Photodisc

Comprehension Check

1. Explain the difference between controllable and uncontrollable risk factors.
2. Describe the three priority healthy lifestyle choices, as well as four or more additional healthy lifestyle choices.
3. Explain how environmental and social factors affect health and wellness.

SELF-ASSESSMENT: Stages of Health Behavior

The questionnaire presented here will help you self-assess your current health behaviors. It does not include all health behaviors but is designed to provide useful information about selected health habits. Record your results as directed by your teacher. A worksheet containing the questionnaire may be provided. Follow these directions.

1. Read the three statements related to each health behavior. Record the number (1 to 5) that best represents your current stage.
2. Add the scores for the three statements for each behavior (e.g., physical activ-

ity, nutrition) to get a score for that behavior.

3. Add the first five health behavior scores to get your overall health behavior score. *Note:* Because of the personal nature of the destructive habits section of the questionnaire, the three-item score for that section is not included in your total score. You should determine your destructive habits score, but you are not required to note your responses on your worksheet.

4. Use table 2.2 to get ratings for each health behavior and for your overall health behavior.

Stages of Health Behavior Questionnaire

Health behavior	Stage 1: Change needed	Stage 2: Thinking about change	Stage 3: Planning for change	Stage 4: Some change made	Stage 5: Regular healthy behavior	Item score
1. Do 60 minutes of activity per day.	1	2	3	4	5	
2. Do vigorous activity three days a week.	1	2	3	4	5	
3. Do muscle fitness and flexibility exercise three days a week.	1	2	3	4	5	
Physical activity score (sum of the scores for items 1–3) =						
4. Eat three well-balanced meals per day.	1	2	3	4	5	
5. Choose fruits and vegetables for half of daily food consumption.	1	2	3	4	5	
6. Balance calories taken in with calories expended.	1	2	3	4	5	
Nutrition score (sum of the scores for items 4–6) =						
7. Have learned stress management skills.	1	2	3	4	5	
8. Manage time effectively.	1	2	3	4	5	
9. Do physical activity or stress reduction exercises to manage stress.	1	2	3	4	5	
Stress management score (sum of the scores for items 7–9) =						

Health behavior	Stage 1: Change needed	Stage 2: Thinking about change	Stage 3: Planning for change	Stage 4: Some change made	Stage 5: Regular healthy behavior	Item score
10. Get nine hours of good sleep each night.	1	2	3	4	5	
11. Floss and brush teeth at least twice a day.	1	2	3	4	5	
12. Wash hands regularly.	1	2	3	4	5	
Personal health habits score (sum of the scores for items 10–12) =						
13. Get regular medical and dental exams and follow the advice of health professionals.	1	2	3	4	5	
14. Wear appropriate safety equipment when biking or participating in a sport and wear a seat belt when driving.	1	2	3	4	5	
15. Drive safely and do not use phone while driving.	1	2	3	4	5	
Safety and medical practices score (sum of the scores for items 13–15) =						
16. Avoid use of tobacco.*	1	2	3	4	5	
17. Do not abuse drugs or alcohol.*	1	2	3	4	5	
18. Avoid risky sexual behavior.*	1	2	3	4	5	
Destructive habits score (sum of the scores for items 16–18) =						

Total health behavior score (sum of the five wellness scores)** =

*Answer these questions for your own use, but responses are not required on your worksheet.

**Your total score does *not* include your destructive habits score (see the note accompanying those questions in the table).

TABLE 2.2 Rating Health Behaviors

Health behavior rating	Three-item score	Total health behavior score
Good	13–15	>65
Marginal	10–12	50–64
Low	<9	<49

Lesson 2.2
Changing Health Behaviors

Lesson Objectives

After reading this lesson, you should be able to
1. describe the four types of groups that, along with personal actions, influence your health;
2. describe the five stages of health behavior and how they relate to change; and
3. describe the theories used to study health behavior change.

Lesson Vocabulary

cognitive theory, community health, global health, health behavior, health psychology, personal health, SMART goal, stages of health behavior change

Health and wellness are important to looking good, feeling good, enjoying life, and preventing disease and illness. Many factors determine your state of health and wellness. For this reason, a person is somewhat—but not totally—in control of day-to-day health and wellness. At the personal level, you can't control your age and your heredity, but you are in control of your personal behaviors that influence your health. This lesson explains the process of behavior change and introduces you to several theories used to help understand **health behaviors**.

Groups and Health

Personal health refers to your own health and wellness. It involves the choices and actions you take as an individual that affect your health. It includes everything from your exercise habits to how often you floss your teeth. Personal health and group health influence each other. As the arrow at the top of figure 2.4 indicates, the personal health of each group member influences the health of the total group. At the same time, as indicated by the arrow at the bottom of the figure, behaviors and interactions within a group affect each member's personal health. For example, if your friends and family practice good health behaviors, you're more likely to adopt good personal health practices as well.

A collection of groups makes up a community— for example, a school, a worksite, a neighborhood, or a town. The health and wellness of a community (**community health**) depend on the personal health

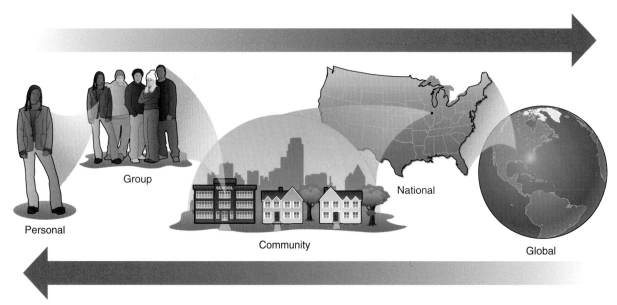

FIGURE 2.4 The relationship between personal health and group health.

of individuals in the community. At the same time, the community's rules, laws, and common practices affect the health of the groups and individuals that make up the community. For example, if a school or workplace limits smoking, the risk of disease is reduced for everyone in that environment. Similarly, if the available food includes healthy options, such as fresh fruits and vegetables, it is easier for people in the community to be healthy.

> " The first wealth is health. "
>
> —Ralph Waldo Emerson, poet

The United States is made up of the communities in towns, cities, and counties that are located in various states. Like communities, nations have health policies and practices that influence the health of their individuals and groups. For example, the CDC works to promote good health and control diseases, and other agencies work to protect food and regulate drugs. Health laws and policies, such as public smoking bans, vary from county to county. As indicated by the top arrow in figure 2.4, the health and wellness of individuals, groups, and communities influence the health and wellness of the nation. As indicated by the arrow at the bottom of figure 2.4, the reverse is also true; that is, national policies and health practices influence the health of individuals, groups, and communities within the nation.

Global health refers to the health of everyone on our planet. In the United States, we are fortunate to live in a nation and in communities that provide treated water, safe waste disposal, and high-quality health care for most (though not all) citizens. But these things do not hold true globally. Many nations still face illness and epidemics not common in the United States. In addition, health practices in one country can influence the health of another nation and its citizens. For example, air pollution created in one nation can affect the entire planet, and an epidemic in one nation can put the health of people in other nations at risk.

Each of us can most influence health and wellness at the personal level. What we do individually also affects the health of people in both smaller and larger groups. Likewise, the health practices and policies in force in our groups, communities, nation, and global population affect us as individuals. This book focuses on enhancing your personal health and wellness. However, you'll also study the effects of social interactions in all types of groups and environments on your personal health and wellness.

Stages of Health Behavior

Researchers know that health behaviors can be changed. They also know that changes occur not all at once but in stages. Dr. James Prochaska and his colleagues developed the "stages of change" idea beginning in the 1970s as a result of research related to smoking behavior; therefore, the example given in figure 2.5 relates to smoking. There are five **stages of health behavior change**, ranging from precontemplation to maintenance. The goal is to move from lower stages to higher stages; the ultimate goal, of course, is stage five.

In the first stage, a person refuses to recognize that change is necessary. For example, a smoker may deny the need to stop smoking. The person might say, "I have no intention to stop." A person at stage 2 is thinking about making a change but has not

Stage 1: Precontemplation
You have no intention to change the behavior.

Stage 2: Contemplation
You acknowledge an intention to change the behavior.

Stage 3: Preparation
You actively plan to change the behavior.

Stage 4: Action
You change the behavior.

Stage 5: Maintenance
You sustain the behavior change for at least six months.

FIGURE 2.5 Stages of health behavior.

⚛ HEALTH SCIENCE

One particular area of the general field of health science is called **health psychology**. Psychology is the study of human behavior, and health psychologists study health behaviors. They are especially interested in finding ways to help people change their behaviors to promote good health. The health psychologists who developed our understanding of the stages of health behavior used information gained from several theories, which are often called **cognitive theories**. The terms *cognitive* and *cognition* refer to thinking and reasoning. Thus cognitive theories address a person's ability to use information to make reasonable decisions and create reasonable solutions to problems. Several theories that are used to explain health behaviors are described in the following discussion.

Transtheoretical Model

The stages of health behavior (stages of change) described in this chapter are based on research that uses a framework called the transtheoretical model. The stages represent levels of motivation for change, ranging from low motivation to high motivation and regular behavior change. Two concepts especially important to this model are self-confidence (also called self-efficacy) and decisional balance. Self-confidence helps you dare to change. Decisional balance involves balancing the positives and negatives of making a change; if there are more positives than negatives, you're motivated to make the change.

Social Learning Theory

According to this theory, also called social cognitive theory, people learn from their interactions with other people. We watch and listen to others, and we shape our attitudes and behaviors based on role models (e.g., parents, friends, teachers). Modeling means imitating or trying out behaviors displayed by those around us. To model a behavior, a person must be motivated—he or she must want to try. So motivation is important to this theory. Self-confidence (self-efficacy) is also

important because it helps you be motivated to try a new behavior and stick with it.

Self-Determination Theory

Human motivation is central to self-determination theory. To be motivated, people have to feel competent, which is similar to feeling self-confident. Also important is autonomy (self-determination)—the freedom to make your own decisions. Autonomy helps people feel internally motivated. A third important feature of this theory is relatedness. People are more likely to be motivated if they feel that they are related to or involved in the world around them.

Theory of Planned Behavior

This theory holds that positive attitudes and personal beliefs motivate people to behave in a certain way. According to the theory, positive attitudes and beliefs help you want to change. People who *state* an intention to change (e.g., make a New Year's resolution) are more likely to actually make changes than people who do not state such an intention. As in social learning theory, feelings of confidence are important here. Having self-confidence helps people both state their intention to change and actually make the change. The theory of planned behavior originated from an earlier theory called the theory of reasoned action. Both theories emphasize the fact that you can use cognitions (thinking) to help motivate your behavior and make good decisions.

Health Belief Model

This model states that people will take action to change their health if they have an interest in health matters, feel susceptible to a particular illness, believe that the benefits of treatment or action outweigh the barriers, or think a potential illness could be serious. The health belief model is often used to determine the likelihood that someone will follow the health recommendations they are given by a health professional.

🔊 HEALTHY COMMUNICATION

Many businesses and schools are smoke-free environments. Some towns, cities, and states now ban smoking in all public places, including outdoor spaces. Do you think such policies designed to protect public health are fair and justified? Why or why not? Share your opinion with a peer or classmate. Support your opinion with facts and respect each other's opinions.

move from a low stage to a higher stage and then fall back to a lower stage. Then they try again, each time moving to a higher stage. Of course, there are exceptions, but gradual change is most common. Since the original research, the stages have been used to help people improve all sorts of health behaviors, including eating patterns, physical activity, adoption of personal health habits, and avoidance of destructive habits other than smoking.

You can find more information about theories of health behavior change in the student section of the Health for Life website.

taken steps to implement it. This person might say, "I'm thinking about stopping." At stage 3, a person has not only thought about changing but also taken steps toward making the change. In the example shown in the figure, the person might have accessed a website for advice about how to stop smoking or investigated joining a smoking cessation group.

By the time a person reaches stage 4, he or she has already made some changes but still needs to make more. The person in figure 2.5 might have cut down the number of cigarettes per day or even stopped smoking for a few days. At stage 5, a person has made a definitive change and is sticking with it. For example, he or she might have stopped smoking for six months or more. This stage is often referred to as maintenance, because the person is adopting the healthy behavior on a regular basis.

It would be nice if people who want to change health behaviors could always move quickly from stage 1 to stage 5. But this is not always the case. For example, smokers who quit (reach maintenance) often do not find success right away. For some smokers, it takes several tries over a period of many months. Others move through the stages more quickly. Regardless of how long it takes, people often

Learning from interactions with other people is part of the social learning theory.

Monkey Business/fotolia.com

Comprehension Check

1. Identify the four types of groups that, along with personal actions, influence your health; also explain how personal health is related to group health.
2. List and describe the five stages of health behavior change; explain how they relate to behavior change.
3. Describe one of the theories used to study health behavior change.

MAKING HEALTHY DECISIONS: Goal Setting

We all know people who have tried to change a health behavior but have not been successful in making permanent change. They are in stage 2 for behavior change. They may have tried to make lifestyle changes but may have fallen short because they failed to set good goals. This feature highlights what are called **SMART goals** for one personal health behavior: sleep.

Ms. Gonzales, the health education teacher, noticed that Emma was not turning in her assignments on time. Emma had always been a good student, but was falling behind and risked getting a poor grade. After class, Ms. Gonzales asked Emma, "Are you okay? You seem a bit tired." Emma said, "I am sorry for getting my homework in late. I have had so much to do lately and I haven't gotten enough sleep. I fell asleep while I was trying to do my homework last night. I'm sorry."

Ms. Gonzales asked Emma if she could stop by after school for a visit. When they met, Ms. Gonzales said, "Maybe you need to make a plan to improve your sleep habits. Maybe setting some SMART goals would help." With Ms. Gonzales' help, they used the acronym SMART to set some goals. Emma prepared several goals to help improve her sleep habits. She made sure that her goals corresponded with each letter in the acronym.

- **S**pecific means identifying very specific things you want to accomplish.
- **M**easurable means being sure you can easily evaluate the goal to see if you have accomplished it.
- **A**ttainable means that they challenge you and are not too hard or too easy.
- **R**ealistic means that they are reasonable for you and that you can expect to accomplish them if you put in the effort.
- **T**imely means the goal can be achieved in the time allotted and the goal is right for you at this time.

Emma wrote down her goals and put them into action.

For Discussion

Why is it important for Emma to use the SMART formula in setting her goals? What are some examples of SMART goals that Emma might write to improve her sleep habits? What are some things that Emma can do to help her implement her goals? In answering these questions, consider the guidelines presented in this chapter's Skills for Healthy Living feature.

SKILLS FOR HEALTHY LIVING: Goal Setting

Now that you know about SMART goals, you can begin developing goals of your own. As you work through this course, you'll have the opportunity to set goals for a variety of health behaviors using the Healthy Living Plan worksheet presented in later chapters. The following guidelines will help you as you identify and develop your personal goals.

- **Use the SMART formula.** Use the formula and goals described by Ms. Gonzales in the Making Healthy Decisions sidebar.
- **Choose a few goals at a time.** This book prompts you to establish goals for adopting a variety of healthy behaviors, but at any given time you should choose a few

goals to focus on rather than working on all of your goals at once. Trying to do too much often leads to failure. Narrowing down to a few goals at a time can help you succeed.

- **Focus on modifying behavior when setting short-term goals.** Short-term goals are goals that can be accomplished in days or weeks. When setting short-term goals, focus on changing your behaviors (e.g., getting in bed by a specific time, eating five servings of fruits and vegetables every day for two weeks or walking 30 minutes every day for two weeks). If you change your behavior, then fitness, health, and wellness will follow.

- **Over the long term you can focus on the process and the product.** As noted, short-term goals focus on behavior change (changing the process). Product goals are outcomes that result from changing the process (behavior). For example, if you do strength training (the process), you will increase the number of push-ups you can do (product). It takes time to change strength (the product), so product goals—such as increasing the number of push-ups you can do—are not especially good as short-term goals.

- **Put your goals in writing.** Writing down a goal represents a personal commitment and increases your chance of meeting that goal. You'll get the chance to write down your goals as you do the activities in this book.

- **Know your reasons for setting your goals.** Those who set goals for reasons other than their own personal improvement often fail. Ask yourself *why* you are setting each goal. Make sure you're setting goals for yourself based on your own needs and interests.

- **Self-assess periodically and keep logs.** Doing self-assessments helps you set appropriate goals and determine whether you've met them. Keeping logs helps you determine whether you're meeting your goals. Focus on improvement by working toward goals that are slightly higher than your current self-assessment results.

- **Reward yourself.** Achieving a personal goal is rewarding. It feels good. Congratulate yourself for your accomplishment.

- **Revise if necessary.** If you find that a goal is too difficult to accomplish, don't be afraid to revise it. Revising a goal is better than quitting because you didn't reach an unrealistic goal.

- **Consider maintenance goals.** Improvement is not always necessary. Once you reach the highest level of change, consider setting a goal of maintenance. For example, if your weight is healthy, then it is a healthy behavior for you to eat food containing enough calories to balance the calories you expend. In this case, it would not be healthy to restrict your calories so that you lose weight. Maintaining a healthy energy balance and a healthy weight are good goals.

 ACADEMIC CONNECTION: Domain-Specific Language

Part of meeting standards in English language arts is demonstrating the acquisition of domain-specific words and phrases. This means that you are expected to learn vocabulary words that are particular to different subject areas, or disciplines. In each lesson of this text, you are provided a list of vocabulary words that are specific to health and wellness. Take the time to study the definition of each vocabulary word (see the glossary or the study section of the website for definitions) and observe how the word is used in its appropriate context (where it appears in the text and how it is used). Try to use each vocabulary word in a new sentence after you have become familiar with it.

Do the Rich Get to Be Healthier?

Having less than a high school education and earning less than US$12,000 annually may increase your risk of heart disease, according to the journal *BMC Cardiovascular Disorders*. Additional published studies also suggest a relationship between heart disease and socio-economic factors such as income, education, and ethnicity. Other conditions that have been associated with lower income include obesity, sleep quality, and diabetes risk (see figure 2.6).

When people can't afford to buy fresh fruits and vegetables, they often opt for cheaper "fast food" that is not optimal for good health. Lower-income workers and blue-collar laborers also often experience impaired sleep quality when they get stuck with night shifts or "swing shifts." In addition, people with more money are more likely to regularly see a doctor and dentist for proper preventive care, more likely belong to a health club, and more likely to get medicine they need.

As health advocate Dennis Carlson has said, "A solid health foundation is built on awareness, information, and then action." But all of these things are harder for people who are poor to sustain, as policy expert Beth Trout points out: "Education and awareness are great, but they do you less good if you live in a dangerous, unwalkable neighborhood with lots of fast food and no supermarkets; if you have little control in your work life; and if you

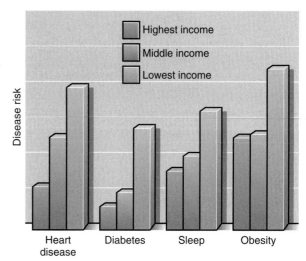

Figure 2.6 The relationship between income level and common health concerns.

are constantly worried about money, housing, and safety."

For Discussion

Brainstorm a list of ways that society could help all people be healthier regardless of economic status. Think of as many realistic examples as you can, then share your ideas with those of a peer or classmate. Compare your ideas and work together to create a list of your top three ideas. Negotiate and compromise as needed to build consensus (agreement).

CHAPTER REVIEW

Reviewing Concepts and Vocabulary

As directed by your teacher, answer items 1 through 5 by correctly completing each sentence with a word or phrase.

1. A collection of groups makes up a _____.
2. _____ _____ refers to the health of everyone on our planet.
3. Short-term goals should focus on changing behavior or goals referred to as _____ goals.
4. Tobacco, alcohol, and drug use are all forms of _____ habits.
5. A _____ factor is anything that increases the chances that you will get sick.

For items 6 through 10, as directed by your teacher, match each term in column 1 with the appropriate phrase in column 2.

6. precontemplation
7. contemplation
8. preparation
9. action
10. commitment

a. making a change such as engaging in physical activity
b. maintaining a behavior change for six months
c. thinking about making a behavior change
d. taking steps toward making a behavior change
e. stage where a person has not yet considered a health change

For items 11 through 15, as directed by your teacher, respond to each statement or question.

11. What does self-determination theory say about behavior change?
12. What are two examples of personal health habits?
13. What is a controllable risk factor? Provide an example.
14. What characterizes a SMART goal?
15. Describe the relationship between process and product goals.

Thinking Critically

Write a paragraph to answer the following questions.

Sheldon is thinking about cutting back on his consumption of sugary drinks. Last weekend, at the grocery store with his dad, he spent some time looking at alternatives, such as naturally flavored water. What stage of change best describes Sheldon's current status? What is one thing you could do to help him move to the next stage?

Take It Home

Teach a parent or guardian what you've learned about the stages of behavior change. Work together with a partner to create an illustration or diagram that explains the stages. Use the illustration or diagram when having the discussion with your parent or guardian. You may want to use an example of a specific behavior (e.g., being more active, eating better).

3

Choosing Healthy Lifestyles

www **Student Web Resources**
www.healthforlifetextbook.org/student

Lesson 3.1

Skills for Healthy Living

Lesson Objectives

After reading this lesson, you should be able to

1. explain the meaning of the term skills for healthy living,
2. explain each of the skills for healthy living, and
3. describe how the skills help you be healthy and well.

Lesson Vocabulary

self-regulation skills, skills for healthy living

Alex went to a lecture about health by Dr. Lazarus. He listened carefully and decided that he wanted to make some changes in his life—and try to help his parents make some changes. Alex felt stressed about his schoolwork. He knew that he had to reduce his stress level and that he needed to establish a more regular routine. He was also concerned because his dad smoked cigarettes and neither of his parents exercised regularly. Alex wasn't sure how to go about making changes in his own life, much less how to help his parents make changes. By consulting with his health teacher, he found out that using **skills for healthy living** would help him.

Experts in health behavior have proven that people who learn skills for healthy living (also known as self-management skills or **self-regulation skills**)—and use them regularly—can make changes in their health behaviors and stick with those changes. A skill is the ability to perform a task well, and a person's skills improve with regular practice.

There are many kinds of skills. For example, typing is a physical skill that helps you use a computer. Playing a musical instrument is a physical skill that helps you create sound. Being able to squat down and back up safely is a physical skill

that helps you with gardening or performing various household tasks. Throwing is a physical skill that helps you participate in various sports. The more you practice a physical skill, the better you get at it. But not all skills are physical. For example, calculation skills are necessary in math, writing skills are important in language arts, and critical thinking skills are necessary in almost all areas of study.

Skills for healthy living are similar to the skills just described. They can help you accomplish a desired goal or keep doing a good thing that you already do. For example, building good time management skills can help you make time to engage in a new activity, such as learning to cook healthy foods. You might also use good time management to help you maintain a workout schedule that you already have in place even when new time demands emerge. Like other skills, skills for healthy living can be learned and improved with practice.

A skill is the ability to perform a task well, and a person's skills improve with regular practice.

Skills for Healthy Living

In this lesson, you'll learn about 14 skills for healthy living, as well as 6 personal characteristics that are similar to skills and that help you make behavior changes. These skills are similar to self-management skills taught in physical education. In health education, they apply to a variety of health behaviors and are called skills for healthy living. The 14 skills for healthy living are described in detail in table 3.1.

TABLE 3.1 Skills for Healthy Living

Skill	Description	Benefits
Self-assessment	A person with self-assessment skill can evaluate his or her current status for markers of health and wellness or particular health behaviors. Examples include assessing your personal fitness, dietary nutrition, and stress level.	• Helps you objectively determine your current status. • Helps you set goals and plan a program to change your health behavior.
Goal setting	A person with goal-setting skill can set goals that are SMART (specific, measurable, attainable, realistic, and timely) for changing his or her health behaviors.	• Provides a road map for change. • Helps you prepare a plan for changing your health behavior.
Self-planning	This skill has five steps (discussed in this chapter's lesson titled Self-Planning) that serve as an outline for planning your personal program for health behavior change.	• Helps you commit in writing to goals and changing your behavior. • Provides a measuring stick for evaluating whether you've accomplished your goals.
Self-monitoring	This skill helps you keep records (logs or a journal) to see whether you're actually doing what you think you're doing—whether you're meeting personal goals and complying with your planned program for changing your health behavior.	• Helps you evaluate your progress in meeting goals and adhering to your program. • Helps you stay motivated to stick with your program. • Helps you keep useful records.
Overcoming barriers	This skill helps you find ways to stick with a behavior change despite obstacles such as lack of time, lack of safe places to be active, and difficulty selecting healthy foods.	• Helps you begin making changes. • Helps you stick with your changes. • Helps you eliminate excuses and succeed.
Time management	This skill helps you schedule time efficiently so that you have more time for the important things in your life.	• Helps you see how you use your time. • Helps you take care of priorities. • Helps you reduce stress.
Relapse prevention	This skill helps you stick with healthy behaviors even when you have problems getting motivated or when other people or situations tempt you to make unhealthy decisions.	• Helps you adhere to healthy behaviors. • Helps you persist and meet your goals.
Finding social support	This skill helps you stick with healthy behaviors by getting support from friends and family members.	• Helps you adhere to healthy behaviors. • Helps you prevent relapse.

Skill	Description	Benefits
Providing social support	Being a healthy citizen includes being able to help others when they are at risk for injury, illness, or death. This skill involves identifying risks, communicating effectively, and finding appropriate resources.	• Helps you build self-confidence and social wellness. • Helps you develop social responsibility.
Saying no	This skill helps you avoid doing things you don't want to do, especially when you're under pressure from friends or other people.	• Helps you adhere to healthy behaviors. • Helps you stay on track to meet your goals.
Conflict resolution	This skill helps you resolve problems that arise at school, at home, or in other circumstances.	• Helps you reduce stress. • Helps you maintain friendships and other good relationships.
Critical thinking	This skill enables you to find and interpret information that helps you make good decisions and solve problems related to your health. For example, one critical thinking skill that you will address in this book is evaluating nutrition information.	• Helps you set goals. • Helps you plan your program. • Helps you be a wise health consumer.
Performance	This type of skill involves performing tasks of daily living (e.g., typing, cooking) and tasks that make your leisure time enjoyable (e.g., playing a sport).	• Helps you enjoy life. • Contributes to healthy living.
Self-help	This type of skill helps you be safe and healthy and able to help others as well. Examples include knowing first aid and CPR, using safety equipment (e.g., helmet and pads for roller blading), and practicing good personal health habits (e.g., tooth brushing and flossing).	• Helps you be healthy and well. • Helps you be safe and avoid injury. • Allows you to contribute to the health and safety of others.

Knowledge is a personal characteristic that functions as a skill for healthy living and it will help you set goals and plan for healthy living.

Photodisc

Personal Characteristics That Function as Skills for Healthy Living

Health scientists have demonstrated that acquiring certain personal characteristics can also help you adopt healthy behaviors. These six characteristics are not exactly skills, but you can improve them with practice, and they do help you adopt healthy behaviors. Therefore, they function as skills for healthy living (self-management) and are considered as such in this book. These six characteristics are described in table 3.2. You can self-assess the six characteristics and the 14 skills for healthy living (20 in all) using the questionnaire in the self-assessment in this chapter.

 Time and health are two precious assets that we don't recognize and appreciate until they have been depleted.

—Denis Waitley, motivational speaker and writer

🔊 HEALTHY COMMUNICATION
Which personal characteristic discussed in this chapter do you think is most important in helping you to be healthy? Force yourself to select only one of the characteristics. Share your selection and the reasons for your selection with a classmate. Engage in active listening and determine where you both agree and disagree. Did listening to your classmate change your perspective?

Though it's important to know about the skills described in tables 3.1 and 3.2, being aware of them doesn't mean that you can automatically use them effectively. You also need to know how and when to use them, and you need to *practice* using them. Throughout this book, you'll learn more about these skills and get the opportunity to practice using them. For best results, practice them on your own as well as in class. For example, the best athletes practice their skills outside of practice sessions—that's part of why they're the best. If you want to be good at using the skills of healthy living, practice them at every opportunity.

TABLE 3.2 Personal Characteristics That Function as Skills for Healthy Living

Skill	Description	Benefits
Knowledge	Knowledge involves more than just knowing and remembering facts. Higher-order forms of knowledge include understanding (ability to interpret, summarize, and explain ideas), application (ability to use ideas), analysis (ability to examine parts of an idea), evaluation (ability to assess an idea), and synthesis (ability to put ideas together). You're developing your knowledge of health throughout this course.	• Helps you make good decisions about health and wellness. • Provides a basis for critical thinking. • Helps you set goals and plan for healthy living. • Helps you be a wise health consumer.
Positive attitude	An attitude is a personal feeling or set of feelings about something. Health scientists know that people with positive attitudes are more likely to adopt healthy behaviors than people with negative attitudes. It's important to learn to take a positive attitude and to change your attitude when needed.	• Helps you enjoy life. • Motivates you to make healthy lifestyle choices. • Helps you stick with your pursuit of your goals.
Ability to identify risk factors	Risk factors are characteristics that make you more likely to have a disease or health condition. You can maximize good health by identifying your risk factors and getting screening to see if you have certain conditions.	• Helps you resist disease and other health problems. • Helps you make changes to reduce them.

Skill	Description	Benefits
Intrinsic motivation	Motivation involves having an incentive or reason for doing a certain behavior. There are two types. *Intrinsic* motivation spurs you to do a behavior because you enjoy it or want to do it. *Extrinsic* motivation encourages you to do a behavior because of a reward or incentive provided by someone else (e.g., being paid for earning a high grade). Over the long haul, intrinsic motivation is more effective in helping you change your health behaviors. Though motivation is not technically a skill, it can be classified as a skill for healthy living because it can help you adopt healthy behaviors.	• Helps you stick with your goals. • Helps you give good effort and enjoy your efforts. • Helps you adopt new behaviors and try new things (e.g., new foods or activities).
Self-confidence (self-efficacy)	Self-confidence is the belief that you can perform a task successfully. People with self-confidence (also called self-efficacy) believe that they will be successful in performing a specific task. It's possible to be confident in one area while not so confident in another. Self-confidence is not exactly a skill, but building your self-confidence can help you adopt healthy behaviors. Practice using positive self-talk and setting SMART goals. Using positive role models can help you build confidence.	• Helps you succeed in your endeavors. • Helps you stick with your pursuit of your goals. • Helps you give good effort and enjoy your efforts. • Helps you adopt new behaviors and try new things (e.g., new foods or activities). • Helps you react positively to criticism.
Positive self-perception	A self-perception is a way of seeing yourself. Types of self-perception include social, scholastic, physical, and global.	• Helps you succeed in your endeavors. • Helps you stick with your pursuit of your goals. • Helps you give good effort and enjoy your efforts. • Helps you adopt new behaviors and try new things (e.g., new foods or activities). • Helps you react positively to criticism.

 ## ADVOCACY IN ACTION: Positive Attitudes

To advocate for something is to publicly recommend or support it. Throughout this book, you're given opportunities to advocate on behalf of a variety of health issues in a variety of ways. We know that positive attitudes can help you make healthy decisions and achieve overall good health. Begin your advocacy work by initiating a positive attitudes campaign. Design posters of inspirational sayings and quotes to place around campus. Include information that helps others understand the link between positive attitudes and making healthy decisions.

HEALTH TECHNOLOGY

An application, or app, is a computer program that allows you to perform tasks on a smartphone or other device. Some apps are designed to help you use skills for healthy living—for example, by self-assessing your food content, self-monitoring your physical activity, or planning healthy meals. If well designed, apps can help you change your health behaviors, but not all apps are based on good health information. Before using an app, determine whether the people who developed it are health experts; ask people you know and trust about the app, and test it out for yourself. For more information about health-related apps, see the student section of the Health for Life website.

 **CONNECT**

Do you currently use any apps to help you live a healthier life? If so, what features do you think make a good health application? If not, what type of app might appeal to you? Can you imagine using a health app in the future?

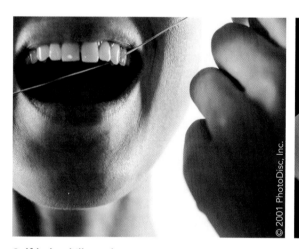

© 2001 PhotoDisc, Inc.

PhotoDisc

Self-help skills such as practicing good personal health habits like flossing and tooth brushing help you to be healthy and well.

Comprehension Check

1. What is the meaning of the term skills for healthy living?
2. List each of the skills for healthy living and explain one of them in more detail.
3. Explain how the skills for healthy living can help you be healthy and well.

The following questionnaire will help you see which of the skills (and characteristics) for healthy living you already possess and which ones you need to develop or improve. As directed by your teacher, record your results. A worksheet may be provided. Follow these instructions.

1. Read each of the 20 skills and characteristics. Circle the number (1 to 4) that best represents your response (use regularly, use rarely, developing this skill, and do not have this skill).

2. Add the scores for the 20 skills and characteristics to get a total score.

3. Use table 3.3 to get your rating for each healthy living skill and for your total score.

Healthy Living Skills Questionnaire

Healthy living skills and characteristics	I have this skill or characteristic and use it regularly.	I have this skill or characteristic but rarely use it.	I am developing this type of skill or characteristic.	I do not have this type of skill or characteristic.	Score
1. Self-assessment	4	3	2	1	
2. Goal setting	4	3	2	1	
3. Self-planning	4	3	2	1	
4. Self-monitoring	4	3	2	1	
5. Overcoming barriers	4	3	2	1	
6. Time management	4	3	2	1	
7. Relapse prevention	4	3	2	1	
8. Finding social support	4	3	2	1	
9. Providing social support	4	3	2	1	
10. Saying no	4	3	2	1	
11. Conflict resolution	4	3	2	1	
12. Critical thinking	4	3	2	1	
13. Performance	4	3	2	1	
14. Self-help	4	3	2	1	
15. Knowledge	4	3	2	1	
16. Positive attitude	4	3	2	1	
17. Ability to identify risk factors	4	3	2	1	
18. Intrinsic motivation	4	3	2	1	
19. Self-confidence (self-efficacy)	4	3	2	1	
20. Positive self-perceptions	4	3	2	1	
Total score and total rating =					

TABLE 3.3   Rating Chart

Wellness rating	One-item score	Total score[*]
Good	4	>80
Marginal	2–3	64–79
Low	<1	<63

[*]It is desirable to be skilled in all areas; therefore, even if you have a good total rating, you should work to improve your skills in any area for which you have a score below 4.

Lesson 3.2

Planning for Healthy Living

Lesson Objectives

After reading this lesson, you should be able to

1. describe the five steps in program planning,
2. describe the SMART formula for goal setting, and
3. explain how you can be accountable for carrying out your plan.

 Lesson Vocabulary

accountability, action steps, enabler, health behavior contract

Living a healthy life isn't always easy. Some healthy behaviors may come naturally to you, and others may be more challenging. For example, you might find it easy to refuse cigarettes if you come from a nonsmoking family and the smell of cigarette smoke is unappealing to you. Other healthy behaviors might be more difficult for you to start doing or to maintain. You might dislike the taste of vegetables and thus struggle to eat enough of them. Or you might feel you don't have the ability to say no to friends who try to convince you to try risky behaviors, such as experimenting with abuse of drugs.

In addition, many healthy decisions are hard to maintain throughout life. You can help yourself maintain healthy behaviors over the long term by learning how to make decisions thoughtfully and plan carefully.

The Five Steps in Making a Healthy Living Plan

Planning for healthy living (program planning) is a skill that takes time to develop and must be intentionally practiced. You'll have opportunities throughout this book to make healthy living plans for various areas of life. All of them will use the five-step process explained here. For an example of a complete plan, see the Sample Healthy Living Plan.

Step 1: Determining Your Personal Needs—Self-Assessment

The first step toward preparing a healthy living plan and making healthy decisions is to collect information about your personal needs. Throughout this book, you'll do many self-assessments that help you understand your current health status so that you can plan where you want to go. Some self-assessments may show you that you're already healthy, and others may draw your attention to areas where you could improve. Even when the results of a self-assessment show you that you're healthy in that area, you can always use the planning process to sustain or enhance your healthy behavior.

Step 2: Considering Your Healthy Behavior Options

After determining your personal needs, the next step is to consider your options for healthy behavior—for example, what types of physical activity are available to you, what changes you can make in your diet, or what approaches are available for ending an unhealthy habit (e.g., nicotine aids, smoking cessation groups). Regardless of the behavior you want to change, explore your options and reflect on which ones might be best for you based on your personal strengths and weaknesses, as well as the barriers you might face in trying to change the behavior.

Step 3: Setting Your Goals

Effective planning involves setting both short-term and long-term goals. Short-term goals are those that you can reasonably achieve in several weeks, whereas long-term goals require months and sometimes even years. Identify both short- and long-term goals for any health behavior you try to change. Remember that all goals should be SMART goals (see figure 3.1).

Sample Healthy Living Plan

STEP 1: Determining Your Personal Needs

The behavior I want to change is: I want to be better prepared for emergencies.

Starting date: April 2

The self-assessment I conducted relating to this behavior is: My Emergency Preparedness.

The results of the self-assessment are: I am not well prepared to meet emergencies.

STEP 2: Determining Your Options

The options available to me for changing this behavior are:

1. Take a first aid and CPR class.

2. Get a first aid kit for my house and car.

One personal strength I possess to help me change this behavior is:

I have good self-motivation and follow through on commitments.

One personal weakness I have that might make changing this behavior difficult is:

I am a little shy and might not be comfortable in a community first aid class.

The barriers I may face in trying to change my behavior are:

1. I live in a small town and there may not be classes available to me.

2. I don't have much extra money for buying supplies.

STEP 3: Setting Goals

Short-term goals (1 day to 1 month):   Target date:

1. Sign up for a first aid or CPR class.   May 10_____

2. Make a list of items for my home first aid kit.   May 6 _____

> continued

Sample Healthy Living Plan > continued

Long-term goal (more than a month):   Target date:

I will *get certified in both CPR and first aid and will have*   July 10 _____

at least one first aid kit made.

_____

STEP 4: Structuring Your Healthy Living Plan and Establishing Accountability

The action steps I need to take first to help me achieve my goals are:

1. *Look up options for CPR or first aid classes in the community.*

2. *Research whether or not there are online CPR or first aid classes I can take.*

3. *Go to the store and make a list of available items and their prices.*

_____

_____

To help me be successful in making this change, I will use the following accountability strategy or strategies:

☑ Behavioral contract

☐ Social support

☐ Behavioral journal or log

☐ Other: _____

Step 5: Implementing Your Plan and Evaluating Your Progress

Short-term goal 1	☑ Met	☐ Not met	Date: **April 21**
Short-term goal 2	☐ Met	☑ Not met	Date: **July 15**
Long-term goal	☑ Met	☐ Not met	Date: **July 15**

If you met your goal, what contributed most to your success?

I was persistent, and my school counselor helped me find a free CPR class in the community.

_____

_____

If you did not meet your goal, what contributed most to your lack of success?

I met all of my goals, but I was late in meeting my second short-term goal because I had a problem

with my car.

_____

_____

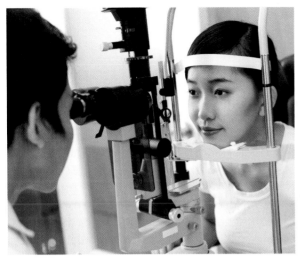

Getting regular check-ups may be one of the healthy options available to you.

© Dragonimages/Dreamstime

S M A R T Goal Reminder

S = Specific

M = Measurable

A = Attainable

R = Realistic

T = Timely

FIGURE 3.1 SMART goal reminder.

Step 4: Structuring Your Healthy Living Plan and Establishing Accountability

In step 4 of the planning process, you use the information that you developed in steps 1, 2, and 3. For each goal, write down **action steps**.

In addition to establishing your action plan, identify the strategy that you'll use for **accountability**. Being accountable means that you follow through with the goals and commitments you make to yourself and others. Two ways to hold yourself accountable are to develop family and peer support and to use self-monitoring strategies. Each of these strategies is discussed in this chapter's Skills for Healthy Living feature.

Step 5: Implementing Your Plan and Evaluating Your Progress

After you've been implementing your action steps for a while, make time to evaluate your progress. Ask yourself whether your goals still seem reasonable. Review your action steps and decide whether they're helping you achieve your goal.

 Good health and good sense are two of life's greatest blessings. **99**

—Publilius Syrus, Roman philosopher

Using Self-Planning Skills

The five steps in planning for healthy living are presented here to help you learn how to plan your own behavior change (self-planning). You'll begin to learn to do self-planning for many kinds of healthy behavior.

⊕ CONNECT

You will benefit from your healthy living plan only if you follow it. How might a person's family help him or her carry out a healthy living plan?

Comprehension Check

1. What are the five steps in planning for healthy living?
2. What does each letter in the SMART (goal setting) formula represent?
3. What is accountability and why is it important in planning?

MAKING HEALTHY DECISIONS: *Self-Planning*

Josefita wanted to change a specific health behavior—her eating. During her annual physical exam, she had been told that her blood sugar level was higher than it should be. It was not high enough for her to be considered diabetic, but the doctor had said that she was prediabetic. High blood sugar is sometimes associated with being overweight, but Josefita was not overweight. However, her doctor and dietitian did advise her to make some dietary changes. Specifically, they recommended that Josefita eat fewer high-fat foods, reduce her consumption of foods high in simple sugar (e.g., candy, doughnuts, pastries), and eat more foods high in fiber (e.g., fruits, vegetables). They also advised her to eat regular, well-balanced meals (rather than skipping meals) and to eat meals rich in nutrients.

For Discussion

How might Josefita be able to use the five steps in program planning to change her eating patterns? How could she use the advice of her doctor and dietitian to carry out the five steps? If Josefita follows her doctor's advice, how might her health improve? Provide one short-term and one long-term example. What is another healthy behavior Josefita might consider adopting? Explain your choice. To guide your thinking about these questions, use the Skills for Healthy Living feature.

 SKILLS FOR HEALTHY LIVING: *Self-Planning*

Now that you know about the five self-planning steps, you can use the following guidelines to help you create plans that work for you over the long term. You can also use the guidelines to help family members and friends who want to change their health behavior.

- **Use the five steps in sequence.** Start with step 1 (determining your needs), then work your way through all five steps.

- **Don't try to do too much.** Plan a program that reasonably challenges you but isn't overly difficult. If you try to accomplish too much all at once, you may not be effective in carrying out your plan. Setting SMART goals is critical to success.

- **Be specific.** Just as SMART goals are specific, your program should be specific. It should clearly lay out (in writing) the actions that you will take to meet your goals.

- **Revise if necessary.** The fifth step in program planning is to try your program and evaluate it. However, you don't have to wait until you've finished your program to revise it. If you find that it isn't working, revise it when you discover the problem.

- **Seek family support.** Tell family members about your plan and ask for their support. Family members may want to help by making health behavior changes themselves to support the changes you're making. This will help you to be accountable.

- **Seek peer support.** Identify a trusted friend or group of people who will help you stay on track as your implement your plan. Choose a buddy or group of friends who will be supportive. Avoid negative "**enablers**"—people who make it easier (enable you) to engage in a destructive habit or make it harder to stay on track with your positive behavior changes. This will help you to be accountable.

- **Self-monitor for progress.** Keep a behavior journal or log. Keeping records not only lets you know if you're successful in your plan; it can also provide reinforcement to help you stick with your plan. Choose a specific time each day to record your progress. Some experts recommend making daily entries in your log just before bedtime. Some plans may require more frequent entries (e.g., recording after lunch, after dinner, and at bedtime). This will help you to be accountable.

Can You Make a Contract for Good Health?

A **health behavior contract** is an agreement you make with yourself to change a specific health behavior. Research shows that behavioral contracts can help you stick with your plan for changing your health behavior. Behavioral contracts have been used in school classes to help students both meet academic goals and adopt healthy behaviors. In many ways, a personal plan based on the five steps for program planning *is* a health behavior contract. It is a written statement of what you plan to do to change your behavior.

Still, some experts recommend supplementing your plan with a health behavior contract to give you another incentive for sticking with your plan. You can do a contract alone or with someone else, such as a parent or teacher. The contract is typically signed and witnessed to give it a prominent place in your life. Here's a sample contract:

Based on awareness of my personal health, I _____ (name) have decided to set the following health-related goal: _____

My health behavior goal is _____ (long-term SMART goal).

My intrinsic (internal) motivation for wanting to achieve this goal is

_____
_____
_____.

The difficulties I anticipate facing in making this change are

_____
_____
_____.

The specific actions or behaviors I will take to reach my goal are (short-term SMART goals)

_____
_____
_____.

I will reward achievement of my goal by _____ (extrinsic motivation). If I fail to achieve my goal I will forfeit this reward.

I will review this contract on (date) _____.

Signature: _____

Signature of witness: _____

For Discussion

What do you think of the idea of a behavioral contract? How might it be helpful? Some contracts include a punishment if the contract is not fulfilled. What do you think of that idea?

Reviewing Concepts and Vocabulary

As directed by your teacher, answer items 1 through 5 by correctly completing each sentence with a word or phrase.

1. Skills for healthy living are also called _____ skills.
2. Skills for healthy living can be _____ with practice.
3. Self-_____ helps you identify your current health status.
4. The skill that helps you solve problems with others is _____ resolution.
5. _____ steps are things that you can do immediately to progress toward a behavior change.

For items 6 through 10, as directed by your teacher, match each term in column 1 with the appropriate phrase in column 2.

6. step 1
7. step 2
8. step 3
9. step 4
10. step 5

a. structuring your healthy living plan and establishing accountability
b. setting your goals
c. determining your personal needs (self-assessing)
d. implementing your plan and evaluating your progress
e. considering your healthy behavior options

For items 11 through 15, as directed by your teacher, respond to each statement or question.

11. Describe three skills for healthy living and explain why they are important.
12. Describe two characteristics that are similar to skills for healthy living and explain why they are important.
13. Describe the five steps in program planning.
14. Describe at least three guidelines for planning for healthy living (self-planning).
15. What is a health behavior contract? Explain.

Thinking Critically

Write a paragraph to answer the following questions.
How is knowledge important to your health? How can it help you achieve positive behavior change?

Take It Home

Share the self-assessment from this chapter with at least one family member. Ask the person(s) to complete the self-assessment, then share information with the person(s) about each of the healthy living skills. Consider setting a family goal that focuses on improving one healthy living skill each week or month.

UNIT II

Preventing Disease and Seeking Care

Healthy People 2020 Goals

- Help people live high-quality, longer lives.
- Reduce disease, injury, and early death.
- Increase awareness and understanding of what determines good health.
- Help people adopt healthy lifestyles for life-time health, fitness, and wellness.
- Create environments that promote health, fitness, and wellness for all.
- Improve emotional wellness.
- Decrease suicide, and suicide attempts, among teens.
- Increase availability of treatment for depression and anxiety.
- Increase counseling and wellness checkups.
- Increase school health education.
- Reduce the rate of HIV transmission among adolescents and adults.
- Increase annual flu and other vaccinations.
- Reduce the proportion of adolescents who are considered obese.
- Prevent inappropriate weight gain among adolescents and young adults.
- Reduce the overall cancer death rate.
- Reduce the percentage of teens who use artificial tanning.
- Increase the proportion of teens who take measures to protect against skin cancer.
- Improve the health literacy of the population.
- Increase the number of teens who have had a wellness checkup in the past year.

Self-Assessment Features in This Unit

- Body Mass Index
- My Disease Prevention IQ
- My Self-Esteem
- My Health Care Consumer Skills

Making Healthy Decisions and Skills for Healthy Living Features in This Unit

- Self-Confidence
- Identifying Risk Factors
- Providing Social Support
- Critical Thinking

Special Features in This Unit

- Diverse Perspectives: Being Overweight
- Consumer Corner: Choosing Hand Sanitizers
- Advocacy in Action: Mental Health Awareness
- Advocacy in Action: Know Your Medical History

Living Well News Features in This Unit

- Yo-Yo Dieting Is Up and Down
- Can Hot Temperatures Make Us Vulnerable to Disease?
- Teens Under the Knife
- What Are the Most Common Types of Health Insurance?

4

Understanding Your Body

In This Chapter

 **Student Web Resources**
www.healthforlifetextbook.org/student

Lesson 4.1
Body Systems

Lesson Objectives

After reading this lesson, you should be able to

1. identify all of the major body systems,
2. identify the major components of each body system, and
3. explain the primary function of each body system.

Lesson Vocabulary

alveoli, cardiac muscle, coronary circulation, cystic fibrosis, gene, hormones, kidney dialysis, nephrons, phenotype, pulmonary circulation, skeletal muscle, smooth muscle, systemic circulation

The human body is an amazing thing. Every second of the day, it sets off electrical impulses and chemical messengers, satisfies its need for oxygen, circulates blood and filters waste products, and regulates its acid–base balance and temperature. All the while, it allows you to think, dream, laugh, cry, jump, play, listen, learn, grow, and do everything else you do.

The intricacy and complexity of the body take years of study to understand, and science is still uncovering the body's many secrets. This lesson introduces you to the 11 major body systems and how they work together to maintain health and functioning. It also introduces the concept of genetics and the role that genes play in regulating major body systems.

Body Systems

The human body's 11 major body systems include the following: respiratory, circulatory, skeletal, muscular, integumentary, endocrine, nervous, digestive, excretory, reproductive, and immune. Each system performs its own specific functions, but all of the systems must also work together and support each other for the body to maintain optimal health and well-being.

For example, in order for you to play soccer on a hot day, your nervous, muscular, skeletal, respiratory, and circulatory systems must work together to create movement and supply your body with needed oxygen; in addition, your integumentary system must function optimally to allow heat to escape through your skin in the form of sweat. In fact, almost every system in your body affects all of the others; some of these interrelationships are summarized in table 4.1.

Circulatory System

Your circulatory system moves blood and oxygen through your body (see figure 4.1). Its operations include three kinds of circulation: pulmonary, coronary, and systemic. **Pulmonary circulation** moves blood from your heart to your lungs and back to your heart; **coronary circulation** provides your heart tissue itself with necessary blood and nutrients; and **systemic circulation** involves all of the arteries and veins that feed the rest of your body. During systemic circulation, your blood also passes through your kidneys and liver, where it is cleaned of toxins and waste products.

Respiratory System

Your respiratory system includes your mouth, nose, trachea, lungs, and diaphragm. Its primary functions are to supply your blood with oxygen and expel carbon dioxide. Oxygen enters your nose and mouth, then passes down through your trachea and into your lungs. More specifically, your trachea divides into two smaller tubes called bronchi, which then divide into smaller tubes. These tubes lead directly to your lungs, where they continue to divide and connect to tiny air sacs called **alveoli**. At this level, oxygen exchange takes place through a network of capillary beds (very small blood vessels). Once fully developed, your lungs contain about 600

TABLE 4.1 Interrelationship of Body Systems

System	Examples of interaction with other body systems
Circulatory	Circulates oxygen from the lungs to muscles to support movement; moves nutrients from the digestive system to all cells in the body; moves hormones through the body for the endocrine system.
Respiratory	Provides oxygen to all systems and removes carbon dioxide from all systems so that cells can survive and function.
Muscular	Moves bones to produce movement and exert force; necessary to produce bone growth for the skeletal system; contracts the heart to provide circulation for the circulatory system.
Skeletal	Bones act as levers to facilitate movement in concert with muscular systems; gives structure to the body; protects the brain for the nervous system; produces blood cells for the immune system.
Nervous	Sends messages to muscles to support movement; controls organs (e.g., stomach, intestines) for the digestive and excretory systems.
Digestive	Breaks down food into nutrients needed by all systems; sustains healthy bacteria in the colon for the immune system.
Excretory	Removes wastes from the body for the digestive system; helps remove water from food and deliver it to the blood for the circulatory system.
Endocrine	Provides hormones needed for the reproductive system; provides chemical messengers needed to regulate the brain and nervous system.
Immune	Protects all systems of the body from disease.
Integumentary	Includes skin, hair, and nails; protects the muscles and bones of the muscular and skeletal systems; protects the organs of the digestive system; protects the body from germs for the immune system.
Reproductive	Secretes (via the testes and ovaries) hormones essential for the maturation of the skeletal and muscular systems during adolescent growth spurts; is intensely interconnected with and mutually supportive of the endocrine system.

million alveoli. The respiratory system is presented in figure 4.2.

Muscular System

Your muscular system is responsible for all movements in your body and consists of more than 650 muscles (see figure 4.3). Muscular tissue falls into one of three categories: cardiac, smooth, and skeletal. **Cardiac muscle** refers to the muscle of your heart, which is distinctive in that it contracts automatically and regularly. On average, the heart contracts 70 times per minute and pumps five quarts (liters) of blood each minute.

Smooth muscle is found in the walls of other hollow organs, such as your esophagus, stomach,

Genetics and Cystic Fibrosis

Cystic fibrosis is a genetic disorder caused by inheriting a particular defective gene from each parent. The genes interfere with the acid balance in the lungs, making it more likely that bacteria will grow. The resulting inflammation leads to the accumulation of mucus, which plugs the airways and causes damage that interferes with breathing and leads to a persistent cough. Cystic fibrosis can affect individuals of all races, but it is five times more common in whites than Hispanics or blacks.

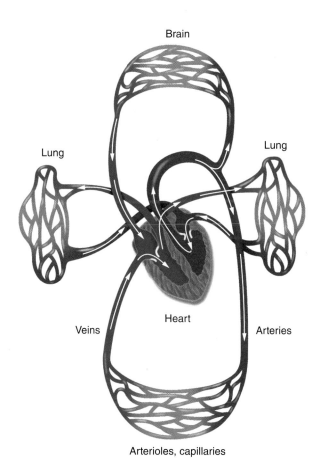

intestines, and (for females) uterus. Its primary role is to contract in order to reduce the size of the organ and create force or movement. As a result, smooth muscle plays a critical role in most body functions. For example, it contracts your esophagus, stomach, and digestive organs in order to push food through your digestive system. It also contracts the uterus to deliver a baby. Smooth muscle function is involuntary, meaning that it contracts automatically in response to stimulation from the nervous system.

Skeletal muscle controls all motor activities and is under your voluntary control. As the name implies, skeletal muscles are attached to your bones in order to give them stability and leverage.

FIGURE 4.1 The circulatory system.

The Skeletal System

Your skeletal system is made up of your bones and the network of tendons, ligaments, and cartilage that connects them. Bones also act as levers. Human infants are born with 300 to 350 bones, some of which fuse together as the body develops. By the time most children reach the age of nine, they have 206 bones. The skeletal system performs vital functions, including support, movement, protection, blood cell production, calcium storage, and hormone regulation.

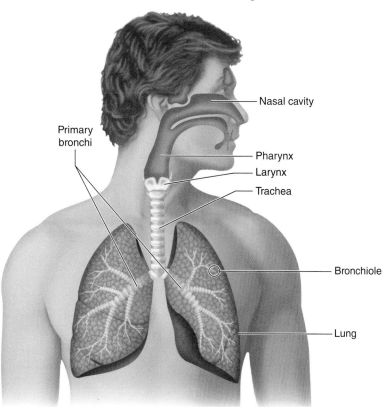

FIGURE 4.2 The respiratory system.

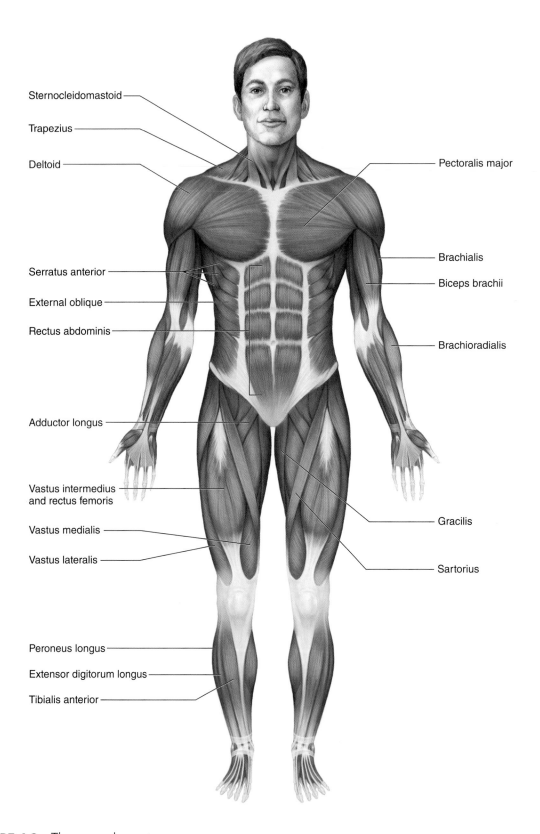

Sternocleidomastoid

Trapezius

Deltoid

Pectoralis major

Serratus anterior

External oblique

Rectus abdominis

Brachialis

Biceps brachii

Brachioradialis

Adductor longus

Vastus intermedius
and rectus femoris

Vastus medialis

Vastus lateralis

Gracilis

Sartorius

Peroneus longus

Extensor digitorum longus

Tibialis anterior

FIGURE 4.3   The muscular system.

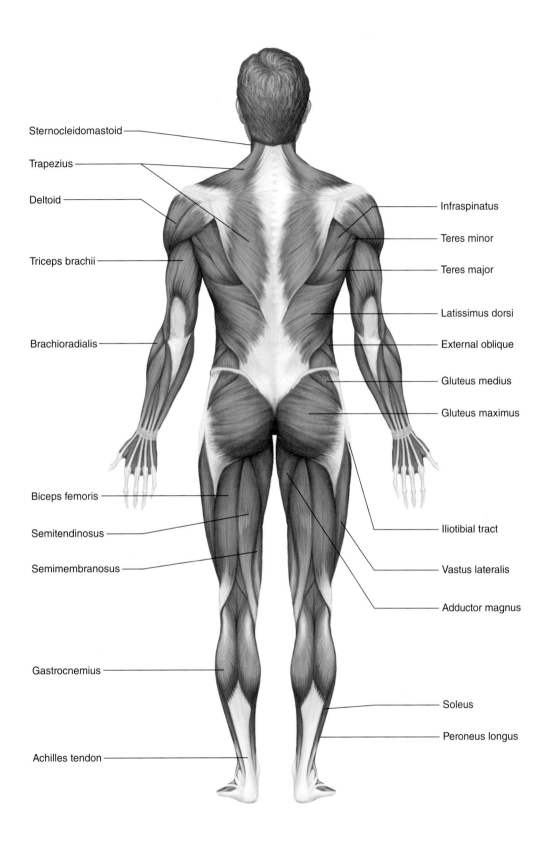

Sternocleidomastoid

Trapezius

Deltoid

Triceps brachii

Brachioradialis

Biceps femoris

Semitendinosus

Semimembranosus

Gastrocnemius

Achilles tendon

Infraspinatus

Teres minor

Teres major

Latissimus dorsi

External oblique

Gluteus medius

Gluteus maximus

Iliotibial tract

Vastus lateralis

Adductor magnus

Soleus

Peroneus longus

A typical bone has a dense and tough outer layer as well as an inner spongy layer that is lighter and slightly flexible (see figure 4.4). In the middle of some bones is the jelly-like bone marrow, where new cells are constantly being produced for blood. Teeth are considered part of the skeletal system, but they are not counted as bones. They are made of dentin and enamel, which is the strongest substance in your body. Teeth also play a key role in your digestive system because they help break down food so that it can be swallowed safely and then transported into the stomach.

Your skeletal system consists of two distinctive parts: your axial skeleton and your appendicular skeleton (see figure 4.4). Your axial skeleton totals 80 bones and consists of your vertebral column, rib cage, and skull. It transmits the weight from your head, trunk, and upper extremities down to your lower extremities at your hip joints. It is responsible for the upright posture of humans. Your appen-

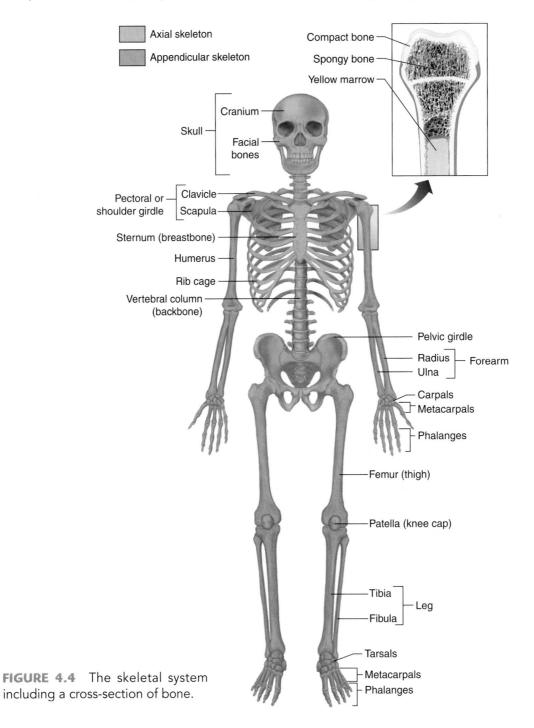

FIGURE 4.4 The skeletal system including a cross-section of bone.

⚛ HEALTH SCIENCE

Your muscular system has strong genetic influences, and the types of muscle tissue that you have can influence your athletic abilities. For example, certain genes are associated with particular muscle proteins that can affect muscle contraction. In fact, one team of Australian researchers discovered the "gene for speed." They studied more than 400 Australian Olympic athletes and another 400 individuals who were not competitive athletes. The gene for speed was missing in 20 percent of the general population but was present in all of the Olympic athletes who competed in power sports (e.g., sprinting, high jumping, long jumping).

dicular skeleton totals 126 bones and is formed by your pectoral girdle (shoulder and shoulder blades), upper limbs, pelvic girdle (hips), and lower limbs. It makes walking, running, and other movements possible and protects the major organs responsible for your digestion, excretion, and reproduction.

Nervous System

Your nervous system provides all of the electrical signals that control your movements. It is made up of two main parts: your central nervous system (CNS) and your peripheral nervous system. Your CNS includes your brain and spinal cord (see figure 4.5). Your peripheral nervous system consists of a network of nerves that link your brain and spinal cord to the rest of your body.

Some of these nerves transmit sensory information from your eyes, ears, skin, and other sensory organs to your CNS. Others communicate with your muscles and glands. You're not aware of all of these actions because many of them (e.g., digestion, breathing) are autonomic, meaning that they happen automatically. Other nerves carry signals that you produce in your brain and control more consciously in order to perform actions such as chewing, walking, picking up a pen, and raising your arm in class.

Digestive System

Your digestive system gets the nutrients you eat into your body, where they are broken down into usable parts and absorbed. Digestion begins in your mouth with chewing and the secretion of saliva, which begins to break down some carbohydrates. It continues in your stomach, where your food

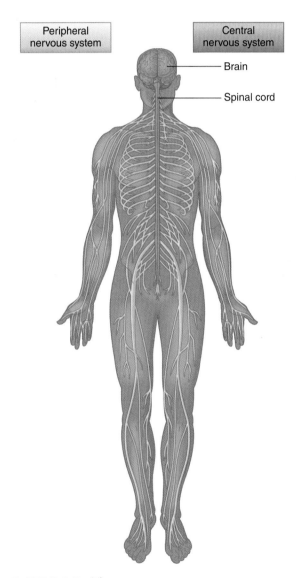

FIGURE 4.5 The nervous system.

is churned and broken down, and in your small intestine, where most nutrients are absorbed by your body. Your large intestine helps extract water from your food and moves waste products out of your body (see figure 4.6). Like other major body systems, digestion depends on the work of the circulatory, endocrine, and nervous systems in order to function properly.

Excretory System

Your excretory system eliminates metabolic wastes from your body and helps maintain proper fluid balance. This system involves the work of your kidneys, bladder, urethra, and skin. Your kidneys play a critical function in this system, since all blood

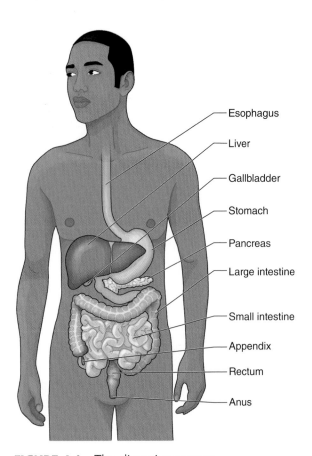

FIGURE 4.6   The digestive system.

passes through them to be cleaned of toxins. Each kidney weighs about 0.25 pound (0.1 kilogram) and contains one million filtering units known as **nephrons**. The glands associated with the kidneys (adrenal glands) also monitor and regulate the fluid balance in your body. Your kidneys deliver unneeded fluid, vitamins, and minerals, as well as toxins, to your bladder for elimination as urine.

Kidney damage can result from chronic high blood pressure, diabetes, and overuse of certain medications (e.g., the painkillers acetaminophen and ibuprofen). Once the kidneys are damaged beyond normal functioning, a person requires kidney dialysis or a transplant in order to survive. **Kidney dialysis** involves running all of the blood in the body through an external filtering system multiple times each week.

Endocrine System

Your endocrine system consists of glands that produce and secrete a variety of hormones throughout your body. **Hormones**, or chemical messengers, communicate information from one cell to another and coordinate functions throughout your body and between body systems. Major endocrine glands include your hypothalamus, pituitary, thyroid, parathyroid, adrenal, pineal, and reproductive organs (see figure 4.7). Disruptions to the endocrine system can affect growth and development, metabolism, and reproductive functions (e.g., ovulation in females, sperm production in males).

Immune System

Your immune system protects you from infection. It is a complex network consisting of your tonsils, lymph nodes, lymphatic vessels, spleen, thymus, and bone marrow. This system fights disease by attacking each threat it faces with a specialized

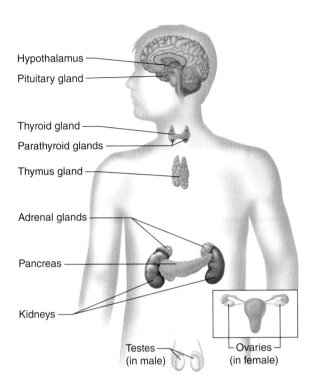

Hypothalamus
Pituitary gland
Thyroid gland
Parathyroid glands
Thymus gland
Adrenal glands
Pancreas
Kidneys
Testes (in male)
Ovaries (in female)

FIGURE 4.7 The major endocrine glands. Two of the most important glands in the body, the hypothalamus and pituitary glands, are located in the brain.

response. As you go through life and are exposed to more threats, your body builds its immunity. When you're exposed to a particular threat, such as chicken pox (not as common anymore because of vaccine), your immune system creates a memory of the threat that enables it to launch a very specific, quick, and aggressive response if the threat returns. Your immune system also plays a role in many disease processes and is discussed further in the chapter titled Diseases and Disability.

Integumentary System

Your integumentary system consists of your skin, hair, and nails. Most important of these is your skin, which is the largest single organ of your body. Your skin protects and cushions your body's organs and provides a physical barrier to keep out foreign materials. It consists of three layers: epidermis, dermis, and subcutis. The epidermis is the outermost layer of your skin. It consists of dead cells on top and live, reproducing cells toward the bottom. Your dermis is your middle layer of skin; it contains its own blood supply and is home to your sweat glands and hair

roots. It also contains collagen, which gives your skin strength and elasticity. Your deepest layer of the skin is the subcutis, where adipose (fat) tissue provides cushioning for your organs and insulation to help your body maintain a stable temperature.

🔊 HEALTHY COMMUNICATION

Select one of the major body systems presented in this chapter. Write one or two verses of a rap song or poem to explain the body system to an elementary or middle school student. Include the system's functions and major organs and give advice for keeping it healthy.

Reproductive System

The human reproductive system allows for the conception, development, and delivery of offspring. It differs, of course, between males and females but ultimately serves the overall purpose of reproduction. In the male reproductive system, sperm is produced in the testicles for release through the penis during sexual activity. The female reproductive system includes the uterus, ovaries, fallopian tubes, vagina, and external genitalia. The female

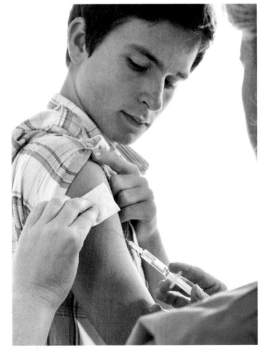

Vaccinations help your body build its immunity.
© Alexander Raths/Dreamstime

Genes and Skin Color

One of the most obvious phenotype characteristics that distinguishes members of our species is skin color. Human skin color covers a tremendous range, and variations can be correlated with factors such as climate, continent, and culture. Still, scientists know very little about the underlying genetics of skin color, and even the number of genes involved in the expression of skin color remains unknown.

menstrual cycle is a monthly cycle that results in the release of a mature egg and prepares the walls of the uterus to implant the egg if it is fertilized by sperm. If fertilization does not occur, the lining of the uterus is shed through menstruation, and the cycle begins again.

Genetics and the Body

Genetics plays a large role in determining how well each of your body systems functions on its own and how well your systems work together. Almost every cell in your body carries a complete set of **genes** (genotype) and all of the information necessary to make you. These instructions are unique to you and are encoded in your DNA—long, twisting, ladder-shaped molecules that store a particular pattern, or code, based on how they are organized. Strands of DNA form your chromosomes, which combine to create your genes, which in turn create the proteins that ultimately affect every aspect of who you are. Thus your genes influence everything about you— for example, what type of muscle cells you have, how well you see and smell, how efficiently your body uses energy, and how you think and solve problems.

We are often most aware of genetic influences when we look at a person's physical characteristics. The way in which your genes are visibly expressed is known as your **phenotype**, which includes, for example, your height, eye and hair color, and skin color. A phenotype has both a genetic and an environmental influence. Height, for instance, is mostly a genetic trait, but it is also affected by the quality of your diet during times of critical bone development, which can also influence how strong your bones become. So genetics and lifestyle choices work together to influence who you are and how healthy you are.

> " Yet this is health: To have a body functioning so perfectly that when its few simple needs are met it never calls attention to its own existence. "
>
> —Bertha Stuart Dyment, author

Genes play a role in determining how well our body systems work together and are visibly expressed through eye, hair, and skin color.

© Stockdisc Royalty Free Photos

❤ HEALTH TECHNOLOGY

Scientists have been working to develop artificial organs since the late 1800s. Many people have benefited from artificial joint replacements, and progress on other organs has been rapid over the last 30 years. For example, the first temporary artificial heart was used in 2007, and a permanent artificial heart was recently approved for use, though its size and life span need improvement before it can be widely applied. Scientists are also developing artificial bladders, skin, blood vessels, and even blood itself. These advances provide hope for people suffering from a fatal or debilitating illness and for those waiting for an organ donation or transplant.

Some research on artificial organs remains controversial, such as the development of artificial wombs and the creation of implantable computer chips that might directly affect brain function. Some biomedical ethicists also question whether the goal of prolonging life through the development of an artificial human body is a good thing, either for individuals or for society.

❸ CONNECT

How do you think your cultural background and personal values influence your thoughts about using artificial organs to prolong life? How do your background and personal values influence your thinking about becoming an organ donor when you die? What other factors go into making the decision of whether or not to become an organ donor?

Photodisc

Comprehension Check

1. Identify the 11 different body systems.
2. Identify and describe key components of each system.
3. Briefly describe the function of each system.

1. Measure your height in inches (or meters) without shoes.

2. Measure your weight in pounds (or kilograms) without shoes. If you're wearing street clothes (as opposed to lightweight gym clothing), subtract 2 pounds (0.9 kilogram) from your weight.

3. Determine your BMI using the BMI calculation chart or either of the following formulas.

$$\frac{weight\ (lb)}{height\ (in.)\ \times\ height\ (in.)} \times 703 = BMI$$

$$\frac{weight\ (kg)}{height\ (m)\ \times\ height\ (m)} = BMI$$

4. Use table 4.2 to find your BMI rating, and record your BMI score and rating.

Height

	90	95	100	105	110	115	120	125	130	135	140	145	150	155	160	165	170	175	180	185	190	195	200	205	210	215	220	225	230	235	240	245	250
4' 6"	25	25	26	26	27	28	29	30	31	32	34	35	36	37	39	40	41	42	43	45	46	47	48	49	51	52	53	54	56	57	58	59	60
4' 7"	24	24	25	25	26	27	28	29	30	31	32	34	35	36	37	38	39	40	41	43	45	46	47	48	49	50	51	52	54	55	56	57	58
4' 8"	23	23	24	24	25	26	27	28	29	30	31	32	34	35	36	37	38	39	40	42	43	44	45	46	47	48	49	50	52	53	54	55	56
4' 9"	22	22	23	23	24	25	26	27	28	29	30	31	32	34	35	36	37	38	39	40	42	42	43	44	45	47	48	49	50	51	52	53	54
4' 10"	21	22	22	23	23	24	25	26	27	28	29	30	31	32	34	35	36	37	38	39	40	41	42	43	44	45	46	47	48	49	50	51	52
4' 11"	20	21	21	22	22	23	24	25	26	27	28	29	30	31	32	33	34	35	36	37	38	39	40	41	42	43	45	46	46	47	48	49	50
5' 0"	19	20	20	21	21	22	23	24	25	26	27	28	29	30	31	32	33	34	35	36	37	38	39	40	41	42	43	44	45	46	47	48	49
5' 1"	18	19	19	20	21	22	23	24	25	26	26	27	28	29	30	31	32	33	34	35	36	37	38	39	40	41	42	43	43	44	45	46	47
5' 2"	18	18	18	19	20	21	22	23	24	25	26	27	27	28	29	30	31	32	33	34	35	36	37	37	38	39	40	41	42	43	44	45	46
5' 3"	17	18	18	19	19	20	21	22	23	24	25	26	27	27	28	29	30	31	32	33	34	35	35	36	37	38	39	40	41	42	43	43	44
5' 4"	17	17	17	18	19	20	21	21	22	23	24	25	26	27	27	28	29	30	31	32	33	33	34	35	36	37	38	39	39	40	41	42	43
5' 5"	16	17	17	17	18	19	20	21	22	22	23	24	25	26	27	27	28	29	30	31	32	32	33	34	35	36	37	37	38	39	40	41	42
5' 6"	15	16	16	17	18	19	19	20	21	22	23	23	24	25	26	27	27	28	29	30	31	31	32	33	34	35	36	36	37	38	39	40	40
5' 7"	15	15	16	16	17	18	19	20	20	21	22	23	23	24	25	26	27	27	28	29	30	31	31	32	33	34	34	35	36	37	38	38	39
5' 8"	14	15	15	16	17	17	18	19	20	21	21	22	23	24	24	25	26	27	27	28	29	30	30	31	32	33	33	34	35	36	36	37	38
5' 9"	14	15	15	15	16	17	18	18	19	20	21	21	22	23	24	24	25	26	27	27	28	29	30	30	31	32	32	33	34	35	35	36	37
5' 10"	13	14	14	15	16	17	17	18	19	19	20	21	22	22	23	24	24	25	26	27	27	28	29	29	30	31	32	32	33	34	34	35	36
5' 11"	13	14	14	15	15	16	17	17	18	19	20	20	21	22	22	23	24	24	25	26	26	27	28	29	29	30	31	31	32	33	33	34	35
6' 0"	13	13	14	14	15	16	16	17	18	18	19	20	20	21	22	22	23	24	24	25	26	26	27	28	28	29	30	31	31	32	33	33	34
6' 1"	12	13	13	14	15	15	16	16	17	18	18	19	20	20	21	22	22	23	24	24	25	26	26	27	28	28	29	30	30	31	32	32	33
6' 2"	12	12	13	13	14	15	15	16	17	17	18	19	19	20	21	21	22	22	23	24	24	25	26	26	27	28	28	29	30	30	31	31	32
6' 3"	11	12	12	13	14	14	15	15	16	17	17	18	19	19	20	21	21	22	22	23	24	24	25	26	26	27	27	28	29	29	30	31	31
6' 4"	11	12	12	13	13	14	15	15	16	16	17	18	18	19	20	20	21	21	22	23	23	24	24	25	26	26	27	27	28	29	29	30	30

Weight

BMI calculation chart. Locate your height in the left column and your weight in pounds in the bottom row. The box where the selected row and column intersect is your BMI score.

TABLE 4.2 Rating Chart: Body Mass Index

	13 years old		14 years old		15 years old		16 years old		17 years old		18 years old	
	Male	Female	Male	Female	Male	Female	Male	Female	Male	Female	Male	Female
Very lean	≤15.4	≤15.3	≤16.0	≤15.8	≤16.5	≤16.3	≤17.1	≤16.8	≤17.7	≤17.2	≤18.2	≤17.5
Good fitness	15.5–21.3	15.4–22.0	16.1–22.1	15.9–22.8	16.6–22.9	16.4–23.5	17.2–23.7	16.9–24.1	17.8–24.4	17.3–24.6	18.3–25.1	17.6–25.1
Marginal fitness	21.4–23.5	22.1–23.7	22.2–24.4	22.9–24.5	23.0–25.2	23.6–25.3	23.8–25.9	24.2–26.0	24.5–26.6	24.7–27.6	25.2–27.4	25.2–27.1
Low fitness	≥23.6	≥23.8	≥24.5	≥24.6	≥25.3	≥25.4	≥26.0	≥26.1	≥26.7	≥27.7	≥27.5	≥27.2

Data based on *Fitnessgram*.

Waist-to-Hip Ratio (Male and Female)

1. Measure your hips at the largest point (the largest circumference of your buttocks). Make sure that the tape is at the same level (horizontal to the ground) in the front, in the back, and on your sides. The tape should be snug but not so tight as to cause indentations in your skin (do not use an elastic tape). Stand with your feet together when making the measurement.

2. Measure your waist at the smallest circumference (called the natural waist). If there is no natural waist, measure at the level of the umbilicus. Measure at the end of a normal inspiration (just after a normal in-breath). Do not suck in to make your waist smaller. This measurement is slightly different from the one used to measure waist girth by itself.

3. To calculate your waist-to-hip ratio, divide your waist girth by your hip girth.

4. Find your ratio in table 4.3 to determine your rating.

5. Record your hip and waist measurements and rating.

To determine your waist-to-hip ratio, measure (a) your hips and (b) your waist.

TABLE 4.3 Rating Chart: Waist-to-Hip Ratio

	Male	Female
Good fitness zone	≤0.90	≤0.79
Marginal	0.91–1.0	0.80–0.85
Low fitness zone	≥1.1	≥0.86

✓ Planning for Health Living

Use the Healthy Living Plan worksheet to make a plan to improve or maintain your weight or body composition. Monitor the steps you take toward meeting your goals and repeat this self-assessment in one to three months to help determine the success of your plan.

Lesson 4.2

Healthy Body Weight

Lesson Objectives

After reading this lesson, you should be able to

1. define *body mass index (BMI)*, *overweight*, and *obesity*;
2. understand the health risks associated with overweight and obesity; and
3. understand the relationship between physical activity, weight, and health.

 Lesson Vocabulary

body composition, body mass index (BMI), essential body fat, lower body fat, obesity, overweight, storage fat, toxic food environment, upper body fat, weight cycling

Have you seen news stories about obesity and disease risk? How about advertisements for weight loss? Do you ever think about your weight or feel pressured to change your weight? Obesity and overweight have increased dramatically in the United States since 1990, and this trend has led to growing concerns about related health risks, such as heart disease and diabetes. This lesson defines overweight and obesity and explores their relationship to health and disease. It also considers the relationships between weight, physical activity, genetics, and society.

The Obesity Epidemic

Obesity is common in American society today. Approximately one-third of all adults are overweight or obese, and 17 percent of children aged 2 to 19 are considered obese. Experts have named this current crisis the "obesity epidemic" because obesity has increased rapidly over the past 20 years. This crisis has many causes, and of the biggest is the rise in physical inactivity; indeed, sedentary living has become the norm. In addition, foods that are high in fat and low in nutrients are more readily available and less expensive than ever before. As a result, it has become easier and easier for people to put on unwanted weight. Reversing this trend is a major public health goal, and experts agree that it is a complex effort requiring many societal changes and individual commitments. For example, in 2013 the American Medical Association formally classified obesity as a disease. The change aids in the fight against obesity-related diseases such as type 2 diabetes and heart disease, and might also improve funding for obesity drugs, surgery, and counseling.

Weight and Body Mass Index

A person's body weight is simply the number of pounds or kilograms he or she weighs, and weight by itself is often of little value in determining health risk. A more useful measure is **body mass index (BMI)**, which is the standard way to measure a person's weight in relation to height. BMI provides a better reflection of health status because it considers the body's overall mass. By definition, the mass of an object is its weight divided by its total volume (the amount of space the body takes up). Body mass index can be calculated by dividing a person's weight (in kilograms) by his or her height (in meters squared); it can also be figured by means of a formula in inches and pounds. BMI can be used to determine whether a person is **overweight**—that is, whether he or she has too much weight per unit of body height or mass. For more information, refer to the BMI chart presented in this chapter's Self-Assessment feature.

Body mass index is a relatively easy and inexpensive way to determine weight status in large populations. As a result, it is often used in large studies that seek to determine the relationship between body weight and health. This type of research has shown that excessive body weight as measured by BMI may be associated with diseases such as diabetes, heart disease, cancer, and arthritis. Very low body weight may also be a sign of disease—or of malnutrition.

These risk assessments are based on the averages of large populations, and individual differences do exist in healthy body weight. For example, BMI does not directly measure body composition (amount of muscle versus amount of fat), nor does it reflect the location of weight on the body, and both of these factors are known to affect health. BMI also does not register a person's lifestyle, in particular diet and physical activity. As a result, it's possible to be overweight as defined by BMI while also being very active and healthy. It's also possible to have a normal weight as defined by BMI and be very unfit and unhealthy. Genetics also plays a large role in size and weight, and individual differences need to be considered when interpreting BMI results.

In spite of the limitations of BMI, there is an established relationship between a high BMI and health risk. As you learned in the self-assessment, the health standards for BMI for teens vary by age and gender. For adults, the CDC uses 25 as the standard for overweight and 30 as the standard for obesity. If you have a high BMI but are very active and eat well, you may want to do follow-up self-assessments to determine your percentage of body fat.

Body Composition

Body composition refers to the ratio of fat to lean tissue in a person's total body mass. A high level of fat, regardless of overall weight, is associated with heart disease, diabetes, and certain cancers. Human beings do need a certain amount of body fat to survive, and this amount is called **essential body fat.** It cushions and insulates organs and aids in nervous system functions. It also plays a role in hormone regulation and reproductive health, particularly in women. Additional body fat (beyond essential fat) is called **storage fat,** and up to a certain point it does not appear to be harmful for health. Healthy body fat levels range from 13 to 31 percent for women and 6 to 25 percent for men. Genetics, physical activity level, and age are examples of factors that can influence total body fat levels.

If a person has too much body fat per unit of body mass, he or she is considered obese. Measuring body fat is more challenging than measuring BMI, and several common methods are used, each of which involves potential error. The most commonly used technique is skinfold measurement, wherein calipers are used to measure subcutaneous fat, which is fat located directly under the skin (see figure 4.8). This technique assumes that about half of a person's total fat is subcutaneous and that the remainder is found in and around the organs.

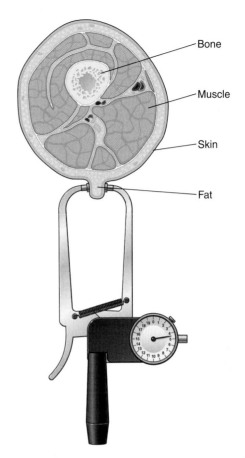

FIGURE 4.8 Using a skinfold measurement caliper.

In addition to special equipment, taking skinfold measurements requires special training. Measurements should be performed by a person who has learned proper technique and practiced this technique to ensure consistency and accuracy.

Another commonly used technique for measuring body fat is bioelectrical impedance analysis. You can read about it in the Health Technology feature presented in this lesson. Getting an accurate assessment of your body fat level can help you determine if other assessments such as BMI are effective for you. If you have a high BMI but a low level of body fat, this indicates that the BMI is not an effective technique for you.

Body Fat Distribution

As you've seen, total body fat provides information about an individual's health risks. However, even greater insight can be gained by noting the location of the fat, which is known as a person's fat distribution pattern. Research shows that fat tissue acts differently depending on where it is located and that different fat distribution patterns come with different degrees of health risk.

When fat is found in the upper body, particularly around the stomach area, it is called an **upper body fat** distribution pattern or apple shape (see figure 4.9). Fat found in this area and around the abdominal organs is very active and responsive to hormones, particularly testosterone. Fat located in the abdominal cavity can enter the bloodstream more easily, which makes it easier to lose, but it also means that the fat can enter the liver and be converted into dangerous cholesterol. As a result, abdominal fat has been associated with high cholesterol and risk for heart disease.

Fat located in the lower body, particularly around the hips and thighs, is called a **lower body fat** distribution pattern or pear shape (refer to figure 4.9). Fat in this location is much less active than abdominal fat. Generally speaking, lower body fat is considered much less harmful than abdominal fat to overall health. As a result, it can often be more resistant to weight loss efforts. The waist-to-hip ratio is a simple measure that can help determine a person's disease risks based on fat distribution (see this chapter's Self-Assessment feature).

> **"** The number of kids affected by obesity has tripled since 1980, and this can be traced in large part to lack of exercise and [lack of] a healthy diet. **"**
>
> —Virginia Foxx, U.S. congresswoman

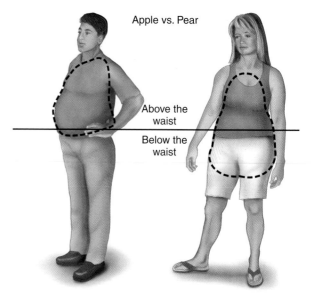

FIGURE 4.9 Apple versus pear body shape.

Health at Every Size

Because weight, body composition, and fat distribution pattern can be associated with disease risk, you need to understand them and evaluate your personal status. Regardless of the results, you also need to understand that none of these factors alone defines a person's total health status. American culture often assumes that fat always means unhealthy and that skinny always means healthy. We also tend to believe that a person's weight is a direct reflection of his or her lifestyle.

These assumptions are simplistic, and believing them can lead a person to make poor health decisions. Research has clearly demonstrated, for example, that individuals of normal weight who are unfit and sedentary face a higher risk for many diseases than those who are slightly overweight but

---

Marion Wear - Fotolia

DIVERSE PERSPECTIVES: Being Overweight

My name is Christian, and I'm overweight. I have struggled with my weight most of my life. I remember being in elementary school and being teased and bullied by other kids. Both of my parents are obese. They're hard on me because they don't want me to be like them. My mom is always on my case to diet and exercise. I try not to be hard on myself, but it's a challenge because I feel like a failure sometimes. Not everyone looks at me like I must be lazy or stupid, but enough people do that it makes me self-conscious. Even when I look happy and okay on the outside, I'm often feeling insecure deep down. I wish people would get to know me before they judge me. I'm a pretty good student and a good musician. I don't really understand why being overweight makes me a bad person in some people's eyes.

physically fit and exercising regularly. In addition, being slightly overweight but having a stable weight may be healthier than engaging in a series of fad diets that result in cycles of weight loss and weight gain. In fact, **weight cycling**—the repeated gaining and losing of weight—may increase weight, fat, and disease risk over time.

Genetic influences on weight, body composition, and body fat are also very powerful. We are not all made to be the same general size. Genetic research has demonstrated that people respond differently to changes in physical activity patterns and diet. Some individuals lose weight or maintain a healthy weight more easily, while others find it more challenging to do so.

In addition, it is generally easier for individuals with higher incomes to take steps such as buying healthy foods, joining a health club, hiring a per-sonal trainer, and purchasing exercise gear. People in better socioeconomic conditions also enjoy greater safety in their parks and greater access to social programs, such as athletic clubs, sport leagues, and parks and recreation programs. Socioeconomic status also makes a difference in how an individual is affected by **toxic food environments**—that is, environments in which food is plentiful and inexpensive but also higher than necessary in calories and fat.

We should encourage all people to seek out their healthiest weight by eating a healthy diet and engaging in regular physical activity and exercise. We should also be compassionate and encouraging to all people and not assume that someone who carries a few extra pounds is simply not trying hard. Reducing obesity over the long term depends on providing both a physically and an emotionally safe place for individuals to pursue a healthy lifestyle.

 ## HEALTH TECHNOLOGY

Body fat scales have become popular in recent years. These scales use bioelectrical impedance analysis to give you an estimate of your body fat level. They estimate your fat level based on how a small amount of electricity moves through your body. In order to use this technology accurately, you need to understand how it works.

When you step onto the electrical sensors on the scale, a small electrical current is sent up one leg and down the other. The scale measures how quickly the current covers the distance and how much of the current is returned. This is relevant because water conducts electrical currents, and your muscle tissue is about 70 percent water when normally hydrated. The scale's program-ming assumes that you're properly hydrated and that the current is traveling through muscle tissue that contains a known amount of water.

However, if you step on the scale after exercis-ing very hard and sweating heavily, your body may be dehydrated. As a result, the current will not move as quickly as it normally would, and the scale will assume that you have less muscle tissue than you actually do. As a result, it will report a higher level of body fat than you really have.

Many consumers fail to understand this basic science and then become perplexed when they measure their body fat after a hard workout only to see that it has apparently gone up! Therefore, being well hydrated is critical for using this tech-nology effectively at home.

⊕ CONNECT

How might using a body fat scale at home affect your feelings about your health? Do you think it would affect your health behaviors? Why or why not?

Comprehension Check

1. What is BMI, and what can it tell you about your health?
2. Why is the location of fat on the body an important factor to consider in determining a person's health risks?
3. Describe the relationship between physical activity, weight, and health.

Olivia has always hated speaking in front of the class and has always doubted her own ideas. As a kid, she would purposefully misspell words in the spelling bee just so she could sit down. Now that she's in high school, it seems like she's expected to speak in front of the class more often.

Group projects and reports also cause Olivia a lot of stress because she feels nervous about sharing her ideas with her group. She's also very self-conscious about her appearance and size: "I don't want to look like an idiot if I'm wrong. I don't want to be blamed for failing, and I don't want people to call me fat or stupid." As a result, she usually doesn't contribute much. Sometimes, she gets angry with herself because she knows that the group is making mistakes or is not doing the task as carefully as she would if she worked alone. Still, she stays quiet.

Will seems just the opposite of Olivia, and she often envies him for how easy it seems for him to be in front of the class. Indeed, Will is a bit of a class clown, always cracking jokes about other people or doing silly stunts. The truth, however, is that Will wishes he wasn't always trying to be funny: "I try to make people laugh because I'm afraid they'll be laughing *at* me if they aren't laughing *with* me." Will is tall and lanky and wears glasses. He feels like a "nerd" and has noticed that no one seems to comment on how he looks because they think of him as "the funny kid" in class. Will does like being popular, but he hates his own appearance, and most of the time he doesn't feel very confident at all.

For Discussion

Despite their differences, both Olivia and Will lack self-confidence. What should Olivia do in order to build her self-confidence? How could others help her? What should Will do to build his self-confidence? Do you think that covering up his insecurity with humor will help him become more confident? When answering these questions, refer to this chapter's Skills for Healthy Living feature for more information.

SKILLS FOR HEALTHY LIVING: Self-Confidence

Everyone suffers from a lack of confidence now and then. Self-doubt can be triggered by uncertainty, competition, or change. For some people, however, a more general lack of self-confidence interferes with daily life and can even lead to social isolation. Building your self-confidence is important to your mental health. It also makes you more likely to be physically active and to resist peer pressure to engage in risky behaviors.

During the teenage years, self-confidence is disproportionately connected to how a person perceives his or her appearance and social status. As a result, teens with body weight issues are more likely to suffer from low self-confidence. A lack of self-confidence is also closely associated with fear of failure.

The good news is that self-confidence is a matter of perception, and building self-confidence is a skill that can be learned. To build your self-confidence, use the following suggestions.

- **Keep a success journal.** Keep track of everything you do well each day. We often focus too much on a few things, such as appearance, and don't pay attention to all of the ways in which we succeed on a daily basis. Focusing on your strengths helps you feel more confident about your abilities.

- **Be your best self.** One quick way to create self-doubt is to compare yourself negatively with others and pass judgment on yourself. No one is good at everything, yet we often compare ourselves with lots of different people—each one very good at something—and assume that we should be better at everything than we are. Stop negatively comparing yourself with others; instead, focus on being the best *you* that you can be.

- **Set small goals that you're sure to reach with effort.** If you set goals that are out of your reach, you won't be able to achieve them, and failing to reach a goal often contributes to low self-confidence. On the other hand, reaching a goal that is well thought out can boost your self-confidence.

- **Work on self-improvements.** We all have weaknesses in our skills and abilities that can contribute to self-doubt. Seek out ways to improve your skills and abilities. If you lack confidence because you aren't good at, say, math or reading, take steps to get help and improve your ability in that area. For example, if you don't feel confident in physical education, practice some of the skills you're learning in class when you're outside of class. You're likely to see improvement in most skills with practice, and when you do your self-confidence will improve.

- **Walk the walk.** If you lack self-confidence, this fact is probably visible to others in the way you carry yourself. Practice holding your head up and using good posture. Standing up straight and walking with a sense of purpose can do wonders for your self-confidence, and it shows others that you're a confident individual.

- **Avoid negative talk.** Try not to think or say negative things about yourself or others. Negative self-talk only serves to reduce your self-confidence, and when you communicate with others in a negative way they often do the same. Positive attitudes are contagious, and surrounding yourself with positive people helps you feel more self-confident.

⊞ ACADEMIC CONNECTION: The Scientific Method

The scientific method is a way to ask and answer scientific questions by making observations and doing experiments. The advancement of science and human understanding relies on the use of an unbiased and fair method of scientific discovery. Sometimes the scientific method yields conflicting results, such as in this chapter's Living Well News feature. When this happens, scientists will seek to replicate (or duplicate) other researchers' findings and add to their discoveries until a more definitive answer is found.

Following are the steps of the scientific method:

1. Ask a question. Every scientific discovery begins with a specific question.

2. Do background research. Sound science depends on knowing and understanding what others before you have learned.

Knowing this information helps you to add to the body of knowledge on a topic in a meaningful way.

3. Construct a hypothesis. A hypothesis is an educated guess about the answer to the question as well as the reason for that guess.

4. Test the hypothesis by doing an experiment. Here, a scientist does the experiment in pursuit of the truth.

5. Analyze the data and draw a conclusion. Once the experiment is concluded, the scientist determines the findings based on careful analysis.

6. Communicate the results. Advancing knowledge depends on sharing what is learned. Scientists communicate their results in academic and scientific journals.

Yo-Yo Dieting Is Up and Down

Yo-yo dieting, also called "weight cycling," can be a frustrating experience for people with weight problems. The term refers to a decrease of 10 pounds (4.5 kilograms) or more of body weight, followed by weight regain after the regimen ends (see figure 4.10). This process can lead to emotional upheaval and health problems.

When a diet includes very low calorie intake, the body first adapts to conserve energy by slowing down its metabolism. When the near-starvation period is then followed by a return to former eating habits, the body reacts by storing fat faster. This is why many dieters end up heavier than they were before their initial weight loss efforts.

Dr. Tracy Bale and her colleagues at the University of Pennsylvania found that dieting itself can change how the brain responds to the process. Based on experiments with mice, the researchers observed that switching from near starvation to overeating can lead to changes in the brain. In other words, the experience of near starvation (severe dieting) effectively taught the rodents to overindulge in high-calorie foods as soon as they had access to them, just in case there would be another period of starvation in the future.

However, not everyone agrees that yo-yo dieting is always unhealthy. At least one study suggests that losing weight, even if it's gained right back, is better than remaining obese all the time. Based on experiments with mice,

researchers found that yo-yo dieters may be healthier and live longer than those who do nothing about their weight. Dr. Edward List, a scientist at Ohio University's Edison Biotechnology Institute and lead author of the study report, concludes that gaining and losing weight by itself does not seem detrimental to one's life expectancy. Still, significant weight changes can result in some damage that is hard to reverse, such as muscle being lost during rapid weight loss and then replaced by fat gain. Another potential problem is the emotional toll of repeated bouts of success followed by failure.

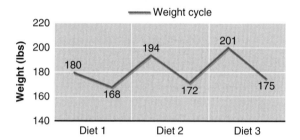

Figure 4.10 Cycle of weight loss and regain.

For Discussion

Given the conflicting research results, do you think it is better for an overweight person's overall health to try to lose weight, even if he or she regains the weight each time? Why or why not?

CHAPTER REVIEW

Reviewing Concepts and Vocabulary

As directed by your teacher, answer items 1 through 5 by correctly completing each sentence with a word or phrase.

1. Your respiratory system includes your mouth, nose, trachea, _____, and _____.
2. Nervous system functions that happen automatically, such as breathing, are called _____.
3. Most nutrients are absorbed through the _____ intestine.
4. Fat tissue is located in the _____ layer of the skin.
5. Repeatedly gaining and losing weight is called _____ _____.

For items 6 through 10, as directed by your teacher, match each term in column 1 with the appropriate phrase in column 2.

6. skinfold
7. bioelectrical impedance
8. body mass index
9. upper body fat
10. essential body fat

a. weight per unit of height
b. measuring subcutaneous fat
c. normal hydration required for accuracy
d. body fat required for normal physiological function
e. fat located around the internal organs

For items 11 through 15, as directed by your teacher, respond to each statement or question.

11. Name the two branches of the nervous system.
12. What is one difference between skeletal and cardiac muscle?
13. Give two examples of how a phenotype may be expressed.
14. Which body fat distribution pattern is more dangerous to health? Why?
15. What is a toxic food environment?

Thinking Critically

Write a paragraph in response to the following questions.

Jenna struggles with her weight. She walks her dog for almost an hour every day after school and goes to aerobics classes at the local gym at least three times a week. Still, most people consider Jenna fat, and sometimes she gets teased at school. She is 5 feet 4 inches (1.6 meters) tall, weighs 170 pounds (77 kilograms), and has a classic pear shape.

What would you tell Jenna about her weight and health? Do you think she is at great risk for disease?

Take It Home

Ask a friend or family member if you can conduct a body weight assessment for him or her. Use the self-assessment presented in this chapter to determine the person's body mass index and waist-to-hip ratio. Once you've gathered and evaluated the information, give the person an interpretation of what the results may mean for his or her health. Write a report presenting your interpretation. If you don't have a scale and tape measure at home, use your own results from this chapter to write your report. If you are comfortable doing so, share your report with a friend or family member and tell him or her what you've learned from doing the self-assessments.

BananaStock

5

Diseases and Disability

In This Chapter

LESSON 5.1
Infectious Diseases

SELF-ASSESSMENT
My Disease Prevention IQ

LESSON 5.2
Chronic Diseases and Disabilities

MAKING HEALTHY DECISIONS
Identifying Risk Factors

SKILLS FOR HEALTHY LIVING
Identifying Risk Factors

 Student Web Resources
www.healthforlifetextbook.org/student

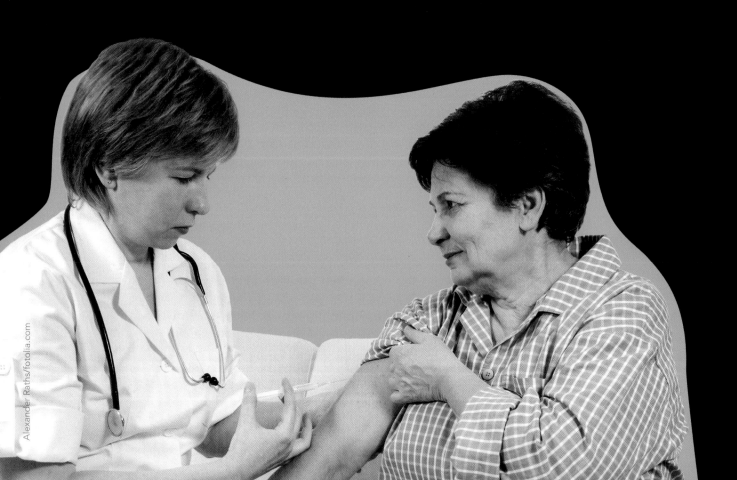

Lesson 5.1

Infectious Diseases

Lesson Objectives

After reading this lesson, you should be able to

1. understand what infectious diseases are and what causes them,
2. give examples of infectious diseases, and
3. understand how to protect yourself from common infectious diseases.

Lesson Vocabulary

acquired immune deficiency syndrome (AIDS), antibiotic, athlete's foot, bacteria, fungi, human immunodeficiency virus (HIV), immune system, influenza, localized infections, pathogen, protozoan, systemic infections, viruses

Have you ever had a cold or the flu? Did you have chicken pox when you were a kid? Have you ever had a bout of food poisoning that caused you to vomit or have diarrhea? If you answered yes to any of these questions, then you've had an infectious disease. These diseases are all around us, and learning about how they are spread and how your body works to fight them can help you reduce your risk of getting sick.

What Are Infectious Diseases?

Living organisms are in the air, on you, and in you all of the time. These small organisms are known as microorganisms. They are not visible to the naked eye and often require powerful magnification in order to be seen. Your mouth, skin, and digestive tract host millions of these microorganisms, which are part of a normal, healthy system. However, some dangerous microorganisms can enter the body, multiply, and cause serious illness. These microorganisms are known as **pathogens**, and the diseases they cause are known as infectious diseases.

Infections can be systemic or localized. **Systemic infections** affect the entire body, not just a single organ or body part; examples include the flu and the common cold. **Localized infections** affect only one body part or organ; examples include athlete's foot and infected wounds.

Methods of Transmission

Pathogens are spread in a number of ways, such as contact with infected people, animals, or objects. Direct contact occurs, for example, from kissing, sharing straws, sexual contact, or even a blood transfusion from an infected donor. Indirect contact

Washing hands with soap and water is one key guideline in preventing infectious diseases.

occurs when you touch an object (e.g., cell phone, computer keyboard, doorknob) where a pathogen is found. One of the most effective ways to reduce your risk of acquiring an infection is to wash your hands regularly.

Pathogens can also spread through airborne transmission. This occurs when a pathogen is in small droplets of water in the air, such as when an infected person sneezes. Germs can also travel through the air as small particles that can be inhaled. Finally, pathogens can travel in hosts, such as insects, animals, and food. As a result, you can be exposed to an infectious disease by coming into contact with an infected animal, being bitten by a pathogen-carrying insect, or eating contaminated food.

CONNECT

Identify three ways in which your friends' and family members' habits can affect your likelihood of getting an infectious disease. How do your own habits influence your susceptibility, or vulnerability, to infectious disease?

Your Body's Defenses

Because pathogens are always in the environment, your body has defenses to protect you against pathogens and the infections they can cause. First, you have physical and chemical defenses that can prevent a pathogen from entering your body. These defenses include your skin, mucous membranes, saliva and tears, and digestive system. Your skin acts as a barrier and contains acids that can kill some pathogens. The skin also sheds regularly, which allows you to shed pathogens as well. Your body's mucous membranes, such as those in your nasal passages, secrete mucus that captures or kills many pathogens, which can then be washed away or expelled from your body. Your tears and saliva work in a similar manner. Your digestive system, including stomach acid, can kill and move some pathogens through your body and eliminate them before they cause severe damage.

The Immune System

If a pathogen gets through your other defenses and enters your body, your **immune system** is designed to attack and kill it. It fights infection and disease by attacking each type of threat it faces with a specialized response that either disables or destroys the pathogen. The organs of the immune system are positioned throughout the body (see figure 5.1). They are called lymphoid organs because they are home to lymphocytes, which are small white blood cells that are the key players in the immune response. Bone marrow—the soft tissue in the hollow center of bones—is the source of all blood cells, including lymphocytes. The thymus is a lymphoid organ that lies behind the breastbone, and the lymph nodes are small bean-shaped glands

You can help prevent airborne transmission of pathogens by covering your mouth and nose with a tissue or handkerchief when you sneeze or cough. If you don't have a tissue or handkerchief, sneeze or cough into your upper sleeve rather than into your hands or directly into the air.

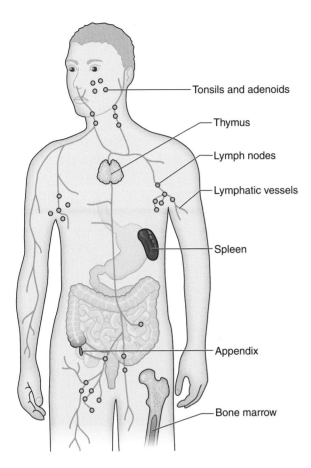

FIGURE 5.1 Your immune system, which consists of numerous components, fights infection and disease.

located throughout the body. Clusters of lymph nodes are in the neck, armpits, abdomen, and groin. The spleen is a flattened organ at the upper left of the abdomen. Like the lymph nodes, the spleen contains compartments where immune cells gather and work. The spleen serves as a meeting ground where immune defenses confront antigens (invaders). Other lymphoid tissues are throughout the body, especially in areas that serve as gateways for the body such as the linings of the digestive tract, airways, and lungs. These tissues include the tonsils, adenoids, and appendix. The lymphatic system mirrors the major blood vessels of the body, which allows cells and fluids to be exchanged between the blood and lymphatic vessels. This enables the lymphatic system to monitor the body for threats. Pathogens that pass through this system are attacked by specialized cells and killed. Together, these systems form your immune response.

Common Causes of Infectious Disease

The dangerous microorganisms called pathogens come in various forms, including bacteria, viruses, and fungi. The following discussion provides more detail, along with some examples.

Bacterial Infections

Bacteria are simple, single-cell organisms found in the air and soil, in food, and on plants and animals. Most bacteria are harmless to your health and some are helpful in digesting your food. Some can be dangerous because they give off poisonous substances known as toxins. About 100 known bacteria are dangerous to people.

One of the most common bacterial diseases that affects teens is strep throat. Strep, or streptococcus, bacteria typically invade the nose and throat and are transferred by contact with the mucus of an infected person. The infection is diagnosed by means of a throat swab performed by a physician. Common symptoms include sore throat, headache, fever, and swollen lymph nodes on the sides of the neck. Other common bacterial infections are lyme disease, bacterial meningitis, and tuberculosis. Most bacterial diseases are treated with an **antibiotic**—a kind of prescription drug that kills or inhibits the bacteria.

Viruses and Viral Infections

Viruses can multiply only once they have entered a living cell. Once inside, they take over the cell's reproductive cycle and ultimately cause cell damage or cell death. Viruses can be airborne, and they can also be found in body fluids, as in the case of **acquired immune deficiency syndrome (AIDS)**. A virus also does not respond to antibiotics. Some of the most common viral infections are described in the following sections.

Influenza and the Common Cold

Influenza, or flu, is a common viral infection that attacks the upper respiratory system. You can catch the flu by breathing in airborne droplets containing the virus or by coming into contact with a contaminated surface and touching the eyes, mouth, or nose. Symptoms include high fever, sore throat, headache, and cough.

⚛ HEALTH SCIENCE

Smallpox is an infectious disease that in earlier times killed millions of people worldwide. In 1796, physician Edward Jenner noticed that people who had contracted a related but less serious disease called cowpox seemed to develop a resistance to smallpox. To test his theory, he exposed a healthy boy to the cowpox disease. Once the boy recovered from that disease, Jenner injected him with the live smallpox virus. The boy did not get sick because he had developed immune defenses from cowpox that destroyed the smallpox virus.

Today, of course, vaccines are common, and they are given in one of two basic forms. Live vaccines are weakened versions of a pathogen, whereas inactivated vaccines consist of dead or incomplete forms of the pathogen. Both forms stimulate the body's immune system to develop antibodies that are associated with the disease in question. If the body is later exposed to the same pathogen, or disease-causing agent, it will recognize it and destroy it.

Vaccination is one of the greatest health science advancements in the modern era; it has helped reduce or eliminate illness and death due to various diseases worldwide. In fact, the U.S. Centers for Disease Control and Prevention (CDC) has identified 28 diseases that are preventable through vaccination, including hepatitis A and B, influenza, human papillomavirus, smallpox, measles, mumps, and yellow fever.

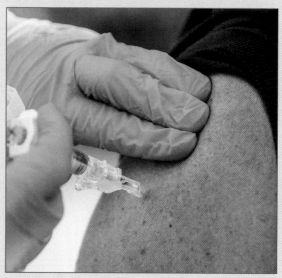

Immunization helps prevent many infectious diseases.

A serious case of the flu can be dangerous, and flu poses a significant threat to infants and elderly people. In the United States, as many as 30,000 people die from influenza each year. In recent years, flu vaccinations have become more common, and their use can help prevent large-scale outbreaks (see this chapter's Health Science feature for more on vaccination).

Many people mistake a common cold for influenza because it can produce similar symptoms; colds, however, are caused by different viruses. In addition, most colds last only 3 to 7 days, whereas the flu can last 10 days or more. Despite the large number of over-the-counter (OTC) cold remedies, there is no cure for the common cold. In fact, viral infections of all types have no known cure. The best-known remedies for overcoming a virus are rest, a balanced diet, and plenty of fluids. Over-the-counter and prescription medications may help you treat the symptoms of a cold or other virus. This can help your body in its own recovery process.

🔊 HEALTHY COMMUNICATION

Influenza is especially dangerous for older adults and young children. Thus it is important for members of both groups to understand how influenza is transmitted and what steps they can take to reduce their chance of getting the disease. If you were given 60 seconds to educate and influence members of each group, what would you say? How would your messages differ between the two groups?

Acquired Immune Deficiency Syndrome

Acquired immune deficiency syndrome (AIDS) is a sexually transmitted infection (STI) caused by the **human immunodeficiency virus (HIV)**. HIV is found in bodily fluids of infected people and can be transmitted to others through sexual contact and in blood (e.g., by sharing a needle). Pregnant women can also transmit the virus to a fetus through shared blood or to an infant through breast milk. HIV gradually attacks the immune system, making the infected person susceptible to many other infections and diseases. In almost all people, HIV progresses to AIDS over time. Remaining abstinent from both sexual activity and drug use is the only way for an adult to eliminate the risk of acquiring HIV and AIDS.

According to the U.S. government's National Institutes of Health (NIH), AIDS is the sixth leading cause of death among people aged 25 to 44 in the United States. Youth aged 13 to 24 account for about 5 percent of all U.S. AIDS cases. You can learn more about HIV and AIDS, other sexually transmitted infections, and their prevention and treatment in the student section of the Health for Life website.

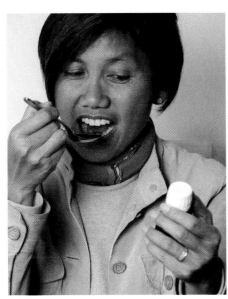

Over-the-counter medications may help relieve symptoms but they do not cure the common cold.

© Ron Sumners/Dreamstime

Hepatitis

Hepatitis is an infection of the liver that results in serious inflammation of that organ. There are five types, the most common of which are hepatitis A, B, and C. The main symptoms of these three types are fever, nausea, abdominal pain, and jaundice (yellowing of the skin).

Hepatitis A is most commonly transmitted in drinking water or food contaminated with the virus. Since the virus is found in feces, it spreads easily in settings marked by poor sanitation or poor personal hygiene. Hepatitis A can also be contracted by eating fruit, vegetables, or other foods contaminated during handling or by eating raw shellfish harvested from contaminated water.

Hepatitis B is spread through contact with blood or body fluid from an infected person; thus common causes of transmission include sharing needles and having unprotected sex. Most cases of hepatitis B are short term, and many infected people are not aware of being sick because the symptoms are generally mild and resemble those of the flu.

Hepatitis C, however, can lead to permanent liver damage as well as cirrhosis (scarring of the liver), liver cancer, and liver failure. Like hepatitis B, hepatitis C is spread through contact with an infected person's blood and produces mild symptoms. Unlike hepatitis B, it is usually chronic (long term), and an infected person typically has it for 15 years before being diagnosed.

Vaccines exist for hepatitis A and B. They are typically required for anyone working in the health care industry. Anyone with hepatitis should seek medical care from a physician.

Fungi and Fungal Infections

Fungi are single-cell and multicell organisms that thrive in warm, humid environments; examples are yeast, mold, and mushrooms. About half of all known fungi are dangerous to humans. Infection is typically caused by a fungus landing on the skin or being inhaled into the lungs, which can result in an internal infection. A fungus can also be ingested in spoiled food. A fungus attacks the body by releasing

Travel-Related Viruses

Severe acute respiratory syndrome (SARS) is a viral disease caused by a coronavirus. It was discovered in Asia in 2003; it then spread to two dozen countries on four continents within a few months. SARS typically begins with a high fever, headache, and body aches. It may result in a dry cough. Most people who contract SARS develop pneumonia or other respiratory infections, and it is considered more dangerous and deadly than common influenza. In fact, SARS is one of several viral diseases that threaten global health. Fortunately, SARS is relatively rare, but it does prove that infectious diseases can spread unexpectedly.

You should also be aware of some other globally active viral diseases when traveling overseas, including avian influenza, yellow fever, and dengue fever. The CDC maintains a database of travel-related health concerns and provides up-to-date recommendations about inoculations and medications needed for safe travel.

enzymes that digest or dissolve cells that it contacts. Fungal infections are treated with antifungal medications and creams.

One common fungal infection is **athlete's foot**. It begins like other fungal infections when a small amount of the fungus lands on the skin. It then multiplies in the warm, moist environment of the sock and shoe. You're more likely to get athlete's foot if you wear closed-toed shoes lacking good ventilation, sweat often, have wet feet for long periods, or get a toenail or skin infection on a foot. To prevent athlete's foot, change shoes often, allow shoes to air out, change socks frequently, and wash your feet thoroughly every day.

Protozoan Infections

A **protozoan** is a single-cell organism that can move through the body in search of food. It attacks the body by releasing enzymes or toxins that can destroy or damage cells. Malaria is a protozoan-based disease that attacks the red blood cells and is common in parts of Africa and many tropical locations. Malaria is transmitted by 50 of the 480 known mosquito species around the globe. In the United States, malaria-carrying mosquitoes were eliminated in the late 1940s and early 1950s. Today, malaria is rare in the United States and is typically seen only in people who have traveled to a malaria-infected country.

Other Types of Pathogens

Infectious diseases can also be caused by larger pathogens, such as lice, mites, and some worms. For example, the trichina worm can live in the muscle tissue of various animals, including bears, foxes, and pigs. If an infected animal is consumed, the worm can invade the person who ate the contaminated meat. It can then cause a foodborne illness known as trichinosis. The best prevention against trichinosis and other pathogens transferred in food and meat products is to ensure that all food is properly handled (cleaned, separated, and stored safely) and that meat is fully cooked at an appropriate temperature.

Preventing Infectious Disease

We're all exposed to potential sources of infection every day. To reduce your chance of becoming ill with an infectious disease, follow these guidelines.

- **Wash your hands with soap and water.** This is especially important before and after preparing food, before eating, and after using the toilet. Use sanitizers when soap and water are not available.

- **Cover your nose and mouth when coughing or sneezing.** Use a tissue or handkerchief to cover your nose and mouth fully, or sneeze or cough into a sleeve. Try to keep your hands clean, or wash them immediately if you must use them to cover your cough or sneeze. Covering properly helps reduce the spread of infection to others.

- **Get vaccinated.** Immunization drastically reduces your chances of contracting many diseases.

CONSUMER CORNER: Choosing Hand Sanitizers

The popularity of alcohol-based hand sanitizers has skyrocketed in recent years. They are readily available in most convenience stores, grocery stores, and pharmacies and can often be found in public restrooms, cruise ship lobbies, schools, hospitals, and even outdoor play areas. Most alcohol-based hand sanitizers offer good protection against a host of germs, including bacteria, fungi, and other pathogens. They typically contain isopropanol, ethanol, n-propanol, or a combination of these ingredients. When selecting and using a hand sanitizer, consider the following points.

- Purchase a sanitizer with an alcohol content of 60 to 95 percent. Anything less makes the product ineffective.
- Sanitizers come in the form of foam, liquid, and gel. Foam sanitizers are excellent but often more expensive. Select a thicker gel sanitizer, since research shows that more of it makes it onto your hands.
- Use an adequate amount of the product to completely wet all surfaces of your hands and fingers. Rub your hands together for 10 to 15 seconds. If your hands dry before then, you haven't used enough.
- If your hands are visibly soiled, don't rely on hand sanitizers to do the job. Research shows that sanitizers are not effective when excess dirt and debris are on the hands.
- When possible, wash your hands with warm soapy water before using an alcohol-based hand sanitizer. This combination is your best bet for killing a wide range of germs.

Use an adequate amount of hand sanitizer to completely wet all surfaces of the hands and fingers.

Consumer Challenge

How should hands be washed in order to provide the best protection against disease? For the answer, visit the CDC website (www.cdc.gov).

- **Stay home.** Don't go to school if you're vomiting, have diarrhea, are coughing and sneezing, or have a fever.
- **Prepare food safely.** Keep counters and other kitchen surfaces clean when preparing meals. Promptly refrigerate leftovers—don't let cooked foods remain at room temperature for extended periods.
- **Remain abstinent or, if sexually active, practice safe sex.** The best method of avoiding any STI is to practice abstinence. If you are sexually active, always use a condom and remain sexually monogamous. You can learn more about the role contraceptives play in disease prevention by visiting the student section of the Health for Life website.

- **Don't share personal items.** Use your own toothbrush, comb, and razor. Avoid sharing drinking glasses or dining utensils.
- **Travel wisely.** Don't travel in confined spaces like trains and planes when you're ill.

Comprehension Check

1. What is an infectious disease? List three types of pathogens that cause infectious disease.
2. Briefly describe two specific examples of infectious disease.
3. Identify four ways to protect yourself from infectious disease.

Indicate your level of agreement with each statement in the questionnaire. Record the number of points associated with each response and add them together for your total. Interpret your disease prevention IQ score using the scale provided at the end of the questionnaire. *Note:* This is for your personal information and is not intended to be turned in to your teacher.

	Always 3	Sometimes 2	Never 1
Behaviors related to chronic disease			
1. I balance calories (calories in equal calories out) to maintain a healthy weight.	3	2	1
2. I participate in moderate to vigorous physical activity for 60 minutes every day.	3	2	1
3. I do muscle-fitness exercises (e.g., push-ups, sit-ups) at least two to three times per week.	3	2	1
4. I don't smoke or use any tobacco products.	3	2	1
5. I eat at least five servings of fruits and vegetables every day.	3	2	1
6. I avoid foods and drinks high in sugar and caffeine.	3	2	1
7. I avoid foods high in fat.	3	2	1
8. I regularly protect myself from the sun by wearing sunscreen, a hat, and long sleeves and long pants.	3	2	1
9. I go to the doctor regularly for checkups.	3	2	1

	Always 3	Sometimes 2	Never 1
Behaviors related to infectious disease			
10. I wash my hands every time I use the restroom and when I prepare or eat food.	3	2	1
11. I get appropriate vaccinations, including a yearly flu shot.	3	2	1
12. I stay home when I am sick and may be contagious.	3	2	1
13. I use only clean surfaces and utensils when preparing or eating food.	3	2	1
14. I avoid sharing personal items (e.g., razors, utensils, drinking cups, bottles).	3	2	1
15. I help keep a clean house, especially the kitchen and bathroom.	3	2	1
16. I cover my mouth with a tissue or handkerchief when I cough or sneeze or use my sleeve or forearm.	3	2	1
17. I protect myself from sexually transmitted infections.	3	2	1

Add up your points.

My disease prevention IQ score is: _____

A score of 40 to 51 indicates lower risk, meaning that your habits and behaviors lower your risk for chronic and infectious diseases. Work to maintain or even strengthen your healthy habits.

A score of 30 to 39 indicates moderate risk, meaning that you have some good habits, but others might be putting you at risk. Try to be more consistent in your habits and adopt more healthy habits.

A score of 29 or lower indicates higher risk, meaning that your habits and behaviors may be putting you at higher risk for chronic and infectious diseases. It's time to make some changes.

✔ Planning for Healthy Living

Use the Healthy Living Plan worksheet to improve one or more of your disease prevention habits.

Lesson 5.2

Chronic Diseases and Disabilities

Lesson Objectives

After reading this lesson, you should be able to

1. identify and describe the most common chronic diseases in our society;
2. describe the consequences of chronic diseases; and
3. define disability and identify common types of disabilities, and differentiate between a disability and a handicap.

Lesson Vocabulary

Americans With Disabilities Act, arteriosclerosis, atherosclerosis, cancer, cardiovascular disease (CVD), chronic disease, coronary heart disease, dementia, diabetes, disability, hypertension, stroke

Most infectious diseases go away once the infection is attacked by your immune system or is properly treated. **Chronic diseases** last a long time, sometimes a lifetime. Most people who live into old age develop at least one chronic disease. If a friend or family member has had cancer or high blood pressure, or if you know someone with diabetes or arthritis, then you know someone whose health has been affected by a chronic disease. In fact, chronic diseases are the most common causes of death in the United States.

Although it's the most serious, death isn't the only consequence of a chronic disease. Chronic disease can progress into disability with time, lack of treatment, or an aggressive form of the illness. But disabilities don't always develop as a result of a chronic disease. Some disabilities may be present from birth. Examples are vision, hearing, mobility, or cognitive impairments. In this lesson you'll learn about common chronic diseases and how to interact respectfully with people who have disabilities.

Chronic Diseases

In the previous lesson you learned about infectious diseases such as the flu and cold. When you get the flu or catch a cold, you have an acute illness, or one that you get over within a relatively short time. Imagine, though, if those cold or flu symptoms never went away, and if the limitations they put on your activities never let up. In the following sections you'll learn about common chronic diseases and what you can do now to avoid them.

Cardiovascular Disease

Cardiovascular disease (CVD) refers to chronic diseases that affect the circulatory system. One in four Americans has one or more cardiovascular diseases, and these diseases contribute to 60 percent of all deaths in the nation. The most common cardiovascular diseases are discussed here; many other forms also exist.

Coronary Heart Disease

The most common form of CVD is **coronary heart disease**, in which the arteries in the heart become clogged or hardened. This is the leading cause of death in the United States. Clogged arteries, a condition called **atherosclerosis** (figure 5.2), can result from eating a high-fat diet, getting too little exercise, smoking, or being very overweight.

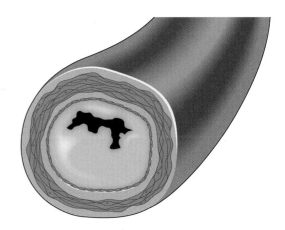

FIGURE 5.2 Plaque buildup in coronary heart disease.

Hardened (inflexible) arteries, a condition called **arteriosclerosis**, tend to occur as we age, but we can limit its effects by living a healthy lifestyle. Both of these cardiovascular diseases can decrease blood flow to the heart muscle, which can lead to chest pain known as angina and heart attacks. A heart attack is a cutting off of blood flow to a portion of the heart, which causes the cells in that area to die. Figure 5.3 shows how a blood clot or piece of plaque can break loose and block blood flow to the heart.

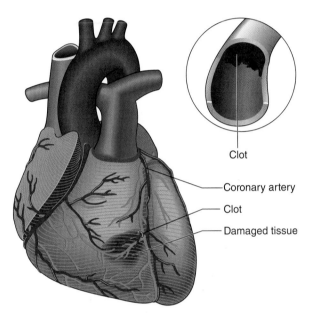

- Clot
- Coronary artery
- Clot
- Damaged tissue

FIGURE 5.3 A blood clot can cause a heart attack by preventing the heart from getting enough oxygenated blood.

Stroke

Inadequate blood supply can also damage the brain. For example, atherosclerosis or a blood clot can block an artery that supplies the brain with blood and cause a **stroke**. This is the most common type of stroke, and it is called an ischemic stroke (inadequate blood supply). A stroke can also occur if a blood vessel in the brain bursts, causing severe bleeding; this type is known as a hemorrhagic stroke. Some strokes are severe enough to cause death, and many others result in disability. This is the fourth leading cause of death in the United States. A person has a **disability** when he or she is unable to perform activities or actions in the way they would normally be performed due to a restriction or impairment (see the Disability section later in this lesson for more information). After a stroke, many people have speech or movement disability due to the damage caused in the brain.

Peripheral Artery Disease

Atherosclerosis can also occur in arteries that take blood to parts of the body other than the heart, and this condition is called peripheral artery disease (PAD). It can compromise circulation to organs and limbs, resulting in symptoms that include leg pain, muscle aches, poor nail or hair growth, decreased temperature in one leg or arm, or sores and wounds on the toes that don't heal properly. About eight million Americans have PAD. The risk of developing it increases with age, and it is more common among people who smoke or have diabetes, high blood pressure, or high cholesterol.

High Blood Pressure

Another form of CVD is high blood pressure, also known as **hypertension**. Each time your heart beats, it moves blood through your arteries at high speed and with a certain amount of force. The amount, or measure, of that force is your blood pressure. People with high blood pressure have higher than normal amounts of force in their arteries, which can damage artery walls as it pushes blood against them. High blood pressure is a risk factor for both coronary heart disease and stroke.

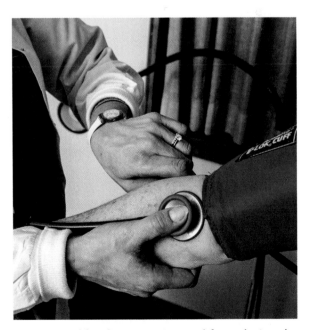

Monitoring blood pressure is a tool for reducing the risk of coronary heart disease and stroke.

PhotoDisc

HEALTH TECHNOLOGY

Scanning and imaging technologies can help determine whether a person has a chronic disease. The common X ray is still useful in assessing damage to bones and other structures. Technological advances have also produced methods for seeing three-dimensional and color images of internal parts of the body. For example, computed tomography (CT) scans provide a series of images stacked together to form a three-dimensional image of an organ or other body area (like slices of bread stacked together to form a loaf). Another technique is magnetic resonance imaging (MRI), which uses a magnetic field and pulses of radio wave energy to form pictures of organs and other structures inside the body. MRI images can show more detail than either conventional X rays or CT scans.

Such technologies have many uses. For example, they can help find cancers and detect blockages in arteries and veins that occur with cardiovascular disease. Ongoing technological advances in scanning and imaging are continuing to make the machines increasingly sophisticated and the resulting images sharper and more useful.

 CONNECT

What if you could have a free medical scan of all your body systems that would locate any infections or diseases and tell you of any physical abnormalities or early signs of disease? Would you want to do it? Could there be any negative aspects to the scan? Do you think medical insurance should pay for this type of preventive screening? Why or why not?

Cancer

The term **cancer** refers to uncontrolled growth of abnormal cells in the body. There are dozens of types of cancer; see table 5.1 for information about some of the more common types. In the United States, the most common types among men are prostate, lung, and colon cancer, and the most common types among women are breast, lung, and colon cancer. Cancer is the second leading cause of death in the United States, accounting for more than half a million deaths per year.

Symptoms, treatment, and survival rate for cancer depend on the type and location of the cancer and how advanced it is at the time of the diagnosis. Though all cancers are different, common symptoms of cancer are fatigue, fever, chills, loss of appetite, weight loss, and night sweats. Regular physical exams and cancer screenings are important for catching cancers in developing stages, when they can often be effectively removed or stopped. Great advances have been made in cancer screenings and treatments, and many common cancers, such as prostate and breast cancer, have increasing survival rates. If left untreated or if treatment is ineffective, cancer can spread to multiple organs. Known risks

Cancer screenings are important for catching cancers in developing stages.

ImageState Photos

TABLE 5.1 Common Types of Cancer

Type of cancer	Description	Risk factors
Bladder	Most commonly attacks the cells lining the inside of the bladder.	Smoking, family history of bladder cancer, exposure to arsenic and other workplace chemicals
Breast	Multiple types exist. This is the most commonly diagnosed cancer among women; men may also get it.	Increasing age, early first menstrual period, family history of breast or uterine cancer, being overweight, physical inactivity, high alcohol consumption, genetics
Colon	Attacks the colon or rectum. It is the third most common type of cancer among women and the second most common among men.	Family history of colon cancer, history of polyps, being over the age of 50, smoking, high-fat diet
Leukemia	Cancer of the bone marrow and blood cells. Multiple types exist, including some that are most common among children.	Genetics, exposure to radiation, smoking, certain related disorders and diseases
Lung	This is the leading cause of cancer deaths among both men and women.	Tobacco smoke, pollution, family history, asbestos and radon exposure, being over age 65
Melanoma	This is a skin cancer caused by excessive sun exposure.	Accumulated sun exposure or tanning bed, severe sunburns that blister (especially before age 18)
Prostate	Attacks the male prostate gland and is the leading cause of cancer among men.	Being over age 65, family history of prostate cancer, being African American, genetics

Preventing Skin Cancer

Only half of all teens report using sunscreen on a regular basis, and 80 percent believe that tan skin makes people look healthier. Although those with light skin are more susceptible to skin cancer, it does not mean that people with dark skin are immune to skin cancer. Unfortunately, sun exposure is especially risky for teens because the teenage years are a time of rapid cell division. Over the long term, tanning reduces skin elasticity, which leads to more wrinkles and can cause uneven skin tones as seen with sun spots and age spots. Tanning also significantly increases the chances of developing skin cancer. To help prevent skin cancer, follow these recommendations from the CDC.

- Seek shade, especially during midday hours.
- Wear clothing that protects your skin, such as long pants, long-sleeve shirts, and hats. You can also wear clothing made with sun-protective fabric (i.e., fabric treated specifically to protect from the sun's rays).
- Wear a hat with a wide brim to shade your face, head, ears, and neck.
- Wear sunglasses that wrap around and block both UVA (long wave) and UVB (short wave) rays. Ultraviolet (UV) rays penetrate the earth's atmosphere and are responsible for damage to the skin.
- Use sunscreen with a sun protection factor (SPF) of 15 or higher and with both UVA and UVB protection.
- Avoid indoor tanning.

for cancer include lifestyle factors such as smoking, physical inactivity, high-fat diet, and exposure to ultraviolet radiation from the sun (e.g., through sunbathing, tanning, or spending time outdoors without using sunscreen and other proper precautions).

Lung Disease

The term *lung disease* refers to a number of conditions that affect the lungs and the ability to take in and use an adequate amount of oxygen. It is the third leading cause of death in the United States. One common lung disease is inflammation of the lungs, or asthma, which can result in spasms of the lung tissue that cause wheezing and breathing difficulty. Asthma can be managed with proper medication, and individuals with this condition can lead normal lives.

Another common lung disease is chronic obstructive pulmonary disease, or COPD. It involves difficulty in exhaling air from the lungs, and the trapped air can cause coughing and tissue damage. Two forms of COPD are emphysema and bronchitis (see figure 5.4). Emphysema occurs when air sacs in the lungs are gradually destroyed, making the person progressively short of breath. In bronchitis, the lung's mucous membrane becomes inflamed, and the swelling causes coughing spells. Both emphysema and bronchitis can be caused by and made worse by smoking.

Lung disease can also result from bacterial infections, such as pneumonia and tuberculosis. Lung cancer, commonly associated with smoking, is one of the most common cancers in the United States. Many other forms of lung disease also exist, and lung disease is the third most common cause of death in the United States.

Dementia and Alzheimer's Disease

Dementia involves loss of brain function over time (see figure 5.5). It can affect memory, thinking, language use, judgment, and behavior. Most causes of dementia are irreversible, meaning that the damage caused to the brain cannot be repaired. The most common cause of dementia symptoms is Alzheimer's disease, which has a genetic component and tends to run in families. It is the sixth leading cause of death in the United States. It is also more common among females, people over age 65, and people with a history of high blood pressure or head trauma. Alzheimer's affects more than five million people in the United States.

Since people with the disease are unable to fully care for themselves, many families are left to provide unpaid and unskilled care for family members with Alzheimer's or another cause of dementia. Caregivers have physical, emotional, and financial strain, which can put their own health at risk. To learn more, visit the student section of the Health for Life website.

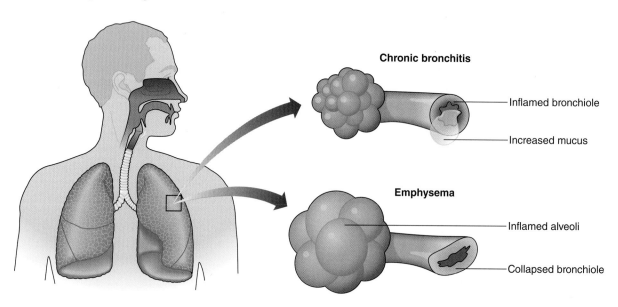

Chronic bronchitis

Inflamed bronchiole

Increased mucus

Emphysema

Inflamed alveoli

Collapsed bronchiole

FIGURE 5.4 In emphysema, the airways collapse and damaged air sacs enlarge, causing shortness of breath and wheezing. In chronic bronchitis, the airways become inflamed and filled with mucus.

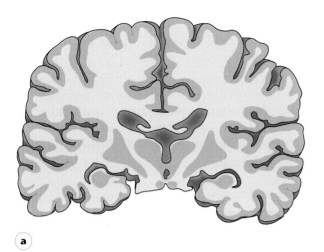
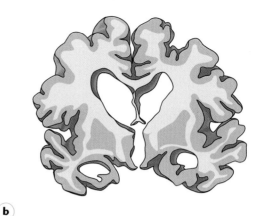

FIGURE 5.5 When compared with (a) a normal brain, (b) a cross-section of brain with Alzheimer's disease is smaller and shriveled.

Diabetes

Diabetes is a chronic disease related to having too much sugar (glucose) in the blood. It is the seventh leading cause of death in the United States. The body is normally able to use blood sugar or store it in muscle and liver cells with help from the hormone insulin. Produced by the pancreas, insulin acts like a key that opens the way for sugar to enter the cells. This process is critical because the human body cannot function properly if cells cannot access needed fuel from blood sugar. Diabetes results from either a lack of insulin (type 1 diabetes) or improperly functioning insulin (type 2 diabetes).

Type 1 diabetes has a strong genetic component and is most likely to develop in childhood, adolescence, or early adulthood. Symptoms include excessive thirst, hunger, weight loss, and frequent urination. Those with type 1 diabetes must monitor blood sugar and take insulin before eating in order to properly use the sugar in their blood.

Type 2 diabetes is strongly related to obesity and can develop at any age. In recent years, type 2 diabetes (formerly referred to as adult-onset diabetes) has become more common in the United States among children, teenagers, and young adults as obesity rates in these populations have increased. It typically requires a combination of medication, exercise, and a healthy diet for management. Many may not exhibit symptoms until the disease is relatively severe. Symptoms can include any of those for type 1 as well as blurred vision and frequent infections. The symptoms of diabetes may not be present in the early stages of the disease. Because many people

with type 2 diabetes are often overweight or obese, weight loss is often effective in treatment. However, diabetes can occur in people who are not obese or overweight.

Pregnant women can also develop a form of diabetes, called gestational diabetes, which can put both mother and infant at risk for immediate and long-term complications. Altogether, according to the American Diabetes Association, about 8 percent of Americans, including 1 in every 400 children, have diabetes.

Monitoring blood sugar is a regular part of managing diabetes.

Phototom/fotolia.com

Osteoporosis

Osteoporosis is a chronic disease in which the bones lose density and become weaker (see figure 5.6). It can result from the body either being unable to

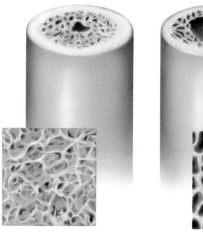

Normal bone   Osteoporotic bone

FIGURE 5.6 Osteoporosis involves a decrease in bone density.

make new bone or absorbing calcium and phosphate from the bones. The disease affects one of every five women and one of every four men in the United States over the age of 50. Its primary cause involves normal changes in the levels of estrogen and testosterone associated with aging. Risk is increased for people who smoke, are underweight, have vitamin D deficiency, or are bedridden. Risk is also higher for women of European heritage.

Some young people can develop osteoporosis if they have an eating disorder for an extended time. This situation is particularly dangerous because their bones are still developing (peak bone density generally occurs between the ages of 25 and 30). You can help your bones develop properly—and reduce your risk of osteoporosis—by engaging in weight-bearing physical activity and eating a balanced diet during your adolescent and early adult years.

Arthritis

Arthritis (Greek word meaning joint and *itis* meaning inflammation) involves inflammation and damage in the joints (see figure 5.7). There are more than a hundred types of arthritis and related joint conditions. Two of the most common forms of arthritis are osteoarthritis and rheumatoid arthritis. Osteoarthritis is also called degenerative joint disease or degenerative arthritis. It affects about 33 million Americans and is the most common chronic joint condition. Osteoarthritis results

from joint overuse. It is most common in joints that bear weight such as the knees, hips, feet, and spine. It often comes on gradually over months or even years. Except for the pain in the affected joint, people generally don't feel sick from osteoarthritis, and there is no unusual fatigue or tiredness as there is with some other types of arthritis.

Rheumatoid arthritis (RA) is a form of inflammatory arthritis and is an autoimmune disease (i.e., a disease in which the body's immune system attacks its own healthy tissues). With rheumatoid arthritis, the immune system attacks the synovium, a thin membrane that lines the joints. The attack causes fluid to build up in the joints resulting in pain and inflammation. Rheumatoid arthritis is a chronic disease that is systemic, meaning it can also attack other parts of the body. Most people with RA have intermittent bouts of intense disease activity called flares. For others, the disease is continuously active and gets worse over time. Some people with RA enjoy long periods of remission where no disease activity or symptoms are present.

Though arthritis is commonly thought of as a disease of older adulthood, some variation of it also affects about 1 in every 250 people under the age of 18. Common symptoms of many types of arthritis are stiffness, swelling, joint pain, and loss of joint mobility. Methods for managing the disease's effects on daily living vary by type and often include exercise, proper diet, physical therapy, medication, and, in some cases, joint replacement surgery. Maintaining

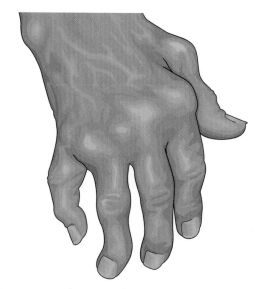

FIGURE 5.7 Severe arthritis can result in deformities and pain that dramatically affect mobility.

a healthy weight, participating in low-impact exercise and physical activity, using good posture and body mechanics when doing active jobs and chores, and appropriately treating joint injuries like sprains and strains can help reduce likelihood of getting arthritis later in life.

Preventing Chronic Disease

Many chapters in this book address ways of preventing chronic disease. For now, review the following suggestions for reducing your risk of chronic diseases such as coronary heart disease, diabetes, cancer, and lung disease. You can find more detailed information about smoking, body weight, exercise, and diet in the chapters dedicated to those topics.

Avoid Tobacco Use

- Avoiding tobacco, especially in the form of cigarettes, is the single most important way to prevent all forms of cardiovascular disease as well as lung disease and cancer.

Get Daily Physical Activity and Limit Screen Time

- Do aerobic exercise: Most of the 60 or more minutes of daily recommended physical activity should be of either moderate or vigorous intensity. Do vigorous physical activity at least three days per week.
- Do muscle-strengthening exercise: As part of the 60 or more minutes of daily recommended physical activity, do muscle-strengthening activity at least three days per week.
- Engage in bone-strengthening exercise: As part of the 60 or more minutes of daily physical activity, do bone-strengthening physical activity (weight-bearing exercise) at least three days per week.
- Limit screen time use (e.g., television, computer and tablet, video game, app) to no more than two hours a day.

Eat a Healthy Diet

- Limit your consumption of saturated fat (e.g., in meat products).
- Eat a generous amount of fruits and vegetables.
- Eat cereal and grain products in their whole-grain, high-fiber form.
- Limit your consumption of sugar and sugar-based beverages.
- Avoid excessive calorie intake from any source.
- Limit your sodium intake.

Disability

Disabilities are reported by about 21 percent of the U.S. population each year. Disabilities can include physical, cognitive or intellectual, emotional, and mobility impairments (see table 5.2). People with a disability share the same hopes and dreams for their lives as people who do not have a disability. One part of our social responsibility to each other is to make efforts to ensure that people with disabilities have the same opportunities available to individuals without a disability.

Some people confuse being handicapped with having a disability. You can have a disability or impairment without being handicapped. Being handicapped limits or prevents the fulfillment of a role.

In the legal arena, the **Americans With Disabilities Act** ensures the civil rights of all Americans who have a mental or physical disability. The law protects individuals with all forms of disability, including those that emerge as part of a chronic disease, such as cancer or AIDS. The law guarantees equal opportunity in employment, public services, public transportation, public accommodations, and communication. A similar law, the Individuals With Disabilities Education Act, ensures equal opportunity in education.

In your own interactions, treat individuals with a disability respectfully. Don't refer to a person in terms of his or her disability. For example, avoid saying, "This is my blind friend Sarah." If it is necessary or helpful to alert others of a person's disability, then introduce the person first. For example, say "This is my friend Sarah; she is visually impaired." Use the person's name first and remember that a person with a disability is a human being, just as you are.

> **❝** All interest in disease and death is only another expression of interest in life. **❞**
>
> —Thomas Mann, author

TABLE 5.2   Common Forms of Disability

Disability	Things to know	Things to consider
Vision impairments	• Visual impairment, including blindness, affects 2 percent of the population. • The chance of vision impairment increases with age. • Common causes of visual impairment include diabetes, cataracts (cloudiness in the eye), glaucoma (pressure in the eye), and macular degeneration (related to aging).	• Avoid startling the person. • Speak up right away. • Speak clearly and pay attention to your use of nonverbal gestures. • Use clear descriptions of where things are located and who is nearby. • Do not touch the person or a guide dog without permission. • If the person asks to be guided, extend your arm and allow him or her to hold on to it.
Hearing impairments	• Hearing impairment affects 3.5 percent of the population. • The chance of hearing impairment increases with age (it affects one-third of adults over age 60). • Listening to loud music through earbuds or headphones might increase your risk of hearing impairment over time.	• Touch the person gently on the arm or shoulder to get his or her attention. • Stand directly in front of the person when speaking so that he or she can see your mouth when you speak. • Do not shout. • Speak slowly and clearly. • Use sign language if you and the person both know it.
Mobility impairments	• Impaired mobility affects about 7 percent of the population. • Mobility impairment can result from disease, injury, or a birth defect. • Mobility aids and prosthetics can help many individuals maintain their independence.	• Be patient and move only as quickly as the individual does. • Give assistance only if asked. • If a person uses a wheelchair or is seated, squat down or sit. When possible, avoid "talking down" to the person. • Be positive and encouraging if the person wants to try an activity, sport, or physical task.
Cognitive impairments	• There are a wide range of cognitive impairments. • Cognitive impairments include conditions such as Down syndrome, traumatic brain injury, autism, and dementia. • Aging contributes to cognitive impairments like dementia.	• Move to a quiet place free of noise and distractions. • Be willing to repeat yourself without becoming frustrated. • Be patient and allow more time for the person to respond to questions or demands.
Emotional impairments	• Emotional impairments can include a wide range of emotional disorders (see chapter on emotional health and wellness). • Emotional impairments can also involve serious sensory impairments such as hearing voices or hallucinating.	• Be patient and empathetic. • If a person seems to suffer from hearing voices or hallucinations, a calm, controlled, and careful approach to interactions is recommended. In these instances avoid physical contact or sudden movements.

Comprehension Check

1. Identify and describe the most common chronic diseases.
2. Describe the consequences of chronic diseases.
3. What is the difference between a handicap and a disability?

Yesenia noticed that her older sister, Selena, had recently gained a little weight and seemed to be sick a lot. In addition, in the last few months, Selena had often complained of being cold and thirsty. Most nights, the sisters were home alone because their mom worked two jobs and their dad had passed away three years earlier due to heart disease. The girls tended to eat fast food or frozen meals for dinner and spent a lot of time in front of the computer. Yesenia did play softball at school, but Selena preferred fashion and art and spent most of her time designing clothes or following the latest trends online.

The girls' older brother, Marcos, weighed 250 pounds (113 kilograms) and had been diagnosed with type 2 diabetes at age 17. His doctor had told him that he needed to lose weight, exercise daily, and go on a special diet if he wanted to improve his health and reduce his own chance of developing heart disease. Since then, Marcos had been pretty good about taking walks and lifting weights at the community center, and sometimes he cooked for himself and his sisters at home.

For Discussion

What chronic diseases and disorders seem to run in this family? What behaviors contribute to their risk for developing chronic disease? Which sister is at increased risk based on her behavior? What healthy behaviors do members of the family practice? What should Yesenia say to Selena about her behavior and health risks? To help you answer these questions, read this chapter's Skills for Healthy Living feature.

SKILLS FOR HEALTHY LIVING: Identifying Risk Factors

To prevent infectious and chronic diseases, you need to recognize and monitor risk factors and take effective action. Take the time to get familiar with common diseases and their risk factors and monitor your decisions and behaviors. Here are some helpful tips.

- **Know your family history.** Spend some time learning about your family history of disease. For relatives who have passed away, find out if any chronic disease contributed to their deaths. For relatives who are still alive, learn about what diseases they have been diagnosed with and at what ages they were diagnosed. Consider your grandparents, parents, and siblings first, but also ask about aunts, uncles, and first cousins. If you're adopted and don't know your family's genetic history, pay extra attention to lifestyle factors and take all of the preventive measures you can in relation to the most common chronic diseases.

- **Learn the risks.** Get familiar with the risks for the most common diseases. Many chronic diseases share common risks, such as physical inactivity, poor diet, and smoking. Some diseases, however, have very specific risk factors. The CDC and the (U.S.) National Institutes of Health are good sources of accurate information about diseases and risk factors.

- **Monitor your behaviors.** We often fail to pay careful attention to our lifestyle behaviors. When you're trying to determine your disease risk, however, you need to assess your behaviors. You can find quizzes on the web or even in smartphone or tablet apps to help you evaluate your behaviors and their associated risks for disease. You can also track your healthy and unhealthy choices in a log or journal in order to see patterns over time—especially in your physical (in)activity and dietary habits.

- **Make healthy decisions.** Once you know which diseases run in your family, the risk factors for common chronic diseases, and the habits and behaviors you already have, you can begin to make informed decisions to improve your health and reduce your risks. It's also useful to consult with experts, such as physicians, dietitians, and trainers.

Can Hot Temperatures Make Us Vulnerable to Disease?

Changing weather patterns are bringing hotter weather to many parts of the United States. According to the National Climatic Data Center, this trend has been most pronounced in the past two decades. More generally, since 1895 the lower 48 states have seen temperature increases of about 0.12°F (0.07°C) per decade, and six of the nation's warmest years on record have occurred since 1998.

How does this warming trend relate to health? For one thing, the adult Culex mosquito that carries West Nile virus does best in hot, dry weather, but water is necessary for the larval stage. As a result, spikes in West Nile cases, such as one that occurred in the summer of 2012, are likely to become more regular occurrences (table 5.3 shows the top four U.S. states for West Nile).

Hot weather creates more warm, damp places in which mosquitoes can lay eggs. The warmth also allows the eggs to hatch faster and the larvae to mature faster. As a result, the mosquitoes spend more of their life span in a flying state, says Janet de la Rossi, and published expert on West Nile virus transmission. Warmer weather also promotes the growth of the virus within the mosquito itself. "Taken together, we see a greater risk for overall transmission to humans," says Michael Smith of the Centers for Disease Control and Prevention.

What can be done about these trends? "Killing mosquitoes that carry disease has been proven to cut down disease rates," said de la Rossi. Most eradication programs spray for mosquitoes at least six times per season, at a cost of US$60,000 to US$100,000 per treatment. Unfortunately, local budget cuts across the country are reducing funds available for mosquito control (abatement) projects. More than 1,100 localities throughout the country currently use mosquito control programs, but most are seriously threatened by budget issues.

In California, the problem is compounded by the large number of foreclosed and abandoned houses, some of which have stagnant swimming pools filled with mosquitoes. These mosquitoes can be pumped out along with the stagnant water—when there is money to pay the cost. "When funds aren't provided, the pumps aren't in the field, and the mosquito population thrives," said Dave White, former mosquito control expert, who was laid off two months ago.

At the same time, Lilly Doppler, a biologist states that "a warm winter, early spring, and hot summer have been so much a factor in a surge in the mosquito population that I honestly don't believe that (cuts have) played a factor with respect to this outbreak." Others in government who are making the budget cuts argue that individuals can take their own precautions against getting bitten by mosquitoes (e.g., applying mosquito repellent, wearing long sleeves and pants, staying in screened areas) and that the government does not need to pay for control programs when other issues are more pressing.

TABLE 5.3 Top Four U.S. States for West Nile Virus

State	Cases of West Nile	Deaths from West Nile
Texas	1,868	89
Louisiana	335	16
South Dakota	203	3
Oklahoma	191	17

Centers for Disease Control and Prevention 2012.

For Discussion

How does the weather affect mosquito outbreaks? Name two things you could do to help reduce the presence of mosquitos in your yard, school, or neighborhood. What steps could you take individually to help prevent yourself from being bit by an infected mosquito?

Reviewing Concepts and Vocabulary

As directed by your teacher, answer items 1 through 5 by correctly completing each sentence with a word or phrase.

1. A dangerous microorganism that causes a disease is known as a _____.
2. When a disease is transmitted by sharing a straw or by kissing, it is being spread through _____ transmission.
3. Yeast, mold, and mushrooms are examples of _____.
4. High blood pressure, also known as _____, is a form of cardiovascular disease.
5. _____ is a chronic disease in which the bones lose density and become weaker.

For items 6 through 10, as directed by your teacher, match each term in column 1 with the appropriate phrase in column 2.

6. lymphocytes
7. arthritis
8. arteriosclerosis
9. atherosclerosis
10. cancer

a. uncontrolled, abnormal cell growth
b. hard, rigid arteries
c. white blood cells that attack pathogens
d. clogged arteries
e. inflammation or damage to the joints

For items 11 through 15, as directed by your teacher, respond to each statement or question.

11. What is an infectious disease?
12. Describe two differences between influenza and the common cold.
13. What is the name of the virus that causes AIDS, and what does AIDS stand for?
14. List four types of cancer.
15. What is a disability? Describe one type of disability.

Thinking Critically

Write a paragraph in response to the following question.

During lunch you overhear your classmate Sarah making fun of another classmate, Martin, who has a mild form of Down syndrome. The things Sarah said about Martin are untrue and cruel. You know Martin to be a kind, funny, and smart person with a really big heart. What would you say to Sarah about the fact that she made fun of someone with a disability?

Take It Home

Share with your family members what you've learned about preventing chronic illnesses. Discuss with them what steps should be taken as a family to help reduce risks for cardiovascular disease, cancer, and diabetes. If a particular disease runs in your family, pay extra attention to the prevention of that disease. Identify three to five action steps that your family can take together to improve overall health and reduce the risk of chronic disease.

6

Emotional Health and Wellness

 Student Web Resources
www.healthforlifetextbook.org/student

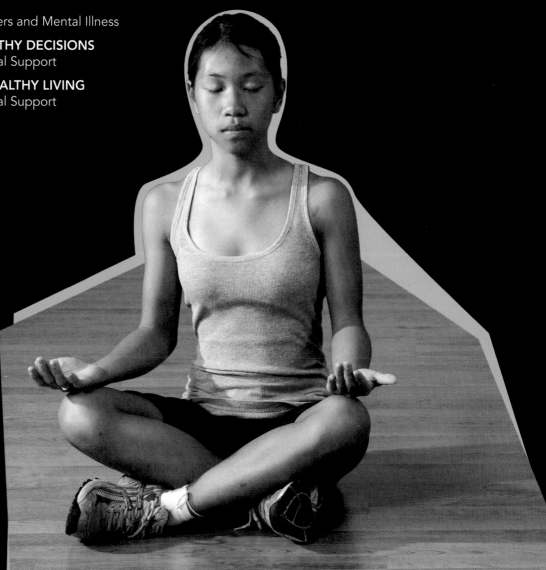

Mental and Emotional Wellness

Lesson Objectives

After reading this lesson, you should be able to

1. identify factors that contribute to emotional wellness;
2. define *personality*, *self-esteem*, and *body image*, and explain their importance to emotional health and wellness; and
3. explain how spiritual health and wellness relate to emotional health and wellness.

Lesson Vocabulary

body image, emotional wellness, personality, self-esteem, spirituality

How would you describe your personality to others? Can you identify your strengths and weaknesses? How do you feel about who you are and how you look? How do you respond when you feel sad or angry? Your answers to such questions can give you insight into your emotional health. This lesson introduces the most important aspects of good emotional health and wellness.

Emotional Health and Wellness

You learned earlier that health and wellness have five components. Emotional health and wellness is one of them. Like health in general, emotional health requires freedom from illness (in this case mental illness) and possession of emotional wellness (emotional well-being). This lesson will focus on emotional (mental) well-being and the next lesson will focus on mental illness. People with emotional wellness have a realistic understanding of their life circumstances and are able to understand and effectively use the options available to them. They can also assess situations accurately and make decisions that are in the best interest of both themselves and others. As a result, an emotionally healthy person can engage fully in life and cope with day-to-day challenges. Some indicators of good emotional health are identified in figure 6.1.

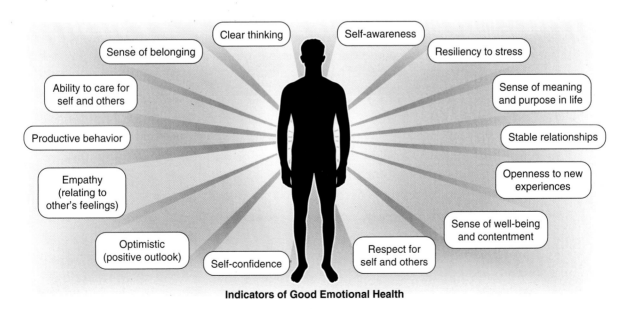

Indicators of Good Emotional Health

FIGURE 6.1 An emotionally healthy person displays some or all of these indicators.

Everyone experiences some challenges in life that might compromise emotional health and wellness. For example, a girl who is emotionally healthy during high school might experience some reduction in health status when she starts college if new academic challenges affect her self-confidence and she feels disconnected from her new community. As a result, she might not feel content, might find herself lacking motivation, and might become easily discouraged. This wouldn't mean that she had a mental illness, but it would mean that her emotional health wasn't as good as it could be. In your own life, you can use many of the skills for healthy living presented in this book to help you develop strong mental health.

Emotional Wellness

Emotion is a normal part of living, and an emotionally healthy person isn't someone who never experiences sadness or fear or who is always happy. What good **emotional wellness** does mean is that you're able to use your thoughts to understand and control the effects that your emotions have on your behavior. It means that you can recognize your own and others' emotional reactions and determine whether a given reaction is helpful—or not. Good health is more than freedom from illness (i.e., mental and emotional illnesses); it includes emotional wellness as shown by being happy and not depressed or sad.

You can also be supportive of your friends and family members and be happy when they exhibit healthy emotional responses. For example, it's okay for you and others to cry in sad situations or feel frustrated when something doesn't go as planned. We all need to allow ourselves and others the time and space to experience healthy emotional responses. However, when an emotional response, such as anger, is expressed in a destructive way—for example, in a violent outburst—it is not emotionally healthy. You can help yourself attain and maintain good emotional health by learning to understand your emotions and control your behavioral responses.

Personality

Think about your close friends and family members. Some are energetic and talkative, some are quieter and more reflective, others are neat and well organized, and still others are spontaneous and messy. Each person you know has a different **personality**—the unique mixture of qualities and traits that distinguishes him or her from others. Personality traits influence how we react to the challenges of life, interpret and express our feelings, and resolve conflicts with others.

Healthy Personality Traits

Many personality traits contribute to your overall emotional wellness. Some traits (such as carefulness) may help you avoid danger, whereas others (such as resilience) may help you resist disease. Here's a sample of healthy personality traits that are often considered to be characteristics of emotional wellness.

- **Conscientiousness**—tendency to conduct yourself according to an inner sense of what is right and wrong; having a strong sense of self-awareness and knowledge
- **Emotional stability**—ability to manage feelings and reactions and behave in a reasoned and consistent manner
- **Openness to experience**—demonstration of curiosity and independence
- **Optimism**—positive outlook on life and tendency to find the positive in various situations
- **Assertiveness**—ability to express emotions, needs, and desires clearly and confidently without impinging on the rights of others
- **Resilience**—ability to adapt to change and stressful events in healthy and flexible ways

---

As a result, your personality plays a role in your emotional health and wellness. Many personality traits exist, but individuals with certain traits seem to have better overall health (see the list titled Healthy Personality Traits). Personality traits are often established early in life, and they are influenced by genetics and by relationships with parents, siblings, friends, teachers, and others. It is possible to influence your personality traits, or to manage a trait (e.g., being disorganized), by working throughout your life to develop healthy life skills—for example, time management.

CONNECT

Do you think you were born with your personality type, or do you think your family environment has created your personality? What personality traits do you share with your family members?

Self-Esteem

Positive self-esteem is foundational to good emotional wellness. **Self-esteem** refers to the way in which a person perceives himself or herself. It is a combination of self-confidence and self-respect. A person exhibits positive self-esteem in feeling that he or she can cope with daily challenges and is worthy of happiness. People with positive self-esteem have confidence in themselves, solve problems effectively without excessive worry, confront or eliminate things that cause them fear or anxiety, take appropriate risks, and nurture themselves and their relationships with others. High self-esteem is not, however, the same thing as arrogance—a sense of superiority over others that results in an overbearing or dominating personality. You can be self-confident and self-accepting without being arrogant.

Research shows that people with positive (or high) self-esteem are more likely to engage in healthy behaviors, such as exercise and healthy

Tips for Healthy Self-Esteem

- **Accept who you are.** Make a list of your good qualities and skills and post it in a location where you will see it every day. Don't be too hard on yourself.

- **Keep track of your accomplishments.** Write them down every day and share them with a supportive friend, teacher, or family member.

- **Develop your own values.** Don't try to be someone else. Know who you are and take healthy pride in your identity.

- **Accept your strengths and weaknesses and set goals for yourself.** No one is perfect. Don't focus on things you can't change about yourself. Instead, think of constructive things you can do to improve in areas that you do control.

- **Don't be afraid to take healthy risks.** It's impossible to make it through life without failure. The important thing is to learn from your failures.

- **Find friends who support you.** Don't allow yourself to be mistreated or constantly put down. Anyone who repeatedly treats you with disrespect does not deserve to be in your life. Similarly, support the people in your life.

- **Respect yourself and others.** People who respect themselves and others are more likely to be respected by others. Don't be judgmental toward yourself or other people. Instead, be encouraging and supportive. You'll feel better about yourself, and others will respond in kind.

- **Join groups that promote your self-esteem.** Participate in clubs and organizations that you enjoy and that use and appreciate your strengths. Accept praise and compliments for the contributions you make.

- **Be careful not to behave arrogantly.** Take pride in your work and who you are without acting as if you're better than others.

eating, and are better able to avoid unhealthy behaviors, such as smoking and excessive drinking. People with low self-esteem, on the other hand, don't have much respect for themselves. They tend to judge themselves harshly and think negatively about their own abilities. Research has shown that low self-esteem is associated with risky and unhealthy behaviors among teenagers, such as drug and alcohol use, dropping out of school, and developing eating disorders.

Body Image

Many people of all ages struggle with body image. Your **body image** includes your thoughts, feelings, and behaviors related to your body size, shape, and appearance. Body image is strongly related to overall self-esteem, especially among teenagers. Many experts believe that young people often struggle with body image due to the pressure they feel when they compare themselves with unrealistic media representations of attractiveness. Other influences on body image include parents, friends, teachers, coaches, and health care workers.

In some cases, a single negative or critical comment about a person's body or appearance can be devastating, especially when it comes from a trusted friend, family member, or role model. When we make negative comments about someone's appearance, or tease someone because of how he or she looks, we contribute to negative body image. Instead, we should celebrate individual differences in appearance and focus on the positive personality characteristics and abilities that each person possesses. You can learn more about body image by visiting the student section of the Health for Life website.

CONNECT

How do you think the media influences your body image? Explain what you see as the three most significant media influences on your body image. Debate your perspective with your peers. Support your position with facts and be respectful of others' opinions.

> " Optimism is the faith that leads to achievement. Nothing can be done without hope and confidence. "
>
> —Helen Keller

Friends, as well as parents, teachers, coaches, health care workers, and the media, can influence body image.

gajatz - Fotolia.com

Spiritual Wellness

In modern society, we often seek to boost our self-esteem or validate our worth by acquiring material possessions. Many people believe that getting more or better stuff will make them happier. Sooner or later, however, most people come to understand that inner happiness is not achieved by simply having more, and they seek out other ways to find or create meaning and purpose in their lives. There's a name for this process. **Spirituality** is defined by the National Center for Complementary and Alternative Medicine as "an individual's sense of purpose and meaning in life, beyond material values." Spirituality is one component of health and wellness and all are interrelated. Spiritual fulfillment specifically relates to emotional health and wellness. It is generally understood to include three facets: relationships, values, and meaningful purpose in life. See the chapter on the introduction to health and wellness for the total health and wellness chain.

- **Relationships.** When we seek to connect with other people, we contemplate who we are in relation to others and what we truly value. When we treat others with respect and dignity, we manifest our own spirituality.

- **Values.** Our personal values are the principles that guide our decisions and actions. Your values are reflected in the rules by which you conduct your own life and the positions you stand for. When we pursue spiritual well-being, we look deeply into our own values and beliefs and seek to align our life choices and actions with them.

- **Meaningful purpose in life.** Why are you here on earth? What is it you're here to do? Spiritual wellness is associated with articulating your individual purpose in life and making choices that align with and develop that purpose. People begin to question their purpose as children and adolescents; they revisit this inner seeking throughout life.

Spirituality is different from religion. A religion is a system of beliefs, practices, rituals, and symbols designed to connect one to a sacred or divine being. Not all human beings participate in organized religion, but all have spiritual needs and longings, and research shows that spiritual well-being is important to physical health. For example, the National Cancer Institute suggests that spirituality contributes to physical health by decreasing anxiety and depression,

Practicing spirituality can be done through physical pursuits, religious practices, and contemplation or mediation.
pixhunter.com - Fotolia

reducing alcohol and drug use, reducing blood pressure and risk of heart disease, and increasing a person's coping ability and overall feelings of hope, optimism, satisfaction, and inner peace.

> continued

> continued

People practice spiritual wellness in a variety of ways. There is no single right way to seek spiritual wellness because spirituality itself is tied to individual values. Here are some common contemporary spiritual practices.

- **Physical pursuits.** Yoga, intentional relaxation, hiking, and other nature activities are common ways that people connect to their own sense of spirituality.

- **Religious practices.** Religious practices, church attendance, retreats, and other religious activities are central to many people's sense of spirituality. Keep in mind that these are often practiced together. Many religious practices also include contemplation and altruism.

- **Contemplation or meditation.** These practices concentrate the mind on a subject, question, object, or "nothingness" (blankness or openness). Often, people keep track of their contemplations and meditations in a journal. Another common spiritual practice is to contemplate gratitude or specific things for which you're grateful.

- **Mindfulness.** This practice involves being fully present in the moment in a non-judgmental state of observation. One way of practicing mindfulness is to awaken fully into an experience such as painting, drawing, music, or sculpting. In fact, anything can be a mindful activity if one is fully immersed in the moment and in touch with his or her innermost feelings.

- **Prayer.** This practice involves focusing oneself in communication with a sacred or divine being. Prayer takes many forms and may include words of praise, sharing of concerns, and petitions for guidance.

- **Altruism.** This is the act of giving yourself or your time due to genuine concern for others. Many people find that practicing altruism connects them to their own spirituality; in practicing selflessness, they get in touch with their deepest personal values.

Comprehension Check

1. Identify factors that contribute to emotional wellness.
2. What is one reason why it's important to have good self-esteem and why is it important to emotional health and wellness?
3. How does spiritual health and wellness relate to emotional health and wellness?

Your level of self-esteem is a good indicator of both your overall emotional health and wellness and your risk for becoming depressed or engaging in unhealthy behaviors. Self-esteem is a complicated thing to measure accurately, and no single test gets at all of its elements. Still, questionnaires like this one can help you get a sense of your overall self-esteem. More important, answering these questions can help you identify any qualities in yourself that could make you vulnerable to low self-esteem.

This questionnaire includes a list of statements addressing your general feelings about yourself. For each statement, circle the response that most accurately reflects how you feel. Try to be honest.

1. I feel like I am a person of worth on an equal plane with others.	Strongly agree	Agree	Disagree	Strongly disagree
2. I feel that I have a number of good qualities.	Strongly agree	Agree	Disagree	Strongly disagree
3. All in all, I am inclined to feel that I am a failure.	Strongly agree	Agree	Disagree	Strongly disagree
4. I am able to do things as well as most other people.	Strongly agree	Agree	Disagree	Strongly disagree
5. I feel I do not have much to be proud of.	Strongly agree	Agree	Disagree	Strongly disagree
6. I take a positive attitude toward myself.	Strongly agree	Agree	Disagree	Strongly disagree
7. On the whole, I am satisfied with myself.	Strongly agree	Agree	Disagree	Strongly disagree
8. I wish I could have more respect for myself.	Strongly agree	Agree	Disagree	Strongly disagree
9. I certainly feel useless at times.	Strongly agree	Agree	Disagree	Strongly disagree
10. At times I think I am no good at all.	Strongly agree	Agree	Disagree	Strongly disagree

To determine your score, complete the following calculations.

For items 1, 2, 4, 6, and 7, give yourself the following points for each response: strongly agree = 3, agree = 2, disagree = 1, strongly disagree = 0.

Item 1:_____ Item 2:_____ Item 4:_____ Item 6:_____ Item 7:_____

For items 3, 5, 8, 9, and 10, give yourself the following points for each response: strongly agree = 0, agree = 1, disagree = 2, strongly disagree = 3.

Item 3:_____ Item 5:_____ Item 8:_____ Item 9:_____ Item 10:_____

Total the points for all 10 items and write your score below.

My Self-Esteem score is: _____.

Higher scores are suggestive of a higher self-esteem. If your score is below 15, consider setting goals to improve your self-esteem. If your score is 15 or higher, consider ways to maintain your self-esteem (see lesson 6.1 of this chapter).

Image from Morris Rosenberg, 1989, *Society and the adolescent self-image, revised edition*. © 1989 by The Morris Rosenberg Foundation. Reprinted by Wesleyan University Press.

✓ Planning for Healthy Living

Use the Healthy Living Plan worksheet to improve your self-esteem.

Lesson 6.2
Mental Disorders and Mental Illness

Lesson Objectives

After reading this lesson, you should be able to

1. identify and describe common mental disorders,
2. recognize the stages of coping with death and dying and know what to do if someone exhibits them, and
3. explain three treatment options for mental disorders.

 Lesson Vocabulary

anorexia nervosa, anxiety disorder, attention-deficit/hyperactivity disorder (ADHD), bulimia, compulsive behavior, depression, generalized anxiety disorder, manic-depressive disorder, mental disorder, muscle dysmorphia, obsession, phobias, post-traumatic stress disorder, psychotherapy, suicide

Do you know anyone who suffers from a mental disorder? Mental disorders affect one in four adults and one in ten adolescents each year and are often left untreated. This lesson introduces some of the most common mental disorders and their treatments.

Mental Disorders

In the previous lesson, you learned about emotional health and wellness. The focus was on the positive and having good emotional wellness. This lesson describes a variety of disorders associated with emotional (mental) health and wellness. Because the term *mental* is commonly used as medical descriptor for these disorders, the terms **mental disorder** or mental illness will be used (rather than emotional disorders).

A mental disorder is an illness that affects a person's mind and reduces his or her ability to function. Mental disorders, or mental illnesses, involve behaviors, thoughts, or emotions (e.g., anger, fear, sadness, envy) that are unusual or inappropriate to a given situation. Many factors can contribute to the development of a mental disorder, and in some cases there is no clear reason why a person develops a disorder. Possible contributing factors include heredity, traumatic experience, and brain damage resulting from injury, accident, heavy alcohol or drug use, or illness. Even today, societies sometimes stigmatize individuals with mental illness; however,

many people will experience some degree of mental illness at some point in life.

Anxiety Disorders

Are you afraid of heights or of flying? What about public speaking? Have you ever experienced sudden anxiety (perhaps a feeling of nervousness or a rapid heart rate or breath rate) for a reason you didn't understand? When such feelings occur regularly or interfere with a person's ability to function normally, they are considered signs of an **anxiety disorder**. **Generalized anxiety disorder** involves feelings of intense worry, fear, or anxiety that do not stem from a specific source or cause. In contrast, intense fear and anxiety that do relate to a specific situation or object (e.g., heights, crowds, spiders) are called **phobias**.

Anxiety disorder can also appear as an unwanted thought or image that takes control of the mind. Such thoughts or images are called **obsessions**, and they can lead to **compulsive behaviors**, which are unreasonable behaviors done in an attempt to prevent a feared outcome. For example, individuals obsessed with germs and a fear of disease may feel compelled to wash their hands many times a day, even when they are already very clean.

Another type of anxiety disorder is called **post-traumatic stress disorder**. In this condition, an individual who has experienced or witnessed a traumatic event, such as a war or terrorist attack,

HEALTH TECHNOLOGY

Treating phobias has traditionally involved repeated exposure to a fearful situation so that the person can gradually adjust and overcome his or her fears. For example, people with a fear of heights (acrophobia) might begin treatment by standing on a platform positioned only slightly off the ground while applying techniques such as deep breathing to reduce their anxiety response, then progressively move higher until they are able to stand on top of a multistory building. This type of therapy can involve tremendous amounts of time and many unpredictable elements.

Advances in computer technology allow a similar process to be performed in a more controlled and safe environment. In virtual reality exposure therapy, the patient wears a head-mounted display and headphones so that both sight and sound are controlled. The virtual world can be precisely adjusted by the therapist to produce the desired exposure and the resulting anxiety, and the patient can revisit the setting or situation as often as needed to successfully conquer his or her fear.

CONNECT

When you immerse yourself in a virtual world by becoming a character in a video game or taking on an avatar, you enter a type of virtual reality. When you are engaged in a virtual reality, do you think it helps or hurts your ability to focus and concentrate? Can you imagine using virtual technology to help you overcome a phobia?

experiences intense flashbacks or nightmares that produce high anxiety and may interfere with his or her sleep, concentration, and relationships.

Eating Disorders

Eating disorders are mental disorders in which anxiety and other emotions are expressed through behaviors related to food and eating. Eating disorders are not simply about appetite and hunger; rather, they are complex psychological disorders. Two eating disorders you may have heard of are anorexia nervosa and bulimia. Individuals with **anorexia nervosa** believe they're fat even when they're dangerously thin; as a result, they may restrict their eating to the point of starvation. Symptoms

What Is a Panic Attack?

Anyone can suffer a panic attack in a life-threatening or otherwise very stressful situation. However, a person with panic disorder (a type of anxiety disorder) experiences regular panic attacks that can come at any time and for no apparent reason. A panic attack can produce the following symptoms.

- Rapid heart rate and breathing
- Pain or discomfort in the chest
- Fear of choking or suffocating
- Uncontrolled trembling or shaking
- Nausea, dizziness, or lightheadedness
- Fear of losing control or dying

Panic disorder often begins during adolescence, and it can be treated with medication and therapy. Left untreated, it can lead to depression, phobia, or substance abuse.

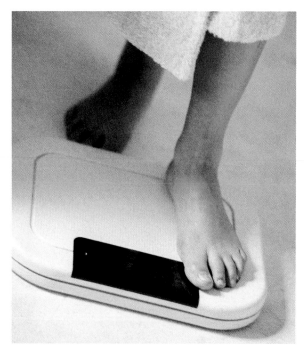

Eating disorders trigger anxiety and other emotions such as body image issues.

Eyewire

include extreme weight loss, dry skin, poor temperature regulation (feeling cold), and body image issues (e.g., feeling fat despite being very thin). Anorexia is a very serious disease that can lead to death if not treated properly. Treatment can be a long process involving multiple health care professionals; to be successful, it must address the underlying anxiety and emotional problems.

Bulimia involves uncontrolled episodes of bingeing (eating a large amount of food) and purging (trying to get rid of the food). Purging sometimes involves forcing the body to vomit but might also include using laxatives, weight loss pills, or even exercise (if it is done for the purpose of getting rid of calories and if the individual has an uncontrollable compulsion to exercise). Individuals with bulimia often eat in order to deal with an unwanted emotion or thought but then feel that they must get rid of the calories in order to remain attractive and in control.

Teenage females are more likely than males to suffer from eating disorders; in fact, about 90 percent of teens with eating disorders in the U.S. are female. Males who experience anxiety about their bodies may engage in different types of unhealthy behavior—for example, consuming excessive protein, obsessively engaging in weightlifting or prolonged training to build muscle, or taking

hormones or unnecessary supplements in order to build muscle or change their body shape. Males who take such actions may have a disorder known as **muscle dysmorphia**, which is not considered an eating disorder per se but is a similar form of mental illness that can have serious consequences for long-term health. This is especially true when people use steroids or other drugs to increase muscle size or enhance performance.

Eating disorders are complex conditions that can be very difficult to understand. If you suspect a friend or family member might have an eating disorder, it is important to recognize that you cannot "fix" or help that person on your own. According to the National Eating Disorders Association, when sharing your concerns with a person who might have an eating disorder, you should avoid placing any blame, shame, or guilt on the other person and avoid being stubborn or forceful with your opinions. Set aside time to talk openly, provide support, express your specific concerns, and be committed to listening to the other person even if they don't seem to understand or agree with what you are saying. If the person is open to the conversation, encourage them to see a doctor or mental health professional. If you try talking to the person and are still concerned, share your concerns with a trusted adult or health professional. For more information about eating disorders and similar conditions, see the student section of the Health for Life website.

Mood Disorders

When a person experiences extreme emotions that prevent him or her from functioning normally, the person may be experiencing a mood disorder. About 10 percent of Americans experience a mood disorder

🔊 HEALTHY COMMUNICATION

You suspect that a friend may have bulimia. She has always struggled with her appearance, and she talks many times a day about being fat. She also makes regular trips to the bathroom after meals and seems very emotional. Lately, she has been excessively hyper and always wants to go work out to "burn off calories." How should you handle this situation? If you chose to confront her with your concerns, what would you say?

each year, and women are 50 percent more likely than men to experience such a disorder at some point in life. A mood disorder can increase a person's risk for heart disease, diabetes, and other diseases. Fortunately, good treatment enables most people with a mood disorder to lead a productive life.

Depression is a mood disorder in which a person feels extreme sadness and hopelessness. The risk of developing depression increases throughout childhood and into adolescence. By the age of 18, about 10 percent of teenagers have experienced an episode of depression. Girls report depression at a higher rate than boys do, and depression is the leading cause of disability among all Americans between the ages of 15 and 44. Depression puts an individual at risk for **suicide** (the taking of one's own life) (see figure 6.2).

In some cases, episodes of depression alternate with periods of extreme excitability and restlessness in a condition known as **manic-depressive disorder** or bipolar disorder. When a person is

Grief, Death, and Dying

When a loved one dies, those left behind often feel extreme grief and sadness. Grief can be intense and last a long time, but it is a normal emotion that differs from depression. The typical stages that people go through when coping with the death of a loved one are illustrated in figure 6.3. Some people go through these stages in a different order than others, and some do not experience all of the stages. The person who died may also have experienced the stages if he or she knew that death was imminent and came to terms with that reality.

Warning signs of depression in teens

- Irritability or anger
- Extreme sensitivity to criticism
- Withdrawing from parents or some friends
- Change in appetite, significant weight loss or weight gain
- Change in sleep patterns (difficulty sleeping or sleeping too much, especially during the day time)
- Changes in activity patterns (becoming sluggish or frantic)
- Loss of energy
- Feelings of worthlessness or guilt
- Difficulty thinking or concentrating
- Loss of interest in usual activities
- Repeated thoughts or statements about death or suicide

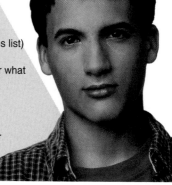

Warning signs of suicide

- A history of depression or the existence of the signs of depression (see previous list)
- Expressions of self-hatred
- Excessive risk-taking behaviors along with a careless attitude ("It doesn't matter what happens to me anyway.")
- A direct statement about committing suicide ("I'm going to end it all.")
- An indirect statement about suicide ("You won't have to worry about me being here by then.")
- Final preparations such as giving away possessions, writing revealing letters, or repairing damaged relationships (before planning to say good-bye)
- A preoccupation with themes of death
- Significant changes to personal appearance

FIGURE 6.2 Depression is a serious illness that can lead someone to commit suicide. Recognizing signs of depression and suicide can help you to help others.

overly excited and restless, he or she may be experiencing a manic episode. People in a manic state may speak so quickly and move around so rapidly that it is difficult to understand them or keep up with their actions. In manic-depressive disorder, manic episodes may last days or weeks and alternate with periods of serious depression. Manic-depressive disorder affects about 2 percent of teens each year.

Self-Injury

Sometimes people cope with emotion, stress, or trauma by injuring themselves through actions such as cutting or burning their skin. This type of behavior is called self-injury. It is a serious problem that can become a compulsive behavior and can be associated with mental disorders such as depression and eating disorders. People who engage in cutting often wear concealing clothing and if confronted may tell lies to cover up the truth. If you or someone you know engages in cutting or other self-injury, tell a trusted adult so that the person can get help in coping with emotions in a healthier way.

Attention-Deficit/ Hyperactivity Disorder

Attention-deficit/hyperactivity disorder (ADHD) is the most common mental disorder diagnosed in children and young adults. Specifically, about 9 percent of teens between the ages of 13 and 18 are diagnosed with ADHD. The disorder can involve a combination of factors, including hyperactivity (excessive energy), inattention (being unable to stay focused), and problems with impulse control (lacking patience and self-control). When ADHD is not properly diagnosed and treated, it can lead to problem behaviors such as drug or alcohol abuse, problems with the law, dropping out of school, and inability to hold down a job. Medications and therapy are used to treat ADHD. Having clear and consistent rules and routines is also helpful to managing the condition.

> If I feel depressed I will sing. If I feel sad I will laugh. . . . Today I will be the master of my emotions.
>
> —Og Mandino, author

Denial
This isn't happening to me!

Anger
Why is this happening to me?

Bargaining
I promise I'll be a better person if...

Depression
I don't care anymore.

Acceptance
I'm ready for whatever comes.

FIGURE 6.3 Stages of coping with death and dying.

ADVOCACY IN ACTION: Mental Health Awareness

Working in a small group, research one of the mental disorders discussed in this chapter. Gather information about the disorder's causes, risk factors, major symptoms, and treatment options. Next, speak to your school's leaders and health providers to gather information about relevant mental health services available on site. Then create a poster or other presentation about the disorder to share the information you've put together. Finally, as a class, share your collective work by organizing a mental health awareness advocacy campaign.

Treating Mental Disorders

Many treatment options are available for mental disorders. The exact treatment or combination of treatments depends on the disorder and the person. Treatment may be provided by a health care team, which can include a physician, a pharmacist, and a mental health professional (e.g., psychologist, psychiatrist, or social worker). Common treatment options include psychotherapy, counseling, medication, and substance abuse counseling. Additional treatments, such as hospitalization, may be used in more severe situations. In some cases, a mental disorder is so severe that a doctor, loved one, or guardian oversees the care until the affected individual is well enough to participate in decision making.

Counseling and Psychotherapy

Psychotherapy and counseling are methods of treating mental disorders that involve talking about the condition and related issues with a mental health care provider. During psychotherapy or counseling sessions, a person learns about his or her condition and his or her moods, feelings, thoughts, and behaviors. The person uses insights and knowledge gained from the treatment to learn coping and stress management skills.

There are many types of psychotherapy, each with its own approach to improving a person's emotional wellness. Psychotherapy can often be successfully completed in a few months, but in some cases long-term treatment is

helpful. It can be done one-on-one, in a group, or with family members.

Medication

Medication does not cure a mental disorder, but it can provide significant relief from symptoms and help the individual function more fully. Psychiatric medication can also help other treatments, such as psychotherapy, to be more effective. The selection of medication depends on the particular situation and how the person's body responds. Here are some of the most commonly used classes of prescription psychiatric medication.

- **Antidepressant medications.** Antidepressants are used to treat various types of depression and sometimes other conditions. They can help improve such symptoms as sadness, hopelessness, lack of energy, difficulty concentrating, and lack of interest in activities. Antidepressants are grouped into more specific categories determined by how they affect brain chemistry.

Psychotherapy helps to treat mental disorders and can be done in a group setting.

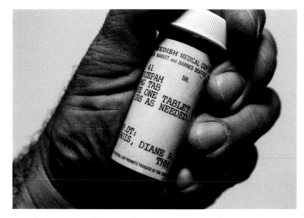

Medication can be used to treat some of the symptoms associated with mental illness.

PhotoDisc

- **Mood-stabilizing medications.** Mood stabilizers are most commonly used to treat bipolar disorder, which is characterized by alternating episodes of mania and depression. Sometimes they are used with antidepressants to treat depression.

- **Anti-anxiety medications.** These medications are used to treat anxiety disorders, such as generalized anxiety disorder and panic disorder. They may also help reduce agitation and insomnia. They are typically fast acting, helping relieve symptoms in as little as 30 to 60 minutes. One major drawback, however, is their potential for addiction.

- **Antipsychotic medications.** Also called neuroleptics, these medications are typically used to treat psychotic disorders such as schizophrenia. Psychotic disorders involve a loss of contact with reality.

Substance Abuse Counseling

Substance abuse commonly occurs along with mental illness; in such cases, it often interferes with treatment and worsens the problem. If an individual cannot stop using drugs or alcohol on his or her own, specialized treatment is needed. For children and adolescents, treatment for substance abuse and mental health issues should include parental and physician involvement. All types of treatment are proven to be more effective when parents or guardians are informed and are actively involved. Substance abuse treatments are discussed in later chapters and include the following:

- Psychotherapy
- Medication
- Hospitalization to address withdrawal (detox)
- Support groups, such as 12-step programs

HEALTH SCIENCE

Brain cells are called neurons, and they communicate with each other by using electrical signals to release chemical messengers from one cell to another. These messengers, called neurotransmitters or neurochemicals, carry out specific jobs and help regulate your body functions and emotions. Some of the most common neurochemicals are serotonin, dopamine, and norepinephrine.

When we are in a state of good emotional health and wellness, this complex communication system works well and without interruption. However, the effectiveness of neurochemicals can be limited by various conditions in the brain. When this happens, normal brain communication breaks down, and mental health may suffer. To learn more about the science of mental health, visit the student section of the Health for Life website.

Comprehension Check

1. Explain three types of anxiety disorder.
2. List the stages of coping with death and dying.
3. List three treatment options for mental disorders and describe one in more detail.

MAKING HEALTHY DECISIONS: Providing Social Support

Anton is a high school senior and star baseball player. You've been Anton's friend since elementary school and have always liked his positive outlook, outgoing nature, and generous spirit. Anton lives with his grandmother and doesn't have any other family nearby. He's always helping his grandma around the house and telling stories about her. He also spends a lot of time with his girlfriend, Zelia.

Lately, however, you've noticed that Anton doesn't talk much about his grandmother and that he seems to be more reserved than usual. In addition, Zelia has mentioned that Anton seems distant with her lately even though they haven't been fighting or having any problems. Last week, you saw Anton hanging out by himself after school even though he was supposed to be at baseball practice. When you asked him about it, he said he was tired and

he acted irritated that you were bothering him. When you asked him to go grab a bite to eat, he shrugged his shoulders and said, "I'm not hungry. What's the point anyway?" And just yesterday, Anton drifted off in class, and when the teacher called on him he didn't know the answer to the question. After class, he said that he was "worthless and stupid" and that he was going home.

For Discussion

What do you think might be wrong with Anton? Is there reason to be concerned for his health? What might you do to help him and provide him with social support? In answering these questions, consider the information presented in figure 6.2 and in this chapter's Skills for Healthy Living feature.

SKILLS FOR HEALTHY LIVING: Providing Social Support

Most people who attempt suicide do not really want to die but see suicide as the only way out of a painful or intolerable situation. Sometimes a person who attempts suicide lacks the support that he or she needs in order to overcome painful circumstances; such a person's suicide attempt is a call for help. With these realities in mind, you can see the value of being able to provide support to someone in need. In order to do so, it is essential to know how to communicate effectively and who to talk to for help. If someone you know displays signs of depression or suicidal thinking, get involved and seek help. Here are some guidelines.

- **Tell a trusted adult about your concerns.** Do not keep your concerns or your knowledge a secret, even if the other person is asking you to. When it comes to depression and suicide, secrets can be deadly, and keeping a friend's secret is not the right or healthy thing to do.

- **Take threats seriously.** If someone you know displays warning signs, don't excuse them or brush them off.

- **Listen and care.** If a person confides suicidal intentions to you, listen for the reasons that the person feels that way. Understanding where the person is coming from can help you convey the situation more effectively to others and may ultimately help the person get the support that he or she needs.

- **Don't belittle or challenge.** If you dismiss a person's threats about suicide, he or she may take that dismissal as a challenge.

- **Monitor the warning signs.** If the person seems to be getting worse, let others know, such as the person's parents, siblings, spouse, or counselor.

If you have serious concerns about a friend and don't know where to turn, call the National Suicide Prevention Lifeline at 1-800-273-TALK(8255).

Teens Under the Knife

If you think plastic surgery is something that only adults do, think again. According to the American Society of Plastic Surgeons, patients aged 18 and younger undergo well over 100,000 plastic surgery procedures each year. Some of the most common types of plastic surgery chosen by teens include nose jobs, breast reduction surgery, and correction of protruding ears, asymmetrical breasts, and scarring caused by acne or injury.

Teens seek such surgeries for many reasons. One often-cited reason is the desire to put an end to cruel comments made by other kids or teens—years of cruel remarks can drive a teen to take surgical action. For example, Jenna, a teenager from Texas, had surgery because she was often on the receiving end of Dumbo jokes about her protruding ears. Such reasons are also given by many adults, but teens often feel even greater pressure to fit in with others in terms of their appearance. For this reason, teens often report that their self-image and self-confidence improve when their perceived physical shortcomings are addressed.

Even so, many psychologists and physicians express concern about teenagers getting elective plastic surgery for any reason. These experts state that peer pressure and peer acceptance are viewed as particularly important among teens. They also note that teens pay a lot of attention to social messaging, social norms, and social expectations that will ultimately fade as they move into adulthood.

It's certainly true that body image plays a particularly prominent role in perceptions of overall health and well-being among teens. Most teens compare themselves and others with media images—often unfavorably, since popular culture tends to promote images and standards of physical attractiveness that are difficult, if not impossible, to attain. These days, computer manipulations, air brushing, and specialty makeup have established flawless skin, eyes, and noses as the norm. In addition, some common media images, such as the bodies of runway models, contradict what can be reasonably attained by most people even if they practice healthy behaviors. For example, fashion models weigh an average of 23 percent less than other U.S. females, but their images are perceived by many people as being normal.

In this environment, going under the knife for a permanent change in appearance may not be wise. "Often, individuals regret their decisions once they've grown into adulthood and found greater self-esteem through their professional and personal accomplishments," said Dr. Priyah Punjab, director of the Adolescent Self-Esteem Center of Los Angeles. Meanwhile, plastic surgeon Dr. Mark Macintosh not only supports plastic surgery for teens—he promotes it. "It's a cruel, competitive world out there, and we should feel obligated to do anything we can to help our kids thrive," said Macintosh. However, the National Institutes of Health (NIH) in the United States raises concerns about the medical risks associated with plastic surgery and also notes that both boys and girls continue to develop and change into their early twenties.

For Discussion

At what age do you think it's okay for a person to have elective plastic surgery? Why? Debate your perspective with a peer whose views differ from yours. Listen to each other's opinions and determine where you agree and disagree.

CHAPTER REVIEW

Reviewing Concepts and Vocabulary

As directed by your teacher, answer items 1 through 5 by correctly completing each sentence with a word or phrase.

1. _____ health is your ability to use your thoughts in order to understand and control the effect your emotions have on your behavior.

2. The ability to adapt to change and stressful events in healthy and flexible ways is known as _____.

3. People with positive _____ are more likely to engage in healthy behaviors such as exercise and healthy eating.

4. _____ is a mood disorder in which a person feels extreme sadness and hopelessness.

5. _____ _____ is an eating disorder that occurs when an individual does not eat enough food to stay healthy.

For items 6 through 10, as directed by your teacher, match each term in column 1 with the appropriate phrase in column 2.

6. conscientiousness

7. body image

8. phobia

9. muscle dysmorphia

10. post-traumatic stress disorder

a. intense fear and anxiety caused by a specific situation or object

b. your thoughts, feelings, and actions about your body shape or size

c. disorder typically seen in males that involves intense desire to become more muscular

d. anxiety disorder in which an individual has intense flashbacks or nightmares related to a traumatic event

e. conducting oneself according to an inner sense of right and wrong

For items 11 through 15, as directed by your teacher, respond to each statement or question.

11. Describe three healthy personality characteristics.
12. What is body image?
13. List two symptoms of a panic attack.
14. Identify and briefly explain one treatment for mental disorders.
15. What are three characteristics of attention-deficit/hyperactivity disorder?

Thinking Critically

Write a paragraph in response to the following statement.
   Identify a positive personality characteristic you possess and use an example to explain how that characteristic helped you make a healthy choice.

Take It Home

Keep an accomplishment journal for one week and ask a family member to do the same. Write down your successes and the things you do well—no matter how big or how small. Each night, share your accomplishments with your family member and ask that person to share his or her accomplishments for the day.

7

Health Care Consumerism

In This Chapter

LESSON 7.1
Health Literacy and Consumer Skills

SELF-ASSESSMENT
My Health Care Consumer Skills

LESSON 7.2
Self-Care and the Health Care System

MAKING HEALTHY DECISIONS
Critical Thinking

SKILLS FOR HEALTHY LIVING
Critical Thinking

 **Student Web Resources**

www.healthforlifetextbook.org/student

Photodisc

Lesson 7.1
. . . .
Health Literacy and Consumer Skills

Lesson Objectives

After reading this lesson, you should be able to

1. explain the importance of knowing your medical history and what should be included,
2. describe your consumer rights in terms of health care, and
3. explain the value of health literacy.

Lesson Vocabulary

culturally and linguistically appropriate services (CLAS), electronic medical records, health literacy, medical history, telemedicine

Chances are good that you've not had to make many choices about your medical or dental care without help from a parent or guardian. Even so, it's not too early to get more involved in your own care. Of course, your parents or guardians have a deep interest in your health. But you, the patient, are the person who actually feels the pain of an illness or injury. Only you know how your condition makes you feel. In addition, the earlier people become actively involved in their own health care, the more likely it is that any necessary intervention will be successful.

This lesson focuses on what it means to have health literacy and explores key issues to help you be an effective consumer of health care. The discussion uses the general term *health care provider* because, depending on the reason you seek treatment, you may visit a doctor, dentist, mental health professional, nurse, dental hygienist, nurse practitioner, pharmacist, physician assistant, physical therapist, occupational therapist, athletic trainer, chiropractor, public health official, or any of many other types of health professionals.

> " I am interested in getting people to use the health care system at the right time, getting them to see the doctor early enough, before a small health problem turns serious. "
>
> —Donna Shalala, former U.S. Secretary of Health and Human Services

How Is a Health Care Consumer Different From Other Types of Consumers?

When you're looking for health care, you have choices to make and questions to answer: what health care professional to see, how much the health care will cost, how to pay for it, where to go if your usual health care provider is not available, and how to get to your health care provider. It's a lot different from buying a video game online or going to a few stores to compare prices and return policies. Here are some more major differences between being a health care consumer and buying other products.

1. *If you have something seriously wrong, you can't afford to put it off like you can if you're buying a new phone or new shoes.* If you're really sick or injured, you need help right away.

2. *You likely don't have the time or the information to comparison-shop.* For many products, it's easy these days to go online, find out what different companies charge for the same product, and choose the least expensive offer. But it's not easy to find out the costs of medical services and determine which health care professional is the best match for your needs—medically or financially.

3. *Unlike shopping for a product online, you generally have to go to wherever the health care professional is located, which can be difficult due to factors such as time, money, and distance.* Of course, some medications and medical equipment can be ordered

online and delivered to your home. However, even with the advent of **telemedicine** and **electronic medical records**—which allow patients to talk with doctors from a distance and access their records online—there will always be a need to see health care providers in person on some occasions.

4. *In medical care your options for bargaining are very limited.* In many commercial transactions, people can bargain for a good deal. For example, when people buy a house or car, or even when they shop at a flea market or garage sale, they can make an offer that the seller will either accept or turn down. One situation in which bargaining might be possible is that of a health care professional not included on an insurance company's list of preferred providers. In this case, the patient could ask (bargain) with the health care professional to accept the same fee that he or she would be paid if included as a preferred provider. Most of the time, however, you do not get to negotiate the price of health care services and products.

5. *In health care, you generally don't have options such as getting two for one, getting a refund, or returning a product you aren't satisfied with.*

For these reasons and others, health care consumer groups and health literacy organizations have developed guidelines and materials to help people navigate the health care system and learn how to stay healthy.

understand basic health information and services needed to make appropriate health decisions." The U.S. Department of Health and Human Services (HHS) further explains that health literacy depends on having good knowledge of health topics, effectively engaging cultural factors (e.g., language differences), knowing how to fill out complex forms and locate health providers and services, engaging in self-care and chronic-disease management (e.g., asthma control), understanding mathematical concepts (e.g., probability, risk), and being able to perform key tasks (e.g., calculating cholesterol and blood sugar levels, measuring medications, understanding nutrition labels).

Health literacy is closely tied to the skill of critical thinking (for more on this connection, see the Skills for Healthy Living feature). It is not something that people just have; it must be acquired and developed. Although health literacy does involve some degree of common sense, many aspects of health care require special—and sometimes technical—knowledge. Generally speaking, the more knowledgeable you are, the more likely you are to have positive health outcomes. On the other hand, if you give vague information to your health care professional, you may get unspecific treatment.

 CONNECT

How do you think the web has influenced health care consumerism? How might it influence the doctor–patient relationship? Think of as many realistic examples as you can, then share your ideas with those of a peer or classmate. Compare your ideas and work collaboratively to come up with a response you agree on. Negotiate and compromise as needed to build consensus (agreement).

Health Literacy

The U.S. government's *Healthy People 2020* report defines **health literacy** as "the degree to which individuals have the capacity to obtain, process, and

Understanding chronic-disease management such as asthma control is just one aspect of health literacy.

Linguistic and Cultural Barriers to Health Literacy

A patient who speaks a different language from the health care provider often has the right to an interpreter (for spoken language) or translator (for written language). Many health care providers and hospitals employ interpreters and translators or subscribe to a service that provides them via telecommunication. Even if a patient speaks the same language as the health care provider, the patient may not always understand the medical or technical language that the health care provider uses. All patients have the right to an explanation that they understand.

In addition, the practice of providing **culturally and linguistically appropriate services (CLAS)** sets standards to ensure that a patient's treatment is not only understandable but also appropriate, whenever possible, within the patient's culture. For example, in some cultures people don't eat certain kinds of food. If a person is put on a special diet for medical reasons, that diet should not include foods prohibited by the person's religion or other cultural tradition.

Knowing Your Consumer Rights and Responsibilities

To participate effectively in your own health care and develop your health literacy, you must know your responsibilities and rights as a health care consumer. For example, you have the responsibility to be honest and forthcoming with your health care providers. You are expected to answer their questions honestly and provide an accurate **medical history**. This history should include all information that can help your medical professional give you the best possible treatment for your specific situation. Information that may be included in a medical history is identified in the accompanying text box. You are also expected to ask questions of your health care provider whenever you need clarification or have a concern.

In addition to these responsibilities, you have certain rights as a health care consumer. In the United States, the Patient's Bill of Rights, created by the government in 1998, affirms the following rights that you hold as a health care consumer.

- **Information.** You have the right to accurate and easily understood information.

- **Choice.** You have the right to a choice of health care providers and to high-quality health care.

- **Access.** If you have severe pain, an injury, or a sudden illness that may put your health in serious danger, you have the right to emergency care whenever and wherever needed.

- **Participation.** You have the right to know your treatment options and to participate in decisions about your care.

Keeping Track of Your Medical History

To ensure that you receive the best possible medical treatment, keep track of your medical history. Specifically, record the following types of information:

- Any prescription medications used during the past six months, including name, dose taken, and reason for taking

- Any over-the-counter (OTC) medications, vitamins, and supplements used during the past six months, including product name, dose taken, and reason for taking

- Any known allergies to medication

- All previous vaccinations and the date of each

- Past major medical events (e.g., surgeries, hospitalizations, tests, treatments, medical problems)

- Known family history of heart disease, cancer, or other disease or disorder (including parents, grandparents, siblings, aunts and uncles, and cousins)

ADVOCACY IN ACTION: Know Your Medical History

Everyone needs to understand his or her health history. As a classroom, design a Know Your Medical History campaign to help your peers gather information about their own health histories. Design a form that can be used to collect critical health information (use the text box titled Keeping Track of Your Medical History as a guide). Set up a table on campus to help fellow students learn why it's important to know their medical history. Provide them with the form you developed and invite them to sign a pledge stating that they will learn their own medical history. Consider providing ribbons, stickers, or pins to all of your peers who sign the pledge. Because of confidentiality issues, however, do not ask anyone to give their medical history to you.

- **Respect.** You have the right to considerate, respectful, and nondiscriminatory care.
- **Confidentiality.** You have the right to talk in confidence with your health care providers.
- **Complaints.** You have the right to a fair, fast, and objective review of any complaints you have against your health care provider or facility.

Trust and Confidentiality

It's crucial that you tell your health care providers the truth, even if it includes something about which you feel embarrassed or the topic is a sensitive one. For example, your providers need to know about medications you are taking, previous illnesses, sexual behavior, and any use of alcohol or other drugs. If you don't tell the truth, you're unlikely to get the treatment you need.

Most state laws provide for special relationships that allow confidentiality between doctors and patients, attorneys and clients, priests and those who confess to them, and guardians and their wards. In health care, such laws mean that your doctor will keep your medical information confidential. This fact can be controversial because some parents and guardians believe that if they are paying the medical bills, the health care professional should not hold back any information about their children. Open communication is encouraged with parents (guardians). Of course, a child is always free to communicate any medical information to his or her parents or guardians. But, for a variety of reasons, they sometimes choose not to.

🔊 **HEALTHY COMMUNICATION**

Do you think it is fair for a minor to be able to keep medical information private from parents or guardians? Why or why not? What personal values influence your perspective? How do you think cultural influences affect your perspective? Share your perspectives with a peer and show respect for each other's opinions.

Comprehension Check
1. Why is it important to know your medical history and what should be included?
2. Describe three rights that you have as a health care consumer.
3. Explain the value of health literacy.

SELF-ASSESSMENT: My Health Care Consumer Skills

For each question, select the answer (yes or no) that best describes you or your situation. Record your results as directed by your teacher.

1. I have access to (or know where to find) my medical history, including my immunization records.

   a. yes

   b. no

2. I have a medical home (a place where I can see the same health care provider) when I need medical care.

   a. yes

   b. no

3. I know what health care services are available at my school.

   a. yes

   b. no

4. If I don't understand my health care professional, I am not afraid to ask for clarification.

   a. yes

   b. no

5. I always tell the truth when my health care professional asks me about my behavior or my medical history, even if it might be embarrassing (e.g., sexual behavior, drug or alcohol use).

   a. yes

   b. no

6. If I am having a problem with my health, I try to learn as much as I can about my condition.

   a. yes

   b. no

7. I feel comfortable talking to my parents or guardian when I am not feeling well.

   a. yes

   b. no

8. When I am told by my health care professional what I should do to get better, I follow all the directions that I am given.

   a. yes

   b. no

9. If my condition gets worse, despite following my health care provider's advice, I have no problem calling for additional help.

   a. yes

   b. no

10. I know where to get medical care if my health care provider is not available.

    a. yes

    b. no

11. I know how to determine whether a website is a reliable source of medical information.

    a. yes

    b. no

12. I understand what patient–doctor confidentiality means.
    a. yes
    b. no
13. I am willing to ask for a medical translator (if needed for me or a friend or family member).
    a. yes
    b. no
14. I believe that it is my responsibility to do what it takes to help myself get well.
    a. yes
    b. no
15. I know where my local public health department is located.
    a. yes
    b. no

To score this self-assessment, count the number of yes answers that you circled. If the total is 12 to 15, you're a very good health care consumer; keep up the good work. If the total is 9 to 11, you can become a very good health care consumer with a little help (e.g., talking to your parents or your school nurse, learning more about your medical history, and so on). If the total is 8 or below, review this chapter to build your skills as a health care consumer.

✅ Planning for Healthy Living

Use the Healthy Living Plan worksheet to improve your skills as a health consumer.

Lesson 7.2

Self-Care and the Health Care System

Lesson Objectives

After reading this lesson, you should be able to

1. explain the importance of personal responsibility when seeking medical care and using the health care system,
2. identify two ways in which a person might get medical insurance, and
3. explain three things you should look for when selecting a physician.

Lesson Vocabulary

medical home, patient education, public health, self-care, support group

In many ways, this entire book addresses self-care. More specifically, the things you learn by reading the book, doing the self-assessments, performing online research, taking quizzes, and making behavior changes all help you take better care of your health.

Self-care does not replace medical care; it complements it. Your self-care is affected in part by the choices you make. It is also influenced by whether or not you have health insurance and whom you select as your health care providers—for example, family physician, specialist, dentist, physician assistant, or nurse practitioner. Your school probably has a school nurse and may even have its own health clinic. Your community may also have a free health clinic or a clinic that charges on a sliding scale according to ability to pay.

You must make many decisions when selecting health care professionals and deciding what type of health care is best suited to you. In this lesson, you'll learn about self-care and health care options.

Self-Care

Self-care involves all of the decisions you make and the actions you take to maintain your health. It includes knowing when you are at risk for a health problem (e.g., asthma increases the risk of complications from the flu). Self-care and medical care work hand in hand. Your health care professional may tell you what to do to get better, but you're responsible for actually doing the things you should do. For example, if you're an athlete with an injury, a physical therapist may assign you exercises, but you're responsible for doing them as directed. That is

one type of self-care. Similarly, although vaccination (which helps prevent disease) is not something you give to yourself, self-care is required in order for you to make and keep an appointment to get vaccinated.

Self-care is often tied to **patient education**. For example, if you have diabetes, you have likely been given education to help you learn to monitor your glucose level, know what your diet and exercise programs should be, and know when and how to take injections or other medications. In this case,

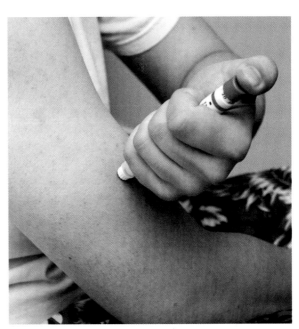

Effective self-care is often based on patient education such as a person who is allergic to bee stings learning how to use an epipen (an epinephrine shot to prevent severe reactions).

Nebojsa Bobic/fotolia.com

self-care involves doing the things you need to do to control your disease, and patient education includes the information, coaching, counseling, and behavior modification techniques provided by your health care provider. Many years ago, the life expectancy for people with type 1 (early-onset) diabetes was not very high. Now, however, when people with diabetes receive patient education and practice self-care, they are able to live as long as people who don't have diabetes.

Support Groups

Support groups, which bring together people who have similar problems, can play an important role in maintaining good health. As discussed in this book's chapters on alcohol and drugs, support groups can help people quit addictive and destructive behaviors. They can also help people meet other goals, such as losing weight, maintaining an exercise program, and learning how to eat well. In fact, just about every health condition or concern you can think of has a support group. For rare conditions, where few people with the condition live near each other, support groups can operate through social media.

As with self-care, support groups do not take the place of medical care but complement it. Most support groups are led not by professionals but by people who have the same problem or concern shared by other members of the group. Some hybrid groups combine medical care with support. For example, a doctor might give a presentation, after which members take the floor and share their problems and successes. In all support groups, members share information, emotional support, moral support, and tactics that enable them to become healthier. We all know that when we have a supportive environment, we are much more likely to succeed in facing difficult situations.

Specialty Camps and Workshops

Many camps and workshops are available for young people who want to learn more about their own health concern in a fun and supportive environment. Thousands of young people have participated in such experiences to learn how to lose weight, control asthma and diabetes, overcome addiction,

and deal with a host of other specific conditions. Some programs incorporate sports, crafts, ropes courses, horseback riding, and other activities. The camps and workshops are typically sponsored by an organization associated with a specific health condition, such as the American Diabetes Association, the American Lung Association, or the American Cancer Society. They may be free or inexpensive for people who qualify.

The Health Care System

The health care system includes all available medical services, the ways in which medical care is paid for, and the programs and services aimed at preventing disease and disability. In the health care system, physicians work with nurses and other health care providers to care for patients.

Medical Home

Patient-centered medicine is a term used to describe a form of medical practice that focuses on the patient's needs and concerns rather than the doctor's. One important part of this approach is to facilitate communication between medical specialists to optimize each person's treatment.

In order for this approach to be successful, each patient needs a primary point of contact in the health care system through which he or she receives medical attention. This point of contact is termed your **medical home**. A patient-centered medical home is a health care delivery system in which patients have an ongoing relationship with a personal physician who provides comprehensive and culturally and linguistically appropriate care. This physician also takes responsibility for coordinating care with other providers.

For many people, their medical home is their primary care physician—a medical doctor who takes care of most routine medical needs. Most primary care physicians have training in family practice, internal medicine, or pediatrics. Your medical home as a student could be your primary care physician, but it could also be your school nurse, and some schools even have their own doctors. Some also have their own school psychologist or psychiatrist. In addition, most high schools have school counselors. All of these professionals can be part of your medical home, depending on your particular needs.

The advantage of having a medical home is that you get to see someone who knows you and your background. Seeing a different person each time you need health care can be more time consuming, and you are more likely to have gaps in the services you receive. Many **public health** departments provide free or inexpensive medical services such as vaccines and testing for sexually transmitted infection (STI). Check to see what medical service your local public health department offers.

Think about it this way: Many people like to get their hair cut by the same person because that person knows what they want. As a result, loyalty often develops between a stylist and a customer. The same kind of relationship—on a deeper level—can develop between a patient and a health care provider who establish a level of trust that enhances their communication. Thus establishing your medical home is one way to enhance your health care experience.

School-Based Health Clinics

Many health care professionals believe that school-based health clinics make sense because children and young adults spend so much of their time at school. In fact, a school-based clinic can be a person's medical home. However, not everyone likes school-based clinics. Some parents and guardians feel that these clinics assume responsibilities that should be their own. Other parents and guardians like school-based clinics because if their child gets sick at school, they don't have to leave work to pick up the child. They know that the child is being taken care of by a health care professional. In addition, medical checkups can be performed at school without making an appointment and an extra trip to another health care provider. And, of course, people can still choose—the presence of a school-based clinic doesn't mean that everyone has to use it.

Emergency Rooms

For a variety of reasons, many people use emergency rooms as their only access to the medical care system. In emergencies, of course, this is exactly what people should do. But many people go to the emergency room for other reasons—for example, because it's always open, they don't have a medical home, their usual health care provider is not open, they don't want to wait for an appointment, an emergency room attends to everyone who shows up regardless of ability to pay, or the person doesn't know of any other options.

Emergency care is much more expensive than care from a primary health care professional, but it is essential in certain circumstances. Examples include when experiencing chest pain, difficulty breathing, severe injury, or poisoning. In many cases, if patients attended to medical problems in their early stages, there would be less need to go to an emergency room.

Selecting a Physician

The relationship you have with your primary care physician can affect the quality of the advice and care you receive. Most people in the United States have a choice when it comes to a selecting a primary care physician. Whether you are part of a health maintenance organization (HMO)—in

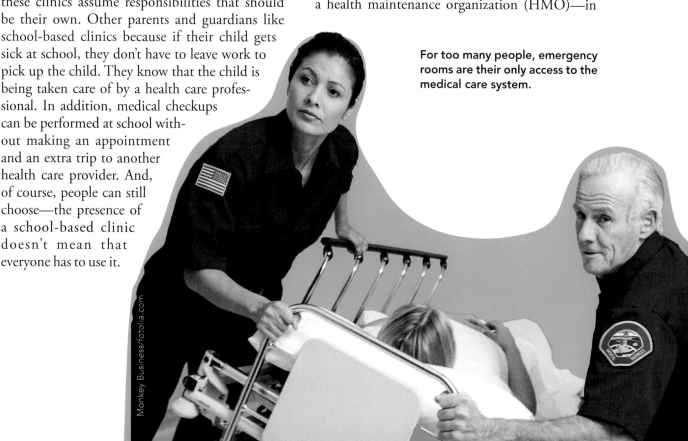

For too many people, emergency rooms are their only access to the medical care system.

Monkey Business/fotolia.com

which all medical services are connected within a network—or are free to choose any doctor in your area, you generally get to pick which doctor is best for you. (See this chapter's Living Well News feature.) Sometimes the choice is a hard one. When selecting a doctor, consider the following factors.

• **Professional ability.** The first and foremost concern on anyone's mind when choosing a doctor should be the physician's credentials. Remember to consider specialties and board certifications.

• **Male or female.** Ask yourself whether you're more comfortable seeing a male or female doctor. Your answer may vary according to the particular medical service.

• **Connection.** Pay attention to how well you connect with your doctor. Do you feel that you are heard? Do you feel respected? Would you recommend this doctor to others?

• **Bedside manner.** Does the doctor have a professional but empathetic tone? Your doctor should listen to what you have to say and respond in ways that show he or she not only hears but also takes seriously what you have to say.

• **Availability.** Is the doctor always booked? Is it hard to schedule appointments? It's important to be able to get care when you need it.

• **Insurance.** Know your insurance and select a doctor who will be covered.

• **Reputation.** It's no longer difficult to find out how others feel about particular doctors. It is easy to get online and do some checking. If doctors are unpopular or have made serious mistakes, they are likely listed with concerns expressed online. However, the Internet can also be misleading on issues like this. A small incident may be overstated or a disgruntled patient may simply lie. For this reason, don't rely solely on online comments when selecting a health care provider. Cross reference them with the other factors.

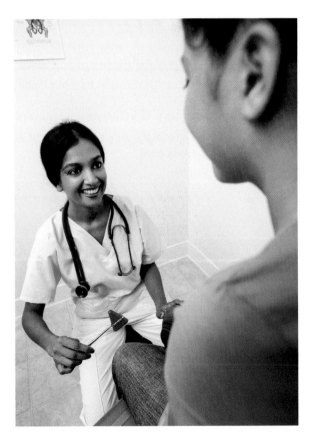

Find a doctor who can communicate well and who makes you feel comfortable about your health care.

© Photographerlondon | Dreamstime.com

Medical Coverage

Part of accessing health care involves making sure you can afford to pay for medical treatment when you need it. One way to meet medical expenses is to purchase medical insurance. According to the U.S. Census Bureau, 84 percent of Americans have some type of health insurance, and those who do are more likely to access the health care system and to have better health. As a teenager, if you have health insurance, you're most likely covered through a parent's or guardian's plan.

Most insured Americans have private group insurance that is provided by an employer, who negotiates the cost of the insurance with the insurance provider and usually helps pay the premium. An insurance premium is a set amount of money paid into the plan up front so that members of the group can have access to financial help and services when they need them. If you're covered on a parent's or guardian's insurance plan, that person is contributing a set amount from each paycheck to cover your premium. As a result, a good health insurance plan is an important benefit to look for when you're considering potential employers.

Other forms of insurance are also available. Plans such as Medicaid and Medicare are subsidized (partially or fully paid) by the U.S. government to help

HEALTH TECHNOLOGY

About two out of three people with Internet access look up medical information online. Two out of five people, for example, use physician rating websites to learn more about their doctor. Unfortunately, only a small number of people rate their doctors online, so the results you find may be based on just a handful of ratings. In addition, since people may be more likely to rate a doctor when they've had a bad experience, you should be careful in judging how accurate online ratings really are. If anyone has ever written bad things about you online, you know that what they say can be wrong or unfair. That's a major problem with online ratings. Some people just like to post negative comments about others, whether or not they're true.

Some health care organizations are rated by groups such as Healthgrades, a health care quality reporting group. Before you use an online ratings site, find out more about the group doing the rating. Is it an independent group, or is it funded by one of the health organizations being rated? Does it have a good system for determining its ratings?

 CONNECT

Have you used a physician rating system when deciding which health care provider to see? Do you think you would do so in the future? Why or why not?

low-income and elderly people obtain affordable medical care. Young, healthy people can also elect to pay for individual insurance plans. Those who don't have access to group care and cannot afford comprehensive individual insurance may choose to purchase catastrophic insurance. This type of plan costs less each month but can be used only if you suffer a very serious health condition.

 The Affordable Care Act (ACA) allows people who don't have insurance from other sources to be able to purchase their own health insurance. The costs vary from state to state and according to income (i.e., people with low incomes may qualify for a subsidy). If people refuse to buy insurance, they must pay a penalty. Insurance companies cannot refuse to insure people because of a preexisting condition, as many companies did before the ACA. Immigrants who are lawfully in the United States can buy health insurance, but immigrants who are undocumented cannot purchase it.

Comprehension Check

1. What role does personal responsibility play in seeking medical care and using the health care system?
2. Identify two ways in which a person can get medical insurance.
3. What are three things to look for when selecting a physician?

Renny was recently diagnosed with a stomach ulcer. Her doctor prescribed medication for her and told her to try to reduce her stress. After the appointment, Renny noticed that her stomach hurt even worse. She stopped taking her medication because she assumed it was causing her increase in pain. Things got so bad that she stopped wanting to eat any solid food. She was able to eat in small amounts over the course of the day and drank mostly fruit juices and soda for the calories.

Renny's aunt told her that she should take a multivitamin and eat licorice because it has an ingredient that helps with digestion. Renny tried that for a while, then started drinking milk after her sister said that it might coat her stomach. The whole situation was making her feel even more stressed out, and the idea of managing her stress was overwhelming. The only thing she found helpful was sleeping, so she was often just lying around and resting.

For Discussion

What weaknesses do you see in Renny's critical thinking about her health problem? Name at least two. What are two specific steps Renny could take to improve her thinking about this issue? To help you answer these questions, refer to the Skills for Healthy Living feature.

SKILLS FOR HEALTHY LIVING: Critical Thinking

Critical thinking is the process of actively and skillfully conceptualizing (generating or creating), applying, analyzing, synthesizing, and evaluating information. Critical thinking is influenced by observation, experience, reflection, reasoning, and communication. Ultimately, it serves as a guide to belief and action. More specifically, it enables you to find and interpret information that helps you make decisions and solve problems in order to live a healthy lifestyle.

Your critical thinking is affected by the work you do as part of your formal education, as well as the way in which you process other life experiences and learn from them. To develop and use critical thinking skills in relation to your health and wellness, consider the following tips.

- **Readily admit a lack of understanding or information and ask questions.** No one knows everything about all aspects of health, wellness, and medicine. Smart people know when to ask others.
- **Be curious.** Health information changes, and you need to stay curious enough to seek updated information on issues related to your health.
- **Be interested in finding new solutions.** Many health issues have more than one solution. Sometimes the ability to try a new approach or solution makes the difference.
- **Be willing to examine beliefs, assumptions, and opinions and weigh them against facts.** The more you learn, the more you're likely to have your previous beliefs and opinions challenged. Accept the challenge and don't be afraid to grow.
- **Listen carefully to others.** Listening to others is essential for your health care. Learn to listen and to follow medical advice.
- **Make critical thinking a lifelong process and self-assess your ability to think critically.** Continually train yourself to think better. Like most skills, developing strong critical thinking takes effort.
- **Suspend judgment until all facts have been gathered and considered.** Jumping to conclusions and making swift judgments shuts off your ability to gather more information and learn. Keep an open mind.
- **Look for evidence to support assumptions and beliefs.** Don't just look at evidence to prove a different point of view wrong. Make a practice of looking

for evidence that supports your health beliefs and assumptions. If you can't find any, consider alternative perspectives.

- **Don't be afraid to update your thinking as you learn more.** It's okay to change your mind on an issue in light of new information.

- **Examine problems closely.** Be sure of what it is you really want to know before you seek solutions.

- **Reject information that is incorrect or irrelevant.** Don't be influenced by scams and quackery.

 ACADEMIC CONNECTION: **Sources of Information**

When reading and analyzing writing and research, you need to recognize the difference between primary and secondary sources of information and use each appropriately. Each is described as follows.

Primary Sources

A primary source is an original object or document—the raw material or firsthand information. Primary sources include historical and legal documents, eyewitness accounts, results of experiments, statistical data, pieces of creative writing, and art objects. Here are some primary sources used in health and fitness:

- Journals or periodicals are the main type of publications in which scientific research is reported. *Exercise and Science in Sports and Medicine* and the *Journal of Health, Physical Education, Recreation and Dance (JOPERD)* are examples of periodicals used in health and fitness.

- These are detailed accounts of research conducted in pursuit of higher academic degrees such as a master of science (MS) degree.

- Conference papers are an important avenue for reporting new research or developments.

- Reports are individual publications containing research. These include many governmental reports. For example, the CDC often reports on data from the Youth Risk Behavior Surveillance System.

Secondary Sources

A secondary source is something written about a primary source. Secondary sources include comments on, interpretations of, and discussions about the original material. You can think of secondary sources as secondhand information. Examples of secondary sources of health and fitness information are articles in newspapers or popular magazines, textbooks, book or movie reviews, and articles in scholarly journals that discuss or evaluate someone else's original research.

What Are the Most Common Types of Health Insurance?

Most people who have a health care policy through their employer (and many who are self-insured) are enrolled in some type of managed care plan—either a health maintenance organizations (HMO) or a preferred provider organization (PPO). A less common alternative is a point-of-service (POS) plan, which combines the features of an HMO and a PPO (see figure 7.1). All managed care plans contract with doctors, hospitals, clinics, and other health care providers such as pharmacies, labs, X ray centers, and medical equipment vendors. This group of contracted health care providers is known as the health plan's network.

In some types of managed care plans, you may be required to receive all of your health care services from providers in the insurer's network. This is the case with HMOs, which require you to select a primary care physician (PCP), who is responsible for managing and coordinating your health care. When you need to see a specialist or receive a diagnostic service (e.g., a lab test or X ray), you must get a referral from your PCP. If you don't have a referral or you choose to see a provider outside of your HMO's network, you will most likely pay most or all of the cost. Even when you see a doctor within your HMO's network, you'll likely make a co-payment (due at the time of service), and you may also have to meet a deductible (a set amount that you pay yourself before your insurance benefits take over).

In other managed care plans, you may be able to receive care from providers who are not

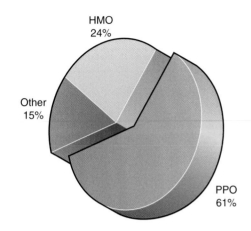

Figure 7.1   Health insurance plans.

part of the network, but you will pay a larger share of the cost to receive those services. A preferred provider organization contracts with a network of preferred providers from whom you can choose. You do not need to select a PCP or get a referral to see other providers in the network. As with an HMO, you will have a co-payment and a deductible to meet.

For Discussion

Are you covered by any health care insurance that you know of? What would be the advantages and disadvantages of getting your medical care from a plan like an HMO? How much of every dollar earned would you be willing to pay in order to have quality medical insurance? Explain your response.

Reviewing Concepts and Vocabulary

As directed by your teacher, answer items 1 through 5 by correctly completing the sentence with a word or phrase.

1. A regular health care provider is referred to as a medical _____.

2. A group of people who get together to discuss health concerns or conditions that they have in common is called a(n) _____ _____.

3. A health care professional who teaches a patient how to take care of his or her condition or disease is providing _____.

4. A person with asthma or diabetes who learns how to manage his or her symptoms is practicing _____ _____.

5. One type of managed care plan is an HMO, which stands for _____ _____ _____.

For items 6 through 10, as directed by your teacher, match each term in column 1 with the appropriate phrase in column 2.

6. CLAS   a. related to the skill of critical thinking

7. specialty camp   b. views health from a collective, group, or population perspective

8. public health   c. more expensive than care from a primary health care provider

9. health literacy   d. culturally and linguistically appropriate services (CLAS)

10. emergency care   e. for young people who want to learn more about their own health concerns

For items 11 through 15, as directed by your teacher, respond to each statement or question.

11. Describe two things you should look for when selecting a physician.

12. List two reasons that a person might choose to get help at an emergency room rather than seeing a regular physician.

13. Why is patient education important?

14. What is critical thinking?

15. What are two steps you could take to improve your critical thinking skills?

Thinking Critically

Write a paragraph in response to the following question.

When José arrived at his doctor's office, the receptionist spoke to him in English, but José's first language was Spanish and he had a hard time figuring out what he was supposed to do. What would be the best solution to José's problem?

Take It Home

Talk with your parents or guardians about your health care insurance. Find out if you have HMO, PPO, or another form of insurance. Learn about your medical co-payments and deductibles and find out what will happen to your insurance if you leave home or go to college.

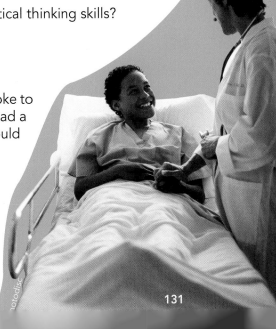

UNIT III

Embracing Priority Lifestyles

Healthy People 2020 Goals

- Increase the number of people at a healthy weight.
- Reduce the number of people, including teens, who are overweight or obese.
- Prevent inappropriate weight gain among teens.
- Reduce disordered eating among adolescents.
- Reduce the percentage of teens who do no leisure-time activity.
- Increase trips made by walking and biking.
- Reduce screen time among teens.
- Improve health literacy.
- Increase fruit, vegetable, and whole-grain consumption.
- Reduce the consumption of calories from saturated fats and added sugars.
- Increase the number of people who get adequate calcium in their daily diet.
- Increase availability of healthy snacks.
- Achieve high-quality, longer lives. Reduce preventable disease, injury, and early deaths.
- Create environments that promote health, fitness, and wellness for all.
- Adopt healthy lifestyles for health and wellness.
- Increase comprehensive school health education.
- Increase the number of teens who do regular muscle fitness exercises.
- Increase out-of-school activities for teens.
- Reduce sports and recreation injuries.
- Increase the percentage of teens and adults who meet national physical activity guidelines.
- Increase overall cardiovascular health.
- Reduce heart disease, stroke, cancer, diabetes, high blood pressure, and osteoporosis.
- Improve teens' comprehension of health promotion and disease prevention concepts.
- Increase education to promote health-enhancing behaviors and reduce health risks.
- Increase availability of stress reduction programs.

Self-Assessment Features in This Unit

- Rate My Plate
- What Motivates Your Eating?
- Physical Fitness Challenges
- Physical Activity Readiness
- Stress Management

Making Healthy Decisions and Skills for Healthy Living Features in This Unit

- Self-Monitoring
- Nutrition Information
- Performance Skills
- Changing Attitudes
- Time Management

Special Features in This Unit

- Diverse Perspectives: Being Vegan
- Consumer Corner: Selecting Diet Products and Services
- Advocacy in Action: Replacing Screen Time With Activity Time
- Consumer Corner: Selecting Proper Athletic Shoes
- Consumer Corner: Can Vitamins Really Reduce Stress?

Living Well News Features in This Unit

- Can a Trip to Your Local Drug Store Help You Lose Weight?
- Eating Out May Be Both Deceiving and Unhealthy
- Physical Activity and Brain Power
- Is Being a Weekend Warrior Bad for Your Health?
- Stress at Work: Can Worksite Health Promotion Help?

8

Nutrition: Foundations for Healthy Eating

www **Student Web Resources**
www.healthforlifetextbook.org/student

Lesson 8.1
Basic Nutrients

Lesson Objectives

After reading this lesson, you should be able to

1. list and describe the three macronutrients,
2. list and describe the two major types of micronutrients, and
3. explain the functions of major macronutrients and micronutrients.

Lesson Vocabulary

calorie, carbohydrate, cholesterol, essential amino acid, insoluble fiber, macronutrients, micronutrients, mineral, nutrient-dense food, protein, saturated fat, soluble fiber, unsaturated fat, vitamins

Sitting down to a meal with delicious food can be a wonderful experience. However, experts tell us that Americans live in a toxic food environment. They mean that large quantities of food are available and that much of it contains added salt, fat, and sugar. As a result, Americans often consume too many daily calories while getting too few of the essential (and other important) nutrients. Perhaps it is not surprising, then, that nutrition has become a national focus in the United States due to rising rates of obesity and illness, such as heart disease and diabetes.

Fortunately, nutrition information is easy to find; unfortunately, the information is not always accurate. This lesson introduces you to the basics of good nutrition and provides you with the foundation necessary for making sense of nutrition information.

Basic Nutrients

Everything you consume can be classified into six major nutrient categories: carbohydrate, protein, fat, vitamin, mineral, and water. Items in the first three categories provide your body with calories and thus are known as energy-yielding nutrients. They are also called **macronutrients** because they are needed in large quantities (macro means large). Items in the remaining three categories—vitamin, mineral, and water—provide no direct energy or calories but are critical to chemical reactions in your body. They are known as non-energy-yielding nutrients and also as **micronutrients** because they are needed in smaller quantities.

Energy-Yielding Nutrients

Carbohydrate, protein, and fat provide your body with energy. Energy is often measured using **calories**. The term *calorie* is short for the proper scientific term *kilocalorie* (abbreviated as kcal), which represents the amount of energy required to raise the temperature of a liter of water one degree centigrade (Celsius) at sea level. The U.S. Department of Agriculture (USDA) recommends that most of the calories in your diet come from carbohydrates and that fewer of your calories come from protein and fat. Figure 8.1 shows the portion of your daily diet that should come from each of these nutrients. Table 8.1 shows recommended daily caloric intake varied by age and gender.

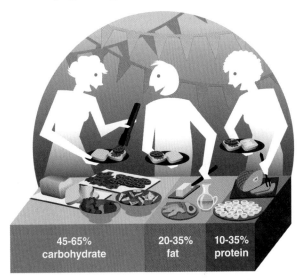

45-65% carbohydrate   20-35% fat   10-35% protein

FIGURE 8.1 Percentage of calories recommended by the USDA for carbohydrate, protein, and fat.

TABLE 8.1   Recommended Daily Caloric Intake by Age and Gender

Gender and age	Estimated daily calories needed by those who are not physically active*
All children 2–3 yrs.	1,000
All children 4–8 yrs.	1,200–1,400
Girls 9–13 yrs.	1,600
Boys 9–13 yrs.	1,800
Girls 14–18 yrs.	1,800
Boys 14–18 yrs.	2,200
Females 19–30 yrs.	2,000
Males 19–30 yrs.	2,400
Females 31–50 yrs.	1,800
Males 31–50 yrs.	2,200
Females 51+ yrs.	1,600
Males 51+ yrs.	2,000

*These amounts are appropriate for individuals who get less than 30 minutes of moderate physical activity on most days. Those who are more active need more total calories and have a higher limit for empty calories. To find your personal total calorie needs and empty calories limit, enter your information into http://MyPlate.gov.

USDA's Center for Nutrition Policy and Promotion.

Carbohydrate

Carbohydrate is your body's main source of energy, and it provides the foundation for a healthy diet. Most of the cells in your body rely on carbohydrate for energy; even the metabolism of fat requires carbohydrate energy. Dietary carbohydrate comes in multiple forms, and not all carbohydrate-rich foods are healthy food choices.

The two main classifications of carbohydrates are simple and complex. Simple carbohydrate, also called simple sugar, is naturally found in foods such as fruits and milk and can also be refined to create products such as table sugar and corn syrup. Complex carbohydrate is found in the starch and fiber contained in foods such as whole-grain breads and vegetables. Most of the sugar in a healthy diet should come in the form of complex carbohydrate. Both simple and complex carbohydrates provide four calories per gram of weight.

The healthiest complex carbohydrate choices are high in fiber. These choices are typically known as **nutrient-dense foods** because they contain high levels of vitamins, minerals, and other important nutrients while remaining relatively low in calories.

Examples of carbohydrate: *(a)* simple sugar (candy); *(b)* complex carbohydrate (beans); *(c)* fiber (fruit).
© 1999 PhotoDisc, Inc.

Apples, whole-grain bread, broiled salmon, steamed vegetables, and black beans are examples of nutrient-dense foods.

Dietary fiber can be soluble or insoluble. **Soluble fiber** is partially digestible and absorbs water as it passes through your digestive system. **Insoluble fiber** is not digestible; it passes through your digestive tract without being broken down or used. Insoluble fiber is often found on the outer layer of fruits, grains, and vegetables. Both types of fiber are important for good health because they help absorb damaging substances in your body and maintain normal digestive function. Both types are contained in most fruits, vegetables, and grains in their natural form.

As a general rule, the more unprocessed a food is, the more likely it is to provide nutrient-dense, fiber-rich, complex carbohydrate. For example, eating a whole apple, including the skin, provides more nutrients, more fiber, and less sugar than eating processed apple sauce. Similarly, bread made from whole-grain flour rather than white flour provides more fiber and more nutrients. White flour is made by removing much of the insoluble fiber from the original grain before grinding it and bleaching it.

Protein

Protein refers to a group of nutrients that build, repair, and maintain your body cells. Protein is easily found in animal products, such as meat, eggs, cheese, and milk; some of these may be high in fat. Some protein can also be found in plants, including grains, beans, and vegetables. Like carbohydrate, protein contains four calories per gram of weight. However, protein is not as easily used by the body for fuel as carbohydrate. As a result, only 12 percent to 15 percent of the calories you eat in the form of protein will be used directly for energy.

Carbohydrate is also used to generate and repair tissue. During digestion, your body breaks down protein into smaller building blocks known as amino acids. Twenty known amino acids are required by the human body for normal functioning, and nine of them must be obtained in the diet because the body cannot make them. If you consume these nine, your body will manufacture the remaining eleven. For this reason, the nine are known as **essential amino acids**.

A food that provides all nine essential amino acids in proper proportion is referred to as a complete protein. Examples include all animal products (e.g., meat, eggs, cheese, milk). A food that provides some of the essential amino acids is referred to as an incomplete protein. Examples include most grains, beans, and vegetables. It is possible to combine incomplete protein sources to make a complete protein; such foods are referred to as complementary protein sources. One example is black beans served with brown rice, which also has the virtue of being high in fiber and low in fat. A vegetarian (a person who doesn't eat meat) must be careful to eat a good variety of incomplete protein sources so that all of the essential amino acids are available for his or her body to use.

Fat

Fat is found in animal products and some plant products (e.g., nuts, vegetable oils). Unlike carbohydrate and protein, fat contains nine calories per gram of weight. As a result, foods higher in fat provide more calories and can be a significant contributor to weight gain if they are not monitored in your diet. However, fat is essential for normal physiological functioning. Specifically, it helps dissolve and carry certain vitamins, aids in the growth and repair of your tissues, and is critical for normal functioning in your nervous system, including brain functioning. As a result, your diet must contain an adequate amount of appropriate fat.

Fat is classified as either saturated or unsaturated. **Saturated fat** is found in animal products and is generally solid at room temperature. Examples include lard, butter, milk fat, and meat fat. **Unsaturated fat** is more typically found in vegetable products (e.g., oils) and tends to be liquid at room temperature. Examples include sunflower, corn, soybean, peanut, almond, and olive oils. Fish also produce unsaturated fat in their cells. Though a healthy diet includes both types of fat, unsaturated fat is considered healthier for the human body. In fact, according to the USDA, less than 30 percent (or up to 35 percent according to the Institute of Medicine) of the total calories you consume should come from fat in general, and no more than 10 percent of your total calories should come from saturated fat.

Sometimes unsaturated fat (e.g., sunflower oil) is chemically altered to look and act like saturated fat; in this case, it is called trans-fatty acid or hydrogenated fat. Trans-fatty acid has been found

DIVERSE PERSPECTIVES: Being Vegan

Karen Struthers/fotolia.com

My name is Erin, and I started eating a vegan diet in college after I took a course on the ethical treatment of animals. As a vegan, I don't consume any animal or animal-derived products, including eggs, milk, cheese, and cereal and bread products that use these ingredients. Some people choose to eat a vegan diet because of a health condition they have, like heart or kidney disease. I'm still young, and I live a healthy lifestyle, so eating vegan is a health choice for me too, but it is also an ethical decision. I am an animal lover and believe that all animals deserve humane treatment. I struggle with the idea of chickens or other animals being raised just to be used for human consumption. I know that my individual decision to be vegan won't change the

world, but it's important to me and my personal sense of values.

Sometimes it's really difficult. A lot of restaurants don't have very many creative or good vegan options, so I prefer to eat a snack before I leave home so that I won't go hungry if that happens. Parties, barbeques, and other celebrations can also be a challenge if there aren't enough options for me. I do have to be careful to get all of the nutrients I need. I see a dietitian once a year to evaluate my diet, and I am also good about getting regular medical checkups. Learning to cook vegan foods has opened my eyes to a wider range of grains, beans, vegetables, and fruits, and I am happy with my decision. I have a lot of energy, my weight is never an issue for me, and I am at peace knowing I am living according to my personal sense of values.

in processed bakery foods (e.g., cakes) and has often been used to prolong a food's shelf life. You can be sure that a food contains trans-fatty acid if you see a term such as "hydrogenated" or "partially hydrogenated" in the ingredient list. The Food and Drug Administration (FDA) has now banned trans fat, but it has been left on the sample food label later in this chapter.

You should also pay attention to your intake of **cholesterol**, which is different from but related to fat. Cholesterol is a waxy, fatlike substance found in the cells of all mammals, including humans. A small amount of cholesterol is needed to make hormones and provide structure to your cell membranes. You consume cholesterol whenever you eat animal products, and even if you don't eat animal products, your body is able to use other fat to make cholesterol in your liver. People who eat a lot of saturated fat or trans-fatty acid are more likely to produce more cholesterol in their liver and thus have more cholesterol in their blood. High blood cholesterol puts you at risk for atherosclerosis and other cardiovascular diseases. To help prevent high cholesterol, and thus reduce your risk for cardiovascular disease, experts recommend consuming a diet that is low in saturated fat, trans-fatty acid, and cholesterol.

Non-Energy-Yielding Nutrients

Vitamins, minerals, and water provide no direct calories, or energy, for your body to use. Vitamins and minerals are also needed in smaller quantities than carbohydrate, fat, and protein. As a result, they are called non-energy-yielding nutrients, or micronutrients. Still, they are essential for normal functioning of your body. They are used in the chemical reactions that break down and release energy from the other nutrients, and they are necessary for the normal growth, development, and maintenance of your body.

Vitamins

Vitamins are organic compounds that are essential to your body's normal growth, functioning, and maintenance. Vitamins support chemical reactions in your body that are necessary for effectively using carbohydrate, protein, and fat. Your body needs many vitamins for healthy functioning, and the actions of vitamins are often interrelated. As a result, a deficiency in just one vitamin can affect the actions of other vitamins and cause profound health problems.

Vitamins are needed, for example, for your body's growth and repair. Vitamin C and the B vitamins are water soluble, meaning that they dissolve in water and are carried to your cells in your bloodstream. Because your body cannot store B and C vitamins, you must eat foods containing them every day. In contrast, vitamins A, D, E, and K dissolve in fat and are stored in fat cells in your liver and fat tissues. They can be dangerous, however, if they build up to excessive levels. For example, consuming vitamin A at a level that exceeds the recommended limit can cause liver scarring and damage. The best way to get the vitamins you need is to eat a well-balanced diet that is rich in nutrient-dense foods. Vitamin functions and food sources are presented in table 8.2.

Minerals

Minerals are essential nutrients that help regulate the activities of your cells. Twenty-five minerals have been identified as important for the human body. Minerals are present in all plants and animals, and a well-balanced diet is likely to provide you with an adequate amount of all necessary minerals. Table 8.3 shows some major functions and food sources of the most important minerals.

Some minerals are especially important for young people—for example, calcium and iron. Calcium helps build and maintain your bones. Sometime between the ages of 20 and 25, your body is still developing its bone structure and has yet to reach its peak bone mass. The body then gradually loses its ability to take calcium from food and store it in the bones. Eventually, the body begins to take calcium out of the bones to help with normal functions. Therefore, it is critical for your bones to reach their maximum possible density during your teenage years. This is particularly important for females, who are at greater risk of losing bone mass later in life. In fact, though osteoporosis (loss of bone mass) is a disease associated with older ages, the framework for prevention is set during your teenage years. You need to get enough calcium and do weight-bearing exercises (e.g., walking, jogging,

TABLE 8.2   Vitamin Functions and Food Sources

Vitamin	Function	Food sources
B_1 (thiamine)	Helps release energy from carbohydrate	Pork, organ meat, legumes, greens
B_2 (riboflavin)	Helps break down carbohydrate and protein	Meat, milk products, eggs, green and yellow vegetables
B_6 (pyridoxine)	Helps break down protein and glucose	Yeast, nuts, beans, liver, fish, rice
B_{12} (cobalamin)	Aids formation of nucleic and amino acids	Meat, milk products, eggs, fish
Biotin	Aids formation of amino, nucleic, and fatty acids and glycogen	Eggs, liver, yeast
Folacin (folic acid)	Helps build DNA and protein	Yeast, wheat germ, liver, greens
Pantothenic acid	Involved in reactions with carbohydrate and protein	Most unprocessed foods
Niacin	Helps release energy from carbohydrate and protein	Milk, meat, whole-grain or enriched cereals, legumes
C (ascorbic acid)	Aids formation of hormones, bone tissue, and collagen	Fruits, tomatoes, potatoes, green leafy vegetables
A (retinol)	Helps produce normal mucus and is part of a chemical necessary for vision	Butter, margarine, liver, eggs, green or yellow vegetables
D	Aids absorption of calcium and phosphorous	Liver, fortified milk, fatty fish
E (tocopherol)	Prevents damage to cell membranes and vitamin A	Vegetable oils
K	Aids blood clotting	Leafy vegetables

TABLE 8.3 Mineral Functions and Food Sources

Mineral	Function	Food sources
Calcium	Builds and maintains teeth and bones; helps blood clot; helps nerves and muscles function	Cheese, milk, dark green vegetables, sardines, legumes
Iron	Helps transfer oxygen in red blood cells and other cells	Liver, red meat, dark green vegetables, shellfish, whole-grain cereals
Magnesium	Aids breakdown of glucose and protein; regulates body fluids	Green vegetables, grains, nuts, beans, yeast
Phosphorus	Builds and maintains teeth and bones; helps release energy from nutrients	Meat, poultry, fish, eggs, legumes, milk products
Potassium	Regulates fluid balance in cells; helps nerves function	Oranges, bananas, meat, bran, potatoes, dried beans
Sodium	Regulates internal water balance; helps nerves function	Most foods, table salt
Zinc	Helps transport carbon dioxide; helps wounds heal	Meat, shellfish, whole grains, milk, legumes

weightlifting)—now and throughout your life—to stimulate your bone development and help prevent osteoporosis later.

Your body needs iron for proper formation and functioning of your red blood cells, which carry oxygen to your muscles and other tissues. Insufficient iron in the blood causes iron-deficiency anemia, which can leave you feeling tired all the time and interfere with your ability to do daily activities. The best dietary source of easily absorbed iron is meat. Some iron can also be obtained from beans, seeds, dark leafy greens, and grains. People who don't eat meat or animal products should make sure to consume other foods high in iron.

Another important mineral is sodium; however, in contrast with calcium and iron, the concern here is getting too much of it. Sodium is naturally present in many foods. Because it is a preservative and also enhances flavor, it is also commonly added to many foods, and it is especially high in some—for example, chips, lunch meat, fast food, processed food, and canned food. As a result, much of the sodium that Americans consume is hidden, and most consume far more than they need. This poses a problem because excess sodium is directly associated with high blood pressure; therefore, people with high blood pressure must take extra precautions to limit sodium in their diet. The best way to reduce your sodium intake is to eat a diet that is high in whole foods—especially fruits, vegetables, and whole grains—and low in processed foods. For more ideas, see table 8.4.

Vitamin and Mineral Supplements

If you're considering a vitamin or mineral supplement, talk to your parent or guardian, physician, or a registered dietitian (RD) first. The American Medical Association does recommend that most Americans take a general vitamin and mineral supplement, but this recommendation exists because most Americans do not eat proper, well-balanced meals. The best approach is to establish a healthy diet first, then consider possible supplements. If you decide to take a supplement, the Academy of Nutrition and Dietetics recommends avoiding any supplement that provides more than 100 percent of the Recommended Dietary Allowance (RDA) for each vitamin or mineral unless prescribed by a physician.

🔊 HEALTHY COMMUNICATION

Do you believe that taking vitamin and mineral supplements is an important part of being healthy? Share your perspective with a friend or classmate in a concise but thoughtful way. Support your position with facts and respect each other's opinions.

TABLE 8.4   Tips for Reducing Sodium Intake

Food source	Tip
Fruits and vegetables	When possible, choose fresh or frozen fruits and vegetables. Rinse canned vegetables in water before cooking.
Breads, cereals, and grains	Compare labels to find products with less sodium. When you cook rice or pasta, don't add salt.
Meat, nuts, and beans	When possible, choose fresh meat (some fresh meat contains added sodium, so always check the label). Avoid heavily processed luncheon meat.
Milk and dairy	Choose fat-free or low-fat milk and yogurt more often than cheese, which can be high in sodium. Milk and yogurt are also good sources of potassium, which can help lower blood pressure.
Dressings, oils, and condiments	When preparing or topping food, choose ingredients that are low in sodium or sodium free, such as unsalted butter or margarine, vinegar, and vegetable oils.
Spices, herbs, and seasonings	When preparing or topping foods, replace salt with herbs and other seasonings or salt-free seasoning mixes. You can also season food with fresh vegetables, garlic, ginger, or citrus.
All foods	Read labels carefully and look for foods that have 5 percent or less of the daily value (DV) of sodium. In any single food, a sodium content of 20 percent of DV or more is high. Look for foods with label markings such as "low sodium," "reduced sodium," and "no salt added."

Water

Depending on age, the human body consists of 50 percent to 70 percent water. As a result, dietitians often say that water is the single most important nutrient. Water carries other nutrients to your cells and helps regulate your body temperature. Almost all foods contain some water, and fruits and vegetables are some of the best sources. However, about

Avoid any supplement that provides more than 100 percent of the Recommended Dietary Allowance for each vitamin or mineral by looking at labels.

HEALTH TECHNOLOGY

Agricultural biotechnology includes a range of techniques that alter organisms or parts of organisms in order to make or modify food products. One aspect of biotechnology is genetic engineering, in which genes are spliced together to introduce or remove particular traits. This process produces a genetically modified organism, also referred to as a GMO.

Scientists have used biotechnology to create crops that are resistant to diseases, bugs, and certain weather conditions, thus allowing farmers to produce more usable food for people in need. Common foods have also been manipulated to add nutrients. For example, a genetically modified form of rice called "golden rice" provides added vitamin A for millions of people who use rice as a dietary staple.

While the best intentions of biotechnology are to improve crops and human health, it also carries potential environmental risks to insects, worms, birds, and other wildlife and thus requires careful monitoring. The USDA oversees agricultural biotechnology efforts and works to provide safe and effective ways for scientists and farmers to make use of these technologies. There are movements to ban or at least label GMOs.

 CONNECT

How do you feel about eating genetically modified foods? Do you think foods that contain genetically modified ingredients should be labeled so that the consumer is informed? Why or why not?

 CONNECT

How do your friends and family influence what drinks you choose? Who influences your choices more—your friends or your family? Explain your answer.

Your body loses two to three quarts (liters) of water each day through sweating, breathing, and elimination through the bowels and bladder. You lose even more water each day if you live in a hot climate or engage in vigorous physical activity. These facts make it essential for you to take in enough fluid on a daily basis.

80 percent of the water you take in each day comes from beverages. The best fluid sources are water, juice, and milk. Other options—such as soda, sport drinks, and coffee—are less beneficial due to their caffeine, sugar, or excess sodium content. Also if you eat lots of fruits and vegetables, you are getting lots of fluids.

 One should eat to live, not live to eat.

—Benjamin Franklin, U.S. Founding Father

Comprehension Check

1. What are the three macronutrients? Describe them in more detail.
2. List the two major types of micronutrients and explain them in more detail.
3. Explain the functions of major macronutrients and micronutrients.

In this self-assessment, you'll track your diet for two days, then analyze trends based on dietary guidelines. Follow these steps.

1. Pick two days to track—one week day and one weekend day. Don't try to alter your regular eating habits during these days; it's important to get a sense of how well you eat on a regular basis.

2. For each day, write down everything you eat and how much of it you eat. Be specific and thorough and indicate measurements that can be used to compare your intake with dietary recommendations. For example, rather than writing "a sandwich and chips," write "ham sandwich on whole wheat bread with mustard (2 slices ham, 2 pieces lettuce, 3 slices tomato) and 20 regular Ruffles potato chips." Where possible, record amounts in specific numbers and units of measure (e.g., tablespoon, cup). Include not only all meals but also snacks and drinks. Add any comments that might help you remember what you ate. For a sample food log, see table 8.5.

TABLE 8.5 Sample Food Log

Food	Amount	Comments
Breakfast		
Frosted Flakes cereal	1 1/2 cups	
Fat-free milk	1 cup	Organic cow milk
Banana	1 medium	
Snack		
Fritos chips	1 bag (2 oz. or 57 g)	
Sprite	Half of a 12 oz. (0.35 l) bottle	Shared with Sarah

3. Use your food log to complete the chart shown in table 8.6. For each food group, determine how much of the food you consumed and compare it with the recommended amount. To help you determine how much of each food you ate relative to the recommended amounts, use the charts provided in the second part of this chapter. For each food group in table 8.6, mark whether you think you were above, at, or below the recommended amount. Record your results as directed by your teacher.

TABLE 8.6 Food Group Diary

Food group	Females aged 14–18	Males aged 14–18	Score		
Day 1					
1. Fruits	1 1/2 cups	2 cups	Above	At	Below
2. Vegetables	2 1/2 cups	3 cups	Above	At	Below
3. Grains	3–6 oz. (85–170 g)	4–8 oz. (113–227 g)	Above	At	Below
4. Protein	5 oz. (142 g)	6 1/2 oz. (184 g)	Above	At	Below
5. Dairy	3 cups	3 cups	Above	At	Below
6. Oils	5 tsp.	6 tsp.	Above	At	Below

> continued

TABLE 8.6 > continued

Day 2					
Food group	Females aged 14–18	Males aged 14–18	Score		
1. Fruits	1 1/2 cups	2 cups	Above	At	Below
2. Vegetables	2 1/2 cups	3 cups	Above	At	Below
3. Grains	3–6 oz. (85–170 g)	4–8 oz. (113–227 g)	Above	At	Below
4. Protein	5 oz. (142 g)	6 1/2 oz. (184 g)	Above	At	Below
5. Dairy	3 cups	3 cups	Above	At	Below
6. Oils	5 tsp.	6 tsp.	Above	At	Below

Alternative Option

If you have access to a computer and the web, your teacher may ask you to analyze your diet using the SuperTracker at www. ChooseMyPlate.gov. Be sure to analyze one day at a time and follow the instructions provided by your teacher.

✔ Planning for Healthy Living

Use the Healthy Living Plan worksheet to set goals and develop a plan to improve one or more parts of your diet. Monitor the steps you take toward meeting your goals and repeat this self-assessment in one to three months to help determine the success of your plan.

Lesson 8.2

Healthy Eating: My Plate

Lesson Objectives

After reading this lesson, you should be able to

1. read and understand a food label,
2. indicate each food group and its recommended intake based on established dietary guidelines, and
3. identify examples of healthy food choices from each food group.

Lesson Vocabulary

empty calories, health claim, nutrient claim, structure/function claim

Eating well day after day can be a challenge. Fortunately, several great resources are available to help you make healthy food choices on a daily basis. Food labels are found on most food products and can be used to help you make informed decisions about which ones to buy and eat. In addition, the USDA and the U.S. Department of Health and Human Services (HHS) work together to develop and issue the Dietary Guidelines for Americans, which are updated every five years. These guidelines help American consumers make informed food choices in order to eat healthier calories, maintain or reduce weight as appropriate, and prevent diseases such as heart disease and diabetes. The guidelines also form the basis for the recommended intake associated with each of the major food groups. The recommended intakes are illustrated in the MyPlate guidelines. Each of these tools and resources is introduced in this chapter.

Selecting Healthy Foods: Using Food Labels

One of the most important tools available to help you select healthy foods is the nutrition facts label found on most food packages. The nutrition label gives you information about the food's serving size and content, including carbohydrate, protein, fat, and selected vitamins and minerals. It also tells you how much carbohydrate, protein, and fat the food has as a percentage of daily intake based on a 2,000-calorie diet. Your individual needs may differ from the label depending on whether you need more

or less than 2,000 calories per day. Each aspect of the food label is explained in figure 8.2.

When reading a food label, consider the suggested serving size and how many servings are contained in the package. Many people make the mistake of assuming that the numbers listed on a food label apply to the entire package. For example, look at the label shown in figure 8.2. It indicates 60 calories per serving, but two and a half servings are contained in the can. As a result, if you ate the whole can, you would be eating 150 calories. In addition, eating the entire can would give you more than a whole day's worth of recommended sodium—just from that one food! As you can see, a food label gives you specific information related to essential nutrients that can be very useful in making dietary decisions. The FDA requires labels such as the one shown in figure 8.2. These labels are different from labels on the front or back of the box provided by manufacturers. Also, trans fat has been banned by the FDA, but it must be included on the label until the trans fat ban is fully implemented.

Nutrient Claims on Food Packages

In addition to the labels required by the FDA, some foods contain additional claim provided by the manufacturer. For example, you may have noticed markings about "fat free" cookies, "lean beef," or "low sodium" canned foods. In the United States, such **nutrient claims** are regulated by the Food and Drug Administration (FDA) and can appear only if the food meets certain standards. Nutrient claims can help you make informed choices, but you need

Chicken Noodle Soup

Nutrition Facts

Serving Size 1/2 cup (120 ml) condensed soup

Servings Per Container about 2.5

Amount Per Serving

Calories 60   Calories from Fat 15

% Daily Value*

Total Fat 1.5g	**2%**
Saturated Fat 0.5g	**3%**
Trans Fat 0g	
Cholesterol 15mg	
Sodium 890mg	**37%**
Total Carbohydrate 8g	**3%**
Dietary Fiber 1g	**4%**
Sugars 1g	
Protein 3g	

Vitamin A 4%		Calcium	0%
Vitamin C 2%		Iron	2%

*Percent Daily Values are based on a 2,000 calorie diet. Your Daily Values may be higher or lower depending on your calorie needs:

		Calories	2,000	2,500
Total Fat	Less than		65g	80g
Saturated Fat	Less than		20g	25g
Cholesterol	Less than		300mg	300mg
Sodium	Less than		2,400mg	2,400mg
Total Carbohydrate			300g	375g
Dietary Fiber			25g	30g

First look at the serving size and the number of servings in the package. To determine the calories for the entire package, multiply the servings per package by the calories per serving (i.e., 2.5 x 60). *Note:* The serving size and your idea of a serving size may be different.

Here you can see how many grams of carbohydrate, protein, and fat are in a serving. You can estimate the number of calories for each by using basic math. Multiply the fat grams by 9 calories, the carbohydrate grams by 4 calories, and the protein grams by 4 calories. These calculations are not exact, but they are a reasonable guide.

Use this as a quick reference to determine how much fat is in the food.

Notice that you can quickly determine if trans-fatty acids, cholesterol, or sodium, are present in the food. In this case, one serving of soup is giving you 37% of the sodium you need all day. If you ate the entire can of soup, you would exceed your recommended sodium intake. *Note:* The FDA has banned trans fat, but it is included on food labels until the ban is fully implemented.

Here you can see the percentages of the daily serving recommendations for 4 of the most important vitamins and minerals.

FIGURE 8.2   Sample food label.

to know their specific meanings and remember that they apply to a single serving (not necessarily the whole packaged amount).

Table 8.7 presents a few sample claims and their real meanings. Notice, for example, that a food may be labeled "fat free" even if it contains a small amount of fat (less than half a gram per serving). Some foods, such as milk and packaged meat, are advertised as being 2 percent fat (or 98 percent fat free). This is true when the calculations are based on weight. For example, 2 percent of the *weight* of a glass of 2 percent milk comes from fat, but more than 30 percent of the *calories* come from fat. Remember, every gram of fat contains 9 calories—more than twice as much as contained in the same weight of carbohydrate or protein. To determine the true percentage of fat calories in a given food, divide the total calories from fat per serving by the overall calorie total per serving, then multiply the result by 100. For the food label shown in figure 8.2, one serving contains 15 calories from fat, and the overall calories per serving is 60 (15 ÷ 60 = 0.25 × 100 = 25), so the fat content is 25 percent.

Disease and Structure Claims on Food Packages

Food packages sometimes also contain health claims such as "heart healthy" or "helps prevent osteoporosis." In the United States, such **health claims** are also regulated by the FDA and can appear on a food only if it meets certain requirements. For example, foods labeled as being good for your heart must be low in fat, saturated fat, and cholesterol.

Vitamin and mineral supplements are sometimes marked with similar claims related to a body

Reviewing nutrient claims on food packages can help you make informed choices.

TABLE 8.7 Examples of Nutrient Claims on Food Packages

Nutrient claim	What it means
Fat free	Less than 0.5 g of fat per serving
Low fat	3 g or less of fat per serving
Lean	Less than 10 g of fat, 4 g of saturated fat, and 95 mg of cholesterol per serving
Light (lite)	1/3 fewer calories or no more than 1/2 the fat of the higher-calorie, higher-fat version; or no more than 1/2 the sodium of the higher-sodium version
Cholesterol free	Less than 2 mg of cholesterol and 2 g or less of saturated fat per serving

structure or function, such as "improves eye sight" or "builds strong bones." However, these **structure/function claims** are *not* regulated; therefore, supplement marketers who use these claims must also include a statement indicating that the claim is not endorsed by the Food and Drug Administration. This statement is often in fine print and is difficult to locate on the package.

Dietary Guidelines for Americans

Dietary Guidelines for Americans is a U.S. government document based on extensive research about foods, their effects on health, and the current strengths and weaknesses of the typical American diet. The guidelines state that a healthy diet should

- emphasize fruits, vegetables, whole grains, and fat-free or low-fat dairy products;
- include lean meat, poultry, fish, beans, eggs, and nuts; and
- be low in saturated fat, trans fat, cholesterol, salt (sodium), and added sugar.

The guidelines are reflected in specific recommendations made for each food group. The 2010 Dietary Guidelines for Americans also have guidelines for vegetarians, vegans, and other special diets. Dietary guidelines also exist that address the different needs of other cultures and countries. To learn more about the Dietary Guidelines for Americans and other dietary guidelines, visit the student section of the Health for Life website.

MyPlate

To help you meet the dietary guidelines, the USDA suggests following the MyPlate recommendations for each major food group (see figure 8.3). Note that half of the plate is made up of fruits and vegetables. Yet studies show that fewer than 5 percent of teenagers eat the recommended amount of fruits and vegetables on a daily basis. Teenage girls should consume 1 1/2 cups of fruit each day, and teenage boys should consume 2 cups daily. All fresh fruits count toward meeting the requirement, though measurements may vary. For example, half a cup of dried fruit (e.g., raisins, dried apples) counts as a full cup of fruit.

Similarly, teenage girls should eat 2 1/2 cups of vegetables per day, and teenage boys should eat 3 cups daily. You should also vary the vegetables you eat. Your diet should include servings of dark green vegetables, red and orange vegetables, beans and peas, and starchy vegetables. All have a role to play in your overall nutrition.

Grains and protein sources make up the other half of the plate. Both of these sources are recommended in amounts referred to as "ounce equivalents" (see tables 8.8 and 8.9 for examples). For grains, teenage girls should eat three to six ounce equivalents per day, and teenage boys should eat four to eight. You should also eat at least half of your grains in the form of whole grain. You can improve your whole-grain intake by choosing whole-grain bread, brown rice, and whole wheat pasta while limiting your consumption of bakery products, white bread, and white rice. For protein sources, teenage girls should consume five ounce equivalents daily, and teenage boys should consume six and a half per day.

The dairy group completes the MyPlate illustration. Both teenage girls and teenage boys need three cups of dairy food each day. Choose low-fat or fat-free options and limit your intake of dairy products containing added sugar (e.g., sweetened milk or yogurt). Vegans should consult the guidelines to determine how they can get the amount of calcium they need.

1 **Balance calories.**
Find out how many calories you need for a day as a first step in managing your weight.
Go to *www.ChooseMyPlate.gov* to find your calorie level. Being physically active also helps you balance calories.

2 **Enjoy your food, but eat less.**
Take the time to fully enjoy your food as you eat it. Eating too fast or when your attention is elsewhere may lead to eating too many calories. Pay attention to hunger and fullness cues before, during, and after meals. Use them to recognize when to eat and when you've had enough.

3 **Avoid oversized portions.**
Use a smaller plate, bowl, and glass. Portion out foods before you eat. When eating out, choose a smaller size option, share a dish, or take home part of your meal.

4 **Eat these foods more often.**
Eat more vegetables, fruits, whole grains, and fat-free or 1% milk and dairy products. These foods have the nutrients you need for health including potassium, calcium, vitamin D, and fiber. Make them the basis for meals and snacks.

5 **Make half your plate fruits and vegetables.**
Choose red, orange, and dark green vegetables like tomatoes, sweet potatoes, and broccoli, along with other vegetables for your meals. Add fruit to meals as part of main or side dishes or as dessert.

6 **Switch to fat-free or low-fat (1%) milk.**
They have the same amount of calcium and other essential nutrients as whole milk, but fewer calories and less saturated fat.

7 **Make half your grains whole grains.**
To eat more whole grains, substitute a whole-grain product for a refined product such as eating whole wheat bread instead of white bread or brown rice instead of white rice.

8 **Eat these foods less often.**
Cut back on foods high in solid fats, added sugars, and salt. They include cakes, cookies, ice cream, candies, sweetened drinks, pizza, and fatty meats like ribs, sausages, bacon, and hot dogs. Use these foods as occasional treats, not everyday foods.

9 **Compare sodium in foods.**
Use the nutrition facts label to choose lower sodium versions of foods like soup, bread, and frozen meals. Select canned foods labeled *low sodium*, *reduced sodium*, or *no salt added*.

10 **Drink water instead of sugary drinks.**
Cut calories by drinking water or unsweetened beverages. Soda, energy drinks, and sports drinks are a major source of added sugar, and calories, in American diets.

FIGURE 8.3 Follow these 10 tips for creating a great plate.
USDA's Center for Nutrition Policy and Promotion.

TABLE 8.8   Ounce Equivalents for Grains

Food	1 oz. (28 g) equivalent	Common portion and number of oz. (28 g) equivalents
Bagel	1 mini bagel	1 large bagel = 4 oz. equivalents
Bread	1 regular slice	2 regular slices = 2 oz. equivalents
Muffin	1 small (2 1/2 in. or 6 1/2 cm in diameter), plain or wheat	1 large (3 1/2 in. or 9 cm) = 3 oz. equivalents
Pancake	1 small (4 1/2 in. or 11 1/2 cm) pancake	3 pancakes = 3 oz. equivalents
Pasta	1/2 cup cooked	1 cup cooked = 2 oz. equivalents
Popcorn	3 cups popped	1 mini microwave bag or 100 cal. bag = 2 oz. equivalents
Rice	1/2 cup cooked	1 cup cooked = 2 oz. equivalents
Tortilla	1 small (6 in. or 15 cm), flour	1 large (12 in. or 30 cm) = 4 oz. equivalents

From U.S. Department of Agriculture 2011.

TABLE 8.9   Ounce Equivalents for Protein Sources

Food	1 oz. (28 g) equivalent	Common portion and number of oz. (28 g) equivalents
Meat	1 oz. cooked meat	1 small steak = 3–4 oz. equivalents
Poultry	1 oz. cooked turkey or chicken without skin	1 small chicken breast = 3 oz. equivalents
Seafood	1 oz. cooked fish or shellfish	1 can tuna = 3–4 oz. equivalents 1 salmon steak = 4–6 oz. equivalents
Eggs	1 egg	1 whole egg = 1 oz. equivalent 3 egg whites = 2 oz. equivalents
Nuts and seeds	1/2 oz. (14 g) nuts or seeds or 1 tbsp peanut butter	1 oz. nuts or seeds = 2 oz. equivalents
Beans and peas	1/4 cup cooked peas or beans	1 cup bean soup = 2 oz. equivalents

From U.S. Department of Agriculture 2011.

 **HEALTH SCIENCE**

Have you ever wondered how scientists figure out how many calories the human body uses for various functions and activities? The answer is calorimetry, which is the measurement of heat released or stored within a closed system. Calorimetry can be used to determine how much heat the human body releases during a given activity. Doing so requires a metabolic chamber large enough for a person to live in during the study. The chamber allows scientists to measure exactly how much heat an individual gives off while eating, sleeping, or engaging in a physical activity.

Since this type of measurement is expensive and not very practical, scientists also estimate calorie expenditure by measuring how much oxygen a person uses. This approach works because every liter of oxygen the body uses requires five kilocalories of energy. As a result, scientists can have people breathe into a special analyzer that compares how much oxygen is inhaled versus how much is exhaled. The difference tells them how much oxygen a person used and therefore how many kilocalories were required. This form of calorimetry allows scientists to measure energy expenditure (calorie use) in a wide variety of settings and activities.

Understanding Empty Calories

Packaged snack foods are often high in empty calories.

Human Kinetics/Kelly Huff

As you may recall, foods that are high in vitamins and minerals and low in calories are known as nutrient-dense foods. But some foods are just the opposite; they contain **empty calories**—calories that come from solid fat or added sugar. Examples of solid fat include trans-fatty acid, butter, beef fat, and shortening. Examples of added sugar include table sugar and corn syrup. These ingredients can be found in many foods, especially processed foods such as cakes, cookies, ice cream, hot dogs, sausages, chips, and soft drinks. Even some fancy coffee drinks (e.g., caramel latte) can be very high in empty calories. Other examples are presented in table 8.10.

You should strictly limit your consumption of empty calories. This doesn't mean that you must avoid the food completely, but a healthier option is often available, such as low-fat hot dogs, fat-free cheese and milk, sugar-free drinks, and baked crackers and chips. Be aware, however, that some of these better options still contain a lot of empty calories or may pose other health risks. If you are considering a food with a lot of empty calories, know that it contributes to overeating and weight gain and provides you with little nourishment.

Recommendations also exist for oils in the diet. Teenage girls should not consume more than five teaspoons of oil each day, and teenage boys should not consume more than six teaspoons daily. Oils are most commonly found in nuts, fish, cooking oil, and salad dressing. The best way to limit your oil intake is to avoid fried food and limit your use of oily dressings and sauces.

TABLE 8.10   Examples of Foods High in Empty Calories

Food and portion	Estimated total calories	Estimated empty calories
1 cup whole milk	149	63
1 cup frozen yogurt	224	119
3 fried chicken wings with skin and batter	478	382
1 medium glazed doughnut	255	170
1 medium order of French fries	431	185
1 slice pepperoni pizza	340	139
1 bottle of regular soda	192	192

From U.S. Department of Agriculture 2011.

Comprehension Check

1. Describe three things you can learn about a food by reading its nutrition label.
2. What do the Dietary Guidelines for Americans say that we should eat less of?
3. What are empty calories? Provide three examples of foods high in empty calories.

Over the past two years, Chloe had gained more pounds than she should have, and she felt more tired and sluggish than she used to. Lately, she'd been trying to eat a healthier diet. However, even though she'd been working on changing her eating habits, she didn't notice any changes in her weight or her energy level. When she wrote about her struggles in an essay for English class, her teacher noted that she had seen Chloe snacking on chips and candy during breaks and afterschool events. She wondered if Chloe was aware of these habits. After considering her teacher's comments, Chloe started keeping track of her food intake. When she reviewed her food log, she noticed that her main meals were pretty healthy but that she was snacking on food with empty calories between meals. This surprised her because she had thought she was just having "a few chips or a couple of pieces of candy" at a time and hadn't thought it was that important.

For Discussion

What did self-monitoring teach Chloe about her habits? What are some other situations where self-monitoring might help someone better understand his or her behavior? Is there a behavior that you might benefit from tracking? Use the guidelines presented in this chapter's Skills for Healthy Living feature to help you begin self-monitoring a health behavior of your own.

Self-monitoring means keeping track of your own behaviors. For example, many people wish to lose weight, but few people keep a detailed log of the calories they eat. Effective self-monitoring involves writing down what you eat, what you're doing while eating, and how you feel before and after eating. Tracking these factors for even a short time allows you to clearly see your own choices and patterns. It also focuses your attention and increases your self-awareness. In short, it brings clarity to exactly what behaviors you're doing and which ones need changing.

You can self-monitor any health behavior or habit for which you have a goal or desired outcome—for example, your diet, physical activity, smoking, drinking, or even time spent watching TV or playing video games. To be effective, you must self-monitor with honesty and without cheating. Done right, self-monitoring is like holding up a mirror to yourself and allowing yourself to see what is really happening and what you need to do to change it. If you decide to self-monitor a health behavior, use the following guidelines as a starting point.

- **Write things down.** Don't assume you can simply remember what you did.

- **Record information as frequently as possible.** Your log will be more accurate if you record your behavior as it happens, or at least several times a day. If you record your behaviors only at night, you might forget something or feel too tired and miss the day entirely.

- **Be honest and record your current behaviors.** Self-monitoring works only if you record what you're actually doing. This is one of the biggest challenges for most people. Sometimes people write down what they wish they had done or what they know they should have done, rather than what they did do. Self-monitoring is useful only if you're willing to look openly and honestly at your choices and actions.

- **Reflect on your behaviors and set goals.** Look over your journal or log after a week or two. What patterns do you see? Can you accurately understand your own behaviors? You may need to continue self-monitoring a while longer, or you may be ready to set goals and begin changing your behavior.

- **As you begin to change, write down your goals and continue to monitor your actions.** Once you see what your behaviors look like, you can set reasonable goals for change. If monitoring your TV watching reveals that you watch an average of five hours each day, you might set a goal of watching no more than three and a half hours daily. Keep monitoring your actions to see if you meet your goal; if so, consider whether or not to change it again. In this case, your final goal might be to watch TV for no more than two hours each day.

- **Take advantage of relevant technology and social support.** Depending on the health behavior you're tracking, you might find that a social support group exists in your community that could help you stay honest and be accountable for your actions. Apps for electronic devices also offer ways to monitor and track a wide range of behaviors. Using one of these options might help you be consistent in your efforts.

Monitoring and tracking health behaviors can be made easier with the use of technology.

Joselito Briones

ACADEMIC CONNECTION: Mathematical Literacy

Developing literacy is an important part of being a good critical thinker. There are various types of literacy. Traditionally, a literate person was considered to be a person who could read and write with reasonable proficiency (ability). Today we speak of literacy in a number of ways. For example, in the chapter on health care consumerism, you will read about what it means to have health literacy. Mathematical literacy (also called qualitative literacy) refers to the knowledge of and confidence with basic mathematical and analytical concepts and operations that are required for problem solving, decision making, economic productivity, and real-world applications. The ability to read information in graphic form is a part of mathematical literacy. This chapter's Living Well News feature uses a bar graph to represent the percentages of obesity in various populations.

A bar graph is especially useful in making comparisons of group information. Each bar illustrates the percentage of a group that has a given characteristic. The height of the bar represents the percentage of a group that has that characteristic. For example, in figure 8.4 the bar for people 60 years of age and older is higher than the bar for other age groups, indicating that a higher percentage of older people (39.7) are obese compared to younger people (32.6 to 36.6).

The ability to interpret the data available in a graph and to decipher trends and patterns that emerge from the graphical representation is a part of mathematical literacy. Developing mathematical literacy requires practice. Whenever you are presented with data in graphs, take the time to read and understand the information.

Can a Trip to Your Local Drug Store Help You Lose Weight?

One in three adults in the U.S. is considered overweight or obese (see figure 8.4). Thus it is not surprising that, according to the U.S. Centers for Disease Control and Prevention, the use of weight loss supplements is on the rise. An article published in the *American Journal of Clinical Nutrition* stated that about 15 percent of Americans have used weight loss supplements (20 percent of women and 10 percent of men). In fact, weight loss supplements are big business. The Nutrition Business Journal, a market research firm, reported that about US$1.7 billion was spent on weight loss pills in 2007. Unlike prescription drugs, however, these products do not require a doctor's prescription; nor are they subject to the same rigorous standards applied to prescription drugs. More alarming, the U.S. Food and Drug Administration (FDA) warns that most over-the-counter (OTC) weight loss drugs are ineffective and that many can carry dangerous side effects.

"I used to think weight loss pills were just harmless pills of hope," said Dr. Anthony Smart, a general physician in the Seattle area. Over the last five years, however, he has seen an increasing number of patients taking weight loss supplements who complain of heart palpitations and chest pain.

Amy Fredlund, CEO of a leading dietary supplement company, states that the majority of weight loss supplements are safe and that the majority of problems that do exist involve obscure imported brands. However, other experts—including physicians, pharmacists, and government scientists—state that even mainstream weight loss supplements could be risky.

Consider ephedra, an herbal stimulant that gained popularity as a weight loss supplement in the 1990s. Ephedra-related problems included heart attacks, seizures, and deaths, leading the FDA to ban the supplement in 2004. As more Americans continue to be obese and the supplement industry continues to grow, the conflict between safety and hopelessness will undoubtedly continue.

For Discussion

What are some alternatives to weight loss supplements that a person could consider if they wanted to lose weight? What individuals or sources of information might a person consult when trying to decide whether or not to use a weight loss supplement? Why do you think some people choose to take these types of supplements?

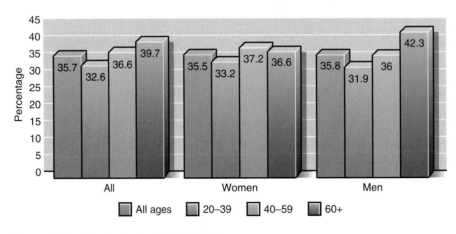

Figure 8.4 Obesity in the United States.
From CDC, NHNES 2009-2010.

Reviewing Concepts and Vocabulary

As directed by your teacher, answer items 1 through 5 by correctly completing each sentence with a word or phrase.

1. Carbohydrate, _____, and fat provide energy to the human body.

2. _____ _____ is unsaturated fat (e.g., sunflower oil) that is chemically altered to look and act like saturated fat.

3. Fat that comes primarily from plant sources and is liquid at room temperature is called _____ fat.

4. Your body needs _____ essential amino acids from the foods you eat.

5. _____ is a mineral necessary for optimal bone growth.

For items 6 through 10, as directed by your teacher, match each term in column 1 with the appropriate phrase in column 2.

6. saturated fat	a. carbohydrate, fat, protein
7. unsaturated fat	b. solid at room temperature
8. macronutrient	c. vitamin and minerals
9. micronutrient	d. chemically altered fat
10. trans-fatty acid	e. most vegetable oils

For items 11 through 15, as directed by your teacher, respond to each statement or question.

11. Explain the difference between soluble and insoluble fiber.

12. What is an incomplete protein?

13. What is cholesterol?

14. Why is calcium an important mineral for teens?

15. What is a nutrient claim? Give one example.

Thinking Critically

Write a paragraph in response to the following questions.

Scott likes to eat hamburgers, fries, and chocolate shakes. For lunch, he often eats pepperoni pizza with extra cheese dipped in ranch dressing. He doesn't like to eat fruits and vegetables. Scott is 17, is not overweight, and has no current health problems. What changes would you advise Scott to make in his diet? Why?

Take It Home

Look through the foods in your house and select five that you might normally snack on. Study each label and complete the following steps.

1. Write down the name of each food, the serving size, and the number of servings in the package.

2. Rank the foods in writing according to the amount of fat per serving (least fat = 1 and most fat = 5). Repeat this process for fat and fiber content.

3. Determine which snack is the healthiest and which is the least healthy. Explain your selections to a family member.

9

Nutrition: Energy Balance and Consumer Nutrition

bilderbox/fotolia.com

Lesson 9.1
Energy Balance

Lesson Objectives

After reading this lesson, you should be able to

1. explain energy balance in relation to nutrition and health,
2. describe the difference between hunger and appetite and how each can affect healthy eating, and
3. explain why diets tend to fail and describe weight gain and maintenance.

Lesson Vocabulary

appetite, hunger, negative energy balance, positive energy balance, resting metabolic rate, satiety

A newborn baby has an innate ability to know when it is hungry and needs food and when it is full. This natural ability to maintain energy balance is the result of a complex set of monitoring and feedback systems in the body. As we grow, we interact with our environment—which includes various societal influences on our diet—and we begin to respond to other types of cues that can influence our eating behaviors. This lesson introduces you to energy balance, hunger, and appetite, as well as the factors that influence them. It also discusses weight loss and dieting.

What Is Energy Balance?

Energy balance is the relationship between energy intake (what you eat) and energy output (what you do). Your energy intake is the total number of calories you consume in the form of carbohydrate, protein, and fat. Your energy output is the total energy you use for digestion, basic body functions, and physical activity. When your energy intake and output are the same, you're in a state of energy balance or equilibrium.

If you take in more calories than you use, you're in a state of **positive energy balance**. This means that you have more energy than you need, and the extra energy gets stored in your body. It's like a bank account balance. If you put more money into the account than you take out, you have a positive balance. However, maintaining a positive energy balance over a period of time causes weight gain and can negatively affect your health. Conversely, if you use more calories than you take in, you're in a state of **negative energy balance**. Over time,

this state results in weight loss; it can also be a sign of starvation, illness, or disease. Energy balance is illustrated in figure 9.1.

Energy Expenditure

To truly understand energy balance, we have to start by understanding energy expenditure or output. Your body's natural way of maintaining balance is to replenish the calories it uses. It does not, however, automatically use whatever energy you put into it. Energy expenditure has three major components.

1. *The energy you need in order to maintain normal functions, such as breathing, circulating blood, and maintaining tissues (e.g., liver,*

Energy in   **Energy out**

FIGURE 9.1   Energy balance.

brain, muscles). The number of calories you use for these functions is called your **resting metabolic rate**, which is influenced by a variety of factors (see figure 9.2).

2. *The energy you need to ingest and digest food.* This process starts with chewing, continues through swallowing, and ends with moving food through your intestines.

3. *The energy you use in movement and physical activity.*

Your body uses most of its energy (60 percent to 70 percent) to maintain normal functions of survival, about 10 percent for ingestion and digestion of food, and the remainder for movement and physical activity (see figure 9.3).

Some stimulants (e.g., caffeine) are marketed as tools for increasing your metabolism—thus helping you burn (use) more calories—but their effect is minimal, and they can cause damaging side effects. A better solution is exercise. The more movement and activity you do, the more your energy expenditure increases. In addition, movement is the source of energy expenditure that you can control directly through your own actions. In fact, an extremely active person might double his or her energy expenditure through activity. In addition, active bodies often consist of more muscle tissue, which naturally raises the metabolic rate, thus using more calories.

number of calories you eat with the number you use in order to remain in energy balance. Recall that calories come from the carbohydrate, fat, and protein you eat. Teenage girls from ages 14 to 18 who are not active need to eat about 1,800 calories each day. Teenage boys from ages 14 to 18 who are not active need to eat about 2,200 calories each day. As just explained, your energy needs will rise as physical activity and exercise levels increase. How much you choose to eat can also be influenced by our hunger, satiety, and appetite. Each of these factors is explained in this lesson.

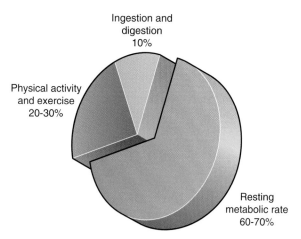

FIGURE 9.3 Contributors to daily energy expenditure.

Energy Intake

Your energy intake, or the number of calories you consume each day, makes up the other half of the energy balance equation. You need to balance the

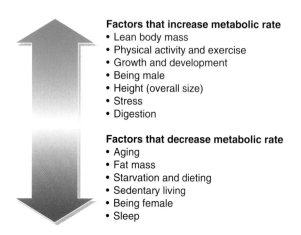

Factors that increase metabolic rate
• Lean body mass
• Physical activity and exercise
• Growth and development
• Being male
• Height (overall size)
• Stress
• Digestion

Factors that decrease metabolic rate
• Aging
• Fat mass
• Starvation and dieting
• Sedentary living
• Being female
• Sleep

FIGURE 9.2 Influences on resting metabolic rate.

Hunger and Satiety

Your body regulates your food consumption through a series of internal and external cues and stimuli. **Hunger** is your physiological drive to eat. When it's time to eat, your body tells you so through a set of internal changes, including a drop in blood sugar and the onset of stomach contractions. Other parts of your body also play a role in establishing your hunger—specifically, your brain, central nervous system (CNS), endocrine system, and digestive system. When you eat, your blood sugar and nutrient levels rise, and your hormone and neurotransmitter levels change, all of which eventually tells your brain and your body that you're full and therefore that it's time to stop eating.

When your body is well balanced and you're comfortable between meals, you're in a state of **satiety**, or fullness. The systems that contribute to hunger and satiety are complicated and very intricate. Studies have shown that certain conditions—for example, imbalances in hormones and neurotransmitters—can make it more difficult for some individuals to feel full. Figure 9.4 shows the relationship between hunger, satiation, and satiety.

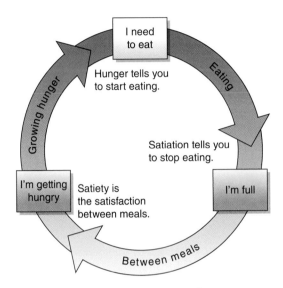

FIGURE 9.4 Hunger, satiation, and satiety are cues that tell you when to start and stop eating.

Appetite

Physiological hunger isn't the only thing that affects your food intake. Have you ever eaten popcorn at a movie or a hot dog at a ball game even though you didn't feel hungry? As these examples illustrate, our choices about what—and when—to eat can be influenced by our psychological needs. Whereas your hunger is your *physiological* drive to eat, your **appetite** is your *psychological* drive to eat. Thus it's different from your hunger. Appetite has to do with the pleasure you derive from food. It can be triggered by the sight and smell of food or even the sound of food cooking. On the other hand, if you're sick with a cold or the flu, the sight or smell of food can make you feel nauseated.

Appetite is influenced by many factors, including traditions. For example, people often associate eating with celebrations, holidays, particular family gatherings, and religious traditions. We may also associate eating with particular circumstances. Some people snack when they watch TV or when they get home from work or school—even if they aren't hungry. Others eat dessert after dinner even if they just ate a very large and satisfying meal.

Appetite is influenced by many factors. We often associate eating with family gatherings for example.

Monkey Business/fotolia.com

Emotions also play a particularly important role in appetite. Is there a food you tend to eat when you feel sad or lonely? How about when you feel happy? Do you eat a lot, or nothing at all, when you feel stressed about a major exam? Most people let emotions affect their eating habits in consistent ways; therefore, understanding what circumstances and emotions trigger you to eat can prevent you from taking in unnecessary calories. Getting control of your appetite is a critical part of establishing and maintaining healthy eating habits.

> **"** If hunger is not the problem, then eating is not the solution. **"**
>
> —Anonymous

Consequences of Energy Imbalance

When energy balance is not maintained, weight loss or weight gain may occur. In American society, many individuals seem to have a chronic (long-term) positive energy balance that results in gradual weight gain during the adult years. This weight gain may result in obesity and may bring many health risks. As a result, many people take various measures to try and lose weight. Other individuals struggle with trying to gain weight even when they maintain a positive energy balance.

Energy Needs Throughout Life

The amount of energy, or the number of calories, a person needs will change as the person goes through life. Infants and children need a lot of energy to support their growing bodies. Teenage girls and boys also use energy to support growth, as well as the changes that occur during puberty. Once a person reaches adult maturity, his or her energy needs stabilize, then gradually decrease (see table 9.1).

Studies show that the average American gains one-half to one pound (about one-quarter to one-half kilogram) per year after the age of 25. The reason for adult weight gain is not fully known, but likely contributors include lack of physical activity combined with poor eating habits, slower metabolism, and gradual loss of muscle mass. The

best way we know of to reduce adult-onset weight gain is to remain physically active throughout life. It also helps to practice healthy eating and engage in regular self-monitoring.

Weight Loss Diets

It's very likely that either you or someone you know has tried to lose weight by going on a diet. In fact, dieting for weight loss is so common in the United States that it almost seems normal, and many people chase after the latest dieting trends year after year. At any given time, as many as 50 percent of American women and 25 percent of American men are reported to be on a weight loss diet. The average age of a first diet among American females is eight years.

Despite these trends, a third of Americans remain obese. How can it be that so many Americans diet while obesity rates remain so high? The fact is, most diets that people try don't work over the long term. Almost any diet, when followed, can result in some weight loss over the first few weeks or months. However, most diets are hard to follow (and many

TABLE 9.1 Energy Needs Across the Life Span

Age (years)	Calories per day (sedentary → active*)
Children 2–3	1,000 → 1,400
Females	
4–8	1,200 → 1,800
9–13	1,600 → 2,200
14–18	1,800 → 2,400
19–30	2,000 → 2,400
31–50	1,800 → 2,200
51+	1,600 → 2,200
Males	
4–8	1,400 → 2,000
9–13	1,800 → 2,600
14–18	2,200 → 3,200
19–30	2,400 → 3,000
31–50	2,200 → 3,000
51+	2,000 → 2,800

*Active means doing daily activity equivalent to walking 3 miles at 3 to 5 miles per hour (4.8 kilometers at 4.8 to 8 kilometers per hour).

From U.S. Department of Agriculture 2005.

are even unhealthy or outright dangerous). As a result, many people "go off" of their diet after a short time and end up returning to the same poor eating habits they practiced before trying the diet. Only about 5 percent of those who do lose weight maintain the weight loss for a year or longer.

The National Weight Control Registry (NWCR) tracks and studies people who have successfully lost weight and kept it off. Though people can be successful using a wide range of diets, the most common behaviors associated with long-term weight loss include reducing overall caloric intake and fat intake, increasing energy expenditure through regular exercise, and having strong social support during the process. We also know that healthy weight reduction should occur slowly—at a rate of one-half to two pounds (about one-quarter to one kilogram) per week. To achieve this reduction, a person needs to expend about 500 more calories per day than he or she eats.

When you consider these findings together, the truth is that the most successful weight loss efforts focus on eating a well-balanced diet and getting enough regular physical activity. This approach

Are Energy Drinks a Good Thing?

Energy drinks are the fastest-growing beverage market in the United States; in 2011, for example, energy drink sales exceeded US$9 billion. Much of the energy drink market is directed at teenagers, and one in three teenagers reports regularly consuming energy drinks. Many young people believe that energy drinks can help them perform better in school, sports, and other activities. Others use energy drinks for the "buzz" or sensation they feel shortly after drinking them. This effect results from a stimulant, usually caffeine, and many energy drinks contain two to seven times more caffeine than a typical can of soda (see table 9.2).

TABLE 9.2 Caffeine Levels of Common Beverages

Beverage	Caffeine (mg)
Coffee—1 cup	115–175
Coca-Cola—12 oz. (355 ml)	47
Energy drink—1 serving	80–360
Hot cocoa—1 cup	10–17
Tea, black—1 cup	32–176
Tea, green—1 cup	25

Even so, because energy drinks are classified as supplements rather than beverages, they fall outside of U.S. regulations governing caffeine. This is no small matter. In 2007, half of all reported cases of caffeine overdose occurred in people under the age of 19, and this risk is increasing with the rise in consumption of energy drinks by teens. Most energy drinks also add herbal stimulants, such as ginseng, ginkgo biloba, and guarana.

While the United States has been slow to study the effect of energy drinks on teenagers, research from several other countries has demonstrated that the side effects of consuming energy drinks can include liver damage, kidney failure, respiratory disorders, agitation, confusion, seizures, psychotic conditions, nausea, vomiting, abdominal pain, abnormal heart rhythms, hypertension, heart attack, heart failure, and even death. High levels of caffeine consumption may also interfere with normal growth and development, particularly of the bones.

In addition, despite their name, energy drinks provide little usable energy for the body. If you're feeling sluggish or tired—or if you want to maximize your performance—the healthiest, safest, and most effective approach is to eat nutrient-dense foods, drink adequate water, do regular physical activity, and get a full eight to nine hours of rest each night. If you consume caffeine on a daily basis and decide to stop, reduce your intake gradually (over a period of one to two weeks) in order to limit withdrawal effects, such as headache and irritability.

🔊 HEALTHY COMMUNICATION

How often do you and your friends use energy drinks? What are the main reasons that you do or don't use them? Do you worry about the short- or long-term health risks associated with drinking these beverages? Share your opinions with your classmates. Support your perspective with facts and be respectful of others' opinions.

is not the same as "going on a diet." Instead, it means adopting long-term health behaviors in line with the prevailing recommendations for diet and physical activity.

Weight Loss Surgery

Many people struggle with issues of weight and associated diseases. Surgery is an extreme approach to weight loss that may be needed by some individuals who are unable to engage in normal activities of daily living and who have related health conditions (e.g., diabetes). Multiple types of weight loss surgery are available. Some use staples or bands to reduce stomach size; others redirect food to enter the intestinal system further along than usual, which reduces the amount of food absorbed by the body. These procedures, known as bariatric surgeries, carry significant risks and should be considered only in extreme cases after noninvasive approaches have been exhausted. Successful weight loss surgery can enable a person to lose as much as half of his or her body weight over a two-year period. However, long-term success still depends on making permanent changes in diet and physical activity.

Gaining Weight

Weight gain (especially as muscle mass) is often desired by certain people such as young males. For those who wish to gain weight, combining proper physical activity with adequate nutrition is the best method. Strength and muscular endurance exercises can help with weight gain. Resistance exercises like weightlifting are especially effective because they help the body build lean tissue (muscle). It is important to remember that physical activity burns calories and that muscle burns more calories than fat. Therefore, if you are trying to gain weight, it is very important to increase your intake of calories as you train and build muscle. A special diet (i.e., one with high protein) is not needed for weight gain and can be dangerous. It is also important to remember that genetic influences play a powerful role in body size and shape. Not everyone is meant to be heavily muscular and not everyone will respond to training or dietary changes in exactly the same way.

🔗 CONNECT

What does growing up in contemporary society teach you about dieting, weight, and health? Which type of media do you think has the biggest effect on people's perceptions of dieting, weight loss, weight gain, and health? Are men and women affected differently by these media narratives? How does the media affect *your* decisions about dieting, weight loss, or weight gain?

Unlike fad diets, regular physical activity can help you lose weight and keep it off.

CONSUMER CORNER: Selecting Diet Products and Services

There is no shortage of diet products and services in U.S. society. The problem is that many of them are not safe or effective, and even among those that are, it can be challenging to know which is the best choice. The following guidelines can help you make an informed decision if you ever need to lose weight.

- **Put safety and effectiveness first.** A safe and effective diet usually results in a loss of one or two pounds (about one-half to one kilogram) per week. Diets that promise rapid weight loss are more likely to be dangerous and less likely to produce long-term benefits.

- **Choose a plan that is flexible.** Not everyone likes the same foods. Any good diet plan allows for personal choice and options.

- **Choose a plan that is balanced.** We all need a balanced diet. No product or service is safe or effective in the long run if it doesn't offer a balance of foods and food groups. Diets that limit choices or focus on only one food group are not likely to provide balance.

- **Choose a plan that is comfortable.** A good diet should be comfortable and even enjoyable. Programs that provide recipes and allow for eating out and attending special functions are more realistic and more likely to help you succeed in the long term.

- **Choose a plan that advocates activity.** Every good weight loss product or service should advocate regular physical activity and provide some basic guidelines to follow.

- **Choose a plan that is educational.** Good weight loss products and services provide information about issues such as how to shop and cook in ways that are sustainable in the long term. Plans that provide you with food or limit you to prepackaged food may be easy, but they don't help you develop the healthy eating skills you need throughout life.

- **Involve your doctor.** Be careful about any plan that includes supplements or limits your food choices. Talk to your doctor before starting any weight loss diet.

- **Consider your needs.** Choose a program or plan that fits your level of commitment, your food preferences, and your budget. You're bound to fail if the program requires too much of your time or includes mostly foods that you don't enjoy.

Consumer Challenge

What diet programs and services are you familiar with? To learn more about some of the best-known options, visit the student section of the Health for Life website.

Comprehension Check

1. What is the difference between positive and negative energy balance?
2. How does hunger differ from appetite?
3. What are some reasons that most diets fail in the long term? Describe weight gain and maintenance.

SELF-ASSESSMENT: What Motivates Your Eating?

What motivates you to eat or not to eat? Do certain situations, emotions, or traditions affect what you choose to eat? This self-assessment will help you better understand what motivates your eating behaviors so that you can better manage them. Indicate your level of agreement with each statement, then total your score from each section and consider your findings. Record your results as directed by your teacher.

Situational factors

When your favorite foods are around the house, do you eat them even if you aren't hungry?

Never 1	Rarely 2	Occasionally 3	Frequently 4	Always 5

When you're eating out, do you try to get the most food you can for the money you're spending?

Never 1	Rarely 2	Occasionally 3	Frequently 4	Always 5

If you see an advertisement for a specific food or restaurant—or if you're passing a bakery, candy shop, or other appealing display—do you stop and get that food?

Never 1	Rarely 2	Occasionally 3	Frequently 4	Always 5

Total your score: _____

3–6: You may occasionally eat when you shouldn't, but overall you're in pretty good control in tempting situations.

7–9: You might want to pay attention to which situations tempt you to eat when you aren't hungry and ask yourself why you eat in these situations.

10–15: Your eating may be too determined by situations. Try to focus on your own hunger cues rather than on what the situation suggests.

Emotional factors

Do you eat when you're bored even if you're not hungry?

Never 1	Rarely 2	Occasionally 3	Frequently 4	Always 5

Do you eat to cope with feelings of sadness, hopelessness, or loneliness?

Never 1	Rarely 2	Occasionally 3	Frequently 4	Always 5

Do you eat when you're happy or excited, even if you're not hungry?

Never 1	Rarely 2	Occasionally 3	Frequently 4	Always 5

Do you eat when you're feeling anxious or stressed?

Never 1	Rarely 2	Occasionally 3	Frequently 4	Always 5

Total your score: _____

4–8: Your emotions don't seem to affect your eating habits very often.

9–12: Your emotions sometimes get the best of you when it comes to eating. Pay attention to how you feel and what you eat and try not to let emotions dictate when or what you eat.

13–20: You're often or always eating in response to your emotions rather than your own hunger. Work on finding healthy ways to cope with your emotions and pay careful attention to your feelings of hunger and fullness.

Social factors

Do you eat when you're at a party or celebration in order to fit in and be social?

Never 1	Rarely 2	Occasionally 3	Frequently 4	Always 5

Do you eat when your friends are eating, even if you're not hungry?

Never 1	Rarely 2	Occasionally 3	Frequently 4	Always 5

Do you feel like you're being rude or disrespectful if you don't eat everything on your plate?

Never 1	Rarely 2	Occasionally 3	Frequently 4	Always 5

Total your score: _____

3–6: You seem not to let social situations control your eating very often.

7–9: Some social situations may be causing you to eat even when you're not hungry. Try not to give in to social pressures to eat if you're not feeling hungry.

10–15: Social situations may be getting the best of you when it comes to eating. Explain to your friends and family members that you're working on improving your eating habits and ask for their support.

✔ Planning for Healthy Living

Use the Healthy Living Plan worksheet to change any negative eating motivation or habit you may have.

Lesson 9.2
Healthy Eating Habits

Lesson Objectives

After reading this lesson, you should be able to
1. identify several ways to plan and shop for healthy foods,
2. make healthy food choices when eating in a cafeteria or restaurant, and
3. identify specific steps to reduce or eliminate the risk of food poisoning.

Lesson Vocabulary

nutritionist, registered dietitian (RD)

Many people know something about basic nutrition and understand some general facts about carbohydrate, fat, and protein. It can be challenging, however, to use that knowledge to make changes in your eating habits. People often struggle with selecting or preparing healthy food options, and some people think they can't make healthy choices when eating out. The challenge is heightened by the fact that much of the information available about nutrition and diet is misleading or inaccurate. As a result, many people don't know who to trust for advice. This lesson provides some practical solutions.

Making Healthy Choices: Planning Ahead

You eat in a variety of places, including your home, school, and car. Since high-fat and high-calorie foods are all around us, it's important to plan ahead to ensure that you have healthy options available. More generally, healthy living requires learning to plan meals, shop for and cook healthy foods, and, when necessary, select the healthiest prepared foods.

When you eat at home, begin by planning your meals. In fact, it's best to both plan meals and do your food shopping *after* eating a good, healthy meal so that you're not hungry—and thus more vulnerable to temptation—while you plan and shop. To plan, think about what you might want to eat for breakfast, lunch, and dinner over the next several days (or week). Write down the meals and add all of the necessary ingredients to your grocery list; include some healthy snack options as well.

At the grocery store, choose the particular ingredients and foods that are tasty and provide the healthiest options for your planned meals. Use food labels to help you select lower-fat and lower-calorie options, consider fresh or fresh-frozen vegetables instead of canned to reduce salt intake, and select leaner cuts of meat or substitute poultry or fish. Lean meats—those with less than 5 grams of fat per 3.5-ounce (100-gram) serving—include eye of round roast and steak, sirloin tip side steak,

It can be a challenge to make healthy food choices when shopping; the fruits and vegetables available in the colorful produce section are a good place to start.

Human Kinetics/Kelly Huff

top round roast and steak, bottom round roast and steak, and top sirloin. Additional suggestions for choosing healthier groceries are found in table 9.3.

While shopping, think also about how you'll cook your meals. If you'd planned to make fried chicken, consider using a baked crust instead. If your planned menu called for frozen fish sticks, consider baked or fresh fish options instead of fried or battered ones. The key to successful meal planning is not to deny yourself particular foods or meals that you enjoy but rather to be intentional in selecting the healthiest ingredients available and choosing the healthiest and tastiest cooking methods you can. Stir frying and sautéing are better options than deep frying; other healthy choices include baking, grilling, steaming, and broiling. When serving food, put cream-based sauces on the side, avoid adding butter to vegetables and breads before they're served, and use salt-free seasonings instead of table salt.

Eating Healthily in a Cafeteria or Restaurant

It can be even more challenging to eat well when you're not in control of the shopping or food preparation. However, if you pay attention to your choices, you can almost always find a healthy food option. You can also reduce the chance of giving in to the temptation of less healthy foods if you observe a few general precautions.

- **Don't skip breakfast.** Eating a healthy breakfast every day can ensure that you're not overly hungry during midmorning breaks and at lunch.

- **Start with a glass of water.** Even if you're having another beverage with your meal, ask for a glass of water and drink it first. We often mistake thirst for hunger. Making sure you're adequately hydrated will help you avoid eating too much.

- **Put vegetables on your plate first.** A fresh salad or fresh steamed vegetables will take up space on your plate and discourage you from filling it up with less healthy choices.

- **Select fresh fruit.** Eating a piece of fruit with your meal can reduce sugar cravings and help you limit sugary drinks or desserts.

- **Carry your own snacks.** Having healthy snacks available can keep you from selecting unhealthy vending machine options and prevent you from getting too hungry. If the cafeteria or restaurant doesn't have as many healthy food options as you'd like, having a healthy snack with your meal might also keep you from making poor choices to satisfy your hunger.

- **Don't start with dessert.** Not only should you not start with dessert; you should also avoid selecting your dessert until you've completely finished your meal and beverage. Once the dessert is on your plate, you're more likely to eat it even if you're not hungry.

TABLE 9.3 Shopping for Healthier Foods

Traditional option	Healthier option
Whole or 2% milk	Fat-free milk or low-fat soy milk
Regular cheese	Low-fat, part-skim, or fat-free cheese
Yogurt	Fat-free yogurt without added fruit (add your own at home to reduce unnecessary sugar)
Meat	Leaner cuts of meat (or removing excess fat at home before cooking), pinto or black beans as substitute in dishes (e.g., chili, tacos)
Salad dressing	Fat-free or low-fat dressing
Canned vegetables	Fresh or fresh-frozen vegetables without added sauce or cheese
Canned fruit in heavy syrup	Fresh fruits or canned fruits in their own juice
Cooking oil, shortening, butter	Olive oil cooking spray for stir-frying or sautéing
Soup	Low-sodium, fat-free (or low-fat) soup; broth-based instead of cream-based when possible
Ice cream	Fat-free yogurt, sorbet, or low-fat ice cream
Potato or tortilla chips	Pretzels, whole-grain crackers, low-fat popcorn, baked chips

Healthy Snacks

Most teenagers snack throughout the day, particularly when they get home from a day at school. The calories you eat in an afterschool snack can add up quickly and contribute to unnecessary weight gain. Try to keep healthy snack options available at home and make an effort to eat them. It might even help to post a reminder in the kitchen about the healthy snack options available to you. Consider simple snacks such as the following items:

- Pretzels
- Carrot or celery sticks dipped lightly in fat-free ranch dressing or teriyaki sauce
- Apples with a small amount of fat-free cheese
- Bananas, oranges, raisins, grapes, and other "grab and go" fruits
- Low-fat or fat-free yogurt without added sugar
- Whole-grain crackers and breads
- Low-fat turkey slices
- A small handful of almonds, other nuts, or seeds
- Air-popped popcorn

Choose your beverage wisely as well. Avoid sugary drinks (e.g., sodas, energy drinks, other non-nutritious drinks). Start with a glass of water to satisfy your thirst. If you still want something more to drink, consider fat-free milk, fat-free soy milk, or fruit juice without added sugar.

• **Don't skimp.** This may run contrary to what you think, but the key to healthy eating is to select healthy foods—not simply to eat less. In fact, eating too little can make you develop cravings and eat worse foods later in the day. Eat a well-balanced meal that includes low-fat, high-fiber foods so that you'll be satisfied without overeating.

• **Stop when you're full.** You don't have to finish everything you ordered. Ask for a takeout box for the portion you don't need. In restaurants that serve large portions, ask for the box at the beginning of the meal and put half of the food in the box before you start eating.

• **Make requests.** When possible, request changes in your food to make it healthier. For example, when ordering a hamburger, eliminate the mayonnaise and cheese (substitute mustard or ketchup). If a fish or meat dish is served with a heavy sauce on top, request that the sauce be served on the side or left off. You can also ask for salad dressings to be served on the side and for vegetables to be steamed and served without butter.

Most states require restaurants to provide nutrition information about their foods. In some cases, this information appears on the menu; in others, you have to ask for it. Don't be shy about requesting the information or using it to help you make good

Make careful choices when eating out or at school.

choices. More and more traditional restaurants, and even some fast food outlets, are providing healthy food options. Eating out today doesn't have to be an unhealthy experience; nor should you take it as a license to ignore nutrition recommendations or common sense.

Although there are many healthy food options when eating out, there is considerable research on the benefits of family dining (i.e., eating together as a family at home). People tend to eat more nutritious foods and they are more likely to share in the food preparation. Also, people are more likely to eat slowly and less likely to watch TV or text while they are eating.

Changing Bad Eating Habits

Changing your eating habits can be hard even if you've moved past the state of contemplation and are ready for action. Don't try to make every desired change at once. Set a reasonable plan that includes weekly short-term goals and celebrate your achievements along the way. Try to avoid using weight loss as a measure of success when making dietary changes; focus instead on your behaviors. For example, if you're trying to reduce overall calories, begin with one or two changes, such as switching from regular to diet soda or from regular cheese to fat-free cheese.

Once you've demonstrated success at those changes, add a few more; for example, consider eliminating a late night snack or switching from a vending machine snack to a healthier one that you bring from home. Such changes add up over time, and you're more likely to be successful over the long term if you avoid taking on too much at once. The idea is not to think of the changes as short-term fixes but to make them last.

Preparing Food Safely

Have you ever had a stomachache or felt nauseous after eating? If so, you may have experienced food poisoning, also known as foodborne illness. This can last from one hour to two days. Each year, one in every six individuals suffers a case of food poisoning and 3,000 people die from it. Preventing foodborne illness at home begins with proper food handling, preparation, and cooking. The U.S.

 HEALTH TECHNOLOGY

Modern research has led to the discovery and isolation of phytochemicals—chemical compounds that occur naturally in plants and perform important functions in the human body. Phytochemicals are not considered to be essential nutrients because we do not develop deficiency diseases if we consume too little of them. However, consuming them can reduce the risks of developing various illnesses, including heart disease, cancer, type 2 diabetes, infections, eye diseases, and other conditions related to premature aging. Today, scientists study the thousands of known phytochemicals and their effects on health while also continuing to discover new phytochemicals.

Phytochemicals tend to be associated with the colors and pigments of fruits and vegetables, and they tend to hold up well when heated (cooked) and stored. Most phytochemicals work in groups, and though it's possible to buy supplements containing phytochemicals, our still-limited understanding of their properties and functions makes eating them in foods a better alternative. Some of the best-known phytochemicals are carotenoids (e.g., lycopene), phytoestrogens (e.g., isoflavones), and flavonoids (e.g., phenols). The best way to benefit from phytochemicals is to eat a good assortment of fruits and vegetables every day.

 CONNECT

Identify two phytochemicals and the specific roles they might play in disease prevention. To help you research your answer, visit the student section of the Health for Life website.

Centers for Disease Control and Prevention (CDC) recommends the following rules.

- **Clean.** Always begin by washing your hands in warm soapy water for at least 20 seconds. Wash all utensils and cutting boards with soapy water and clean all surfaces with a bleach solution after using them. Wash all fruits and vegetables—even those that you peel, to prevent bacteria from spreading to the inside during peeling or cutting.

- **Separate.** When shopping for food and when storing food in your refrigerator, separate produce from meats, eggs, and poultry. When preparing foods, use separate utensils and cutting boards for produce and meats. Using the same cutting utensils and surfaces can result in cross-contamination with bacteria and other pathogens.

- **Cook.** Cook foods to their proper temperatures (see table 9.4); where necessary, use a food thermometer to check the food's internal temperature. Serve foods immediately, making sure to keep them warm—above 140°F (60°C). Cold and uncooked foods (e.g., coleslaw, dips, and salads) should be kept chilled and should not be left out at room temperature for more than two hours.

- **Chill.** When a meal is finished, place leftovers in the refrigerator immediately. When cooling hot foods, use shallow dishes to allow the food to cool thoroughly, quickly, and evenly. When marinating foods, place them in the refrigerator and dispose of unused marinade. Respect expiration dates and inspect foods for mold and foul odors before eating them, since foods can spoil even when properly chilled.

TABLE 9.4 Proper Cooking Temperatures

Food	Temperature
Ground beef	165°F (74°C)
Fresh meat, lamb, poultry	135° F (58°C) for steak, 165°F (74°C) for all others
Pork	145°F (63°C)
Eggs and egg dishes	Until yoke and white are firm for eggs; 140°F (60°C) for egg dishes
Seafood	145°F (63°C) or until flesh is opaque and separates easily with a fork
Leftovers	165°F (74°C)

Trustworthy Sources of Nutrition Information

Anyone can *claim* to have nutrition knowledge, and in many states anyone can use the term **nutritionist** without having to meet specific educational standards. In contrast, a person who has studied nutrition at a recognized college or university, holds a certification in the field, and possesses full knowledge of nutrition is either a **registered dietitian (RD)** or a dietetic technician, registered (DTR). Other health professionals may possess nutrition knowledge, but be careful about assuming that their education has been formal or that they are as knowledgeable about all aspects of nutrition as they could be.

Comprehension Check

1. List five healthy choices a person can make when shopping for groceries.
2. What are three things a person can do to eat healthily in a cafeteria or restaurant?
3. What are the four steps to prevent food poisoning when preparing, cooking, and serving food?

Sarah is a high school sophomore who is interested in nutrition and tries to eat healthily. Lately, however, you've noticed that Sarah has stopped eating certain foods and that she makes all sorts of strange claims that she never used to make. For example, she won't eat any fish because she heard that fish is contaminated with mercury, she eats only raw vegetables because she heard that cooked ones lose their nutritional value, and she stopped eating citrus fruits because she heard from her mom that they cause diabetes.

Sarah has also started taking various vitamins in her drinks a few times a day. When you ask Sarah why she believes all these things are beneficial, she said "because my mom told me." When you ask her about her new vitamin supplements, she says that her mom has been buying them from a neighbor who says he is a nutritionist. It seems, however, that Sarah's habits are getting worse—not better—and that she thinks her vitamins are more important than the food she eats.

For Discussion

What concerns do you have about Sarah's choices? Do you think she should question the information she's hearing? Why or why not? Where would you recommend that Sarah go to get better information? How should she decide whether nutrition information is accurate? When answering these questions, consider the guidelines in this chapter's Skills for Healthy Living feature.

It's not hard to find nutrition information. If you search the web for information about most any health topic, you're likely to get thousands of hits. Sometimes it seems that everyone has an opinion or perspective about what to eat, how to eat, when to eat, and so on. Unfortunately, much of the information out there is not rooted in good science; instead, it's often profit driven or based on individual experiences that don't apply to other people. Use available resources such as food labels, food charts in restaurants, and MyPlate resources. When you look for nutrition information, use the following guidelines.

- **Consider the URL address.** Sites with the suffix *.gov* (governmental), *.edu* (education), or *.org* (organization) are often the most reliable sources of nutrition information. Sites with the suffix *.com* (commercial) may or may not be reliable and are more likely to use biased information to sell a product or service.

- **Consider the author or publisher.** Is the website written or published by a reputable organization, such as the CDC, the Academy of Nutrition and Dietetics, or the U.S. National Institutes of Health?

What are the author's or organization's credentials? Remember—anyone can claim to know about nutrition, but registered dietitians are the most qualified to present information about nutrition.

- **Consider the date.** Is the website current? Has the site been updated lately? Nutrition information changes, and U.S. guidelines are updated every five years. Make sure the information you're reading is as current as possible.

- **Consider the motivation.** Is the website aimed at selling a supplement, program, or other product? If so, compare the information you find there with information from more neutral sites. Sites designed to sell a product often use only the research they have sponsored or other findings that support their interests—even if that information is not well supported by other studies. There are no quick fixes or miracles in dieting and nutrition. Such claims should be a warning to scrutinize the information carefully. Also be very cautious about sites featuring extensive testimonials without research to support them.

Eating Out May Be Both Deceiving and Unhealthy

When you sit down at a family restaurant or place an order at your favorite fast food spot, chances are that your food will *not* meet federal nutrition recommendations. In fact, researchers from Tufts University in Boston tested 157 meals from 33 individual or small-chain restaurants and found the average meal contains two to three times the calories a person needs at a single sitting, and more than half of what is needed for an entire day (see table 9.5 for examples).

An 'On the Menu' report issued by the National Restaurant Association states that the industry is "employing a wide range" of healthy living strategies, including putting nutrition information on menus and order boards. It references Kids LiveWell, the first voluntary national program to encourage restaurants to offer healthful children's menu items. The report says, "We launched with 19 restaurant companies two years ago and now have more than 140 companies representing more than 40,000 locations."

Medical professionals, however, say that restaurant industry standards are out of line. For example, the industry-favored "Healthy Dining" seal of approval allows up to 2,000 milligrams of sodium per entrée, even though the standard recommended *daily* allowance for adults is only 2,300 milligrams.

A related study showed that kids and teens who eat in a restaurant on any given day consume more fat and sugar than they do when they eat at home. Of the 9,000 teens studied, 24 percent had eaten at a takeout or fast food restaurant on each day they were questioned. The study showed that adolescents ate an additional 310 calories on days when they ate at a takeout or fast food restaurant. Drinks proved to be a major culprit; regular menu drinks (e.g., sodas, shakes) had an average of 310 calories. In some regards, full-service restaurants proved to be even worse than takeout and fast food spots; in particular, entrées at family style restaurants averaged more calories, fat, and sodium than fast food options.

For Discussion

What is your favorite restaurant? What is your favorite meal there? Have you evaluated the fat and sodium content of the meal? If it were high in fat and sodium, would that influence your choice? Why or why not? Nutrition information for fast food restaurants can be found online.

TABLE 9.5 Nutritional Content of Sample Restaurant Dishes

Dish	Calories	Fat (% RDA)	Sodium (% RDA)
Domino's Ultimate Pepperoni Pizza—1 slice	280	13 g (20)	650 mg (27)
Famous Dave's Sampler Platter with Boneless Wings	2,880	181 g (278)	7,580 mg (316)
McDonald's Sausage Biscuit With Egg	560	33 g (51)	1,170 mg (49)
Ruby Tuesday Parmesan Chicken Pasta Without Biscuit	1,345	74 g (114)	3,481 mg (145)
Subway 6" Spicy Italian on Wheat Bread	480	24 g (37)	1,520 mg (63)
Taco Bell XXL Grilled Stuft Burrito	880	42 g (65)	2,020 mg (84)

Reviewing Concepts and Vocabulary

As directed by your teacher, answer items 1 through 5 by correctly completing each sentence with a word or phrase.

1. Your _____ can be influenced by circumstances, emotions, and traditions.
2. Most people who go on a diet do not keep the weight off for longer than _____ _____.
3. A _____ _____ is a licensed professional and a good source of nutrition information.
4. Substances found in plants, called _____, perform important functions in the human body.
5. The sensation of fullness is known as _____.

For items 6 through 10, as directed by your teacher, match each term in column 1 with the appropriate phrase in column 2.

6. positive energy balance   a. the calories you burn each day just to survive
7. negative energy balance   b. the physiological need to eat
8. hunger   c. taking in more calories than you use
9. appetite   d. the psychological drive to eat
10. resting metabolic rate   e. using more calories than you take in

For items 11 through 15, as directed by your teacher, respond to each statement or question.

11. How is age related to a person's energy needs?
12. What does the National Weight Control Registry teach us about effective long-term weight loss?
13. Describe two ways to make healthy choices when shopping for groceries. Give specific examples.
14. How long can you safely leave cooked food out at room temperature?
15. Describe two guidelines for evaluating nutrition information online.

Thinking Critically

Write a response to the following prompt.
You and some friends are planning a birthday party and want it to be a fun and healthy event. Make a list of eight healthy snacks you could serve at the party. For each snack, identify all of the ingredients and explain how to prepare it. Include tips for making sure the food preparation is safe.

Take It Home

Pick a meal that you and your family eat on a regular basis. Ask a parent or guardian for the recipe or look it up in a cookbook. Write down all of the ingredients, then identify at least two ways to make the meal healthier. Write down the changes and explain why they would be healthier. Share your modified meal idea with a family member and encourage your family to try the healthier option.

10

Physical Activity: Health and Fitness Basics

In This Chapter

 **Student Web Resources**
www.healthforlifetextbook.org/student

Lesson 10.1
Physical Fitness and Health

Lesson Objectives

After reading this lesson, you should be able to
1. describe the six parts of health-related and five parts of skill-related physical fitness,
2. explain how the four categories of fitness rating help you determine your health-related fitness, and
3. identify factors that contribute to fitness.

Lesson Vocabulary

agility, balance, body composition, cardiorespiratory endurance, coordination, criterion-referenced health standards, flexibility, functional fitness, health-related physical fitness, maturation, muscular endurance, physical fitness, power, reaction time, skill-related physical fitness, speed, strength

Physical activity is fun whether it is playing a sport or simply hiking or walking. The more fit we are, the more opportunities we have for fun and enjoyment. Our bodies are designed to move and they function best when we act on that movement. **Physical fitness** is the ability of your body systems to work together efficiently to allow you to be healthy and effectively perform activities of daily living. Being efficient means doing daily activities with the least effort. A fit person can perform schoolwork and fulfill home responsibilities and still have enough energy and vigor to enjoy sports and other leisure activities. A fit person can also respond to normal life situations, such as raking leaves at home, stocking shelves at a part-time job, and riding a bike to school. And a fit person can respond effectively in emergency situations, for example by running to get help or aiding a friend in distress.

The Parts of Physical Fitness

When you see a person who is good at a sport, do you assume that the person is physically fit? You might be surprised to know that this assumption is not always correct. It's true that a person who excels at a sport needs a certain degree of physical fitness. However, being good at a specific skill, such as running, is not necessarily a good indicator of total physical fitness; in fact, some sports require only certain parts of physical fitness.

Physical fitness is made up of 11 parts—six related to health and five related to skill. As the terms imply, **health-related physical fitness** helps you stay healthy, and **skill-related physical fitness** helps you perform well in sport and other activities that require certain skills. This chapter's self-assessment feature will help you better understand the differences between the 11 parts.

Health-Related Physical Fitness

Imagine a runner. She can probably run a long distance without tiring. Therefore, she has good fitness in at least one part of health-related physical fitness. But does she have good fitness in all six parts? Running is indeed an excellent form of physical activity, but being a runner doesn't guarantee fitness in all parts of health-related physical fitness. Similarly, you may be more fit in some parts of fitness than in others. Table 10.1 describes the six parts of health-related fitness; as you read about each part, ask yourself how fit you are in that part.

> **"** If you don't do what's best for your body, you're the one who comes up on the short end. **"**
>
> —Julius Erving (Doctor J), Hall of Fame basketball player

How much of the health-related parts of fitness do you have? To be healthy, you should have some of each. Good health-related fitness helps you resist disease and promotes your wellness. Later in this chapter, you'll learn how physical activity promotes good health-related fitness.

TABLE 10.1   The Six Parts of Health-Related Fitness

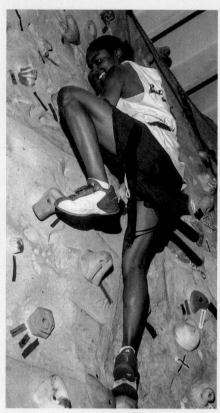

Cardiorespiratory endurance is the ability to exercise your entire body for a long time without stopping. It requires a strong heart, healthy lungs, and clear blood vessels to supply your large muscles with oxygen. Examples of activities that require good cardiorespiratory endurance are distance running, swimming, snowshoeing, and cross-country skiing.

Strength is the amount of force your muscles can produce. It is often measured by how much weight you can lift or how much resistance you can overcome. Examples of activities that require good strength are lifting a heavy weight and pushing a heavy box.

Muscular endurance is the ability to use your muscles many times without tiring—for example, doing many push-ups or curl-ups (crunches) or climbing a rock wall.

Skill-Related Physical Fitness

Just as the runner may not rate highly in all parts of *health-related* physical fitness, she also may not rate the same in all parts of *skill-related* physical fitness. Different sports and activities require different parts of skill-related physical fitness, and some require several parts (see table 10.2). Skill-related fitness also plays a role in many daily activities, such as driving a car (**coordination** and **reaction time**) and climbing stairs (coordination and **balance**). Balance is particularly important in preventing falls

(especially among older adults), and **agility**, **speed**, and reaction time are important if you need to avoid dangers such as moving or falling objects.

Any given sport requires certain parts of skill-related fitness. For example, a badminton player might have good coordination but might not be very powerful. Most people have more natural ability in certain areas than in others. No matter how you score on the skill-related parts of physical fitness, you can enjoy some type of physical activity. Keep in mind that good health does not come from skill-related physical fitness. Health and wellness are improved by doing activities that contribute to

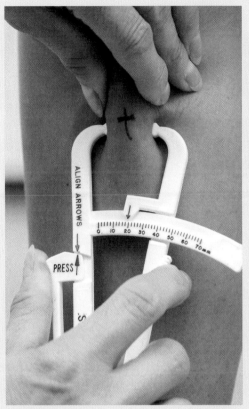

Flexibility is the ability to use your joints fully through a wide range of motion without injury. You are flexible when your muscles are long enough and your joints are free enough to allow adequate movement. Examples of people with good flexibility include dancers and gymnasts.

Body composition refers to the different types of tissues that make up your body, including fat, muscle, bone, and organ. Your level of body fat is often used to assess the component of body composition related to health. Body composition measures commonly used in schools include body mass index (based on height and weight), skinfold measures (which estimate body fatness), and body measurements such as waist and hip circumferences.

Power is the ability to use strength quickly; thus it involves both strength and speed. It is sometimes referred to as explosive strength. People with good power can, for example, jump far or high, throw a javelin, and speed-swim.

your health-related physical fitness. They can be enjoyed both by people who consider themselves poor athletes and by those who see themselves as great athletes. These skill-related fitness components can help to prevent injuries (e.g., having good balance that can prevent a fall, good reaction time and speed while driving).

Health-Related Fitness and Performance

Health-related fitness also helps you perform well in sport and other activities. Thus it offers double

benefits—it helps you both stay healthy and perform well. For example, **cardiorespiratory endurance** helps you resist heart disease and perform well in sports such as swimming and cross country running; **strength** is associated with strong bones but also is important in sports such as football and wrestling; **muscular endurance** benefits back health but also aids in performing well in in soccer and tennis; **flexibility** aids your posture and also helps you in sports such as gymnastics and diving; **power** also benefits the bones and helps you in track activities such as the discus throw and long jump; and keeping your **body composition** at a healthy level helps you be efficient in many activities.

TABLE 10.2   The Five Parts of Skill-Related Fitness

Balance is the ability to keep an upright posture while standing still or moving. People with good balance are likely to be good, for example, at gymnastics and ice skating.

Coordination is the ability to use your senses together with your body parts or to use two or more body parts together. People with good eye–hand or eye–foot coordination are good at hitting and kicking games, such as soccer, baseball, volleyball, tennis, and golf.

Speed is the ability to perform a movement or cover a distance in a short time. For example, people with good leg speed can run fast, and people with good arm speed can throw fast or hit a ball that is thrown fast.

Reaction time is the amount of time it takes you to move once you recognize the need to act. People with good reaction time can make fast starts in track and swimming and can dodge fast attacks in fencing and karate.

© Alberto Pomares

Agility is the ability to change the position of your body quickly and control your body's movements. People with good agility are likely to be good, for example, at wrestling, diving, soccer, and ice skating.

HEALTH SCIENCE

Experts in physical education and exercise physiology have worked together to develop various physical fitness test batteries—that is, groups of tests designed to assess all parts of physical fitness. For example, Fitnessgram is a fitness test battery used in many schools across the United States and throughout the world. It includes several tests of health-related fitness (e.g., 1-mile walk or run, curl-up, push-up) and uses **criterion-referenced health standards**. Associating health risk factors such as blood pressure, blood sugar level, and body fat level determines how much fitness is enough for good health. People who take the Fitnessgram test can get a report that tells them their scores and indicates whether they are in the healthy fitness zone for each part of health-related fitness. The report also provides suggestions for improving fitness.

Other test batteries have been created by various organizations, such as the YMCA and groups in Canada and Europe. These batteries contain some similar tests and some different ones. You might want to try the tests in Fitnessgram or another battery such as the ALPHA-FIT test used in Europe. With practice, you can learn to test yourself (i.e., perform self-testing). You can then use your self-testing results to assess your personal needs. The goal is to use the information to build a personal fitness program. Please note that fitness test results are personal, and anyone's results that are shared with you should be kept confidential.

Functional Fitness

Functional fitness refers to the ability to function effectively when performing normal daily tasks. You have functional fitness if you can do your schoolwork, get to and from school and participate in leisure-time activities without fatigue, respond to emergency situations, and perform other daily tasks (e.g., drive a car, do housework or yardwork) safely and without fatigue. Functional fitness involves both health- and skill-related fitness. Health-related fitness, of course, helps you stay healthy and well and also helps you function (e.g., avoid fatigue when working or playing). And skill-related fitness helps you not only perform well in sport but also function well (e.g., stop quickly when driving a car).

Fitness, Health, and Wellness Are Interrelated

Fitness, health, and wellness are all states of being, and you can improve all three by practicing a healthy lifestyle. For example, if you're active on a regular basis, your health-related fitness improves, thus reducing your risk of disease, which improves your health. Your wellness and quality of life are also improved because you feel better and can better enjoy the activities of your daily life. The interrelationship of fitness, health, and wellness is illustrated in figure 10.1. Health, including wellness (the positive component of health), is depicted in blue and green on the left. Fitness is depicted in red on the right. Fitness affects health and wellness, and health and wellness are important to fitness.

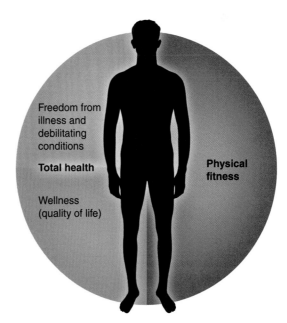

FIGURE 10.1 The interrelationship of fitness, health, and wellness.

How Much Fitness Is Enough?

Sometimes people judge their fitness by comparing themselves with others. If they score higher on a fitness test than most other people, they consider themselves fit. This type of comparison creates several problems. First, it suggests that only a few can be fit; second, it suggests that only people with high test scores have good fitness. Neither of these assumptions is true. Most experts agree that you should use criterion-referenced health standards to determine whether you have enough fitness. These ratings require you to have enough fitness to

- reduce your risk of health problems,
- achieve wellness benefits,
- work effectively and meet emergencies (functional fitness), and
- be able to enjoy your free time.

CONNECT

Most people rate better in some parts of health-related fitness than in others. What do you think accounts for these differences the most—genetic influences or training? Debate your perspective with a peer who feels differently than you. Listen to each other's positions and determine where you agree and disagree.

Figure 10.2 describes four rating categories that you can use to determine whether you have enough fitness for good health. Fitness test batteries may use slightly different rating categories, but all suggest

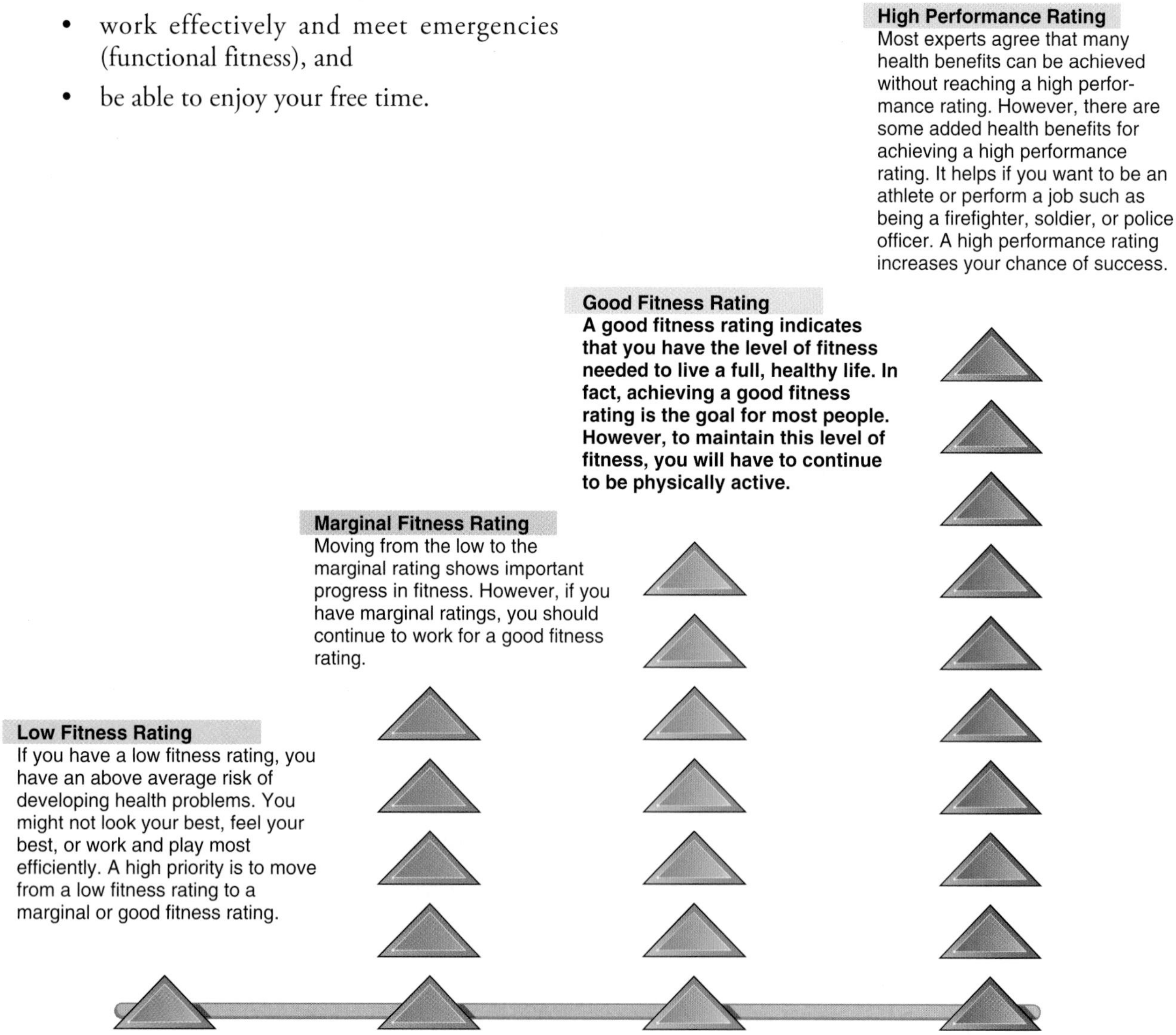

High Performance Rating
Most experts agree that many health benefits can be achieved without reaching a high performance rating. However, there are some added health benefits for achieving a high performance rating. It helps if you want to be an athlete or perform a job such as being a firefighter, soldier, or police officer. A high performance rating increases your chance of success.

Good Fitness Rating
A good fitness rating indicates that you have the level of fitness needed to live a full, healthy life. In fact, achieving a good fitness rating is the goal for most people. However, to maintain this level of fitness, you will have to continue to be physically active.

Marginal Fitness Rating
Moving from the low to the marginal rating shows important progress in fitness. However, if you have marginal ratings, you should continue to work for a good fitness rating.

Low Fitness Rating
If you have a low fitness rating, you have an above average risk of developing health problems. You might not look your best, feel your best, or work and play most efficiently. A high priority is to move from a low fitness rating to a marginal or good fitness rating.

FIGURE 10.2 Do you have enough fitness for good health?

that low or marginal ratings are associated with poor health, that a good fitness rating (sometimes called a healthy rating) is adequate for most people, and that a high performance rating is necessary for doing certain activities, such as sports and physically active jobs.

Factors Influencing Physical Fitness

Physical activity is the most important thing you can do to improve and maintain your health-related physical fitness, and it is discussed in greater detail in the next lesson of this chapter. Physical activity is something that you can control—you can choose the activities you want to do and schedule a regular time to do them. However, as illustrated in figure 10.3, physical activity is not the only factor that contributes to your physical fitness. Other important factors include **maturation**, age, heredity, and the environment.

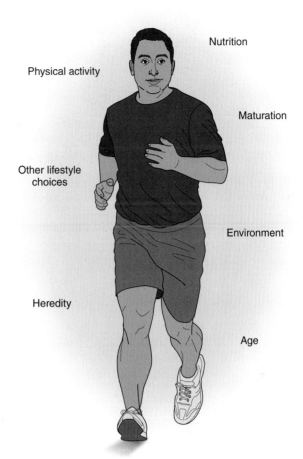

FIGURE 10.3 Factors that influence your physical fitness.

Maturation

Physical maturation is the process of becoming physically mature, or fully grown and developed. In your early teens, you begin to mature physically (maturation). Hormones are produced that promote the growth and development of tissues such as muscle and bone. Some people mature earlier than others, and individuals who mature faster than their peers will perform better on fitness tests in the short term. People who mature later will catch up, though.

Age

Studies show that older teens perform better on fitness tests than younger teens. Even within the same school class, those who are older typically do better than those who are younger. This difference results mostly from the fact that the older you are, the more you've grown and the more mature you're likely to be. However, some people mature earlier than others and therefore could have an advantage in physical fitness tests.

Compare your fitness with established health standards—not with your friends' fitness.

Your friends (and other environmental factors) can indirectly affect your physical fitness.

people have more of the muscle fibers that help them run fast, whereas other people have more of the muscle fibers that help them run a long time without fatigue. Still others have more fat cells because of heredity. Fortunately, fitness is composed of many parts. Your heredity partly determines the areas of fitness in which you do well and those in which you don't do as well; for each person, heredity enables better performance in some areas and makes others more challenging.

Environment

Your fitness is also affected by various environmental factors. Examples include where you live (e.g., city, suburbs, country), your school environment, the availability (or lack) of places to play and do other types of physical activity, and even your social environment, including the friends you choose.

Heredity

Heredity refers to the characteristics we inherit from our parents, and these characteristics influence how we do on physical fitness tests. For example, some

🔊 HEALTHY COMMUNICATION

Which factor do you think has the greatest effect on a person's physical fitness—maturation, age, heredity, or environment? Share your perspective with a classmate. Compare your ideas and work together to agree on an answer. Negotiate and compromise as needed to build consensus (agreement).

Comprehension Check

1. What are the six parts of health-related and five parts of skill-related physical fitness and how are they defined?
2. What are the four categories of fitness rating, and how do they help you determine whether you have enough health-related fitness?
3. What are some factors that contribute to fitness?

In this self-assessment, you'll try 11 challenges. They're called challenges rather than tests because *they are not meant to be tests of fitness; nor are they meant to be exercises that you do to get fit.* Instead, trying these challenges is a fun way to better understand the differences between the various parts of physical fitness. Please do not draw conclusions about your fitness based on your performance in these challenges.

The cardiorespiratory endurance and flexibility challenges will help you warm up before performing the other challenges. You may also want to consider additional warm-up exercises recommended by your teacher.

Part 1: Health-Related Physical Fitness Challenges

Running in Place (cardiorespiratory endurance)

1. Determine your resting heart rate for one minute. To do this, use your fingers to feel your pulse at your wrist or neck, then count your pulse (heartbeats) for one minute.
2. Run 120 steps in place for one minute. Count one step every time a foot hits the floor.
3. Rest for 30 seconds, then count your pulse (heart rate) for one minute. People with good cardiorespiratory endurance recover quickly after exercise. Is your heart rate after this exercise within 15 beats per minute of your resting heart rate before running in place?

This challenge focuses on cardiorespiratory endurance.

Two-Hand Ankle Grip (flexibility)

1. Squat with your heels together. Lean the upper body forward and reach with your hands between your legs and behind your ankles.
2. Clasp your hands in front of your ankles.
3. Interlock your hands for the full length of your fingers. Keep your feet still.
4. Hold the position for five seconds.

This challenge focuses on flexibility.

Single-Leg Raise (muscular endurance)

1. Bend forward at your waist so that your upper body rests on a table and your feet are on the floor.
2. Raise one leg so that it is extended straight out behind you. Complete several such raises with each leg. Performing multiple repetitions (8 or more) requires muscular endurance. Stop if you reach 25 with each leg.

This challenge focuses on muscular endurance.

Arm Skinfold (body fat level)

1. Let your right arm hang relaxed at your side. Have a partner gently pinch the skin and the fat under the skin on the back of your arm halfway between your elbow and shoulder. Together the skin and fat under the skin is called a skinfold.
2. Several skinfolds in different body locations can be used to determine the total amount of fat in the body. At this point there is no need to measure the skinfold. The skinfold on the arm is used only to illustrate the concept of body composition.

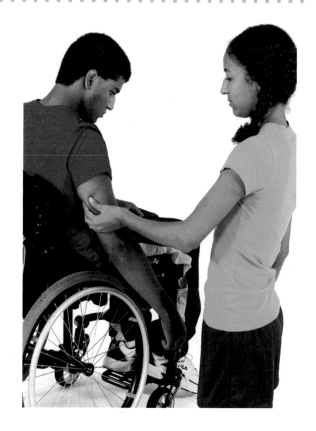

This challenge focuses on body composition.

90-Degree Push-Up (strength)

1. Lie facedown on a mat or carpet with your hands under your shoulders, your fingers spread, and your legs straight. Your legs should be slightly apart and your toes should be tucked under.

2. Push up until your arms are straight. Keep your legs and back straight—your body should form a straight line.

3. Lower your body by bending your elbows until your upper arms are parallel to the floor (elbows at a 90-degree angle), then push up until your arms are fully extended. Do one push-up every three seconds. You may want to have a partner say "up-down" every three seconds to help you. Performing up to five push-ups requires muscular strength.

This challenge focuses on strength.

Knees-to-Feet (power)

1. Kneel so that your shins and knees are on a mat. Hold your arms back. Point your toes straight backward.

2. Without curling your toes under you or rocking your body backward, swing your arms upward and spring to your feet.

3. Hold your position for three seconds after you land.

This challenge focuses on power.

Part 2: Skill-Related Physical Fitness Challenges

Line Jump (agility)

1. Balance on your right foot on a line on the floor.
2. Leap onto your left foot so that it lands to the right of the line.
3. Leap across the line onto your right foot; land to the left of the line.
4. Leap onto your left foot, landing on the line.

This challenge focuses on agility.

Double Heel Click (speed)

1. Jump into the air and click your heels together twice before you land.
2. Your feet should be at least three inches (eight centimeters) apart when you land.

This challenge focuses on speed.

Backward Hop (balance)

1. With your eyes closed, hop backward on one foot five times.
2. After the last hop, hold your balance for three seconds.

This challenge focuses on balance.

Double-Ball Bounce (coordination)

1. Hold a volleyball in each hand. Beginning at the same time with each hand, bounce both balls at the same time, at least knee high.
2. Bounce both balls three times in a row without losing control of them.

This challenge focuses on coordination.

Coin Catch (reaction time)

1. Point your right elbow outward in front of you. Your right hand, palm up, should be beside your right ear. If you're left-handed, do this activity with your left hand.
2. Place a coin as close to the end of your elbow as possible.
3. Quickly lower your elbow and grab the coin in the air with the hand of the same arm.

This challenge focuses on reaction time.

✔ Planning for Healthy Living

Use the Healthy Living Plan worksheet to help you develop the six parts of health-related fitness. Monitor the steps you take toward meeting your goals and repeat this self-assessment in one to three months to help determine the success of your plan.

Lesson 10.2
Physical Activity and Health

Lesson Objectives

After reading this lesson, you should be able to

1. describe the health and wellness benefits of physical activity,
2. discuss the three basic principles of physical activity,
3. describe the FITT formula and explain how the shorter FIT formula helps you build each part of health-related physical fitness, and
4. describe the types of physical activity included in the various steps of the Physical Activity Pyramid.

Lesson Vocabulary

FITT formula, frequency, hypokinetic disease, intensity, Physical Activity Pyramid, principle of overload, principle of progression, principle of specificity, target ceiling, target fitness zone, threshold of training, time, type

In 1996 the U.S. Surgeon General issued a report titled *Physical Activity and Health* that clearly established the importance of regular physical activity to health and wellness. Since that report, growing scientific evidence has continued to drive the point home. Regular physical activity leads to good fitness of the body systems (e.g., heart, lungs, blood, blood vessels, brain, muscles). Active people with good fitness are less likely to have a **hypokinetic disease** (see figure 10.4). *Hypo* means too little, and *kinetic* means movement; thus hypokinetic diseases are caused by too little movement or activity—for example, heart disease, stroke, cancer, diabetes, osteoporosis, and Alzheimer's disease. Active people also possess better wellness, as evidenced by looking good, feeling good, and enjoying the other factors shown in figure 10.5.

> " In the United States, physical inactivity is the biggest health problem of the 21st century. "
>
> —Dr. Steven Blair, past president of the American College of Sports Medicine

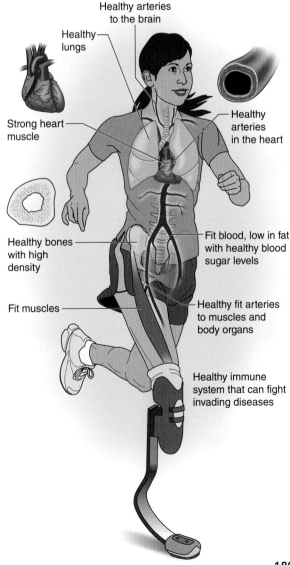

Healthy arteries to the brain

Healthy lungs

Strong heart muscle

Healthy arteries in the heart

Healthy bones with high density

Fit blood, low in fat with healthy blood sugar levels

Fit muscles

Healthy fit arteries to muscles and body organs

Healthy immune system that can fight invading diseases

FIGURE 10.4 Physical activity reduces the risk of hypokinetic disease.

189

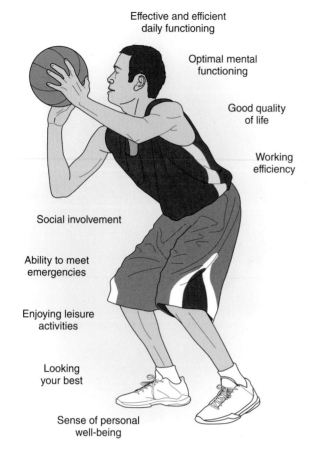

Effective and efficient daily functioning

Optimal mental functioning

Good quality of life

Working efficiency

Social involvement

Ability to meet emergencies

Enjoying leisure activities

Looking your best

Sense of personal well-being

FIGURE 10.5 The relationship between wellness and physical activity.

Basic Principles of Physical Activity

How do you know if you're doing enough physical activity? To answer this question, you need to understand three basic principles of physical activity: overload, progression, and specificity.

Principle of Overload

The **principle of overload**—the most basic law of physical activity—states that the only way to produce fitness and health benefits through physical activity is to require your body to do more than it normally does. Increasing the demand on your body (i.e., overloading it) forces it to adapt. Your body was designed to be active; therefore, if you do nothing (underload), your fitness will decrease and your health will suffer.

Principle of Progression

The **principle of progression** states that the amount and intensity of your exercise should be increased gradually. After a while, your body adapts to an increase in physical activity (load), and that amount of activity becomes easy. When this happens, increase your activity slightly.

As shown in figure 10.6, the minimum overload you need in order to build physical fitness is your **threshold of training**. Activity above this threshold builds your fitness and gives you health and wellness benefits.

It is possible to go above your upper limit of activity, also called your **target ceiling**. Ideally, you should exercise above your threshold of training and below your target ceiling. This correct range of physical activity is called your **target fitness zone**. When you do physical activity in your target fitness zone, you build fitness and other benefits. However, when you go above your target ceiling, you increase your risk of injury and can develop muscle soreness. In other words, the principle of progression rejects the "no pain, no gain" approach to exercise. If you experience pain when you exercise, you're probably overloading too quickly for your body to adjust.

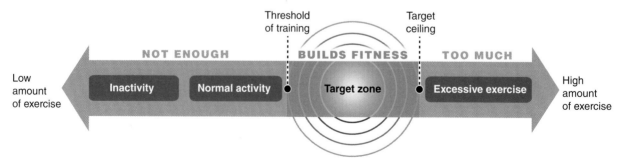

Threshold of training

Target ceiling

NOT ENOUGH BUILDS FITNESS TOO MUCH

Low amount of exercise

Inactivity Normal activity Target zone Excessive exercise

High amount of exercise

FIGURE 10.6 Exercising in your target fitness zone builds your fitness and promotes your health and wellness.

Principle of Specificity

The **principle of specificity** states that the specific type of exercise you do determines the specific benefit you receive. Different kinds and amounts of activity produce very specific and different benefits. An activity that helps you in one part of health-related fitness may not be equally good in another part. For example, jogging improves cardiorespiratory endurance but does not improve flexibility. Finally, exercises for specific body parts (e.g., calf muscles) may provide benefits only for those body parts. To give an obvious example, exercises for your calf muscles will not build the muscles of your back and shoulders.

FITT Formula

To apply the basic principles of exercise, use the **FITT formula** (sometimes called the FITT principle). Each letter in the acronym FITT represents

The principle of specificity indicates that specific types of exercise produce specific types of benefits.

Anton

one of the following factors in determining how much physical activity is enough: frequency, intensity, time, and type. When you apply the formula to one specific type of fitness or a specific type of activity, you can drop the last T and use only FIT (see Physical Activity Pyramid later in this lesson).

Frequency refers to how often you do physical activity. For physical activity to be beneficial, you must do it on multiple days per week. The proper **frequency** depends on the type of activity you're doing and the part of fitness you want to develop. For example, to develop strength you might need to exercise two days a week, but daily activity is recommended for losing fat.

Intensity refers to how hard you perform physical activity. If your activity is too easy, you won't build fitness or gain other benefits. But remember—extremely vigorous activity can be harmful if you don't work up to it gradually. **Intensity** is determined differently depending on the type of activity you do and the type of fitness you want to build. For example, if you're building cardiorespiratory endurance, you can determine intensity by counting your heart rate; if you're building strength, you can determine intensity by the amount of weight you lift.

Time, of course, refers to how long you do physical activity. The length of **time** for which you should do physical activity depends on the type of activity and the part of fitness you want to develop. For example, to build flexibility, you should exercise for 15 seconds or more for each muscle (or muscle group); to build cardiorespiratory endurance, on the other hand, you need to be active continuously for at least 20 minutes.

Type refers to the kind of activity you do in order to build a specific part of fitness or gain a specific benefit. Any given **type** of activity may help you build one part of fitness but not another part. For example, doing active aerobics builds your cardiorespiratory endurance but does little to develop your flexibility.

The Physical Activity Pyramid

Established physical activity guidelines recommend at least 60 minutes of physical activity each day for teens. The five steps of the **Physical Activity Pyramid** (figure 10.7) are designed to help you

HEALTH TECHNOLOGY

Heart rate monitors help you track your heart rate during exercise or other physical activity. They are sometimes called heart rate watches because they can be worn on your wrist. Most heart rate monitors include a band that you wear around your chest. A transmitter in the chest band sends a signal to a receiver in the device on your wrist, which displays your heart rate. Some monitors don't include a separate chest band but instead pick up your heart rate at your wrist by using sensors built right into the device. Heart rate monitors are readily available at most major sporting goods stores.

You can program a heart rate monitor to tell you when you're training at the appropriate intensity for building cardiorespiratory endurance (target heart rate zone). The American College of Sports Medicine recommends two different methods of determining target heart rate. For simplicity, see table 10.3 for a chart based on one of these methods (heart rate reserve method—HRR). If you want to know more about how to calculate your target heart rate using the two different methods, go the student section of the Health for Life website.

CONNECT

Do you think heart rate monitors influence people's motivation to participate in physical activity? Would owning one affect how hard or often you work out? Why or why not?

TABLE 10.3   Calculating Heart Rate Target Zone (% HRR Method)

Threshold HR	Step 1:	204 (max HR)*
	Step 2:	− 67 (resting HR)
		137 (HRR)
	Step 3:	× 0.6 (threshold %)
		82
		+ 67 (resting HR)
		149 (threshold HR)
Target ceiling	Step 1:	204 (max HR)*
	Step 2:	− 67 (resting HR)
		137 (HRR)
	Step 3:	× 0.8 (ceiling %)
		110
		+ 67 (resting HR)
		177 (target ceiling HR)
Target HR zone	149–177 beats per min	

*The example is for a 16-year-old with a resting HR of 67 with cardiorespiratory endurance in the good fitness zone.

understand the five kinds of physical activity, which build different parts of fitness and produce different health and wellness benefits (recall the principle of specificity). To meet the recommended 60 minutes of daily activity, you can choose from the different types of activity. For optimal benefits, you should perform activities from all parts of the pyramid each week. Information about the FIT formula for each type of activity in the pyramid is presented in figure 10.7.

Moderate Physical Activity

This is the first step in the Physical Activity Pyramid, and you should do it daily or nearly every day. Moderate activity involves exercise equal in intensity to brisk walking. It includes some activities of normal daily living (also called lifestyle activities), such as walking to school, doing yardwork (e.g., raking leaves, mowing the lawn), and doing housework (e.g., mopping the floor).

Energy balance

Energy out
(Activity)

Energy in
(Diet)

F = 3+ days per week
I = Stretch overload
T = 10-30 sec, 2-4 reps of major muscle groups*

STEP 5
Flexibility exercises
• Stretching exercises
• Yoga
• Gymnastics

F = 2-3 days per week
I = Muscle overload
T = 8-12 reps, 2-4 sets of major muscle groups*

STEP 4
Muscle fitness exercises
• Resistance training
• Calisthenics
• Wall climbing
• Plyometrics

F = 3+ days per week
I = Reach target heart rate
T = At least 20 min/day*

STEP 3
Vigorous sport and recreation
• Play sports (e.g., tennis, soccer)
• Skating
• Skiing
• Dancing

F = 3+ days per week
I = Reach target heart rate
T = At least 20 min/day*

STEP 2
Vigorous aerobics
• Jog
• Aerobic dance
• Bike
• Swim
• Stair stepper

F = Daily
I = Equal to brisk walking
T = At least 30-60 min/day*

STEP 1
Moderate physical activity
• Walk
• Do yardwork
• Go bowling
• Do active household chores

*For teens, at least 60 minutes of moderate to vigorous activity is recommended each day. Activities from the pyramid can be combined to meet this recommendation.

Avoid inactivity

FIGURE 10.7 The new Physical Activity Pyramid for Teens.
Source: C.B. Corbin.

Moderate activity is a good way to accumulate some of the recommended 60 minutes of daily activity. At least 30 minutes a day is recommended for adults. It should be performed at least five days a week. It is associated with reduced risk of hypokinetic disease and enhanced wellness. It also helps you control your body fat level and is well suited for people of various abilities.

Vigorous Aerobics

Step 2 of the Physical Activity Pyramid represents vigorous aerobics, which includes any activity that you can do for a long time without stopping and that is vigorous enough to increase your heart rate and make you breathe faster. Thus these activities are more intense than moderate activities, and they are typically continuous (e.g., jogging, aerobic dance). Like moderate activity, they provide many health and wellness benefits, and they're especially helpful for building a high level of cardiorespiratory endurance and controlling body fat.

You should perform vigorous aerobics and vigorous sport and recreation activities (see step 3) at least three days a week for at least 20 minutes each to meet national activity guidelines.

Vigorous Sport and Recreation

Like vigorous aerobics, vigorous sport and recreation (represented in step 3 of the Physical Activity Pyramid) require your heart to beat faster than normal and cause you to breathe faster. Unlike vigorous aerobics, however, vigorous sport and recreation often involve short bursts of activity followed by short bursts of rest—as, for example, in basketball, football, soccer, and tennis. When done for at least 20 minutes a day in bouts of 10 minutes or more at a time, these activities provide fun, fitness, health, and wellness benefits similar to those of vigorous aerobics. They also help you build motor skills and contribute to healthy weight management. Like vigorous aerobics, they should be done at least three days per week for at least 20 minutes.

Vigorous aerobic activity helps you build cardiorespiratory endurance.

Muscle Fitness Exercises

Step 4 in the Physical Activity Pyramid represents muscle fitness exercises, which build your strength, muscular endurance, and power. Muscle fitness exercises include both resistance training (with weights or machines), moving your own body (as in calisthenics and rock climbing), and doing activities that build power such as jumping. These types of exercise produce general health benefits (e.g., reduced risk of disease, a healthier back, better posture, stronger bones), wellness benefits (e.g., look good, feel good, enjoy life), as well as better performance. These exercises can be used to meet established activity guidelines and should be performed on two or three days a week.

Flexibility Exercises

The fifth step of the Physical Activity Pyramid represents flexibility exercises, which help you have a healthy back, good posture, and improve your performance in activities such as gymnastics and dance. Flexibility is also beneficial in jobs that require reaching and bending. Also, stretching exercises that build flexibility can help you relax and may reduce risk of injury. They are also used in therapy to help people who have been injured. Two examples of flexibility exercise are stretching and yoga. To build and maintain flexibility, perform flexibility exercises at least three days a week.

Avoiding Inactivity

Just below the Physical Activity Pyramid, you'll notice pictures of a TV set and a video game controller with an X over them. This illustration emphasizes the fact that being sedentary, or inactive, poses a health risk.

Just as you should do 60 minutes of daily physical activity, drawing from the five types of activity presented in the pyramid, you should also avoid the inactivity that is common among people who log too much "screen time" in front of a TV or other device. We all need to take time to recover from daily stresses and prepare for new challenges, so periods of rest and sleep are important to good health. Some low-key activities of daily living—such as studying, reading, and even a moderate amount of screen time—are appropriate. But general inactivity or sedentary living is harmful to your health. Your choices from active areas of the pyramid should exceed your choices from the inactivity area.

ADVOCACY IN ACTION: Replacing Screen Time With Activity Time

A recent survey of children and teens in the United States found that they watch TV for an average of nearly 4 hours a day. Sixty-eight percent of teens have a TV in their room, and of course many also spend screen time on computers, video games, and cell phones, thus more than doubling the amount of time they spend watching a screen. Research shows that screen time results in inactivity and increases your health risk.

Develop a script for a 90-second public service announcement (PSA) that advocates reducing screen time and increasing physical activity among youth. Include compelling facts and a relevant story or testimonial. If possible, record your PSA and share it with your class. If you cannot record it, develop a poster that captures the message.

Comprehension Check

1. What are some health and wellness benefits of physical activity?
2. What are the three basic principles of exercise?
3. What is the FITT formula, and how does it and the shorter FIT formula help you build physical fitness?
4. What types of physical activity are represented in the Physical Activity Pyramid?

To enjoy a physical activity, it helps to have the skills needed for that particular sport or game—for example, kicking, throwing, hitting, and swimming. Learning such skills is easier for some people than for others, but anyone can get better with practice.

Zack felt that he was never really good at sports. He had tried several activities and found that he was not as good at any of them as the other people he knew. He had even tried out for the soccer and swim teams at school but didn't make either one. His biggest problem was that he hadn't learned to play any sports when he was young, and now he was behind his friends and peers.

Zack wanted to learn a sport but was afraid that he would be unsuccessful again and that his friends might laugh at him. Still, he did a self-assessment of his skill-related abilities and was surprised to find that he did pretty well on most of the assessments. His power was not especially high, but he did well in coordination and agility.

Before trying out for a team again, Zack thought it would be best to try to learn some skills used in a sport that matched his abilities. Being over 6 feet (1.8 meters) tall and weighing 180 pounds (82 kilograms) seemed to give him an advantage, but he wanted to get stronger. And he still wasn't sure which sport would be best for him. He wanted to be on a team, but he also wanted to learn something that would be fun and interesting. An alternative to trying out for a team would be to participate in an individual sport like mountain biking or dancing.

For Discussion

What advice would you give Zack for choosing a sport? Once he chooses, what steps could he take to improve his performance skills? How might Zack's life be different in the long term if he develops his sport skills now? Who could he talk to for help? Zack knew that he needed to practice but wasn't sure exactly *what* to practice. What practice advice would you give him? Consider the guidelines presented in this chapter's Skills for Healthy Living feature to help you answer the questions.

SKILLS FOR HEALTHY LIVING: Performance Skills

Sport educators and researchers have studied various ways to learn sport skills. Based on their findings, they've developed the following guidelines to help you improve your skills.

- **Get good instruction.** If you learn a skill incorrectly, it will be hard to improve, even with practice. Good instructors provide feedback that you can use to correct errors and help you improve your performance.

- **Practice.** Good practice is the key to improving your skills. Good practice involves repeating a performance with a focus on correct technique. Good instruction helps you practice right. Many people don't like to practice skills—they just want to play the game—but just playing the game doesn't allow you to practice a particular skill. In addition,

when you play a game without having the proper skills, you often develop bad habits that hinder your success.

- **Practice all skills, not just those that you already do well.** Any sport requires more than a few skills to become proficient. For example, basketball requires skillful shooting, dribbling, passing, catching, and defense. Practice each of the different skills that are important to your activity.

- **At first, don't worry about details.** When you first learn a skill, concentrate on the skill as a whole. You can deal with the details after learning the main skill.

- **As you improve, concentrate on one detail at a time.** If you try to concentrate on too many details at once, you may develop what is called analysis paralysis. This condition occurs when you analyze an activity and try to correct several problems all at once. For example, if you're learning the tennis serve, it's not wise to work simultaneously on your ball toss, grip, backswing, and follow-through. It's more effective to practice changes one at a time.

- **Avoid competing while learning a skill.** Although competition can be fun, competing while you're learning a skill is stressful and does not promote optimal learning.

- **Think positively.** Experts have shown that if you think negatively, you're likely to perform poorly. On the other hand, if you think positively while you practice, you'll learn faster and become more confident in your ability.

ACADEMIC CONNECTION: Measures of Central Tendency

Understanding mathematical and statistical concepts can help you interpret health and fitness test scores. In a group of people, each person can have a different score on the test. Most people have scores around the middle of the distribution, but some have low scores and some have high scores. In the following example, each number represents a score on a health or fitness test.

An average score can be indicated by the mean (sum of all scores divided by the number of scores), the median (the middle score in a number of scores), or the mode (the most common score in a number of scores). Determine the average score (mean, median, and mode) for the example given. The scores with bold numbers get a good fitness (healthy fitness) rating. Scores higher than those in bold get a high performance rating (also considered to be healthy). Scores below the bold numbers get a marginal rating. Is an average score for this group good enough to be considered healthy?

Distribution of Fitness Scores for One Group

					8					
					8					
				7	8	**9**	**10**			
			6	7	8	**9**	**10**			
		5	6	7	8	**9**	**10**	11		
	4	5	6	7	8	**9**	**10**	11	12	
3	4	5	6	7	8	**9**	**10**	11	12	

Physical Activity and Brain Power

Scientists at the U.S. Centers for Disease Control and Prevention (CDC) reviewed more than 400 studies and found that in addition to health benefits, regular physical activity can "help improve academic achievement, including grades and standardized test scores." The CDC also concluded that physical activity has a positive effect on cognitive skills and academic behavior, including enhanced concentration and attention, as well as improved classroom behavior.

The idea that physical activity helps students concentrate on academic tasks is supported by research from Dr. Chuck Hillman and colleagues at the University of Illinois. They found, for example, that 20 minutes of walking stimulates areas of the brain that increase classroom concentration and attention (see figure 10.8). The studies looked at children involved in recess, physical education classes, and physical activity breaks during the school day.

Similarly, Dr. Edward Johnson, from Columbia University, found that students who performed well on fitness tests also performed better on math and reading exams than students who did not perform well on the fitness tests. Another research study showed that students who had 5- to 10-minute activity breaks throughout their school day also had higher standardized test scores, better school attendance, and fewer disciplinary problems than students with more limited opportunities for physical activity.

Thus, even as many school districts around the United States are eliminating physical education and reducing recess periods to increase time spent on core subjects, more and more research is showing that physical activity—whether in the form of recess, physical education, or physical activity breaks—aids students' overall cognitive functioning and can improve their test scores.

For Discussion

Do you notice a difference in your ability to pay attention in class after engaging in moderate to vigorous physical activity?

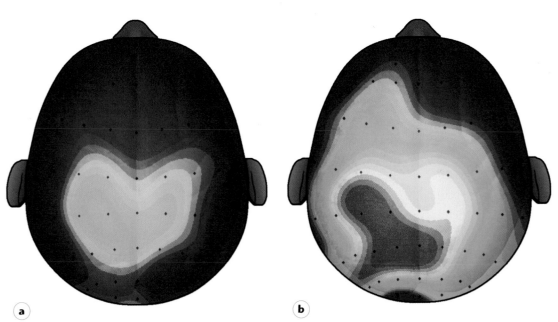

Figure 10.8   Activation of the brain (a) while sitting and (b) after walking. The red and yellow areas indicate activation of the brain after exercise.

CHAPTER REVIEW

Reviewing Concepts and Vocabulary

As directed by your teacher, answer items 1 through 5 by correctly completing each sentence with a word or a phrase.

1. The diagram with five steps that helps you understand the types of physical activity is called the _____ _____ _____.

2. The minimum amount of overload needed to achieve physical fitness is called _____ _____ _____.

3. Age, maturation, _____, and the environment are factors that affect your physical fitness.

4. If you achieve a _____ _____ rating, you probably are at the level of fitness needed to live a full, healthy life.

5. The type of standard used to rate fitness based on health is called a _____ _____ _____.

For items 6 through 10, as directed by your teacher, match each term in column 1 with the appropriate phrase in column 2.

6. target ceiling   a. how hard you perform physical activity
7. intensity   b. increasing exercise gradually
8. progression   c. the upper limit of your physical activity
9. specificity   d. doing more exercise than you normally do
10. overload   e. exercise for one part of fitness

For items 11 through 15, as directed by your teacher, respond to each statement or question.

11. How do age and maturation affect physical fitness?
12. Describe each step of the pyramid and provide examples of specific activities.
13. Explain what the acronym FITT stands for and how it is different from FIT.
14. Describe several guidelines for building performance skills.
15. Explain why you should not compare yourself with others when assessing your fitness.

Thinking Critically

Write a paragraph in response to the following situation.

A friend tells you that he thinks it's important for everyone to attain a high-performance fitness rating. He says that if a good rating is the goal for all people, then a high performance rating must be even better for everyone. How would you respond? Explain your answer.

Take It Home

Show the Physical Activity Pyramid to a member of your family. Ask if she follows the FIT formula for that type of activity. If she is a child or teen, ask if she does at least 60 minutes of activity from the pyramid every day. If she is an adult, ask if she does at least 30 minutes of physical activity from the pyramid every day. Prepare a report based on the information from the interview.

199

11

Physical Activity: Getting Started With Your Plan

In This Chapter

 Student Web Resources
www.healthforlifetextbook.org/student

Valeriy Pistryy/fotolia.com

Lesson 11.1

Physical Activity: Getting Started

Lesson Objectives

After reading this lesson, you should be able to

1. explain medical readiness and how it is determined,
2. explain how the environment affects physical activity, and
3. describe steps for dressing appropriately for physical activity in normal environments.

Lesson Vocabulary

air quality index, frostbite, heat index, humidity, hyperthermia, hypothermia, Physical Activity Readiness Questionnaire (PAR-Q), warm-up, wind-chill factor

Whether you're a beginner or have been physically active for some time, you need to be prepared and know how to exercise safely in all conditions. If you're a beginner, the first step is to be physically and medically ready. As a young person, you may have no problem in this regard, but you should answer some simple questions about yourself just to be sure. You should also be ready for a variety of environmental conditions—such as heat, cold, pollution, safety, and high altitude—that might require a change in your exercise plans. In this lesson, you'll learn the ins and outs of preparing yourself for physical activity.

> **"** An ounce of prevention is worth a pound of cure. **"**
>
> —Benjamin Franklin, U.S. Founding Father

Medical Readiness

Before you begin a regular physical activity program for health and wellness, assess your medical and physical readiness. Experts have developed a seven-item questionnaire called the **Physical Activity Readiness Questionnaire (PAR-Q)**. If you answer yes to any of the questions, consult with a doctor before beginning or continuing a program. You can try the PAR-Q in the self-assessment for this chapter. You might also want to show the PAR-Q to your parents or other adults who are important to you. Older people are more likely to be at risk when doing exercise, and you may be able to encourage

them to answer the PAR-Q questions before they begin an exercise program.

You may be required to have a medical exam if you're going to participate in an interscholastic sport or an activity of similar intensity (e.g., a community sport or rigorous personal challenge). The exam is intended to make sure that you're free from disease; it can also help prevent health problems. Even if you get a medical exam, you may still benefit from answering the questions in the PAR-Q as well as the questions included in the Physical Readiness for Sports or Vigorous Training section of the self-assessment at the end of this lesson to help you determine whether you're ready for sport competition.

Later in life, you may want to do a graded exercise test, sometimes called an exercise stress test, which is administered by a health professional. This test, done on a treadmill, can help identify people who are at high risk for health problems such as heart attacks. Even seemingly fit athletes can be at risk, though the test is typically recommended for people with risk factors for heart disease. More information is available in the student section of the Health for Life website.

Readiness for Extreme Environmental Conditions

Whether you're a beginner or an experienced exerciser, environmental conditions affect your body; therefore, they play an important role in determining when and how strenuously you should exercise. Your body is able to adapt to environmental factors, such as heat, cold, altitude, and air quality. As a result, people who've been exposed to an environment for a long time function better in it than those who have just become exposed to it. This discussion provides guidelines for adapting to weather and environmental factors in order to help you prevent injury and health problems. All people should follow these guidelines, and they're especially important for people who are new to exercise or to a particular environment.

Hot, Humid Weather

Be careful when doing physical activity in high heat, especially when it is accompanied by high **humidity**. These conditions can cause **hyperthermia**, or overheating, in which body temperature gets too high. Exercising in the heat, of course, causes your body temperature to rise. As a result, you start to perspire (sweat), and when your sweat evaporates, your body is cooled. But when the humidity is high, evaporation is less effective in cooling your body, thus increasing your risk of overheating. Hyperthermia causes three main conditions—heat cramps, heat exhaustion, and heatstroke—which are described in table 11.1.

To prevent and cope with heat-related conditions, follow these guidelines.

- **Begin gradually.** As your body becomes accustomed to physical activity in hot weather, it becomes more resistant to heat-related injury. Start with short periods of activity, then gradually increase your exercise time.

- **Drink water.** During hot weather, your body perspires more than usual in order to cool itself. Therefore, you need to drink plenty of water to replace the water that your body loses through sweat.

- **Wear proper clothing.** Wear porous clothing that allows air to pass through and cool your body. Also wear light-colored clothing; lighter colors reflect the sun's heat, whereas darker colors absorb it.

- **Rest frequently.** Physical activity creates body heat. Periodically stop and rest in a shady area to help your body lower its temperature.

- **Avoid extreme heat and humidity.** You can use the heat index chart (figure 11.1) to determine whether the environment is too hot and humid for activity. If the **heat index** is too high (in the danger zone), postpone or cancel your activity. You should do physical activity in the caution zones only if you've adapted to hot environments, and you should follow all basic guidelines. The amount of time it takes to adapt to these conditions varies with each person.

- **Get out of the heat and cool your body if heat-related injury occurs.** Find shade; apply cool, wet towels to your body; spray your body with water; drink water; and seek medical help if heatstroke occurs.

To help cool your body when exercising in hot weather, wear light-colored clothing and drink water.

TABLE 11.1 Heat-Related Conditions

Condition	Definition
Heat cramps	Muscle cramps caused by excessive heat exposure and low water consumption.
Heat exhaustion	Syndrome caused by excessive heat exposure, in which body temperature is normal or slightly higher, and characterized by paleness, clammy skin, profuse sweating, weakness, tiredness, nausea, dizziness, muscle cramps, and possibly vomiting or fainting.
Heatstroke	Serious, potentially fatal condition caused by excessive heat exposure that requires prompt medical attention and is characterized by high body temperature, up to 106°F (41°C); hot, dry, flushed skin; rapid pulse; lack of sweating; dizziness; and possibly unconsciousness.

Reprinted, by permission, from C. Corbin, G. Le Masurier, and K. McConnell, 2014, *Fitness for life*, 6th ed. (Champaign, IL: Human Kinetics), 74.

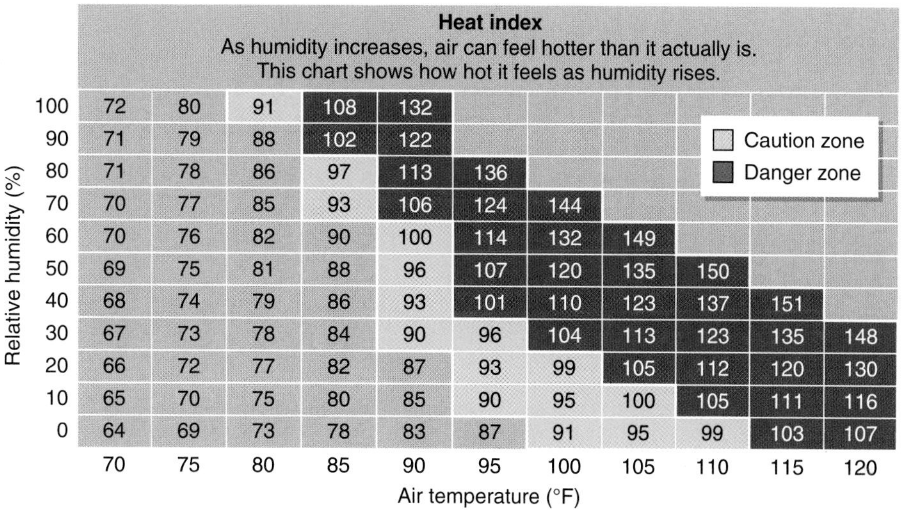

Heat index
As humidity increases, air can feel hotter than it actually is.
This chart shows how hot it feels as humidity rises.

Relative humidity (%)	70	75	80	85	90	95	100	105	110	115	120
100	72	80	91	108	132						
90	71	79	88	102	122						
80	71	78	86	97	113	136					
70	70	77	85	93	106	124	144				
60	70	76	82	90	100	114	132	149			
50	69	75	81	88	96	107	120	135	150		
40	68	74	79	86	93	101	110	123	137	151	
30	67	73	78	84	90	96	104	113	123	135	148
20	66	72	77	82	87	93	99	105	112	120	130
10	65	70	75	80	85	90	95	100	105	111	116
0	64	69	73	78	83	87	91	95	99	103	107

Air temperature (°F)

☐ Caution zone
■ Danger zone

FIGURE 11.1 Heat index chart.

 ## HEALTH TECHNOLOGY

Modern technology has produced clothing that is especially good for cold weather. For example, a shirt made of wicking fibers (e.g., polypropylene, Capilene) absorbs moisture from your skin and transfers it (wicks it away) to the next layer of clothing. A windbreaker made of synthetic material (e.g., Gore-Tex) blocks the wind. This type of garment is especially effective as an outside layer in cold weather. These fabrics can help prevent emergencies related to cold weather, such as frostbite and hypothermia.

 ## CONNECT

How might a person's access to high-tech fabrics (e.g., Capilene, Gore-Tex) influence his or her choice of physical activity? What factors might prevent a person from using high-tech fabric?

Cold, Windy, and Wet Weather

Exercising during cold, windy, and wet weather can be dangerous. Extreme cold can result in **hypothermia**, or excessively low body temperature. Hypothermia is accompanied by shivering, numbness, drowsiness, muscular weakness, and confusion or disorientation. Extreme cold can also cause **frostbite**, in which a body part becomes frozen. This condition is made especially dangerous by the fact that it often causes no immediate pain. It can, however, cause the symptoms shown in the accompanying list titled Symptoms of Frostbite. Follow these guidelines when exercising in cold, windy, and wet weather.

- **Avoid extreme cold and wind.** Exercising in cold, windy weather is especially dangerous because the wind makes the air feel colder than indicated by the standard temperature. Before dressing for physical activity, determine the **wind-chill factor**. The chart presented in figure 11.2 indicates how quickly various wind-chill levels can cause frostbite. Experts agree that if the time to frostbite is 30 minutes or less, you should postpone activity. If you are active when the wind-chill factor is high, dress properly and be aware of the symptoms of hypothermia and frostbite.

- **Dress properly.** Wear several layers of lightweight clothing rather than a heavy jacket or coat. The clothing closest to your body should be made from a fiber that wicks or transfers the moisture away from your skin to the next layer of clothing. Good options include silk, wool, and many synthetic garments. Cotton is not a good inner layer because it tends to absorb water rather than transfer it away from your skin. Garments made of nonabsorbent material (e.g., plastic, nylon) should not be worn as the layer closest to the skin. Do wear a high collar on one of your inner layers. The outer layer should be made of a material (e.g., nylon) that

Allow your body to adjust to a higher altitude by first exercising at low intensity for limited periods.
Krzysztof Tkacz/fotolia.com

will stop the wind. As needed, wear a knit cap, ski mask, and mittens (which keep hands warmer than gloves do).

- **Avoid exercising in weather that is icy or cold and wet.** Special problems can occur during these types of weather. For example, your shoes, socks, and pant legs can get wet, increasing the risk of foot injury and falls.

Pollution and Altitude

The effectiveness and safety of your exercise can also be affected by conditions other than weather. For example, high levels of air pollution affect your ability to breathe, and experts have identified levels of pollution (ozone and particulate matter) that are unhealthful. Pollution is rated according to an

---

Symptoms of Frostbite

- Skin becomes white or grayish yellow and looks glossy.
- Pain is sometimes felt early but subsides later (often, feeling is lost and no pain is felt).
- Blisters may appear later.
- The affected area feels intensely cold and numb.

Temperature (°F)

Wind (mph)	30	25	20	15	10	5	0	−5	−10	−15	−20	−25
5	25	19	13	7	1	−5	−11	−16	−22	−28	−34	−40
10	21	15	9	3	−4	−10	−16	−22	−28	−35	−41	−47
15	19	13	6	0	−7	−13	−19	−26	−32	−39	−45	−51
20	17	11	4	−2	−9	−15	−22	−29	−35	−42	−48	−55
25	16	9	3	−4	−11	−17	−24	−31	−37	−44	−51	−58
30	15	8	1	−5	−12	−19	−26	−33	−39	−46	−53	−60
35	14	7	0	−7	−14	−21	−27	−34	−41	−48	−55	−62
40	13	6	−1	−8	−15	−22	−29	−36	−43	−50	−57	−64
45	12	5	−2	−9	−16	−23	−30	−37	−44	−51	−58	−65
50	12	4	−3	−10	−17	−24	−31	−38	−45	−52	−60	−67
55	11	4	−3	−11	−18	−25	−32	−39	−46	−54	−61	−68
60	10	3	−4	−11	−19	−26	−33	−40	−48	−55	−62	−69

Frostbite occurs in 30 minutes or less

FIGURE 11.2 Wind-chill chart.

air quality index that includes levels ranging from good to very unhealthful (see figure 11.3). When pollution is high, radio and television stations often make warning announcements. During these times, avoid exercising outdoors.

People who live at high altitude may be able to exercise there with little trouble; however, people who live at lower altitude may have trouble adjusting to a higher altitude. Even if you're physically fit, allow your body to adjust to a higher altitude by first exercising at low intensity for limited periods. For example, snow skiers should avoid hard skiing and limit the length of ski sessions for a day or two in order to become accustomed to the higher altitude.

Air quality index	Levels of health concern	Color	Ozone	Particulate matter
0-50	Good	Green	None	None
51-100	Moderate	Yellow	Unusually sensitive people should consider limiting prolonged or heavy exertion.	Unusually sensitive people should consider limiting prolonged or heavy exertion.
101-150	Unhealthy for sensitive groups	Orange	Active children and adults, and people with respiratory disease such as asthma, should limit prolonged outdoor exertion.	People with heart or lung disease, older adults, and children should reduce prolonged or heavy exertion.
151-200	Unhealthy	Red	Active children and adults, and people with respiratory disease such as asthma, should avoid prolonged outdoor exertion. Everyone else, especially children, should limit prolonged outdoor exertion.	People with heart or lung disease, older adults, and children should avoid prolonged or heavy exertion. Everyone else should reduce prolonged or heavy exertion.
201-300	Very unhealthy	Purple	Active children and adults, and people with respiratory disease such as asthma, should avoid all outdoor exertion. Everyone else, especially children, should limit outdoor exertion.	People with heart or lung disease, older adults, and children should avoid all physical activity outdoors. Everyone else should avoid prolonged or heavy exertion.
301-500	Hazardous	Maroon	Everyone should avoid all physical activity outdoors.	Everyone should avoid all physical activity outdoors.

FIGURE 11.3 Air quality index.

HEALTH SCIENCE

Health scientists recently discovered that the wind-chill factors they had used for years were incorrect because they overemphasized the importance of wind. Canadian experts, with help from U.S. scientists, developed a new formula, which is used in the wind-chill chart presented by figure 11.2.

General Readiness: Dressing for Physical Activity

Even under normal circumstances, the way you dress has a lot to do with your comfort and enjoyment during physical activity. Consider the following guidelines.

• **Wear comfortable clothing.** Tight clothing can restrict your blood flow or limit your motion during vigorous exercise. Your body cools itself better if your clothing fits loosely.

• **Wash exercise clothing regularly.** Clean clothing is more comfortable than soiled clothing, and it reduces chances of fungal growth and infection.

Wearing specially engineered clothing can help you when you exercise in the heat or cold.

• **Dress in layers when exercising outdoors.** You can remove layers of clothing as you become warmer while exercising, then put them back on when you cool down.

• **Wear proper socks.** Thick sport socks provide a cushion, help prevent blisters, and absorb perspiration from your feet.

• **Wear proper shoes.** Most people can use a good pair of multipurpose exercise or sport shoes. However, if you plan to do special activities, you might prefer shoes designed specifically for them. Be sure to look for shoes with the features listed in the Consumer Corner sidebar.

• **Consider lace-up ankle braces.** Ankle braces can help prevent ankle injuries, especially during activities that involve quick changes in direction (e.g., basketball, racquetball). Studies show that lace-up ankle braces reduce the number of ankle injuries among those who have a history of ankle injury. Also consider wearing high-top shoes for ankle support.

☻ CONNECT

How do media images influence your perception of athletic shoes? Do you think the quality of shoes is related to the quality of advertisements? Why or why not? Share your perspectives with your peers. Work on active listening and respect each other's opinions.

Other General Preparation Guidelines

So far in this lesson, you've learned about medical readiness, environmental factors that affect activity, and how to dress appropriately for activity. The following are some additional steps you can take to make your activity sessions safe and effective.

CONSUMER CORNER: Selecting Proper Athletic Shoes

Shopping for athletic shoes can be an overwhelming experience. You can narrow the options by focusing on shoes that are appropriate for the activity in which you plan to participate. Each type of athletic shoe is structured to meet the demands of the activity for which it is intended. For example, running shoes have more flexibility to allow your foot to bend and create push. On the other hand, cycling shoes are rigid along the bottom to allow the force generated in your legs to move down into the bike pedal. When selecting athletic shoes, use the following basic guidelines; also see figure 11.4.

- Go to a reputable store with a wide selection of brands and styles.
- Shop for shoes at the end of the day when your feet tend to be a bit larger.
- Wear the same type of socks you plan to wear when using the shoes.
- Don't get hung up on a certain size. Shoe manufacturers differ, and you may need a slightly different size in one brand than in others.
- If your feet are wide or narrow, look for shoes that come in an appropriate width.

- Bring your old shoes with you. The wear pattern of your shoes may help you decide which new shoe is best. A shoe store can help you with this.
- Replace shoes when they get old. Each component of a shoe is designed for a reason and if one or more components wear out, the shoe does not function as designed.
- People who perform many activities can consider cross-training or multipurpose shoes. They have many of the same features as running shoes, but typically have less heel padding and provide more stability for lateral movements.
- For daily wear (i.e., not for a specific activity), running shoes or cross-training shoes are appropriate; expensive high-performance shoes are typically not necessary. New shoe models are introduced regularly to encourage people to get the latest styles. Older models are often just as good as the newer ones and are usually sold at discounts.

Find a firm sole that flexes with reasonable ease.

A firm, thick sole and good arch support are essential.

Look for a shoe with a well-padded heel and a firm heel counter (i.e., the part that surrounds your heel; it should provide a snug fit to help control your foot's movement).

Figure 11.4 Characteristics of proper shoes.

• **Get fit for your workout.** You do your workout to get fit, but you also need to be fit enough to do your workout without getting hurt. When you begin a new program, start gradually. As your fitness improves, do more. Good health-related fitness of all kinds is important to safe exercise.

• **Warm up before your workout.** Recent research indicates that the type of **warm-up** that you perform should be based on the type of workout that you plan to perform. For moderate activity, no warm-up is required in most cases. Before vigorous activity, a general warm-up of moderate full-body movement (e.g., walking, easy jogging) for 5 to 10 minutes is recommended. In addition, you may want to perform a stretching or dynamic warm-up before some vigorous activities that required strength, speed, and power. For more information visit the student section of the Health for Life website.

• **Cool down after your workout.** Gradually reduce the intensity of your activity until your heart rate returns to a normal level. Stretching as part of a cool-down can also help you maintain or improve flexibility.

Stretching as part of your cool-down can help maintain or improve flexibility.

Comprehension Check

1. What is medical readiness and how can you determine it?
2. What environmental factors can make activity unhealthy or unsafe?
3. What are some guidelines for dressing properly for physical activity in normal environments?

In this self-assessment, you will complete the Physical Activity Readiness Questionnaire (PAR-Q). Record your results as directed by your teacher.

Physical Activity Readiness
Questionnaire - PAR-Q
(revised 2002)

PAR-Q & YOU

(A Questionnaire for People Aged 15 to 69)

Regular physical activity is fun and healthy, and increasingly more people are starting to become more active every day. Being more active is very safe for most people. However, some people should check with their doctor before they start becoming much more physically active.

If you are planning to become much more physically active than you are now, start by answering the seven questions in the box below. If you are between the ages of 15 and 69, the PAR-Q will tell you if you should check with your doctor before you start. If you are over 69 years of age, and you are not used to being very active, check with your doctor.

Common sense is your best guide when you answer these questions. Please read the questions carefully and answer each one honestly: check YES or NO.

YES	NO		
☐	☐	1.	Has your doctor ever said that you have a heart condition <u>and</u> that you should only do physical activity recommended by a doctor?
☐	☐	2.	Do you feel pain in your chest when you do physical activity?
☐	☐	3.	In the past month, have you had chest pain when you were not doing physical activity?
☐	☐	4.	Do you lose your balance because of dizziness or do you ever lose consciousness?
☐	☐	5.	Do you have a bone or joint problem (for example, back, knee, or hip) that could be made worse by a change in your physical activity?
☐	☐	6.	Is your doctor currently prescribing drugs (for example, water pills) for your blood pressure or heart condition?
☐	☐	7.	Do you know of <u>any other reason</u> why you should not do physical activity?

If you answered

YES to one or more questions

Talk with your doctor by phone or in person BEFORE you start becoming much more physically active or BEFORE you have a fitness appraisal. Tell your doctor about the PAR-Q and which questions you answered YES.

- You may be able to do any activity you want — as long as you start slowly and build up gradually. Or, you may need to restrict your activities to those which are safe for you. Talk with your doctor about the kinds of activities you wish to participate in and follow his/her advice.
- Find out which community programs are safe and helpful for you.

NO to all questions

If you answered NO honestly to <u>all</u> PAR-Q questions, you can be reasonably sure that you can:
- start **becoming** much more physically active — begin slowly and build up gradually. This is the safest and easiest way to go.
- take in part a fitness appraisal — this is an excellent way to determine your basic fitness so that you can plan the best way for you to live actively. It is also highly recommended that you have your blood pressure evaluated. If your reading is over 144/94, talk with your doctor before you start becoming much more physically active.

→

DELAY BECOMING MUCH MORE ACTIVE:
- if you are not feeling well because of a temporary illness such as a cold or a fever — wait until you feel better; or
- if you are or may be pregnant — talk to your doctor before you start becoming more active.

PLEASE NOTE: If your health changes so that you then answer YES to any of the above questions, tell your fitness or health professional. Ask whether you should change your physical activity plan.

<u>Informed Use of the PAR-Q:</u> The Canadian Society for Exercise Physiology, Health Canada, and their agents assume no liability for persons who undertake physical activity, and if in doubt after completing this questionnaire, consult your doctor prior to physical activity.

No changes permitted. You are encouraged to photocopy the PAR-Q but only if you use the entire form.

NOTE: If the PAR-Q is being given to a person before he or she participates in a physical activity program or a fitness appraisal, this section may be used for legal or administrative purposes.

"I have read, understood, and completed this questionnaire. Any questions I had were answered to my full satisfaction."

NAME _____

SIGNATURE _____ DATE _____

SIGNATURE OF PARENT _____ WITNESS _____
or GUARDIAN (for participants under the age of majority)

Note: This physical activity clearance is valid for a maximum of 12 months from the date it is completed and becomes invalid if your condition changes so that you would answer YES to any of the seven questions.

 CSEP | SCPE
THE GOLD STANDARD IN EXERCISE
SCIENCE AND PERSONAL TRAINING

© Canadian Society for Exercise Physiology www.csep.ca/forms

From *Physical Activity Readiness Questionnaire* (PAR-Q) © 2002. Reprinted with permission from the Canadian Society for Exercise Physiology. www.csep.ca/forms.asp.

Physical Readiness for Sports or Vigorous Training

Answer the PAR-Q before using this chart. If you had one or more "yes" answers, follow the directions for the PAR-Q concerning consulting with a physician. If you had all "no" answers on the PAR-Q, answer the additional questions below before beginning intensive training, especially for sports.

If your answer to any of these questions is "yes," then you should consult with your personal physician to determine if you have a potential problem with vigorous involvement in physical activity.

Yes	No	Question
☐	☐	1. Do you plan to participate on an organized team that will play intense competitive sports (i.e., varsity team)?
☐	☐	2. If you plan to participate in a contact sport (even on a less organized basis), such as football, boxing, rugby, or hockey, have you been knocked unconscious more than one time?
☐	☐	3. Do you currently have pain from a previous muscle injury?
☐	☐	4. Do you currently have symptoms from a previous back injury, or do you experience back pain as a result of involvement in physical activity?
☐	☐	5. Do you have any other symptoms during physical activity that give you reason to be concerned about your health?

✓ Planning for Healthy Living

Use the Healthy Living Plan worksheet to set goals to improve your physical activity readiness, or revisit the Healthy Living Plan worksheet from the chapter on physical activity: health and fitness basics, and update it with more detailed information. You can use the Physical Activity Pyramid (figure 11.5) to help you in this process.

Lesson 11.2
Physical Activity Guidelines and Attitudes

Lesson Objectives

After reading this lesson, you should be able to

1. describe the types of activities in the Physical Activity Pyramid and the FIT formula for each,
2. identify some of the activity options from the pyramid for inclusion in your plan,
3. describe how energy balance relates to maintaining a healthy body composition, and
4. describe several positive and negative attitudes toward activity and explain how they relate to being active or sedentary.

Lesson Vocabulary

anaerobic activity, attitude, energy balance, 1-repetition maximum (1RM), progressive resistance exercise (PRE), proprioceptive neuromuscular facilitation (PNF), weekend warrior

Established physical activity guidelines indicate that teens should get 60 minutes or more of physical activity on each day of the week. This daily activity should be of moderate to vigorous intensity, and vigorous activity should be performed at least three days a week. In addition, on at least two days a week, you should perform activities designed to build your muscle fitness. Exercises can be modified for special conditions such as asthma, injury or disability, diabetes, and so on. Consult with your medical professional for ways to modify exercises.

The Physical Activity Pyramid (figure 11.5) identifies five types of physical activity. The FITT formula stands for frequency, intensity, time, and type of physical activity. Here, the pyramid takes care of activity type, so this lesson looks at each of the five types simply in terms of frequency, intensity, and time (FIT). Each type has its own FIT formula and provides unique and specific benefits. The amount of physical activity you do depends on the type of activity that you perform. The following sections of this lesson present guidelines for performing each type of physical activity in the pyramid. In addition, you can use the FIT formula for each type of activity in the pyramid to help you determine areas of need for your personal physical activity plan. The pyramid also provides you with various options of activity to consider when planning.

 Walking is [humanity's] best medicine.

—Hippocrates

Moderate Physical Activity

Moderate physical activity, represented in the pyramid's first step, is performed by more people than any other type of activity in the pyramid. It's popular because it provides many health and wellness benefits with a relatively low amount of effort. Walking, for example, is a moderate physical activity that is also the most popular of all forms of physical activity. Consider these guidelines as you do moderate physical activity.

1. **Adhere to the FIT formula** (see the box by step 1 in the pyramid). Moderate activity should be performed on all or most days of the week and is included as part of the recommended 30 to 60 (or more) minutes of daily activity.

2. **Choose activities that are at least equal in intensity to brisk walking.** Less intense activities are considered to be light activity. Such activities are better than none at all, but not as good as moderate activity.

Energy balance

Energy out
(Activity)

Energy in
(Diet)

F = 3+ days per week
I = Stretch overload
T = 10-30 sec, 2-4 reps of major muscle groups*

STEP 5
Flexibility exercises
• Stretching exercises
• Yoga
• Gymnastics

F = 2-3 days per week
I = Muscle overload
T = 8-12 reps, 2-4 sets of major muscle groups*

STEP 4
Muscle fitness exercises
• Resistance training
• Calisthenics
• Wall climbing
• Plyometrics

F = 3+ days per week
I = Reach target heart rate
T = At least 20 min/day*

STEP 3
Vigorous sport and recreation
• Play sports (e.g., tennis, soccer)
• Skating
• Skiing
• Dancing

F = 3+ days per week
I = Reach target heart rate
T = At least 20 min/day*

STEP 2
Vigorous aerobics
• Jog
• Aerobic dance
• Bike
• Swim
• Stair stepper

F = Daily
I = Equal to brisk walking
T = At least 30-60 min/day*

STEP 1
Moderate physical activity
• Walk
• Do yardwork
• Go bowling
• Do active household chores

*For teens, at least 60 minutes of moderate to vigorous activity is recommended each day. Activities from the pyramid can be combined to meet this recommendation.

Avoid inactivity

FIGURE 11.5 The Physical Activity Pyramid.
Source: C.B. Corbin.

3. **Consider lifestyle activities.** Lifestyle activities are moderate activities done as part of normal daily living. Examples include yardwork, moderate housework (e.g., mopping), and walking to the store or to school.

4. **Consider moderate sport and recreational activities.** Many sports and some recreational activities are considered to be vigorous. Others, however, are considered to be moderate; examples include golf, bowling, slow-pitch softball, recreational biking, and fishing.

Vigorous Aerobics

Vigorous aerobic activities are represented in the second step of the pyramid. *Aerobic* means "with oxygen," so aerobic activity refers to activity during which your body can supply adequate oxygen to continue for an extended time. **Anaerobic activity**, on the other hand, is activity that you can perform for only about 30 seconds because it is so vigorous that your body cannot provide enough oxygen for you to continue longer. An example of anaerobic

Walking is a moderate physical activity that is also the most popular of all forms of physical activity.

totti/fotolia.com

activity is the 100-meter dash. We can run at maximal speed for a few seconds, but we can't maintain it for very long.

Vigorous aerobic activities are more intense than moderate activities—but not so intense as to be anaerobic. They provide benefits similar to those of moderate activity but are especially good for building cardiorespiratory endurance and health. Consider these guidelines as you do vigorous aerobic physical activities.

1. **Adhere to the FIT formula** (see the box by step 2 in the pyramid). On at least three days a week, do vigorous activity (e.g., vigorous aerobics) as part of the daily 60 (or more) minutes of recommended activity.

2. **Choose activities that are more intense than brisk walking—but not so intense that you cannot perform them continuously for at least 20 minutes.** You can use your heart rate to determine the intensity of your activity. You can also use an established formula to determine your own target heart rate zone. In general, the target heart rate zone for teens (13 to 18 years old) ranges from 125 to 175 beats per minute.

3. **Consider all types of aerobic activity.** Unlike many sports and some other forms of vigorous recreation, vigorous aerobic activities are typically done continuously. Some of the most popular forms are jogging, aerobic dance, biking, swimming, skating, and backpacking. However, any type of aerobic activity done with adequate intensity provides fitness, health, and wellness benefits.

Aerobic dance is especially good for building cardiorespiratory endurance and health.

4. **Aim for bouts of activity that last at least 10 minutes each.** When performing vigorous aerobic activity, bouts of 10 minutes or longer are recommended for optimal fitness, health, and wellness benefits. Thus two bouts of 10 minutes are equivalent to one bout of 20 minutes.

5. **Avoid being a "weekend warrior."** The term **weekend warrior** refers to people who do no regular physical activity on most days of the week, then do a lot of activity on one day (typically a weekend day). This pattern of activity is discouraged (to find out why, see this chapter's Living Well News feature). The American College of Sports Medicine recommends that you perform vigorous activity on at least three days a week.

Vigorous Sport and Recreation

Vigorous sport and recreation activities are presented in the third step of the pyramid. Unlike vigorous aerobic activity, which is continuous (e.g., jogging, aerobic dance), vigorous sport involves spurts of very vigorous activity (anaerobic activity) followed by rest periods. For example, basketball players sprint up and down the court but rest during free throws and time-outs. Examples of vigorous recreational activity include kayaking and skiing. Some of these may involve spurts of anaerobic activity (e.g., kayaking) but many do not (e.g., hiking). Vigorous sport and recreation activities provide benefits similar to those of vigorous aerobic activity when appropriate guidelines are followed.

1. **Adhere to the FIT formula** (see the box by step 3 in the pyramid). On at least three days a week, do vigorous activity (e.g., vigorous sport or recreation), as part of the daily 60 (or more) minutes of recommended activity.

2. **Perform activities of adequate intensity.** The activities must keep your heart rate in the target zone (generally, 125 to 175 beats per minute for teens) for most of the time during the activity. Your heart rate may go higher at times because of spurts of very vigorous activity; it may also drop below the target zone during rest period (e.g., time-outs).

3. **Consider all vigorous sport and recreation activities.** Popular forms of vigorous sport include tennis, basketball, volleyball, and soccer. Popular recreation activities include hiking and mountain biking. Various other sport and recreation activities can provide similar benefits.

4. **Avoid being a weekend warrior.** As with vigorous aerobic activity, this pattern is discouraged (see the Vigorous Aerobics section for more detail).

Vigorous sport and recreation activities provide benefits similar to those of vigorous aerobic activity when appropriate guidelines are followed.

Suprijono Suharjoto/fotolia.com

Muscle Fitness Exercises

Activities for building muscle fitness are typically referred to as exercises because they are designed specifically to build strength, power, and muscular endurance. Of course, they also provide health and wellness benefits (e.g., heart health, healthy bones). Here are some guidelines for doing muscle fitness exercise.

1. **Adhere to the FIT formula** (see the box by step 4 in the pyramid).

2. **Allow rest days between muscle fitness workouts.** The proper frequency of muscle fitness exercise is two or three days a week. Your muscles need about 48 hours to recover in order for your next workout to be effective.

3. **Consider a 1RM test for determining exercise intensity.** The term **1-repetition maximum (1RM)** refers to the amount of resistance you can overcome (the weight you can lift) in one maximum lift. You may want to consult your instructor about estimating your 1RM for specific muscle groups. You can then set appropriate intensity for your muscle fitness exercises as a percentage of 1RM (use a higher percentage to build strength than to build muscular endurance). If a 1RM test is not possible, begin with a low resistance. Gradually increase resistance until you experience fatigue (but not failure to perform) at the end of the last repetition of your last exercise set.

4. **Use sets and repetitions (reps) when determining the time of muscle fitness exercise.** For moderate and vigorous activities, you use time in minutes to determine the length of a workout. For muscle fitness exercises, you determine time by means of sets and repetitions. A repetition (rep) refers to performing an exercise one time; for example, 1 push-up is 1 repetition. Performing a series of repetitions constitutes a set. So performing 10 push-ups followed by a rest is one set. The number of sets ranges from one to four, depending on your personal goals and the part of muscular fitness you want to develop. Repetitions range from 10 to 25 for most people. For strength, perform fewer reps with higher resistance; for muscular endurance, perform more reps with lower resistance. Consult your instructor for more information.

5. **Progressively increase resistance (intensity) as you improve.** Exercises for building muscle fitness are called **progressive resistance exercises (PREs).** You determine intensity for PRE based on a percentage of your 1RM. Beginners use 50 to 70 percent, intermediates use 60 to 80 percent, and advanced use 70 to 85 percent of 1RM. As your fitness improves, you gradually (progressively) increase the resistance.

6. **Perform exercises for all major muscle groups.** See the book's chapter on understanding your body.

Muscle fitness exercises are designed specifically to build strength, power, and muscular endurance and they also provide health and wellness benefits.

7. **Consider a variety of progressive resistance exercises.** The most common types of PRE are resistance machines, free weights (barbells, dumbbells), calisthenics (push-ups, curl-ups), exercise bands (elastic band exercises), isometrics (static contractions), plyometrics (jumping activities), and isokinetics (exercises using special machines).

8. **Learn to perform exercises properly.** Here are some of the more important guidelines for proper PRE: lift at a moderate speed (not too fast), use smooth and steady movements, and exercise through a full range of joint movement (e.g., don't go only part of the way up or down when doing a biceps exercise). Learn good technique from an expert, such as your physical education teacher.

9. **Use a spotter for safety.** A spotter stands by when you do PRE to make sure that you are doing the exercise correctly and to help you if you lose control while doing an exercise. A spotter is especially important when using free weights.

10. **Do not compete when doing muscle fitness exercises.** Competition encourages incorrect form and leads to using inappropriate weights or amounts of resistance.

🔊 HEALTHY COMMUNICATION

Look over the types of physical activity found in the pyramid as described in this chapter. Select one that you think is especially important for your personal overall health. Find a classmate or classmates who selected a different type of activity and debate your perspectives. Support your opinion with facts and respect the opinions of others.

Flexibility Exercises

Like muscle fitness exercises, activities for building flexibility are typically referred to as exercises, but of course they also provide health and wellness benefits (e.g., back health, good posture). Here are some guidelines for doing flexibility exercises.

1. **Adhere to the FIT formula** (see the box by step 5 in the pyramid).

2. **Stretch your muscles and tendons to improve flexibility.** If you have good flexibility, you can move each joint through a full range of motion. On the other hand, if your muscles and tendons (tissues that connect muscles to bones) are too short, your range of motion is reduced. Appropriate stretching increases your muscle and tendon length and thus improves your range of motion. For optimal benefits, stretch to a longer-than-normal length—to a point of tension but not pain.

3. **Consider a variety of flexibility exercises.** The most common flexibility exercises are static stretch, in which you stretch and hold for at least 15 seconds; **proprioceptive neuromuscular facilitation (PNF)**, in which you contract the muscle, then do a static stretch for at least 15 seconds; dynamic stretch, which involves movement during the stretch; and ballistic stretch (bouncing stretch). Flexibility can also be improved through various activities, including yoga, tai chi, and gymnastics. Each has its advantages and disadvantages.

4. **Flexibility exercises can be performed daily.** Exercises for flexibility can be performed daily and should be performed on at least three days a week.

Flexibility can also be improved through various activities, including ballet, yoga, tai chi, and gymnastics.

5. **Use sets and repetitions (reps) to determine the time of flexibility exercise.** For static stretch, each rep is held for 15 to 30 seconds. For stretches involving movement, reps typically range from 10 to 15 in either two or three sets.

6. **Perform exercises for all of your major muscle groups and joints.**

7. **Learn to perform exercises properly.** Here are some of the more important guidelines for proper flexibility exercise: avoid overstretching, avoid dangerous exercises (e.g., deep knee bends, back arching, excessive flexion), avoid stretching injured muscles, and use care when doing ballistic stretching. Learn good technique from an expert, such as your physical education teacher.

Exercise for Healthy Body Composition

All types of physical activity presented in the pyramid can contribute to healthy body composition—that is, a healthy proportion of muscle and fat. All types of exercise expend calories, so they all play a role in **energy balance**. The figure at the top of the Physical Activity Pyramid illustrates the need for balance between the energy you expend in physical activity (i.e., energy out or calories expended) and the energy you consume in food (i.e., energy in or calorie intake). Energy balance is critical to maintaining a healthy weight and healthy amount of body fat. Here are some specific guidelines.

1. **Consider moderate activities.** Moderate physical activities (step 1 of the pyramid), such as walking, are especially effective in helping you maintain a healthy body weight because they're popular and relatively easy. In fact, walking is the top activity (chosen by 52 percent) of participants in the National Weight Control Registry (NWCR), who have all maintained a healthy weight for a long time.

2. **Consider vigorous activities**. Vigorous activities (steps 2 and 3 of pyramid) are good options for many people because they expend more calories than moderate activities do in the same period of time. People who have maintained a healthy weight throughout life often cite aerobic dance, vigorous sport, and swimming as regular activities. Less popular but still common choices include jogging,

running on a treadmill, long-distance biking, and stair stepping. One advantage of vigorous activity is that it elevates your metabolism to expend more calories, and that elevation continues for several hours after exercise.

3. **Consider muscle fitness activities.** Because muscle burns more calories at rest than fat does, more muscular people expend more calories at rest. This is one reason that NWCR members list muscle fitness training as a primary activity. In fact, progressive resistance exercise has increased dramatically among NWCR members in recent years.

4. **Balance the calories in what you eat with the calories you expend in activity.** The most recent version of the Dietary Guidelines for Americans points out the importance of energy balance in maintaining a healthy weight.

Muscle fitness exercises help build lean body mass which burns more calories at rest.
Photodisc

Prepare a Plan

Once you have determined your needs (i.e, if you meet the FIT formula for each step in the pyramid) and have considered options for activity from the pyramid, set some personal goals, select activities from the options you have available, and prepare a written plan. Try out the plan. Evaluate and revise after you try it.

Attitudes Toward Physical Activity

Exercise psychologists have been studying physical activity for years; as part of that work, they use surveys to determine how people feel about physical activity. Another word for your feelings about something is **attitude**. We all have attitudes about a wide variety of topics—for example, food, school subjects, and physical activity. In fact, active people have more positive attitudes in general. If you follow certain guidelines (addressed in this chapter's Skills for Healthy Living feature), you can improve your positive attitudes and get rid of negative ones.

Improving Positive Attitudes

The following list presents some reasons that people like to be physically active. Think about these attitudes and how you might make some of them your own.

"Physical activities are a great way to meet people." Many activities provide opportunities to meet people and strengthen friendships. For example, aerobic dance and team sports are good social activities.

"I think physical activity is really fun." Many teenagers do activities simply because they're fun. Participating in activities you enjoy also helps you reduce stress.

"I enjoy the challenge." When the famous mountain climber George Mallory was asked why he climbed Mount Everest, he replied, "Because it's there." Many people welcome a challenge.

"I like the rigor of training." Some people enjoy doing intense training. For these people, competition and winning can be secondary to training.

"I like competition." If you enjoy competition, sport and other physical activities provide ways to test yourself against others. You can even compete against yourself by trying to improve your score or time in an activity.

"Physical activities are my way of relaxing." Physical activity can help you relax mentally and emotionally after a difficult day—for example, a day of demanding schoolwork.

"I think physical activity improves my appearance." Physical activity can help you build muscle and control body fat. Remember, though, that even regular activity cannot completely change your appearance.

"Physical activity is a good way to improve my health and wellness." As you've learned from this book, regular physical activity helps you resist illness and improves your general sense of well-being.

"Physical activity just makes me feel good." Many people just feel better when they exercise, and many have a sense of loss or discomfort when they don't exercise.

Changing Negative Attitudes

The following list shows you some negative attitudes, along with suggestions for turning them into positive ones. To decrease any negative attitudes you may have, give some thought to the suggested alternative for it.

Negative: "I don't have the time."

Positive: "I will plan a time for physical activity." If you planned time for physical activity, you would feel better, function more efficiently, and therefore have more time to do other things you want to do. Also, you can take the stairs instead of elevators, walk or bike to school or the store, stretch while watching television, and so on.

Negative: "I don't want to get all sweaty."

Positive: "I'll allow time to clean up afterward." Sweating is a natural by-product of a good workout. Allow yourself time to change before exercising and to shower and change afterward. Focus on how good you'll feel.

Negative: "People might laugh at me."

Positive: "I'm not going to dwell on what people might think. Besides, when they see how fit I get, they might wish they were exercising too." Find friends who are interested in getting fit. Anyone who does laugh may simply be jealous of your efforts and results.

Physical activity can be a great way to meet new people.

Negative: "None of my friends work out, so neither do I."

Positive: "I'll ask friends to join me, and we'll work out together." Talk with your friends. Some of them may be interested in working out or doing lifestyle activities together.

Negative: "I get nervous and feel tense when I play sports and games."

Positive: "Everyone gets nervous sometimes. I'll try to stay calm and do the best I can." Many athletes need to learn techniques to reduce their stress level. You can learn them, too (see this book's chapter on stress management).

Negative: "I'm already in good condition."

Positive: "Physical activity will help me stay in good condition." Do the self-assessments in this book, then take an honest look at yourself. Are you as fit as you thought? Physical activity can help you get in shape *and* stay in shape.

Negative: "I'm too tired."

Positive: "I'll just do a little to get started, then as I get more fit I'll do more." You'll probably find that once you get started, physical exertion gives you *more* energy. Begin realistically, then gradually increase the amount of activity you do.

Comprehension Check

1. What are some of the types of activities in the Physical Activity Pyramid and what is the FIT formula for each?
2. What are some of the activity options from the pyramid that you can consider for inclusion in your personal plan?
3. What is *energy balance* and how does it relate to maintaining a healthy body composition?
4. What are several positive and negative attitudes toward activity and how do they relate to being active or sedentary?

Most people have some positive attitudes and some negative attitudes toward physical activity. Active people have more positive attitudes than negative attitudes.

"Allen, I don't want to play tennis now," said Matt, as he put down his tennis racket and walked into the family room. "Anyway, there's a good show on TV."

Allen followed him. "I think you just don't want to lose again."

"You're right," Matt admitted. "I hate losing."

"You win sometimes, Matt. The competition is what makes tennis fun."

"Not when I lose," Matt replied.

Allen thought for a minute. "How about taking a jog around the block?" he asked. "There'll be no winner or loser that way."

"I don't want to get all sweaty," Matt replied. "I'd rather relax watching TV."

"Oh, come on, Matt. Jogging will help you relax. We need to stay in shape."

Matt paused, then smiled at Allen. "I'm thinking about it."

For Discussion

What does Allen like about being physically active? What does Matt like—and not like—about physical activity? How could Matt change his negative attitudes and become more active? What would be one short-term benefit Matt would experience by changing his attitude? What about a long-term benefit? What are some positive attitudes that help people stay active? Consider the guidelines presented in this chapter's Skills for Healthy Living feature.

SKILLS FOR HEALTHY LIVING: Changing Attitudes

Most of us have had both positive and negative attitudes toward physical activity at one time or another. Experts have shown that people with more positive attitudes than negative ones are likely to be active. Use the following guidelines to build positive attitudes and get rid of negative ones.

- **Assess your attitudes.** Make a list of your positive and negative attitudes. You can use the ones described in this lesson to help you make your list.

- **Identify reasons for negative attitudes.** Your self-assessment will help you identify any negative attitudes you hold. Ask yourself why you feel negatively about physical activity. If you can find the reason, it may help you change. For example, you may not have liked playing a sport when you were young because you didn't like a particular coach or player. Maybe you can now find a situation that will make an activity more fun. Consider the alternatives to negative attitudes presented in this chapter.

- **Find activities that bring out fewer negative attitudes.** People have different attitudes and feelings about different activities. For example, maybe you don't like team sports but you do enjoy recreational activities. List your negative attitudes, then ask yourself, "Are there activities that you like?" If so, consider trying them.

- **Choose activities that accentuate the positive.** If you really like certain activities and feel good about them, focus on these activities rather than ones you don't like as much.

- **Change the situation.** You may feel negatively about an activity because of things unrelated to the activity. For example, if you hated playing basketball because you had too little time to get dressed and groomed after participating, maybe you can find a situation in which you can do the activity and also have more time to shower and dress.

- **Be active with friends.** Activities can be more fun when you do them with friends. Sometimes just participating with other people you like is enough to change your feelings about an activity.

- **Discuss your attitudes.** Sometimes it helps just to talk about your attitudes. People sometimes think that they're the only ones who have problems in certain situations. Talking about it with others can relieve stress and help you change the situation to make it more fun for everyone concerned.

- **Help others build positive attitudes.** The ways in which others react can affect a person's feelings about physical activity. This means that your positive reactions might help others change negative feelings about physical activity. Consider the following suggestions when you interact with others in physical activity.

  ○ **Instead of laughing, provide encouragement.** Do you remember how difficult it is to start something new or different? You can encourage others by saying things like, "Good to see you exercising. Way to go!"

  ○ **Try to make new friends through participation in physical activities.** Introduce yourself to others and offer to help other people when it seems appropriate.

  ○ **Don't hesitate to ask for help from others.** Start or join a sport or exercise club at school. An activity club can be a great way for you and your friends to combine socializing with physical activity. Check with your school's activity coordinator about any applicable rules.

  ○ **Be sensitive to people with special needs.** Some people need certain accommodations or modifications when performing physical activity. People with no special needs can help by participating with those who have special challenges and by being sensitive to their needs.

  ○ **Be considerate of cultural differences.** The popularity of physical activities varies from culture to culture. What is popular in one culture is not necessarily popular in another. For example, field hockey and curling are not popular in the United States but are very popular in some other countries. Similarly, what one person enjoys may not be so enjoyable to another. Learning to accept cultural and personal differences helps all people enjoy activity and contributes to better interpersonal understanding.

ACADEMIC CONNECTION: Understanding Quartiles

Various statistics can be used to describe scores for a group of people. The term *quartile* is used to describe the scores for each quarter or one quarter of a distribution. In the following example, each number represents a score (in inches) on the waist girth test for 36 different 15-year-old females. The distribution is divided into quartiles (25 percent of scores per quartile, listed in different colors).

A good fitness rating for waist girth for 15-year-old females is 32 inches or less. Which quartile includes scores for the good fitness range (indicate color)? What percentage of girls were in the good fitness zone for waist girth? What percentage of girls had scores that did not qualify them to be in the good fitness zone? Is the average waist girth for this group a healthy score?

Distribution of Waist Girth Scores (Inches) for 15-Year-Old Females

					34											
				33	34	35										
			32	33	34	35	36									
	28		30	32	33	34	35	36	37	38	39	40				
27	28	29	30	32	33	34	35	36	37	38	39	40	41	42	43	

Is Being a Weekend Warrior Bad for Your Health?

More than a few people don't do regular activity during the week but play a full game of soccer or run a 5K race on the weekend (see figure 11.6). These people are referred to as "weekend warriors." Exercising vigorously once a week or less can increase your risk of injury, according to Dr. Jeffrey Spang of the UNC School of Medicine. In fact, according to the U.S. Centers for Disease Control and Prevention, more than 10,000 Americans visit an emergency room for a sport- or exercise-related injury every day. Injuries can happen to weekend warriors of all ages and fitness levels but are most likely among those over age 30. The most common injuries are muscle strain, tendonitis, and Achilles tendon injuries.

According to Spang, many people hurt themselves when they have been inactive and then suddenly take on a major exercise program, such as training for a marathon. Spang states, "The most common mistake is to get out there and to do too much, too fast." It is common for people to get injured in the first few training sessions and then they are unable to train again for a while. A better plan is to break your sessions into smaller, more frequent increments and to avoid exercising too much, too soon. Spang also states, "Gradually increase the amount that you're working out—and the intensity level—on a week-to-week basis." Following the FIT formula for each type of activity in the pyramid during the week will help prevent injury and maximize performance. "It is important to build up gradually and give your body recovery time," said Spang.

For Discussion

Do you know any people who are weekend warriors? If so, what do they do? Why do you think people engage in weekend warrior activities? How might a person's work, family life, and friends contribute to them becoming a weekend warrior?

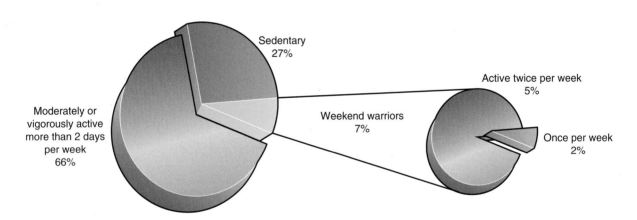

Figure 11.6 Weekend warriors compared to sedentary and active populations.

Reviewing Concepts and Vocabulary

As directed by your teacher, answer items 1 through 5 by correctly completing each sentence with a word or phrase.

1. The seven questions used to determine readiness for physical activity are called the _____.

2. The two factors used to determine the heat index are _____ and _____.

3. One measure you can use to determine whether it's too cold to exercise is the _____ factor.

4. Symptoms of frostbite include _____.

5. The level of pollution can be determined using the _____ _____ _____.

For items 6 through 10, as directed by your teacher, match each term in column 1 with the appropriate phrase in column 2.

6. 1-repetition max
7. progressive resistance exercise
8. energy balance
9. hypothermia
10. PNF

a. exercises for building muscle fitness

b. form of stretching in which you contract the muscle, then do a static stretch for 15 or more seconds

c. amount of resistance you can overcome (weight lifted) in one maximum lift

d. extremely low body temperature

e. calories in equal calories out

For items 11 through 15, as directed by your teacher, respond to each statement or question.

11. Describe the five steps in the Physical Activity Pyramid.
12. What is the FIT formula for moderate physical activity?
13. How do vigorous aerobics and vigorous sport and recreation differ?
14. What are two guidelines to consider when doing muscle fitness exercise?
15. Identify two examples of a negative attitude and describe how you would try to change them.

Thinking Critically

Write a paragraph to answer the following question.

How does having positive attitudes affect a person's physical activity level and choices?

Take It Home

Share what you've learned about exercising in hot and cold weather with a family member. Work together to identify important steps you can take to prevent cold- and heat-related illnesses. Consider your unique circumstances (e.g., the climate where you live, the types of activity you engage in). Make a list of at least five prevention strategies that you and your family can use.

Valeriy Pistryy/fotolia.com

12

Stress Management

 Student Web Resources
www.healthforlifetextbook.org/student

EastWest Imaging/fotolia

Lesson 12.1

Understanding and Avoiding Stress

Lesson Objectives

After reading this lesson, you should be able to

1. explain how the body responds to stress,
2. identify the positive and negative aspects of stress, and
3. understand how different people can react differently to the same stressor.

Lesson Vocabulary

assertiveness, distress, eustress, fight-or-flight response, stressor

When someone asks how you're feeling, do you ever answer by saying that you're stressed or "stressed out"? Do you ever feel like there are too many demands on your time? Do you worry about your performance on tests and homework? Everyone experiences stress, and the teenage years can be particularly stressful. This lesson introduces you to the concept of stress and discusses how the body reacts to stress. Understanding stress, its causes, and its symptoms can help you learn to manage it more effectively.

Understanding Stress

Stress is the body's reaction to a difficult or demanding situation. Renowned stress researcher Hans Selye defined stress as the "nonspecific response of the body to any demand or change." Selye named this response the general adaptation syndrome. His theory (see figure 12.1) described the general way in which all people respond when they experience a **stressor**—something that causes or contributes to stress. Stressors can be physical (e.g., pain, thirst, hunger, illness), emotional (e.g., worry, fear, anger, love), or social (e.g., relationships). Some stressors—for example, flying, taking a test, speaking in public, and facing schedule or financial demands—are common among most people. Others vary by the individual. People tend to be stressed whenever a situation feels out of their control—when they feel that they don't have the ability to cope with or manage the situation effectively. Regardless of the particular stressor, the general adaptation syndrome is the set of physiological reactions we all experience in response to stress.

The first stage of the general adaptation syndrome is the alarm reaction. Any stressor that you experience starts your body's alarm response (see figure 12.2), also known as the stress response or the **fight-or-flight response**. The term *fight-or-flight* reflects the fact that these physiological changes prepare the body to either engage in a physical fight

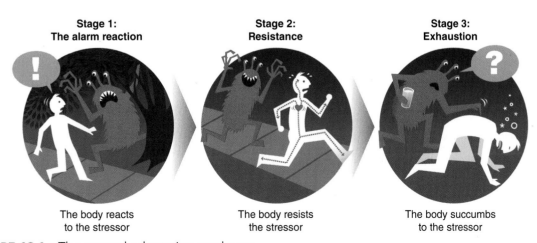

Stage 1: The alarm reaction	Stage 2: Resistance	Stage 3: Exhaustion
The body reacts to the stressor	The body resists the stressor	The body succumbs to the stressor

FIGURE 12.1 The general adaptation syndrome.

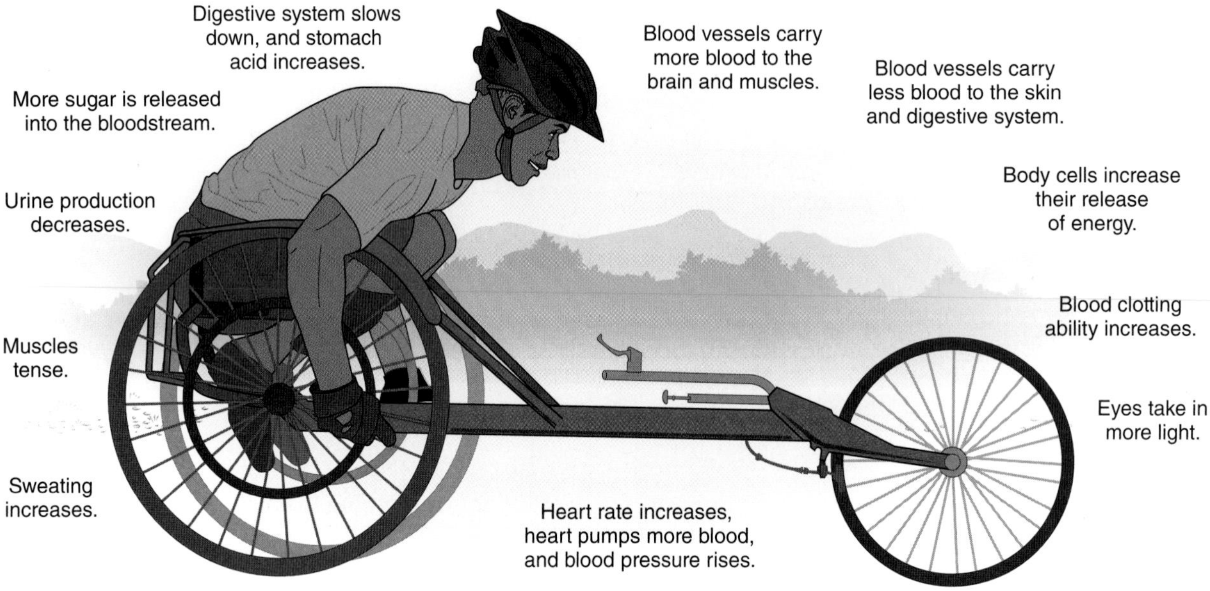

FIGURE 12.2 The stress response.

Labels on figure:
- Digestive system slows down, and stomach acid increases.
- More sugar is released into the bloodstream.
- Urine production decreases.
- Muscles tense.
- Sweating increases.
- Blood vessels carry more blood to the brain and muscles.
- Blood vessels carry less blood to the skin and digestive system.
- Body cells increase their release of energy.
- Blood clotting ability increases.
- Eyes take in more light.
- Heart rate increases, heart pumps more blood, and blood pressure rises.

or flee (run) from a stressful situation. Fighting and fleeing can be appropriate in some life-and-death situations. If a car is racing toward you, you need to flee—to get out of the way. If a big dog backs you into a corner, you may have no choice but to fight. In such circumstances, fleeing or fighting can save your life.

In modern society, most of our stressors are not immediately life threatening. Even so, your body acts as if you're preparing for a physical response: blood flows to your muscles, your pupils get bigger, your blood pressure increases, your heart beats faster, and your breathing rate goes up.

The second stage of the general adaptation syndrome is resistance. In this stage, your body works to resist or minimize the potential long-term effect of the stress response on your systems. If stress is not effectively managed, it can cause a wide range of negative symptoms (see table 12.1).

Extreme cases—in which the body is not able to effectively manage stress over a long time, or in which the stressor itself is ongoing or chronic—can lead to the exhaustion stage of the general adaptation syndrome. In this stage, illness and disease can occur. In fact, chronic stress can play a role in the development or progression of several diseases and disorders, including coronary heart disease, diabetes, depression, and Alzheimer's disease.

Stress and Performance

Though we often categorize all stress as negative stress, or **distress**, not all stress is bad. Stress can be a challenge that helps us learn, grow, and develop. Indeed, a certain amount of stress is desirable because it helps us be alert and prepares our bodies for optimal performance. This type of stress is called **eustress**, or positive stress.

TABLE 12.1   Effects of Stress on the Body

Type of impact	Symptoms
Cognitive	Headaches, insomnia, difficulty remembering things, inability to concentrate
Physiological	Increased heart rate, hypertension, gastrointestinal problems, frequent illness, increased respiratory rate, disruption of metabolism
Behavioral	Disrupted eating habits, grinding of teeth, hostility, increased use of substances, difficulty communicating with others, social isolation
Emotional	Crying, fatigue, anxiety, depression, hypervigilance, impulsiveness, irritability

Feeling some stress will motivate you to practice before your concert performance.

Photodisc

For example, if you're preparing for a big exam and you experience no stress at all, you might be lazy and lack the motivation to study. As a result, you might perform poorly. On the other hand, if you feel overly stressed—if you experience distress—you might have too much nervous energy to concentrate while studying or you might be unable to remember the things you did manage to study. In this situation, as in many others, an ideal amount of stress will optimize your performance. Feeling some stress will motivate you to study and heighten your brain function and your senses during the exam, thus allowing you to perform at your best. Figure 12.3 illustrates the relationship between stress and performance.

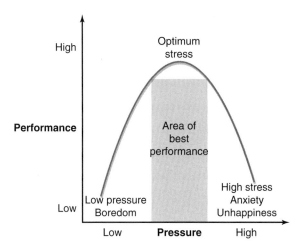

FIGURE 12.3 The relationship between stress and performance.

> **Stress is the spice of life; the absence of stress is death.**
>
> —Hans Selye, stress researcher

Sources of Stress

As you probably already know, you'll face many stressors during high school in particular and during your teenage years overall. The number one stress reported by middle and high school students is academic pressure (e.g., getting good grades, preparing for college). The second-leading source of stress reported among these groups involves relationships—with parents, romantic partners, and friends. Other commonly reported sources include financial concerns, responsibilities at home, body image struggles, peer pressure, popularity concerns, bullying (including cyberbullying), and criticism and disapproval. Though you can't always control the daily stressors you face as a teenager, you can learn to manage your emotional reactions in stressful situations, build your coping skills, and learn relaxation techniques that can help you minimize the effect of stress. In some ways stress is similar to pain. You are the one who experiences it and despite the saying "I feel your pain," you really don't. You can feel your own pain, but not the pain of others. Likewise, you perceive a stressor, but others may view the same situation in a very different manner. One person may see a snake and immediately run

Academic pressure is the number one stressor reported by middle and high school students.

Monkey Business - Fotolia.com

away; another person may see the same snake and want to pick it up and learn more about it. Previous knowledge and experience and coping skills will determine why two people react so differently to the same stimulus. The remainder of this lesson and all of the next lesson provide you with important information and help you learn skills that can help you better manage stressors in your life.

CONNECT

How much do you think peer pressure influences your individual stress level? What are the most common stressors you feel as a result of peer pressure? Explain each stressor and analyze how it affects your stress level.

Avoiding Stressful Situations

The next lesson addresses stress management techniques that can help you handle stressful situations—something we all need to be able to do. But sometimes the best thing you can do is avoid a stressor altogether. Skills that you can use to stay out of stressful situations include assertiveness, avoidance decision making, and time management.

Assertiveness

Has anyone ever sabotaged your studying by coaxing you to play video games or go to the mall instead? If so, you can benefit from learning to say no or offer a better alternative, such as "I'll meet up with you later after my homework is done." Doing so requires **assertiveness**—standing up for your own needs, interests, and desires. Assertiveness is not the same as aggressiveness. Both are direct forms of communication, but aggressive behavior is direct communication without regard for the rights and feelings of others, whereas assertive behavior is direct while respecting others. Passive behavior, in contrast, involves not standing up for your rights—for example, not doing or saying anything even when you believe someone is taking advantage of you.

Most people have to practice becoming assertive. People often mistakenly believe that being assertive means being rude. In reality, assertive behavior means simply and directly stating your feelings. For example, if a classmate asks you to lend him or her your homework, you can answer by saying, "That makes me feel uncomfortable. I can't do it." This is a direct and honest response. An aggressive response, on the other hand, would involve saying something like, "You're stupid. Do your own homework." And a passive person would likely give the homework to the classmate because he or she doesn't want to "cause trouble" or thinks something like, "If I don't give him my homework, he won't like me."

Remember—your feelings are your feelings, and you have a right to express them. This doesn't mean that you'll always get what you want, but at least it lets others know where you stand. Most people admire someone who can be honest and forthright in a respectful manner.

Like most things in life, being assertive gets easier with practice. It may seem uncomfortable at first, but you can practice assertive responses in front of a mirror when no one else is around. If you can't be assertive in a practice situation, it's unlikely that you'll be assertive in life situations. You might want to start with some easier scenarios, such as how you would respond if you ordered food and received the wrong order. A passive response would be to say nothing and accept the order as it is. An aggressive response would be to say something like, "Can't you get anything right? This is not what I ordered!" An assertive response would be something like, "This is not what I ordered. Would you please take it back and bring me my order?"

Developing assertiveness skills is one way you can avoid some of the potential stressors in your life. Being assertive helps you stand up for yourself and effectively defuse potential conflicts. As a result, it allows you to avoid getting yourself into situations that you don't want to be in.

Avoidance Decision Making

You can also avoid some situations simply by making smart choices. For example, if getting caught in heavy traffic causes you to feel stressed, you can try to run errands at less busy times of the day. If your

HEALTHY COMMUNICATION

What are some situations in which it's important to be assertive? What are some things that make a person assertive and not aggressive? Do you think assertive behavior is interpreted differently in males than in females? Support your opinions with facts and be respectful of others' opinions.

home environment is stressful and studying at home causes you stress, you might choose to study in the library before or after school. If you're at a park and see someone who makes you feel uncomfortable, you can choose to leave the park and go home. The key is to avoid getting yourself into situations that you know will be stressful and to remove yourself from situations that might become uncomfortable or stressful.

Time Management

Many stressors are related to time constraints—for example, being overscheduled, running late to an important meeting, and forgetting to study for an exam. All three are examples of how poor time management skills can create stressful situations that you might otherwise avoid. Teach yourself to take on the most important or pressing tasks first. For example, first do your homework that is due tomorrow, then tackle the big paper due in two weeks. If you're faced with a large or tedious task, break it down into smaller parts or spread the project over

HEALTH SCIENCE

Neuroscientists (scientists who study the brain) have documented the effects of stressful events on brain circuits and brain development. Stressful events experienced early in life can affect the brain's networks in ways that help or hurt how a person might react to stressful events later in life. Stressful or traumatic events can also inhibit the brain's reward system. This system normally makes us feel pleasure when, for example, we eat a nice meal or spend time with good friends. But individuals who undergo extreme stress, such as war veterans, often report a lack of pleasure from normal activities. Scientists are working to develop medications that can repair or mimic the reward system in order to more effectively treat mental health conditions that might result from stress.

Time management is a key to avoiding stressful situations.

diego cervo/fotolia.com

a longer period of time. If you have to memorize twenty new vocabulary words by next week, learn three words per day rather than trying to learn them all at once.

Other ways to decrease stress by managing your time effectively including making a list of things to do and keeping a schedule to organize your daily life. Even if you're the type of person who thrives on pressure and likes to press right up to a deadline, you'll find it beneficial to allow for the unexpected—the computer glitch, the traffic jam, the unexpected homework assignment. In this way, good time management can help you avoid stress and maximize your performance. For more information about time management, see this chapter's Skills for Healthy Living feature.

CONSUMER CORNER: Can Vitamins Really Reduce Stress?

Many vitamin and supplement products are marketed as helping people reduce or manage stress and its symptoms. Unfortunately, most of these claims are supported by little or no scientific evidence that they hold true in healthy individuals. The stress response can reduce some vitamin levels in the blood, and it is important to restore them to normal levels through either a healthy diet or a modest vitamin or multivitamin supplement. But no vitamin can keep stress out of your life, and the best way to reduce stress is to learn how to recognize its symptoms and causes and how to manage it through a variety of strategies like those presented later in this chapter.

If you're thinking of taking a vitamin to reduce stress (or for some other reason), are you assertive enough to discuss it with your personal health care professional or school nurse? When considering taking a vitamin, ask yourself the following questions.

- Does this vitamin offer a proven health benefit?
- Does the research support the use of this vitamin for people with my health status?
- Is this vitamin known to treat a medical condition or help prevent disease?
- What is the recommended dose for this vitamin?
- When and for how long should I take this vitamin?

Comprehension Check

1. How does the body respond to stress?
2. What are the positive and negative aspects of stress?
3. Explain how the same situation might be a stressor to one person but not to another.

Indicate how frequently each of the following statements applies to you. Total the points associated with your responses to get your stress management score. Then use the descriptions accompanying the table to interpret your score.

SELF-ASSESSMENT QUESTIONNAIRE

	Rarely	Sometimes	Frequently	Always
I feel pressure to do things I don't really want to do.	1	2	3	4
I am anxious about doing well in my classes.	1	2	3	4
I feel like there's no one I can turn to who will understand how I feel.	1	2	3	4
I'm so busy, I rarely have time for myself.	1	2	3	4
I drink lots of caffeine to maintain my energy throughout the day.	1	2	3	4
I eat fast food that's not good for me because I don't have the time for anything else.	1	2	3	4
I cannot find the time or energy to enjoy the activities that are important to me.	1	2	3	4
I get less than six hours of sleep at night.	1	2	3	4
It is necessary to multitask to accomplish everything I need to do.	1	2	3	4
I feel guilty if I relax and do nothing.	1	2	3	4
My stress management score is _____.				

A score of 10 to 19 = lower risk. You have a low risk for stress-related health problems. Keep up the good work, but consider learning and practicing a stress management technique or two in case things change.

A score of 20 to 29 = moderate risk. You have a moderate risk for stress-related health problems. You should practice a stress management technique two or three days per week.

A score of 30 to 40 = higher risk. You are at high risk for stress-related health problems. It's time to make some changes. It would be great if you could practice a stress management technique on a daily basis.

Adapted, by permission, from American Hospital Association. Available: http://student.aahanet.org/eweb/dynamicpage.aspx?site=student&webcode=stressquiz.

✓ Planning for Healthy Living

Use the Healthy Living Plan worksheet to set goals and develop a plan to help you control and manage your stress through stress management techniques. Monitor the steps you take toward meeting your goals and repeat this self-assessment in one to three months to help determine the success of your plan.

Lesson 12.2

Stress Management Techniques

Lesson Objectives

After reading this lesson, you should be able to

1. describe a variety of stress management techniques,
2. explain how physical activity and exercise can help you manage stress, and
3. describe a method of practicing mindfulness.

 Lesson Vocabulary

asanas, biofeedback, mindfulness, reframing

Many methods are available to help you successfully manage stress. Some are mainly physical, and some are mostly mental, but the fact is that your mind and body are connected. What affects your mind affects your body, and what affects your body affects your mind. We tend to talk about mind and body as if they are totally separate, perhaps because we have separated them through our language—different words describe different parts, functions, and concepts. The reality, however, is that these parts, functions, and concepts often overlap or coordinate with each other. Therefore, learning stress management techniques helps your whole human system operate more efficiently. Stress management is a type of fine tuning that helps us better cope with the stressors of daily living.

Reframing

Because stress involves perception, one way to deal with it is to change your perception or reframe the situation. For example, if you think a teacher is being too hard on you, you might consider the possibility that the teacher is not picking on you but is devoting time to you because he or she thinks you can do better. Or, if you believe you have to dress like people in a certain group at school, you might consider the fact that it's more important to be who you are than what others might like you to be.

Of course, **reframing** doesn't always solve a problem. There are times when people are just plain mean spirited and you can't reframe them into being nicer. You can, however, reframe your response to mean people. You can practice not letting anger, vengefulness, or jealousy get the best of you. As the saying goes, when life gives you lemons, you can choose to make lemonade. For example, when you have to wait in a long line, instead of complaining about the wait, you can find a productive way to use your time—perhaps listening to your favorite song, reading a book, or practicing deep breathing.

Mindfulness

Mindfulness means being in the moment. Too often, our thoughts dwell on the past or on the future. Of course, we should learn from the past, and we should plan for the future, but many people seem to ignore the here and now. When is the last time you were lost in the moment, or when time seemed to stand still? These are examples of being mindful—times when you are fully present and immersed in a particular moment.

Mindfulness means being fully present and immersed in a particular moment.

Andres Rodriguez - Fotolia

One way to practice being mindful is to put a single raisin, grape, or sunflower seed in your mouth. Take a few minutes to explore the texture, the aroma, the feel, and the taste. More than likely, you will find this experience far different from your usual eating. In fact, in daily life, it's not unusual for people to eat without even noticing it, because they may be multitasking—watching TV, playing a video game, or texting while eating.

Although multitasking is common, we all need at least a little time each day when we can be more aware of what is going on in our bodies. Ask yourself, "Are my muscles tense? Am I breathing rapidly? Is my heart rate fast?" If so, you can consciously let go of the tension, slow down your breathing and lower your heart rate. They are all under your control, and the more you practice, the better you get at being in control and being in the moment. Sometimes we just need time to be, not do. As some popular motivational speakers like to say, "We are human beings, not human doings." Since we spend plenty of time doing, it's important to devote some time to just being.

Breathing

To a large extent, if you can control your breathing, you can control your stress. It may seem strange to pay attention to breathing; after all, you've been doing it all your life. But there are special kinds of breathing that can help you better handle stress. Practices that use breathing to manage stress include yoga, tai chi, and some types of meditation.

A good way to start using breathing as a stress management technique is to simply observe your breathing. Find a quiet place, sit in a comfortable position, and close your eyes. Now, just pay attention to five to ten cycles of your breathing. What did you notice? Did anything surprise you—for example, noticing a space between your inhalation and your exhalation? Did you feel silly? Did your thoughts wander? Did you notice whether or not you were breathing through your mouth or your nose? Was your breathing faster or slower than you expected?

Simply becoming aware of your breathing can help you focus. In addition, once you know how you normally breathe, you can experiment with a special kind of breathing called "so hum" breathing. To use this technique, say the word "soooo" (to yourself, not out loud) as you inhale (for the length of the inhalation) and say to yourself the word "hummmm" for the length of your exhalation. Even though it may seem strange to do this, after repeating the so hum breathing for several cycles, you will become more relaxed. And as with most things that are new, you'll find that the more you practice this type of breathing, the better you get at it—and the more in control of your stress you become.

Some people prefer to do this type of breathing by simply saying the "so" and the "hum" as just described. Others like to fill in the space between the inhalation and the exhalation with the word "and." Thus they say "soooo" internally on the inhalation, then "and" in the space between inhalation and exhalation, then "hummmm" on the exhalation, then "and" again, and so on. Try each method to see which you prefer. If you don't have allergies, asthma, or a cold, inhale through your nose and exhale through your mouth.

Another breathing technique used for stress reduction is called breath counting. It involves simply counting your exhalations, up to ten, then starting over. If your thoughts wander or you forget which breath you were on, just start over at one. It's very common to lose track or to find your thoughts wandering—and it's perfectly okay. Some people do this practice for as long as twenty minutes, but if you have less time, try five minutes. Like so hum breathing, it may seem a bit strange at first, but it is very relaxing to most people who give it a chance.

Practices that use breathing to manage stress include yoga, tai chi, and some types of meditation.

Guided Imagery

This practice involves allowing someone to guide you to a relaxing place in your mind. It is similar to controlled daydreaming. Using a prompt—whether it be a computer application, video game, podcast, digital audio recording, or skilled teacher—you can allow yourself to be led to a safe and relaxing place in your mind, no matter where you are. You can find many guided imagery programs and activities by doing a web search for the phrase "guided imagery." Although the word *imagery* suggests something visual to many people, guided imagery can also involve your other senses, as in the smell of a rose, the taste of chocolate, the feel of sand on your toes, or the sound of a gentle rain.

Body Scanning

Most people can manage their stress simply by scanning their body for any unwanted or unneeded tension. To try this technique, start from your head and end at your toes. Focus on the muscles of your forehead. Check for any unwanted or unneeded tension. You can wrinkle your forehead to see what your tension feels like, then consciously let go of it. You can follow this same pattern for other muscle groups. Next, for example, check the muscles around your closed eyes. When you find any unwanted or unneeded tension, let it go. Release it. Progress through your jaw muscles; your tongue muscles; your shoulder muscles; the muscles of your arms, hands, and fingers; your back muscles; the muscles of your chest and stomach; the muscles of your hip girdle (hips and buttocks); and, finally, the muscles of your legs, feet, and toes.

Physical Activity

Physical activity and exercise are natural mechanisms for managing stress. Taking a brisk walk or a jog, or doing some resistance or stretching exercises, or yoga or tai chi, can help your body balance the naturally occurring changes that result from the fight-or-flight response (see figure 12.2).

Noncompetitive physical activity, especially when done slowly (e.g., yoga), allows your body to return to its normal physiological state more quickly following stress.

For stress management purposes, deemphasize competition when engaging in physical activity. Competition causes stress in most people. This doesn't mean that you should always avoid competition, which actually meets other human needs. It just means that if you're exercising to relieve stress, it's better to stick to noncompetitive activities. Moderate physical activity performed a few hours before bedtime also helps you get to sleep.

Yoga

Yoga has been around for thousands of years, and in recent years it has become very popular in the United States. Yoga positions (**asanas**) use sustained stretching to help people become more flexible; as a result, many people use yoga as a type of exercise. However, yoga is much more than a stretching exercise; some types of yoga also involve breathing and body awareness. Therefore, if you like to combine physical and mental types of stress management, you'll probably be attracted to yoga. Yoga classes are now available in many settings across the United States, including preschools; elementary, middle, and high schools; and colleges and universities. In addition, many businesses offer yoga classes or encourage their employees who work at desks or work stations to practice "desktop yoga" (i.e., yoga-like exercises that can be done while sitting at a desk) in order to reduce muscular tension.

Tai Chi

Tai chi chuan, usually referred to in the United States simply as tai chi, has been around for hundreds of years. It involves a series of movements performed in a slow, focused manner accompanied by deep breathing. It is a noncompetitive and self-paced system of gentle physical exercise and stretching. Each posture flows into the next without pause, ensuring that the body is in constant motion.

♥ HEALTH TECHNOLOGY

Many technological applications are now available to help people control stress. **Biofeedback** machines, for example, are very popular and range from very expensive to very inexpensive. These machines allow you to monitor body systems and functions such as muscular tension, heart rate, blood pressure, electrical conductance on the skin, skin temperature, and brain waves. The *bio* part of the name means life, and *feedback* means information—in this case, about your performance. So biofeedback machines measure your physiological (life) functions and give you information about them that can help you gain better control over your body in order to reduce stress. Some biofeedback devices look very much like medical devices, whereas others look more like video games. Biofeedback devices can be purchased through major online retailers.

⊙ CONNECT

Are you interested in trying biofeedback as a way to learn how to control your stress? What about this technology do you think would (or would not) help you?

Tai chi is a self-paced system of gentle physical exercise and stretching that keeps the body in constant motion.

EastWest Imaging

Comprehension Check

1. Describe two stress management techniques that do not involve physical activity.
2. Explain how physical activity and exercise can help you manage stress.
3. Describe a method of practicing mindfulness.

MAKING HEALTHY DECISIONS: Time Management

Alexis was one of those people who was always going from one commitment to the next. Her friends rarely saw her sitting still, and she often complained about having too much to do. Alexis played on the softball team and volunteered at her church on the weekends. She also helped out around the house with cleaning and cooking. When her friend Deborah asked her to go to yoga class together as a way to manage stress, she said, "I totally want to—it would be really great—but I just don't have any free time." Later in the conversation, Deborah noticed Alexis talking about TV shows she'd been watching and showing off a new video game she'd been playing. Deborah wondered if Alexis was as busy as she seemed to be. Deborah herself worked two jobs, was an honor student, ran cross country, and played in the school orchestra.

For Discussion

What could Deborah suggest that Alexis do to make time for yoga class? What could Deborah say to Alexis that might help her better understand her time management needs? To help you answer these questions, review this chapter's Skills for Healthy Living feature.

SKILLS FOR HEALTHY LIVING: Time Management

How you manage your time is an important part of your overall health. If you struggle with time management, you may have higher levels of stress and you may end up coping with your stress by engaging in destructive habits that seem to provide quick fixes, such as smoking or drinking alcohol. Poor time management can also interfere with your ability to create time for healthy pursuits, such as exercise.

Young people, like adults, often tend to book their schedules solid with work, school, errands, and other tasks they deem important. For example, you may be involved in a community organization, spend time tending to a school garden, play a sport, or care for an aging relative. The time you spend doing all of these activities is referred to as your committed time. What's left over is your free time. Learning to manage your free time can help you manage stress, avoid destructive habits, and make time for healthy habits. The following tips can help you with your time management:

- **Monitor your time.** Write down what you do during the course of each day. Record when you sleep, when you eat, when you're at school, when you're at work, and when you do all of the other things you do. Most people who track their use of time are surprised by the findings.
- **Evaluate your use of time.** Once you've tracked your time for several days, review your records to see how many hours you spend in various types of activities. For example, you can arrange all your activities into three categories: school and work, committed time, and free time. Then you can evaluate whether there is a good balance between the categories. Alternatively, you can think of all of your activities as fitting into three drawers: the lower drawer (not important or urgent), the middle drawer (important but not urgent), and the top drawer (urgent and important). If any drawer is overflowing, you may need to re-evaluate your commitments and priorities. Evaluating your time can help you decide whether you're using your time the way you want and need to use it. Having a lot of important and urgent things to do can add to your stress levels significantly.
- **Plan a schedule.** After you determine how much time you spend on various activities, work on creating a time management plan for yourself. Efficient time management means you get to do all the things you think are important so that you don't feel rushed or anxious, and it also allows you to make time for those things that you value, such as relaxation and recreational activities. Begin by blocking out your committed time (school, work, practice time). Then, make decisions about your free time.

When making decisions about your time, consider some of the following tips:

o First, schedule time for those things that are most important and most urgent (for example, an assignment worth a lot of points that is due tomorrow is important to your academic success and has a clear, time-sensitive deadline). It is typically better to allot more time than you think you might need to get these tasks done.

o Second, make a plan to complete those items that are important to you but may not be as urgent. Plan ahead and schedule in the time you need along the way. Most important, follow through with your plan so that you don't end up in a bind.

o Third, schedule in and plan time for yourself to do the things that you value (even when they don't seem important or urgent), such as exercising, reading a novel, or playing a musical instrument. Ensuring you are balanced and have the opportunities to relax and recover from the demands of life is critical to overall health. Often people do not take the time for these important activities unless they plan for them. It is also important to ensure that these activities do not interfere with obligations such as schoolwork.

o Finally, schedule some time every day for the unexpected. Meetings, appointments, and practices can run late, unexpected opportunities can arise, or other scheduled tasks can take longer than expected. Allowing some flexibility in each day can help you adjust your schedule to adapt to changing demands.

 # ACADEMIC CONNECTION: College and Career Skills

Being able to respond to precise instructions is an important skill for college and career readiness. For example, if you were asked to *analyze* how physical activity contributes to overall health, would you know how to respond? Would you be confident in your ability to *compare* carbohydrate and protein? What about your ability to *contrast* them? Each of these is different, and you must first understand what is being asked before you can accurately respond. The following are some of the most valuable skills for successful college admissions (performance on standardized tests like the SAT or ACT as well as for writing college admissions essays) and job performance.

- *Analyze:* Explain how each part functions or fits into the whole. For example, how does each type of physical activity (see the Physical Activity Pyramid) affect each component of health?

- *Persuade:* Take a stand on one side of an issue and convince others of the validity of that stance. Use facts, statistics, beliefs, opinions, and your personal view. Showing passion for your point of view can help you be persuasive.

- *Compare:* Find the common characteristics between two things. For example, carbohydrate and protein are both energy-yielding nutrients, and both contain 4 calories per gram.

- *Contrast:* Identify how people, events, or objects are different from one another. For example, carbohydrate is primarily used as fuel for the body, whereas protein is primarily used to build and repair tissues in the body.

- *Describe:* Present a clear picture of a person, place, thing, or idea. Try to write or speak so that the reader or listener could accurately visualize what you are saying.

- *Summarize:* State the meaning in a concise way (e.g., describe each of the factors that lead to teen stress and explain the relative importance of each).

Stress at Work: Can Worksite Health Promotion Help?

According to the American Psychological Association, 69 percent of people report that their work is a significant source of stress, 41 percent report feeling stressed at work on a regular basis, and 51 percent report that stress reduces their work productivity. According to the U.S. Bureau of Labor Statistics, people suffering from stress, anxiety, and related disorders miss an average of 25 work days each year. In contrast, the average number of days missed due to physical illness or injury is only 6. And according to health economist Dr. Roesch, job stress is estimated to cost the U.S. industry more than US$300 billion a year in absenteeism; turnover; diminished productivity; and medical, legal, and insurance costs.

What can be done about these costs? According to the U.S. Centers for Disease Control and Prevention, health care spending can be reduced by implementing and expanding evidence-based programs to promote workplace health, which would also improve the health of many Americans. Evidence shows, for example, that workplace health programs can positively influence social norms; help establish effective health policies; promote healthy behaviors such as practicing stress management techniques; improve people's health knowledge and skills; provide needed health screenings, immunizations, and follow-up care; and reduce on-the-job exposure to substances and hazards that can cause disease or injury. And when done well—using evidence-based best practices—comprehensive worksite health programs can yield an average $3 return on every $1 spent over a two- to five-year period (see figure 12.4).

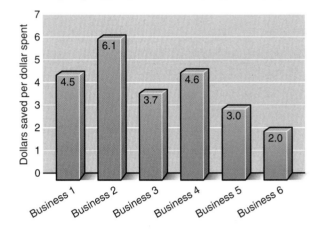

FIGURE 12.4 Return on investments for worksite health promotion programs.

For Discussion

How important do you think it is for employers to provide health promotion programs at work? What services and benefits do you think should be part of a good worksite health promotion program?

CHAPTER REVIEW

Reviewing Concepts and Vocabulary

As directed by your teacher, answer items 1 through 5 by correctly completing each sentence with a word or phrase.

1. The practice of using your imagination, or an actual visual or sound presentation, to help you relax is known as _____ _____.

2. If you're often late or tend to wait until the last minute to complete your homework, the best stress management technique for you would be _____ _____.

3. Identify two types of stress management breathing discussed in this chapter: _____ _____ and _____ _____.

4. Identify two physiological changes that happen in people who are under stress: _____ _____ _____ and _____ _____.

5. _____ involves paying close attention to what you're doing at the moment.

For items 6 through 10, as directed by your teacher, match each term in column 1 with the appropriate phrase in column 2.

6. yoga
7. tai chi
8. body scanning
9. reframing
10. guided imagery

a. changing the way you view a situation
b. uses asanas or postures
c. slow, flowing movements done in sequence
d. focusing step by step on different body parts
e. using soothing words or images to help manage stress

For items 11 through 15, as directed by your teacher, respond to each statement or question.

11. Explain the relationship between performance and stress.
12. Briefly describe the fight-or-flight response.
13. How does assertiveness differ from aggression?
14. What is mindfulness?
15. Describe one breathing exercise for stress management.

Thinking Critically

Write a paragraph in response to the following questions.
Stress is something that most people think of as a negative aspect of life. However, it would be dangerous or even deadly if people did not have a stress response. Why?

Take It Home

Select a relaxation technique from this chapter and explain it to at least one of your family members. Then work together to try out the technique. Rate your stress before and after the session. Make a family relaxation plan that will help you build relaxation into your daily lives.

EastWest Imaging/fotolia

UNIT IV

Building Relationships and Lifelong Health

● ●

Healthy People 2020 Goals

- Increase the proportion of pregnant women who receive early and adequate prenatal care.
- Reduce sexual violence.
- Reduce the rate of all infant deaths and death among children.
- Reduce the rate of adolescent and young adult deaths.
- Increase the proportion of adolescents who are connected to a parent or other positive adult caregiver.
- Reduce adolescent and young adult perpetration of and victimization by crimes.
- Increase the proportion of adults who report having someone with whom they can talk about their health.
- Increase the proportion of teens that prohibit harassment based on a student's sexual orientation or gender identity.
- Reduce bullying and fighting among adolescents.
- Increase the proportion of older adults with reduced cognitive functioning who engage in light, moderate, or vigorous leisure-time activities.

Self-Assessment Features in This Unit

- Rate Your Relationships
- My Spiritual Wellness

Making Healthy Decisions and Skills for Healthy Living Features in This Unit

- Conflict Resolution
- Intrinsic Motivation

Special Features in This Unit

- Diverse Perspectives: Sexual Orientation
- Diverse Perspectives: Being an Older Parent

Living Well News Features in This Unit

- Changing Marriage Patterns
- Does a High-Carbohydrate Diet Contribute to Mild Cognitive Impairment?

13

Family Living and Healthy Relationships

Stewart Cohen/Digital Vision

In This Chapter

(www) **Student Web Resources**
www.healthforlifetextbook.org/stude

Lesson 13.1

Family Life and Family Structure

Lesson Objectives

After reading this lesson, you should be able to

1. describe types of family in contemporary society,
2. define gender roles and explain how they have changed over time,
3. explain three factors that contribute to marriage success, and
4. describe the difference between divorce and separation.

Lesson Vocabulary

blended family, culture, divorce, empty nest, extended family, family role, gender, nuclear family, role model, separation, sex, traditional family

The family has historically been viewed as the most important force in shaping human development. Family offers a place of security and stability for people, each with his or her own roles. In this lesson, various types of families and the roles fulfilled by family members will be described. Marriage, parenting, and family dynamics will be discussed as well.

Family and Family Types

Family is defined in many different ways. One definition is a group of people who are related to each other. Another refers to a group of people living under one roof. Many definitions exist and we'll explore some of them.

The term **nuclear family**, sometimes referred to as a **traditional family**, is commonly defined as a father and mother with children. In this family unit, the mother was often seen as the primary caretaker of the children who stayed at home to care for the household while the father went to work each day. The most recent census indicates that less than half of all households now have both a husband and wife, and not all households have children. Roles have changed over the years for many reasons, one of which is the fact that in many families both parents now work full time outside of the home. This arrangement means that the caretaking of children is often a shared responsibility between parents and others, such as **extended family** members (e.g., grandparents, aunts, uncles), as well as babysitters, day care providers, neighbors, friends, and after-school program providers.

Today more than a quarter of all households have only one person. Also, many households have only two people under the same roof (without children), but those in the household consider themselves to be a family. People in one- or two-person family households are typically part of an extended family, but those other family members do not live under the same roof. These people may include those older in age with grown children, those who have no children, or those who have children who do not live with them.

Families with children now have a variety of different forms, including single-parent, adoptive (i.e., with at least one adopted child), divorced, blended (formed when a parent remarries), and gay and lesbian families. Thus the term *family* has broadened and now refers not only to bloodlines but also to an individual's living and social arrangements, which often consist of more than those people who are related by blood.

Families with children, regardless of type, tend to cycle through four stages of development: beginning, parenting, **empty nest**, and retirement (see figure 13.1). The beginning stage is the time when the newly united couple, or the individual, creates the home and adjusts to the new personal and social status. In this stage, people plan their future and move forward to realize their dreams. The parenting stage begins, of course, with the birth or adoption of the first child and lasts until the youngest child leaves the family home. Today many parents stay in this stage for a longer time than was traditionally the case, since adult children are more often living at home longer or returning home after college.

It is now fairly common for sons and daughters to live at home with parents into their young adulthood.

When the last child leaves home, parents find themselves in the empty nest stage. Traditionally, parents have been middle aged when they arrive at this point. Some parents have difficulty adjusting to this period of their lives, whereas others enjoy their new freedom. In the retirement stage, adults are typically ending their careers and enjoying the freedom of no longer having to be responsible for a job. However, in today's society, more people are continuing to work at an older age, and some even launch second careers. During this stage, a new role as a grandparent is common. Many indicate that being a grandparent has the benefits of a loving bond with grandchildren without the day-to-day responsibilities of parenting.

Whatever family type you find yourself in, a healthy family provides you with love and support. Generally, our first lessons about relating to others come from our family members. Young people tend to model their behavior on the examples they see most often—those of their parents, siblings, and extended family members, who fill similar functions and roles across family types. That is, individuals fulfill child-rearing roles whether they are part of a two-parent family, a single-parent family, a **blended family**, a divorced family, or a gay or lesbian family.

> ## ⊕ CONNECT
>
> In what ways do you model the behaviors and relationships you see in your family? Do you treat your friends or your dating partner in ways that mirror what you see in your home? Overall, are these influences more positive or more negative?

Family Roles

Most families share similar roles in that they teach family members about love, respect, responsibility, social interaction, communication, and other life skills necessary for living apart from the family, coping with change, and being financially independent. However, roles for each family member vary from family to family. In today's society **family roles** aren't as clear-cut as they may have been for previous generations. There was a time when society expected only the adult male in the household to work each day while the adult female stayed home to take care of the house and children.

Today both adults (in two-parent and blended families) in the household often work outside of the home and share the financial duties, household chores, and child rearing. In single-parent families, of course, one individual is primarily responsible for all aspects of breadwinning, finances, chores,

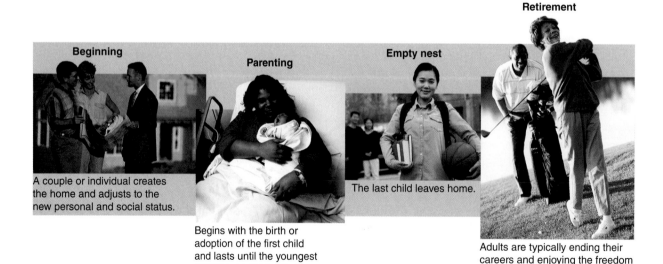

Beginning

A couple or individual creates the home and adjusts to the new personal and social status.

Parenting

Begins with the birth or adoption of the first child and lasts until the youngest child leaves the family home.

Empty nest

The last child leaves home.

Retirement

Adults are typically ending their careers and enjoying the freedom of no longer having to be responsible for a job.

FIGURE 13.1 Four stages of development of families.

and child rearing. Most gay and lesbian families consist of two adults and function in much the same manner as heterosexual two-parent and blended families. Familial roles and responsibilities will continue to evolve in response to changes in economic conditions, in the definition of family roles, and in society more generally.

Role Models

Parents serve as **role models** who impart values and information to their children. Parenting also requires a set of skills that are learned on the job—for example, patience, emotion management, health promotion, disease prevention, time management, and communication. The lessons that a child needs to learn often come through trial and error; therefore, a parent must have plenty of patience to allow the process to happen. Children can be very trying, and parents must know how to keep their frustration and other emotions in check while disciplining with love.

Parents also need to know how to handle various kinds of hurt—whether it be first aid situations, colds, the flu, bruised feelings, or emotional distress—in their children. They must model a healthy lifestyle for their children to emulate. Many of the diseases and illnesses experienced by average Americans result directly from poor lifestyle habits (e.g., poor eating, sleeping, and exercise patterns). Parents are called on to provide their children with the best environment possible and to help them develop the necessary tools for meeting the ever-changing world around them. One of the most important tools parents can give their children is the ability to communicate effectively. Good communication—both within and outside of the family—can go a long way toward preparing family members for a lifetime of success and happiness.

Parents are not the only role models for children. The learning that takes place outside of the home and the classroom is often the most influential in the lives of young people. This is the case due to the constant flow of information received from teachers, friends, peers, and the media. Such sources provide young people with a continuous

stream of information that sometimes includes questionable information. This misinformation is often not discussed fully with parents or educators. As a result, the misinformation is often regarded as accurate when it really is not. The importance of good role models outside the family cannot be underestimated.

Gender Roles

Our ideas of what it means to be male or female are structured by the messages—both direct and indirect—that we receive from family, friends, and the media. In considering these messages, it is useful to understand the distinction between sex and gender. **Sex** refers to the biological factors (male or female) that influence your fitness, health, and wellness. The word **gender** has a similar but slightly different meaning. It refers to social and cultural roles of people (masculine or feminine). For example, in the past, some roles were identified as gender appropriate for males only (masculine) or females only (feminine). Generally speaking, males were (traditionally) expected to be independent and physically active, whereas females were traditionally expected to be more social and cooperative. For example, young boys may be encouraged to play sports while young girls may be encouraged to play with dolls. Society

Parents serve as role models who impart values and information to their children.

Photodisc

asserts and reinforces such expectations even before children are born (e.g., blue for baby boys and pink for baby girls). This type of socialization continues for a lifetime. It is, among other things, the basis for the stereotypes that we see in our **culture**.

> " What can you do to promote world peace? Go home and love your family. "
>
> —Mother Teresa

Over time, stereotypes have diminished, especially in Western culture. For example, girls and women who often did not have opportunities to participate in sports prior to the 1970s now are regular participants. Activities previously considered appropriate only for males are now considered to be appropriate for both sexes (male and female).

Roles in a family or social group are influenced by gender stereotype. As noted earlier, some roles have traditionally been considered to be masculine (to be fulfilled by males) or feminine (to be fulfilled by females). Some families adhere to strict role expectations, whereas others do not. For example, in some families the man works and the woman stays home. Over time, role expectations have changed, as is the case when parents both work outside the home or the father stays home as the primary care giver. In today's society, men and women can both pursue most any desired career, educational path, or role (whether in a relationship or in society more generally). In other words, we are much less bound by traditional roles than people were in previous generations.

Family Dynamics and Stability

Marriage plays an important role in most cultures around the world. In the United States, it is a legal bond that typically involves permanence and sexual and emotional exclusivity. Marriage provides stability and fulfills many social, emotional, financial, and sexual expectations and needs. According to a study done by the Pew Research Center to determine why people get married, the top three factors are being in love, making a lifelong commitment, and companionship. Ninety-three percent of the people interviewed felt being in love was the number one reason for marriage; 87 percent felt making a

🔊 HEALTHY COMMUNICATION

How do you feel about traditional gender roles for males and females? Do you seek relationships where traditional gender-specific behaviors are expected? Why or why not? Share your perspective with a friend or classmate. Support your perspective with reasons and facts and be respectful of other opinions.

lifelong commitment was important while 81 percent felt having a companion was significant. Couples who get married are also more likely to live longer compared to their single counterparts.

The term *marriage* was traditionally used to describe only a legal union between a man and a woman, but that is no longer the case. In June 2013, the U.S. Supreme Court declared part of the Defense of Marriage Act (DOMA) unconstitutional, which had defined marriage solely as a legal union between a man and a woman. The Supreme Court ruling declared that same-sex couples who are legally married deserve the same legal rights enjoyed by other married couples under federal law. There are a number of states that are legalizing gay marriage. States that may not yet recognize gay marriage may recognize civil unions or domestic partnerships. Civil unions provide legal recognition to a couple's relationship and provide some legal rights similar to those given to spouses in marriages. Domestic partnerships are broadly defined as a committed relationship between two adults of the same sex.

Marriage is a legal bond that provides stability.
iofoto/fotolia.com

⚛ HEALTH SCIENCE

According to researchers at Harvard University, individuals who have strong relationships with family, friends, and their community experience happier and healthier lives. Such people live longer and experience fewer health problems. For example, connecting with others reduces the effects of stress and improves the functioning of the coronary artery, digestive, and immune systems. Research also shows that exhibiting caring behavior triggers hormones that reduce stress. This means that when people take action to promote social support and express affection, they bring about life-enhancing effects. This is encouraging news for families, because every day provides an opportunity to engage with other human beings and practice this proven strategy for improving the health of both the caregiver and the receiver.

Marriage success can be attributed to a variety of factors including the age of the individuals; the length of the relationship and the engagement; the presence or absence of shared interests, values, and goals; the attitudes of each individual's parents or guardians toward the marriage partner; and the individuals' views about having and raising children. For more information related to marriage, see the student section of the Health for Life website.

Although marriage is a lifetime commitment for some, the expectations associated with marriage may be difficult to maintain, and married couples may go through periods where their happiness alternately diminishes and increases. The highest degrees of happiness are typically found in the beginning stages of the relationship and upon the birth of the first child. Happiness tends to level off as the couple raises adolescents. It increases again as children reach young adulthood and move out, and as the retirement years get closer.

Some couples who experience trouble in their relationship try separation rather than divorce. The most common type of **separation** is a test period that is not legally recognized. In this approach, any shared property or possessions are still co-owned by the couple. Couples may use a separation to assess their relationship and decide whether they want to work at staying together.

Though many marriages last, others end in **divorce**, which is a legal termination of the marriage, wherein the property, the custody and support of any children, and possibly spousal support are negotiated by the divorcing individuals or decided by a judge or court. According to the American Psychological Association, approximately 40 to 50 percent of married U.S. couples divorce, and for people who marry again the divorce rate is even higher. Divorce rates also tend to be higher for younger individuals.

Most people marry with the intention of having a permanent relationship. When divorce happens, it often results from multiple causes, and it differs for each couple. Divorce also goes beyond the termination of the marriage itself; it often has a ripple effect and influences every aspect of a person's life. Divorced individuals often have to establish their individual identity all over again, since changes take place in their financial status, living arrangements, friendships, family relationships, and possibly even work situations. Children are also affected by divorce and may not understand why their parents are divorcing. While children may initially feel fearful of the changes associated with divorce, they can overcome the anxiety and grow up having very positive relationships with both their mother and their father, as well as with a spouse of their own.

Comprehension Check

1. Describe the types of family in contemporary society.
2. Define gender roles and explain how they have changed over time.
3. Explain three factors that contribute to marriage success.
4. Describe the difference between divorce and separation.

✔ SELF-ASSESSMENT: Rate Your Relationships

Think about a family member, friend, or boyfriend or girlfriend you are close to. Select the answer (yes or no) to the following questions. Record your results as directed by your teacher.

1. This person encourages me to try new things.
   a. yes
   b. no

2. This person is supportive of the things I do.
   a. yes
   b. no

3. We have similar common interests and values.
   a. yes
   b. no

4. It is easy to share my feelings (e.g., happy, sad, frustrated, and so on) with this person.
   a. yes
   b. no

5. This person respects me and our relationship.
   a. yes
   b. no

6. This person is not liked very well by my other friends.
   a. yes
   b. no

7. This person gets jealous when I talk with or hang out with other people.
   a. yes
   b. no

8. This person thinks I'm too involved in different activities.
   a. yes
   b. no

9. This person puts me down or criticizes me.
   a. yes
   b. no

10. This person pressures me to do things I don't want to do.
    a. yes
    b. no

✔ Planning for Healthy Living

Use the Healthy Living Plan worksheet to improve your relationship skills.

Lesson 13.2

Relationships

Lesson Objectives

After reading this lesson, you should be able to

1. describe the three main qualities that most people value in their friendships,
2. explain how peer pressure can be both positive and negative,
3. describe the four roles that people may play in a bullying situation, and
4. list at least four healthy dating expectations that you have for yourself.

Lesson Vocabulary

assertive behavior, bullying, casual friendship, close friendship, cyberbullying, date rape, dating violence, harassment, manipulation, online dating, peer pressure, platonic friendship, refusal skills, sexual coercion

Humans are social beings; we have an innate desire to belong, feel accepted, and be wanted. In fact, your ability to relate with others often determines how happy and successful you will be throughout your life. More specifically, your ability to give and receive love and support is related to your attainment of a healthy and productive life. Relationships can bring much sorrow—and much joy—to your life. Entering into any relationship demands that we take risks. These risks frequently put us outside of our comfort zone, but without them our growth and development would be stunted. In this lesson, you'll learn about different types of relationships and some of the characteristics that define them.

What Is a Relationship?

Relationships are connections between people. They can be strong and last a lifetime (e.g., a parent–child relationship) or short and superficial (e.g., a relationship with a short-term employer). Relationships can involve romance or be based on friendship. A friendship is likely to be based on shared interests and values. Friends play an important role in helping us grow and mature.

Different people look for different qualities in friends. The most valued qualities are honesty, confidentiality, empathy, and tolerance. Trustworthiness is valued and expected because we want our friends to be fair, sincere, and straightforward. We want to know that we can confide in our friends

and not worry that they will disclose information (confidentiality). Empathy is the ability to understand how another person feels; without this trait, it would be difficult for friends to understand one another. Tolerance allows friends to remain friends through adversity. Friends do not always get along, but good friends find a way to work through the rough patches.

Long-standing mature relationships provide an opportunity for mutual caring, openness, disclosure, commitment, trust, and tenderness. As people mature, they have more opportunity and capacity for relationships on many levels.

Safe and Healthy Peer Relationships

As you mature, your peer relationships will take on different aspects. Many young people maintain friendships initiated during their school years, while others focus on new relationships as they enter college or the work force. Friendships also vary in commitment and level of significance, and they are dynamic and may continue to evolve over time. Many people enjoy friends that include both males and females, and interacting with a range of peers can enrich your life and encourage your growth and development beyond young adulthood.

Three basic types of friendship are casual, platonic, and close. **Casual friendship** occurs between individuals who share some commonalities (e.g., classmates or co-workers); it is not characterized by the formation of a deep bond. **Platonic friendship** often involves a member of the opposite sex and is characterized by affection but not romantic involvement. **Close friendship** is punctuated by emotional ties and the sharing of intimate personal information. When problems arise, it is generally to these close friends that we turn for support and guidance.

Regardless of the type, positive friendships are built on shared morals and values and common interests. They are characterized by trust, dependability, predictability, and accountability. Maintaining such a friendship, requires work and loyalty. Loyal friends are respectful of each other. They encourage and support one another in both easy and difficult times.

Peer pressure can affect one's decisions and actions including relationships with friends. On the positive side, peer pressure can encourage us to try new things and be better in some way. Our peers can also serve as role models for us to emulate, thus helping us grow. Negative peer pressure, on the other hand, encourages us to make poor decisions and behave badly and thus ultimately leads to negative consequences. People of all ages can be influenced by negative peer pressure, which is often exerted through **manipulation**—indirect pressure to get you to do something inappropriate or harassing. **Harassment** often includes name calling, teasing, or **bullying**.

Resisting Negative Peer Pressure

One way to address negative peer pressure is to try to avoid it. For example, we know that teens with friends that have destructive health habits (e.g., smoking, use of drugs) are more likely to adopt these habits than people with friends who do not have destructive habits. Finding friends with similar values reduces chances for negative peer pressure. Whenever possible, try to develop and maintain friendships with people that you know share your values and interests. Be true to yourself and your beliefs by asserting your goals and values; this may reduce your risk of potentially harmful consequences.

Being assertive and practicing refusal skills can be very helpful in standing up for yourself if needed. **Assertive behavior** involves making a firm verbal statement that lets another person know how you feel. **Refusal skills** are techniques for saying no and sticking with it. The following three steps help you to be assertive and use refusal skills.

1. **State your position.** Demonstrate that you mean no. You can do this both verbally and through nonverbal cues. For example, you might say no and state a reason, or you might say no and raise your hand to signify clearly that you are not interested.

Close friendships are punctuated by emotional ties and the sharing of intimate personal information allowing friends to turn to each other for support and guidance.

2. **Suggest an alternative activity.** If you are being pressured to take part in an activity you are not comfortable with, suggest an alternative. You might also provide reasons for doing so.

3. **Stick with your position.** Stay positive and firm while you make clear that you are not interested in the suggested activity or behavior. Use strong words and body language and look your friend in the eye. If this does not work, remove yourself immediately from the situation. In the best case scenario, your friends will honor your requests. Occasionally, you may have friends who are aggressive and who continue to apply pressure and make you uncomfortable. If your personality tends toward being passive, you may find it difficult to refuse your friends. Assertive behavior takes practice. With practice, you get better at it and it will serve you well throughout your life.

Bullying

Bullying involves an imbalance of power between a bully and his or her victim. It is the act of repeatedly doing or saying something to intimidate or dominate another person. It might involve making threats, spreading rumors, physically or verbally attacking someone, or purposefully excluding someone from a group. Bullying takes three main forms: (1) verbal, in which someone says or writes mean things; (2) social, which involves hurting someone's reputation or relationships; and (3) physical, which includes hurting a person's body or damaging his or her possessions. Bullying is covered under the federal civil rights laws enforced by the U.S. Department of Education and the U.S. Department of Justice. Punishment varies from a fine or imprisonment of up to one year (or both). If bodily injury results or if an act includes the use, attempted use, or threatened use of a dangerous weapon, punishment can be a fine or imprisonment up to ten years (or both).

Bullying may involve only the bully and the person being bullied, or other people. Other people can play a variety of roles in bullying, including assistant, reinforcer, outsider, and defender. An individual who assists the bully (assistant) does so by encouraging him or her and perhaps even joining in the act of bullying. A person who reinforces the bully's behavior (reinforcer) does so by being part of the audience; this person doesn't participate in

Bullying can take three main forms: verbal, social, or physical.

the bullying itself but does encourage the bully to continue. An outsider neither encourages the bully's behavior nor defends the individual being bullied. In contrast, a defender helps the person *being* bullied by comforting him or her and perhaps by coming to his or her defense during the bullying incident itself.

Stopping bullying can be a difficult task, since much of it happens subtly and often isn't noticed. Aside from witnessing an incident of bullying, how can you know when there is a problem? Here are some signs that a person may be getting bullied: unexplainable injuries; lost or destroyed clothing, electronics, or other personal items; changes in eating habits, such as coming home from school hungry (because a bully took his or her lunch or lunch money); difficulty with sleeping; decline in grades or desire to go to school; participation in fewer school activities than usual; and self-destructive behaviors (e.g., cutting). There are also signs that a person may be acting as a bully. They include getting into physical or verbal fights; having friends who are bullies; being more aggressive than normal; being sent to the principal's office for being verbally or physically aggressive; having unexplained money or belongings; and blaming others for their actions. The following are some statistics about bullying.

- Approximately one in seven students in grades kindergarten through 12 is either a bully or has been bullied.

- About 56 percent of students have witnessed a bullying crime at school.

- Approximately 71 percent of students report that bullying is an ongoing problem.

- One out of every 10 students drops out or changes schools because of repeated bullying.

- Revenge for bullying is one of the strongest motivations for school shootings.

A person who is bullied may not want to go to school—just one of several signs of bullying.

Photodisc

If you are being bullied, try the following tips.

- If you feel safe, talk to the bullying student and tell them in a strong, calm voice to leave you alone.

- Walk away from the bully.

- Tell an adult right away about the incident. While this may feel like you are tattling, adults can't help unless they know it is happening.

- If possible, try to avoid the bully and make sure you have a friend with you. Many bullies are less likely to bully multiple people.

Cyberbullying

Cyberbullying involves electronic technology, such as cell phones, computers, tablets, and social media sites. It can happen 24-7, since messages and images can be posted anonymously and distributed quickly to a large audience at any time. In addition, once a message or image is posted, it can be difficult or impossible to fully remove.

The signs of cyberbullying are much the same as those for bullying in general. The main difference involves the consistency and amount of bullying that can be done via technology. It isn't done just on the school playground, in the lunchroom, or between classes. Rather, it can happen all day and all night long, and many more people can see the bullying when it is posted to a social media website or distributed electronically. Cyberbullying can lead to anxiety, depression, and even suicide due to the ongoing bullying. Students must also realize that what they post online can have lasting consequences when they apply for college or a job. Recruiters will search for people to see the kinds of posts they make as well as the posts that are made about them. Cyberbullies and their parents may also face legal charges for cyberbullying. For more information about cyberbullying, see the student section of the Health for Life website.

Dating Relationships

Dating can be described as an extension of a friendship. Dating allows students an opportunity to strengthen self-esteem; being liked by a friend encourages people to gain confidence in how they feel about themselves. Dating also helps to improve social skills and assists in students understanding personal needs.

The dynamics of dating relationships are similar to those of a friendship-based relationship, except for the level of intimacy that is shared. In fact, a dating relationship often begins as a friendship, then develops into a relationship that includes another level of intimacy when two people share a physical attraction. Dating relationships are nonmarital—usually exclusive—relationships between two people that may or may not include a sexual relationship.

As a dating relationship becomes more serious, trust becomes more and more important. Trust is established over time and is earned as a result of proven commitment. When this kind of trust is experienced by two individuals who are capable of an emotionally mature and physically satisfying relationship, it can be one of the most gratifying experiences in life. When you enter into any type of relationship, your personal values will be questioned, affirmed, and challenged. You must

Dating relationships are similar to a friendship-based relationship, except for the level of intimacy that is shared.

Photodisc

consider your own values when making decisions about relationships. If you decide to behave in ways that conflict with your values, you will cause yourself distress and feelings of guilt, shame, and loss of self-respect.

Setting Limits

Dating can be an enjoyable experience; it can give you opportunities to develop your social skills and

learn more about yourself. Some people, for example, discover new interests and ways of expressing themselves through dating. At the same time, dating can put you at risk for unwanted peer pressure—for example, pressure to participate in sexual activity or other high-risk activities such as using drugs. It is important to remember that abstinence in both sexual activity and drug use is the only prevention method for not getting pregnant, not getting sexually transmitted infections, and not using and abusing drugs. It is also the only prevention method that works 100 percent of the time. Therefore, before you go on a date, you should determine who else will be present, what time you and your date need to be home, and how you will get from one place to another. Plan for your safety and self-control. First and foremost, avoid places where there will be alcohol or other drugs. Also avoid being alone with a date or in an isolated place.

Parents and other caregivers often set limits on where you can go, who you can go with, and how late you can stay out. In most cases, however, it is ultimately up to you and your date to make the final decisions because your parents or caregivers aren't around. As a responsible individual, you will set your own limits about where you will go and what you will do on dates. Communicating these limits to your date before going out helps you avoid risky and sometimes embarrassing situations.

DIVERSE PERSPECTIVES: Sexual Orientation

PhotoDisc/Barbara Penoyar

My name is James, and I am gay. I knew I was different from most of my friends early in my life. I remember having a crush on another boy when I was in middle school, and I remember not knowing what to do, what to think, or who to talk to. My family is very traditional and conservative. I was raised in a faith tradition that isn't always very accepting of gays and lesbians, and I am from a small town where everyone seems to know everyone else's business. This made it really difficult.

I came out in high school, and at first most of my family members and friends weren't accepting. I moved out and lived with a friend whose parents were more tolerant. I went through a time

of depression and even had a failed suicide attempt after that. Even though society has changed some of its views and I can see role models on popular television shows or among great athletes, I still felt like I didn't belong, or like I wasn't valued. The family I lived with saved my life and gave me a sense of inner strength and self-confidence. They also helped build bridges for me with my own family. I was lucky to have them when I did.

I realized later on that being a gay teenager is harder than being a gay adult. The pressures are greater, and the challenges to fit in and be accepted are just worse at that time in life for everyone. I want my story to be a sign of hope for other teens who may struggle like I did. It gets better.

Avoiding being alone with a date is just one limit you could set when dating.

Monkey Business/fotolia.com

Healthy dating begins with your own expectations. Expect to be treated with consideration and respect. Expect that your partner respect your values. Expect that you have the courage—and remember that you have the right—to say no to any activity or behavior for which you are not ready. Remember: no one has the right to force unwanted advances on you. These expectations may seem obvious, but dating can sometimes obscure the obvious.

Satisfying and secure relationships take skill and effort and often share certain identifiable traits. Key traits include trust, predictability, and faith. In fact, trust is punctuated by a sense of predictability, meaning that you can predict your partner's behavior based on the fact that you have witnessed consistent positive behavior from him or her in the past. When your partner demonstrates consistent dependability, you know that you can rely on him or her, particularly when you need support the most. Having faith in your partner allows you to feel that you are certain about his or her intentions and principles. These characteristics—trust, predictability, and faith—are crucial to a satisfying relationship, and can be used as a measuring stick for deciding whether a given relationship is a healthy one.

Teens should also consider dating a variety of people as they begin to date. Too often, teens think that they will be with the first person they date for the rest of their life, which is usually not the case. Dating is one part of the high school experience, whether it is for a one-time trip to the movies or a school dance or lasts for an extended period of time. It should not be an all-consuming experience. The person you date should be supportive of you and the activities you are involved with; should encourage you to be the best person you can; and should hold values and goals similar to yours. Too many teens "fall in love" only to find that the person they are dating does not share their values and goals for their future. Teens need to understand that while breaking up is difficult to do, many of the dating and friendship relationships they have in high school will change, and the qualities they are drawn to in a partner may also change dramatically as they continue to mature.

Breaking Up

When ending a relationship, break up with the person face to face rather than through texting, social media, or e-mail. While breaking up in person may be more difficult to do, it is also more respectful and less hurtful. It may feel easier to hide behind a phone or computer, but it is also much easier to be hurtful through media than it is in person.

In addition, break up with the person sooner rather than later. You cannot change the other person, and thinking that you can will lead only to arguments and hurt feelings. Breaking up is not the time to pick a fight or blame each other; in fact, it is often just time to move on. Finally, before breaking up, make sure of what both you and the other person need—is it time to talk with each other, or is it time for a clean break to get away from each other?

Also, if someone breaks up with you, it is important to respect their decision. While it may be painful, moving on and giving the person the space they request is part of being a mature and responsible person.

Valuing Your Social Health

Dating relationships during the teen years can support healthy growth and development and lead to life-changing experiences. People who enter into such relationships with strong values and morals often fondly remember their first dating relationships. If you can resist the hormone-influenced urges and social pressures that tend to lead people toward high-risk behaviors—including sexual activity and drug and alcohol use—your dating relationships are likely to generate positive feelings of self-respect and self-esteem.

On the other hand, overcoming a bad reputation (whether it is based on real or assumed behaviors) is a difficult task. Teens are often judged not only by their peers but also by their teachers and other adults in the community. Family relationships can also become strained and difficult when parents learn that their children have stepped past the limits they set to protect them. When faced with the question of whether or not to become sexually active or partake in other risky behaviors, think critically, evaluate the risks, and ask yourself, "How will this activity affect my goals for my future?" It is important to remember that remaining abstinent when dating is the only way to ensure that there won't be unintended consequences such as pregnancy and sexually transmitted infections. Your teacher may provide you with more information on this topic.

Dating Violence

Dating violence occurs in the form of various kinds of physical, emotional or psychological, and sexual abuse within a dating relationship, and unfortunately it occurs more often than was once assumed. In fact, adolescents and young adults sometimes misinterpret abusive behavior by a dating partner as a sign of caring. In reality, a dating partner should never disrespect, dominate, or exert force or

excessive control over you. Here are some sobering statistics about dating violence from the U.S. Centers for Disease Control and Prevention.

- One-fourth of high school girls have been abused physically or sexually.
- Young women between the ages of 16 and 24 are roughly three times more likely than the rest of the population to be abused by an intimate partner.
- Half of males and females who experience rape or physical or sexual abuse attempt to commit suicide. Rape is any kind of penetration of another person regardless of gender without the victim's consent. **Date rape** is the same as rape except it is committed by a person known to the victim in a dating situation.
- About 1.5 million high school boys and girls report being intentionally hit or physically harmed in the last year by someone with whom they were romantically involved.
- At least half of all violent crimes occur after the offender, the victim, or both have been drinking alcohol.
- In one in three sexual assaults, the offender was intoxicated. Sexual assault is any type of sexual contact or behavior that occurs without the clear consent of the receiver.

Basic signs that a relationship may be headed for trouble include manipulation, put-downs, excessive control over the dating partner's behavior, control over the partner's outside friendships, jealousy and possessiveness, scaring or threatening the partner, and general lack of respect. A healthy relationship should never involve **sexual coercion** (i.e., the unwanted sexual penetration that occurs after a person is pressured in a nonphysical way) or sexual violence (i.e., any sexual act that is committed against someone's will). If you find yourself in a situation characterized by one or more of these factors, seek outside help from parents, teachers, or school counselors. Like all forms of violence, dating violence traumatizes victims and leaves emotional scars. It can also result in unintentional pregnancy and sexually transmitted infections such as HIV. Your teacher may provide you with more information on this topic.

It is also critical to take measures that reduce your risk of experiencing dating violence. Make sure that your dates take place in well-lit public areas. Encourage your date to invite others. Date as part of a group until you know him or her better. Avoid using alcohol and other drugs on dates and immediately remove yourself from any situation involving alcohol or drugs—they increase your risk for violence and trouble. Always tell a parent or guardian who you are with and where you intend to go on your date. Bring a cell phone and some extra money in case you need to get home on your own.

 HEALTH TECHNOLOGY

While traditional dating is the best option for many, online dating is an increasingly popular alternative. **Online dating**, also called Internet dating, involves searching for a romantic partner on the Internet. This practice has grown in popularity due to social media sites, including some teen dating sites. As always, you need to be very careful about any information you consider providing and you should talk with a parent or guardian before using an online dating site. Online dating can be very risky. Here are some tips to help keep you safe.

1. **Protect your personal information.** Never give out your real name, address, or phone number online to a person you don't know. Also do not give out other personal information, such as where you go to school or the names of teams or organizations of which you are a part. Choose an online dating name that cannot be linked to your real name.

2. **Read all information available.** Start out slowly by reading all of the profile information about other members along with carefully evaluating the information. Then trust your instincts about what you find. Remember that not everything put on the Internet is the truth. People will exaggerate the truth about themselves as well as lie about who they really are.

3. **Protect your privacy.** Create a new e-mail account that you use only for online dating. Make sure that you sign your e-mail only with your dating name.

4. **Don't be afraid to stop.** If a conversation ever becomes uncomfortable, terminate it and contact the dating site's administrators about it.

5. **Share photo with care.** Use extreme caution if you are asked to share a photo with someone you don't know. Always ask to see a current photo of that person as well and be aware that he or she may send a fake photo.

6. **Use alternate forms of communication.** If you are going to talk on the phone with someone you met online, protect yourself. Do not give out your phone number. Enter *67 before dialing so that the other person won't be able to see your number. Consider using a communication app (e.g., Skype) as a way to avoid using your phone number.

7. **Meet in public.** If you get to the point in your relationship where you want to meet face to face, never allow the person to pick you up at home, school, or work. Schedule a meeting during the day at a public place where there are a lot of people around who could help you if needed; in addition, consider bringing a friend with you to the date. Make sure to tell a friend or family member about your date and give them a phone number, information about the meeting time and place, and a picture of the person you are meeting.

As with any relationship, you need to get to know the person you're talking with before telling too much about yourself. Be cautious about online dating. You never know who may really be at the other end of the computer connection.

CONNECT

What could be some benefits of online dating? What are some risks of online dating? If you haven't already, do you think you will participate in online dating? Why or why not?

Overcoming Abuse

For those who have suffered abuse or dating violence, it is important to remember that they have not done anything to justify being treated in an abusive way. All forms of abuse are illegal and should be reported to the authorities. Reporting such an incident can be instrumental in preventing further abuse. All U.S. states have laws and policies to facilitate the reporting of abuse, often anonymously. In addition, help for victims of abuse is also offered by health care facilities, educational institutions, and places of worship. Victims should seek out this assistance in order to protect themselves and others from future abuse and to receive emotional and spiritual support. According to the Centers for Disease Control and Prevention, approximately one in five women and one in seven men who experienced rape or physical violence by an intimate partner first experienced some form of partner violence between the ages of 11 and 17.

Abusers also need help; in fact, they are likely to have been victimized in their own past. According to a research study, 35 percent of abusers had also been victims of abuse. Abusers often see violence as a way of life and view it as normal behavior. Support and counseling provided by mental health professionals can help both the abuse victim and the abuser. To prevent and overcome abuse, all individuals need to learn skills for developing and maintaining healthy and safe relationships.

> " You don't develop courage by being happy in your relationships every day. You develop it by surviving difficult times and challenging adversity. "
>
> —Epicurus, ancient Greek philosopher

It is possible to have a healthy relationship even if you've been abused.

Photodisc

Comprehension Check

1. Describe the three main qualities that most people tend to value in their friendships.
2. Explain how peer pressure can be both positive and negative.
3. Describe the four roles (other than the bully) that people may play in a bullying situation.
4. List at least four healthy dating expectations that you have for yourself.

MAKING HEALTHY DECISIONS: Conflict Resolution

Sofia and Ariana have been best friends since third grade. When they began their first year of high school, Sofia began dating Mateo, a senior, and spending less time with Ariana. Mateo convinced Sofia that she should stop playing soccer in order to spend more time with him. He has a reputation for being a partier and getting in trouble at school. Sofia now seems to be spending more and more of her time with Mateo, and when Ariana tries to talk to Sofia at school or on the phone, Mateo pressures Sofia to stop talking. He also seems to dictate to her who she can and cannot talk to, as well as what she can and cannot do.

Ariana decided she would stop by Sofia's house one day after soccer practice to talk with her about Mateo's controlling behavior. As soon as Ariana told Sofia that she didn't think Mateo was good for her and that he

was controlling her life, Sofia started yelling at Ariana, and they ended up in a big fight. It has now been over a week since Ariana tried to talk with Sofia about Mateo, and they haven't spoken to each other. In fact, Sofia has begun telling their friends that Ariana is the one trying to control her life.

For Discussion

Using the seven skills for conflict resolution (see the Skills for Healthy Living feature), explain how Ariana could have approached Sofia about her relationship with Mateo in a principled manner rather than being confrontational. How would you rewrite the scenario between Sofia and Ariana using the seven steps of conflict resolution?

SKILLS FOR HEALTHY LIVING: Conflict Resolution

Conflict is a part of life. It happens between friends and family members, as well as with individuals we don't like and may not even know. Although most people don't like conflict and tend to ignore it, others are confrontational. Thus it's important to know how to resolve conflict through constructive engagement, which can produce better outcomes and relationships. You can use conflict resolution skills to settle a disagreement in a responsible way. Conflicts should be resolved through conversation—not violence.

Conflict resolution approaches can be classified into three primary groups: soft, hard, and principled. Soft and hard responses tend to lead to winners and losers rather than resolution. People who approach conflicts with a soft response tend to withdraw or avoid conflict and may even deny that a conflict exists. On the other hand, people who approach conflicts with a hard response tend to be confrontational and aggressive. These individuals have the goal of winning the conflict rather than resolving it through a cooperative resolution. In contrast, people who approach conflicts with a principled response seek a resolution that preserves the relationship and

addresses the needs of both parties. Ideally, a person who falls into the soft or hard group will use the following seven skills to become more of a principled responder when handling a conflict.

- **Remain calm.** Be patient and stay in control of your emotions. If you are calm, you are less likely to harm yourself or others.
- **Set a positive tone.** Avoid blaming and shaming, using put-downs, and making threats. Instead, show that you want to be fair as you work together to resolve the conflict.
- **Define the conflict.** Have each person describe the conflict, either in conversation or in writing. Be brief and to the point.
- **Take responsibility for personal actions.** Do not cover up any of your behavior. Apologize if any of your actions were wrong or may have contributed to the conflict.
- **Listen to the needs and feelings of others.** Do not interrupt when another person is speaking. When it is your turn,

use "I" messages (i.e., state your needs and feelings and do not focus on the traits or behaviors of someone else). Show respect.

- **List and evaluate possible solutions.** Identify as many solutions as possible. Then examine each solution to determine whether it is healthful, safe, legal, in accordance with family guidelines and good character, and nonviolent.

- **Agree on a solution.** Select a responsible solution. State what each party will do. Make a written agreement, if necessary. Restate and summarize the agreement to help each person honor it.

These steps give you a healthy way to help resolve conflicts. Realize that not every conflict will require using all seven steps; nor will you always use them in exactly the order in which they are listed here. Each conflict, each situation, is different, as is each individual. The goal is to use conflict resolution skills appropriately in order to contribute to a cooperative resolution for all.

 ACADEMIC CONNECTION: Relationships Between Concepts and Terms

Part of meeting the standards for English language arts is the ability to understand the relationships between concepts and terms. In this book you have worked with groups of different but related concepts and terms such as bullying, cyberbullying, sexting, sexual coercion, and sexual assault as well as drug addiction, drug dependence, and drug tolerance. Do you understand the differences between these related sets of terms? Are you able to appreciate why they are similar and how they are different? Use the glossary or the study section of the website to look up each term to help you distinguish between them. Can you identify another set of related terms you have learned in this book?

Changing Marriage Patterns

In 1960, 72 percent of U.S. adults aged 18 or older were married. Today that figure is just 51 percent. According to U.S. Census data, the age at which people elect to get married for the first time is also increasing. In 1960, the median age at first marriage was 20.3 for females and 22.8 for males. By 2012, these ages had risen to 26.6 for females and 28.6 for males.

Age at first marriage varies greatly between countries. Compared with other regions of the world, the United States and northwestern Europe are characterized by relatively later ages of first marriage, as well as a larger proportion of the population who remain single and more emphasis on nuclear family rather than extended family.

Traditionally, marriage has served to mark the transition to adulthood and the beginning of a new family. Over the last half century, however, family dynamics have changed, as more young adults have cohabited and delayed marriage. Many young people are now comfortable with delaying marriage until their late 20s or early 30s (see figure 13.2). Today, in fact, only 20 percent of those aged 18 to 29 are married, compared with 59 percent of that same group in 1960.

"There may be some wisdom in waiting," says sociologist Rebecca Johhanson. "The likelihood that a first marriage will break up within 10 years is highest among those individuals who get married under the age of 18 and lowest among those who are married after the age of 25."

On the other hand, "delayed marriage increases the number of years when a nonmarital pregnancy might occur and decreases the likelihood of starting a family," states marriage and family therapist Bill O'Reilly.

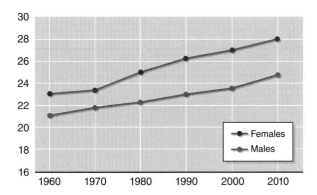

Figure 13.2   Increasing marital age.

For Discussion

Why do you think more young people are waiting longer to get married than in previous generations? What benefits do you see in marrying later? What disadvantages?

Reviewing Concepts and Vocabulary

As directed by your teacher, answer items 1 through 5 by correctly completing each sentence with a word or phrase.

1. A _____ family—consisting of a mother, a father, and at least one child—has been the typical depiction of the American family.
2. _____ refers to the biological factors (male or female) that influence your fitness, health, and wellness.
3. _____ is a set of rules governing behavior in a society. It is influenced by morals, values, and religious beliefs.
4. _____ is a characteristic valued by most people that involves the ability to understand how another person feels.
5. Techniques used to help an individual say no and stick with it are referred to as _____ skills.

For items 6 through 10, as directed by your teacher, match each term in column 1 with the appropriate phrase in column 2.

6. manipulation
7. separation
8. gender
9. online dating
10. platonic friendship

a. relationship, often with a member of the opposite sex, in which there is no romantic involvement
b. social and cultural roles of people
c. searching for a romantic partner on the Internet
d. indirect pressure to get you to do something inappropriate
e. test period for couples that is not legally recognized

For items 11 through 15, as directed by your teacher, respond to each statement or question.

11. List and briefly explain the four stages of development that all families tend to cycle through.
12. What is the primary difference between bullying and cyberbullying?
13. Why do you think the divorce rate is higher among people who get married at a younger age?
14. List the factors that predict marriage success.
15. Explain the three steps for using refusal skills.

Thinking Critically

Write a paragraph in response to the following question.

Have you ever really thought about the characteristics that your perfect partner might have? What characteristics do you value the most? List four characteristics and indicate why they are so important to you.

Take It Home

Talk to a parent, guardian, or other trusted adult about online dating. Make a list of the pros and cons of online dating as compared with traditional dating. Discuss any differences in rules or parameters (e.g., appropriate age to start dating) between the two types.

Stewart Cohen/Digital Vision

14

Health and Wellness Throughout Life

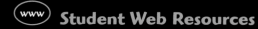 **Student Web Resources**
www.healthforlifetextbook.org/student

Joggie Botma/fotolia.com

Lesson 14.1

Healthy Children and Adolescents

Lesson Objectives

After reading this lesson, you should be able to

1. identify major developmental milestones in infants and young children,
2. describe puberty and list the secondary sex characteristics of males and females, and
3. identify career options in health and wellness.

Lesson Vocabulary

abstract thinking, adolescents, cognitive development, developmental milestones, growth spurts, impulse control, physical development, puberty, reasoning skills, secondary sex characteristics, socioemotional development

What do you remember about yourself as a young child? How have you changed over the years? Childhood and adolescence are times of tremendous change. Infants, children, preadolescents, and adolescents all experience rapid—and normal—changes in physical, cognitive, social, and emotional development. Developing fully in each of these areas helps us achieve wellness in all stages of life.

The Life Span

The average adult life span in the United States is 82 years for females and 76 years for males. Over the course of an average life span, a person passes through six developmental phases (see figure 14.1). Each phase is marked by unique factors related to well-being. In infants, children, and adolescents, growth and developmental factors are most prominent as the body and brain reach maturity. During young adulthood and middle adulthood, factors related to maintaining emotional and physical health and managing stress become prominent. The older adult years are often marked by declining physical, emotional, and mental health; challenges to social well-being; and the stress associated with these changes.

Infants and Children

The first two stages of the life span are infancy and childhood. Two of the most obvious markers of **physical development** in infants and children are weight and height. Parents and physicians track changes in weight and height to make sure that the child is properly nourished and healthy. Physical development also involves changes in motor skills (movement abilities) and sensory perceptions. It is particularly rapid during the first two years of life.

Infancy	Childhood	Adolescence	Young adulthood	Middle adulthood	Older adulthood
• 0-1 years	• 1-10 years	• 10-18 years	• 18-39 years	• 40-65 years	• 65+ years

FIGURE 14.1 Stages of the life span.

Learning to crawl is just one of many developmental milestones expected in a typically developing infant.

Each physical change brings new abilities and new learning.

Cognitive development is the acquisition and development of skills such as language use, problem solving, and reasoning. Emotional and social development involves expressing feelings about self, others, and things. It also involves relating well to others. Because emotional development and social development are closely related, they are often referred to as **socioemotional development**. Markers of socioemotional growth are self-esteem, empathy, and friendship.

Developmental milestones are the physical and behavioral signs one expects to see in a typically developing infant or child during a period or at a particular age. Table 14.1 presents some of the major physical, cognitive, and socioemotional milestones for infants and young children.

TABLE 14.1 Developmental Milestones for Infants and Young Children

Age	Milestones
0–6 months	Grows rapidly (doubles birth weight), follows objects with eyes, reaches with both hands, places objects in mouth, turns over unassisted, recognizes parents with smile at 2 to 3 months, responds to adult interaction by 6 months.
7–12 months	Triples birth weight, doubles birth length, begins to grow teeth, stands up, crawls and begins to walk unassisted, begins to distinguish strangers, experiments with sounds, develops sense of self, distinguishes between good and bad, begins to attract attention with giggles and shouting, has sense of humor, demonstrates separation anxiety from parents.
1–3 years	Continues to grow and gain weight (at a slower rate), has emerging teeth, runs, climbs, pushes and pulls, can learn taught skills, has fully developed range of emotions, moves from playing alone to having a set of friends, understands friendship, uses short sentences such as "me want cookie."
4–6 years	Continues to grow 2 to 3 inches (5 to 7.5 centimeters) per year; legs lengthen; eats and drinks independently; hops, skips, and throws; has emerging molars and some permanent teeth; generally wants to please others; can follow rules and play in groups; selects own friends; uses a vocabulary of 2,100 words.

Caring for Infants

If you're caring for an infant, talk with his or her parents or guardians for guidance. Make sure you know what to do and what not to do.

Be sure to know

- what to do when the baby cries,
- what to do if you suspect that the baby is sick,
- how to properly put on a diaper,
- how to bathe the baby safely,
- how to give the baby a bottle and burp the baby safely, and
- how to properly pick up and hold the baby.

Do not

- leave the baby alone,
- hit or shake the baby,
- yell or scream at the baby, or
- give the baby any toys or objects that could be swallowed.

Adolescence

The third stage of the life span is called adolescence. **Adolescents** are individuals between the ages of 10 and 19. The period in which the body undergoes sexual development is known as **puberty**. Puberty begins sometime between the ages of 10 and the late teens. Physical changes that occur during puberty include the development of **secondary sex characteristics** (see figure 14.2), and the start of ovulation in girls and sperm production in boys. At this time, the body can undergo rapid **growth spurts**. During this time, bone length increases; this growth can cause aches and pains as well as muscle cramps.

Physical changes can also alter how the body moves and reacts. As a result, it can sometimes feel awkward to do activities and sports that are normally easy or familiar. Both girls and boys may also feel self-conscious about their appearance during this time. Rest assured that it's normal for adolescents to feel self-conscious about changes in body size, shape, and appearance. The physical changes that accompany puberty are normal. They can occur at different times and rates in different people.

Girls are particularly at risk of dropping out of physical activity as they progress through adolescence. At this time they typically have an increase in overall body fat, develop breasts, start menstruating, and undergo changes in body shape. These developments can cause self-consciousness and a perceived drop in skill or ability. Don't let this stop you from being active. While boys are more likely than girls to remain active during the teenage years, activity rates among boys also decline during adolescence. Continuing to be physically active throughout your teenage years helps you practice healthy habits in adulthood. Being physically active also helps prevent weight gain and can improve self-esteem. Be supportive of friends and encourage each other to stay active.

Because growth takes a great deal of energy, both boys and girls experiencing puberty often notice an increase in appetite. Though it's normal to eat more during this time, you should select healthy and nutrient-dense foods that give your body the nourishment it needs.

You also experience cognitive changes during adolescence as parts of your brain change and grow. For one thing, you improve considerably at **abstract thinking**—the ability to consider things that are not visible, immediate, or concrete. You also improve your **reasoning skills**—your ability

Boys

Girls

Acne increases

Skin becomes
more oily

Voice deepens

Hair appears on
face and chest

Perspiration
increases

Shoulders broaden

Pubic hair appears

Skin becomes
more oily

Breasts develop

Body fat increases

Pubic hair appears

Perspiration increases

Hips widen

Acne increases

FIGURE 14.2 Secondary sex characteristics.

to solve problems and make decisions. Together, these changes allow you to think more critically and evaluate ideas more carefully. As your brain matures and develops, you may notice improvements in your ability to do math, solve scientific questions, and express complex ideas.

Adolescence can also bring uncertain and changing emotions. Many preteens and teenagers have emotions that at times seem uncontrollable. This emotional uncertainty results in part from an increase in hormones, such as estrogen and testosterone. As a result, despite adolescents' maturing cognitive abilities, they may also have challenges with **impulse control**—the ability to resist making rapid decisions without fully considering the consequences. It's important to think twice about any sudden or rash decisions you are tempted to make. You also need to consider the possible effects on your health and wellness. Examples include driving aggressively, drinking, using drugs, and being violent.

In addition, adolescence is a time of intense self-discovery and searching. This search for identity and self-expression is a normal part of the

adolescent experience. You may find yourself seeking meaning and purpose in your life. You may question your values and beliefs as you work to define what's important to you. You may also feel like experimenting with your identity and personality. For example, you might try different clothing and hairstyle choices and other forms of expression. All of this emotional change—along with the physical changes your body is going through—can make your teenage years a turbulent yet exciting time.

CONNECT

What are some of the ways in which you express your individuality? How do your peers influence how you choose to express your individuality? Does peer pressure make it easier or harder to express your individuality as a teenager? Debate your perspective with your peers. Support your position with facts and be respectful of each other's opinions.

> " Adolescence represents an inner emotional upheaval, a struggle between the eternal human wish to cling to the past and the equally powerful wish to get on with the future. "
>
> —Louise J. Kaplan, psychologist and author

Adolescence is also a stage when you begin to define goals and plans. Deciding on a potential job path or career can be overwhelming and stressful. As you explore your interests, consider the following tips and suggestions:

- **Explore career clusters.** Explore clusters or groups of occupations with common features first. Once you see which clusters appeal to your interests, you can explore specific options in more detail.

- **Take skills and interest assessments.** Taking assessments will help you discover your interests, skills, values, or other traits. You can complete self-assessments in each chapter.

- **Understand needed skills.** Knowing about specific skills that are needed for jobs and careers will help you to make informed decisions when choosing college and job training options.

- **Set goals and stay positive.** Use the skills you have learned in this book to help you set career goals and to stay positive as you work to achieve them.

- **Study career and labor market information.** Spend some time getting to know labor market information. This includes data about occupations, industries, skills, salaries, job openings, and job satisfaction. Updated, local labor market information is a critical part of the puzzle when planning for a career.

- **Don't overlook unique or nontraditional career paths.** Make sure you consider all the options before deciding on a career path. Nontraditional careers, military options, and self-employment are often overlooked.

One example of a career cluster includes jobs related to health and wellness (see table 14.2). Many of these involve working directly with a variety of people in health care settings. Other options (e.g., medical research, laboratory work) are more removed from the general public. You can learn about more career options in health and fitness, as well as in other areas, by visiting the student section of the Health for Life website.

Young Adulthood

The fourth stage of the life span is young adulthood. This is marked by major milestones including beginning a career, college graduation, marriage, and the birth of children. During this time, self-identity is more firmly set. People begin to establish themselves as contributing members of society. You're likely to enjoy good physical health during these years if you follow recommendations for physical activity and nutrition.

Defining moments for many people during young adulthood include beginning a career, college graduation, marriage, and the birth of children.

Christoph Hohnel - Fotolia

TABLE 14.2 Careers in Health and Wellness

Career	What do they do?	Who do they serve?
Chiropractor	Preserves and restores health through structural manipulation.	The general public and those with chronic pain or illness, typically in a private practice
Dentist	Preserves and restores oral health.	The general public, typically in a private practice
Dietitian PhotoDisc	Uses nutrition to maximize health and aid recovery from illness.	Variable by interest and specialty (e.g., the general public, children, athletes, people in hospital and rehabilitation settings)
Exercise physiologist	Specializes in the role of exercise for prevention and treatment of disease or enhancement of athletic performance.	Variable by interest and specialty (e.g., people with illness or injury, the general public, elite athletes)
Forensic scientist	Applies scientific methods to the investigation of legal problems; may be a doctor, dentist, pathologist, or other health care specialist.	Law enforcement officials, attorneys, crime victims and their families
Health education specialist Monika Adamczyk/fotolia.com	Encourages healthy behaviors through education and health promotion.	Variable by interest and specialty (e.g., schoolchildren, underserved populations, older people, other subgroups); typically in schools, public health offices, or private settings
Laboratory technician	Conducts laboratory tests to aid in the diagnosis and treatment of disease.	The general public at hospitals and medical clinics (e.g., conducting tests); other technicians and professionals in laboratory settings (e.g., analyzing blood work)
Medical researcher	Uses science and experimentation to advance the field of medicine and health care.	Other researchers in a lab; the general public when conducting clinical trials

Career	What do they do?	Who do they serve?
Naturopathic doctor	Focuses on whole-patient wellness through a practice of medicine that blends ancient natural therapies with current medical advances.	The general public (may specialize in children, pregnant women, aging people, other subgroups)
Nurse michaeljung - Fotolia	Provides focused, hands-on, highly personalized care to promote health, prevent disease, and help patients cope with illness.	The general public in hospitals and clinics (may specialize in children, pregnant women, aging people, other subgroups)
Personal trainer iofoto/fotolia.com	Designs and oversees personalized fitness and exercise programs; motivates and monitors improvements in health and fitness.	The general public (may specialize in strength and conditioning for athletes)
Pharmacist	Specializes in medications; dispenses prescription medications and works with doctors to determine proper medications and dosages for patients.	The general public through pharmacies located in a variety of settings
Physical or occupational therapist	Diagnoses and treats injuries and pain; oversees rehabilitation efforts.	The general public (may specialize in children, aging people, athletes, other subgroups) in a variety of settings (e.g., hospitals, private practices)
Physical education teacher	Uses scientific and education programming knowledge to teach physical activity, sport, and exercise and to promote healthy living.	School-aged children, families, and communities

> continued

TABLE 14.2 > continued

Career	What do they do?	Who do they serve?
Physician Photodisc	Diagnoses disease and prescribes treatments; may practice in a specialty (e.g., general medicine, surgery, dermatology).	The general public in settings ranging from private practices to hospitals and clinics
Psychologist or psychiatrist	Provides counseling and sometimes medical care to promote positive mental health; may be a medical doctor.	The general public or those who have mental illness in private practice, hospitals, and clinics
Public health professional	Works with populations of people; conducts research; plans, implements, and evaluates prevention and other health-related programs; oversees health promotion initiatives.	The general public in settings ranging from schools, public health departments, neighborhoods, communities, and even national and international programs
Social worker	Counsels individuals, families, and communities in need and provides a range of assistance and support.	The general public (often people with particular needs, such as children, poor people, and elderly people)
Wellness coach	Provides guidance, motivation, and support for positive behavior changes related to wellness; often holds certain health credentials.	The general public through private practice

However, since major life transitions during these years can be stressful, young adults are more susceptible to sadness and depression than younger or older people. Common sources of stress are financial strain and relationship challenges. If you develop a strong sense of identity and good coping skills now, you'll position yourself to make your early adulthood a positive and productive time.

Comprehension Check

1. Identify three major developmental milestones that occur during the first year of life.
2. List the secondary sex characteristics that develop during puberty for boys and girls.
3. Compare two careers related to health and wellness.

Spiritual wellness plays a significant role in many of life's developmental stages. Whether you are coming to terms with your sense of identity as an adolescent, negotiating with a spouse on how to raise a child as a young adult, or grappling with death and dying in older adulthood, your spirituality will impact your decisions and your overall wellness.

Spiritual wellness depends on many qualities, traits, and actions. Some experts in spiritual health refer to these elements as your "spiritual muscles" because they provide the foundation necessary for developing a strong sense of spiritual wellness. This self-assessment will help you examine your spiritual muscles. Respond to each statement honestly and openly, then calculate your score and evaluate it according to the guidelines at the end of the assessment.

I have a good sense of humor and giggle or laugh often. (humor)

Never	Rarely	Occasionally	Frequently	Always
1	2	3	4	5

I am able to forgive others if they've hurt my feelings or wronged me in some way. (forgiveness)

Never	Rarely	Occasionally	Frequently	Always
1	2	3	4	5

I am a curious person—I ask questions, seek out options and ideas, and am generally interested in learning. (curiosity)

Never	Rarely	Occasionally	Frequently	Always
1	2	3	4	5

I stick to the things I start and am persistent in pursuing my goals. (persistence)

Never	Rarely	Occasionally	Frequently	Always
1	2	3	4	5

I can move forward and make progress even if I feel scared. (courage)

Never	Rarely	Occasionally	Frequently	Always
1	2	3	4	5

I am able to wait for the right time to move forward or to seek acknowledgement for the things I do. (patience)

Never	Rarely	Occasionally	Frequently	Always
1	2	3	4	5

I feel a sense of purpose in my life. (optimism)

Never	Rarely	Occasionally	Frequently	Always
1	2	3	4	5

I have a general belief that things end up well and that there is a purpose for all things. (faith)

Never	Rarely	Occasionally	Frequently	Always
1	2	3	4	5

> continued

> continued

I trust my intuition and listen to my gut. (intuition)

Never	Rarely	Occasionally	Frequently	Always
1	2	3	4	5

I am able to care for someone or something without expecting recognition or reward for my actions. (compassion)

Never	Rarely	Occasionally	Frequently	Always
1	2	3	4	5

I am honest in my daily life and live according to a personal code of conduct. (integrity)

Never	Rarely	Occasionally	Frequently	Always
1	2	3	4	5

I treat others as I would like to be treated and seek to be kind and serve others. (humility)

Never	Rarely	Occasionally	Frequently	Always
1	2	3	4	5

I am imaginative and creative. (creativity)

Never	Rarely	Occasionally	Frequently	Always
1	2	3	4	5

I can love others without conditions and accept them for who they are. (unconditional love)

Never	Rarely	Occasionally	Frequently	Always
1	2	3	4	5

Total your score: _____

If your total score is 56 to 70, your spiritual muscles are strong. Continue seeking ways to cultivate your spirituality. If your total score is 29 to 42, your spiritual muscles are fairly strong, but something is holding you back. Reflect on your responses and identify three areas where you can improve. Write down what you can do to exercise those spiritual muscles more often and set some short- and long-term goals for doing so. If your total score is 14 to 28, your spiritual muscles are not as strong as they could be. Reflect on the list and identify five or more areas where you can improve. Write down what you can do to exercise your spiritual muscles more often and set some short- and long-term goals for doing so.

✔ Planning for Healthy Living

Use the Healthy Living Plan worksheet to focus on developing one or more aspects of your spiritual health.

Lesson 14.2
Aging Well

Lesson Objectives

After reading this lesson, you should be able to
1. identify the benefits of regular physical activity during the aging process,
2. understand how aging affects dietary needs and preferences, and
3. identify common sources of stress for aging individuals.

Lesson Vocabulary

activities of daily living, chronological age, physiological age

We're all growing older every day, but aging is a slow process that affects each of us differently. As a result, it is somewhat subjective. Most young people consider anyone who is 10 to 20 years older than themselves to be old, and many people over 60 still think of themselves as young and vital. In reality, decisions you make now can affect the aging process that you'll experience decades from now. For example, eating a balanced diet and doing weight-bearing exercises can help you develop strong bones that protect you from osteoporosis later in life and keep you safe if you fall or have a traumatic accident.

Conversely, if you choose, for example, to start smoking at a young age, you can accelerate the aging process of your skin and organs, making you look and feel older. You can also begin a slow process of damaging your lungs in a way that results in cancer 20 years down the road.

This lesson explores some of the ways in which aging is affected by healthy lifestyles choices and how the aging process affects healthy lifestyle recommendations.

Middle and Older Adulthood

The fifth and sixth stages of the life span are middle and older adulthood. At these stages, it is important to maintain emotional and physical health. Managing stress is also an important factor at this age, too. Adults have more care and support responsibilities for themselves, children not quite on their own, or parents in older generations. There can be changes in oneself with new career and personal goals or in a relationship with children moving out of the

---

DIVERSE PERSPECTIVES: Being an Older Parent

Our names are Madeline and Steve. We are both almost 60, and we have a son in high school and a daughter in junior high school. We met at work when we were both in our 30s and got married at almost age 40. Both of us wanted children earlier in life but had been committed to our careers; we also wanted to spend the first few years of our marriage traveling.

Having children in our mid-40s was difficult physically—we didn't have as much energy as

we'd once had. But we've both noticed that we don't seem to get as stressed out about parenting as younger parents do, and we're financially more secure than a lot of younger parents. Our kids are great, but I know they think we aren't as cool as some of their friends' parents. When the kids were younger we often felt uncomfortable around much younger parents as well. We know it embarrasses our kids when strangers say, "Are these your grandparents?" That's probably one of the hardest parts.

house. As for physiological changes, some people start getting back or joint pain, wrinkles, or vision loss. Women experience menopause at this time, too. Although there can be many changes at these stages, people generally feel more established.

Physical Activity and Aging

Regular physical activity is beneficial to people of every age. A person is never too old to participate in some sort of physical activity. Still, as people move through the middle-age years and into the senior years, the habits they developed in their teens and young adulthood have a considerable effect. Regular physical activity has been shown to delay the onset of most chronic diseases, reduce adult weight gain, improve mood, and delay disease- and illness-related death (see figure 14.3). Regular exercise has also been shown to help reduce the risk of dementia—the leading cause of disability among people over 80.

Just as important, when older people engage in physical activity and exercise, they retain a higher level of fitness and are generally more mobile. As a result, they are better able to manage **activities of daily living**, such as bathing, preparing food, eating, and dressing. This ability allows them to remain independent, productive citizens for longer periods of time. Active older adults can also play more with their grandchildren and great-grandchildren, travel more often and more easily, participate in more leisure activities, and remain more socially engaged

and connected to their communities. Physical activity and exercise recommendations for older adults are presented in figure 14.4. In short, being active throughout your life is one of the most important things you can do to ensure wellness as you age.

Nutrition and Aging

Eating well throughout your life also plays a critical role in how well you will remain as you age. Overall, people's nutritional needs are similar at all ages. All teens, adults, and older adults should eat a balanced diet of nutritionally dense foods. They should all minimize intake of saturated fat and sodium, eat plenty of fiber and foods rich in antioxidants, and limit their intake of alcohol.

Some differences, however, do exist. For example, most adults require fewer daily calories as they age because of decreased metabolic rate. After the age of 19, the recommended daily calories decrease by 10 per year for men and by 7 per year for women. As a result, by the time a person reaches age 70, daily need is about 350 to 500 calories lower than it was at age 20. But if a person remains physically active throughout life, and therefore loses less muscle, his caloric need will be a bit higher than that of a sedentary person.

Though caloric need may drop with age, some nutrient needs may increase—for example, calcium and vitamins B_6, B_{12}, C, and D. As a result, older people need to eat high-quality, nutrient-dense

Provides opportunities for social engagement

Helps reduce the impacts of stress

Helps speed the recovery from injuries and illnesses

Helps prevent depression

Helps prevent chronic disease

Helps prevent dementia and Alzheimer's disease (a cause of dementia)

Helps maintain muscle mass, metabolism, and strength

Helps maintain independence

FIGURE 14.3 The benefits of physical activity for older adults. Some of these could apply to middle adulthood, too.

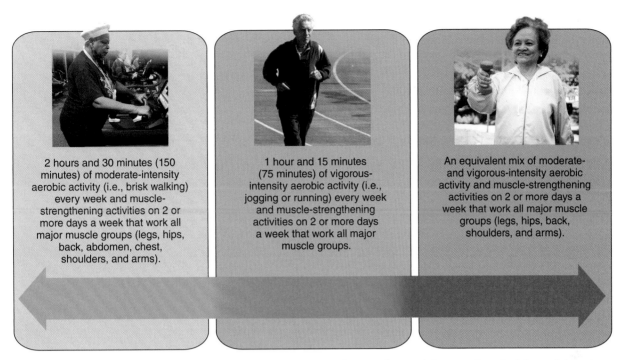

2 hours and 30 minutes (150 minutes) of moderate-intensity aerobic activity (i.e., brisk walking) every week and muscle-strengthening activities on 2 or more days a week that work all major muscle groups (legs, hips, back, abdomen, chest, shoulders, and arms).	1 hour and 15 minutes (75 minutes) of vigorous-intensity aerobic activity (i.e., jogging or running) every week and muscle-strengthening activities on 2 or more days a week that work all major muscle groups.	An equivalent mix of moderate- and vigorous-intensity aerobic activity and muscle-strengthening activities on 2 or more days a week that work all major muscle groups (legs, hips, back, shoulders, and arms).

FIGURE 14.4 Physical activity and exercise recommendations for middle-aged and older adults: three options.

foods. Dietary needs and nutrition status can also be affected by many diseases and health conditions. In addition, an aging person's ability to get proper nutrition can be hindered by poverty or economic struggle, tooth loss, certain medications, lack of social support, and loss of independence.

What Does It Mean to Grow Old?

In 2011, a Londoner named Fauja Singh completed his seventh marathon at the age of 100; he had run his first at the age of 89. We often think of aging as

Most adults require fewer daily calories as they age because of decreased metabolic rate.

robert lerich/fotolia.com

a process of becoming weaker and frailer. However, people like Fauja Singh have demonstrated that the fact of aging itself is not nearly as important as how we choose to age. Research shows that the lifestyle choices we make throughout life affect our health and wellness more strongly than our **chronological age** (numeric age) does. This is particularly true as we move through midlife and into older ages. Maintaining a healthy lifestyle can keep your **physiological age**—the effective age of your body based on its ability to function well—lower than your chronological age.

Throughout this book, you're reading about various aspects of health and wellness and considering what affects your health in all the components of wellness. As you continue through life and eventually enter old age, making healthy lifestyle choices is critical to your ability to stay healthy, maintain your independence, and enhance your quality of life.

Stresses of Aging

Albert is a retired military officer who lost his wife two years ago. He has no children and was an only child. Albert has arthritis and takes several medica-

⏵) HEALTHY COMMUNICATION

How are older adults portrayed in the media? Do you think media stereotypes influence your perceptions of older adults? What experiences do you have with older adults? How do you think those experiences influence your views of aging? Share your perspectives with a friend or classmate. Use facts to support your position, and be respectful of each other's perspectives.

tions for heart and blood pressure problems. When his wife, Patricia, was alive, she picked up his medications, helped with meal preparation, and managed some of the household tasks. As a result, Albert rarely felt uneasy or alone. Now, without her help, Albert now finds himself struggling. He doesn't have money to hire help and he has to ask neighbors to pick up his medications. He stresses for days about whom to ask and hates to inconvenience his busy, younger neighbors. His pain is sometimes so bad that he struggles to prepare his meals, and he feels he has no one to turn to. Figuring out what to eat and getting groceries are also sources of stress.

Stress is a part of all stages of life. In Albert's younger years, he might have felt stress mostly in relation to his military job. As an older adult, his stress relates largely to managing his pain and living in daily isolation. Understanding stressors and managing stress effectively are part of a lifelong process that can greatly affect how well we age.

Older adults do experience some common, and sometimes unfamiliar, stressors (see figure 14.5). However, many studies have shown that older adults report less stress overall. It's possible that older adults have the same degree of stressful situations but have learned to deal with stress better and become more resilient over time. The wisdom that comes with age can help a person put common stressors in perspective. An older adult who has managed difficult times in the past may not seem as bothered by stressful experiences in older age.

Lifestyle choices we make throughout life affect our health and wellness more strongly than our chronological age does.

Death of spouse or lifelong friends

Financial strains

Health issues and problems

Depression and social isolation

Fear of loss of memories and concentration

Pain and discomfort from illness or treatments

Loss of independence

FIGURE 14.5 Common causes of stress in older adults.

Learning to cope with stress in the earlier stages of life—and doing so throughout life—not only helps you slow down the aging process and reduce your risk of disease, but it can also help you be more resilient later in life.

> " I think that age as a number is not nearly as important as health. You can be in poor health and be pretty miserable at 40 or 50. If you're in good health, you can enjoy things into your 80s. "
>
> —Bob Barker, entertainer

HEALTH TECHNOLOGY

Homes that can respond to the environment on their own used to be a futuristic idea, but that is changing. Now technologies make living at home possible for more people who are dealing with disability or age-related changes. For example, in-home monitoring systems help caregivers and health care workers see and talk with people even if they're not nearby. They can conduct basic physical exams, track medication use, and monitor vital signs from a distance.

In addition, computer technology now allows a person to control the home's temperature, lighting, security, and electronics using voice commands or applications without needing to get up. Devices such as lighting and temperature sensors and controls can even be programmed to make adjustments as a person moves around in the home. And voice commands or remote con-

trols can fill a bathtub with water, raise a toilet seat, or turn on a faucet.

Soon, the integration of global positioning system (GPS) technology will create even more options. For example, smart home controls could notify someone when public transportation (e.g., a bus) is approaching the house. As new technologies are integrated into home living, the possibilities will continue to grow for people to remain independent and age comfortably and safely within their own homes.

 CONNECT

How do you think technology will affect the way you live in the future? Do you think technology will help you live a longer and better life? Why or why not?

⚛ HEALTH SCIENCE

Studies show that pet owners are more likely than other people to live longer and to recover from major health events, such as heart attacks. Research has also shown that interaction with animals can lower blood pressure and reduce feelings of anxiety and stress. Incorporating animals into the care of people with disease, disability, or aging-related impairment is referred to as animal-assisted intervention (AAI). A variety of populations have benefited, including elderly people, cancer and cardiac patients, those with autism, and people with anxiety or social disorders.

Some animals are used specifically for therapeutic purposes and can help patients relax and engage more fully in therapy. Animals can also provide direct assistance, as in the case of dogs that help people with vision impairments. Service dogs can also directly assist people by opening doors and cabinets or retrieving items such as phones or clothing. Many types of animals—including cats, fish, and birds—can provide companionship to aging people whose circumstances limit their interactions with people. Regardless of whether the animal is a beloved family pet or a working therapy dog, they provide unconditional love and a steady presence that can benefit the health of their human companions.

Photodisc

Comprehension Check

1. What are the benefits of physical activity in older adults?
2. What is one physical change that occurs with aging that might influence a person's diet or eating habits?
3. What are five common stressors that older adults may encounter?

Damon is a high school senior who loves to win. Recently, his school sponsored a Walk the Globe challenge, and Damon was excited to participate. The walk raised money for Alzheimer's disease research. He thought it might help him get in shape, and he also had his heart set on winning the grand prize—a new iPad. The idea of the challenge, sponsored by the school's wellness club, was to see who could walk enough steps to make it "around the world" the fastest.

Damon was one of the first students to register and pick up his pedometer and walking chart. Every time you saw Damon, in school or around the neighborhood, he was walking and bragging about how he was going to win the prize. He seemed highly motivated, and he even lost a few pounds and gained a little more energy. As it turned out, he finished in second place and won a free water bottle. Despite his strong result, Damon stopped walking and actually seemed to sulk a little. Other students were surprised because he had seemed so motivated during the contest.

For Discussion

Does Damon seem to be intrinsically or extrinsically motivated? How can you tell? (To learn about these kinds of motivation, see the Skills for Healthy Living feature.) What are some things that Damon could do to become more intrinsically motivated? How might the campus wellness club help students build intrinsic motivation when they put together their next campus challenge?

 SKILLS FOR HEALTHY LIVING: Intrinsic Motivation

Intrinsic motivation involves doing something not because it brings recognition or reward but because you enjoy it or value it. For example, people who participate in healthy activities (e.g., exercise, healthy eating) for intrinsic reasons do so because they value the health benefits and enjoy the active lifestyle.

Extrinsic motivation, on the other hand, refers to doing something to get an external reward or avoid a punishment. Extrinsic motivation can sometimes motivate someone to begin a healthy behavior or avoid an unhealthy behavior, but it eventually fades away when the reward is achieved or is no longer valued.

As a result, change in health behaviors depends on intrinsic motivation. Here are some tips to help you develop your intrinsic motivation:

- **Learn and understand the benefits of healthy behaviors.** Knowledge can be a factor in developing internal reasons for choosing to live a healthy lifestyle.

- **Appreciate the effects of healthy living over your life span.** Talk to people who are older than you and are healthy and energetic. Compare them with others who are unhealthy. Think about how you would like to be in 5, 10, 20, or 30 years. Use that vision to motivate your choices now.

- **Give yourself credit for trying.** Sometimes the greatest reward comes from doing something challenging, even if you don't fully succeed. Commend yourself for having courage, persevering, and keeping a positive attitude. Believing that success is all or nothing is a quick way to undermine your own intrinsic motivation.

- **Set achievable goals, not just aspirations.** It's okay to dream big and hope for great things. Set small, realistic goals for yourself. Doing so can help you reach your dreams and build your intrinsic motivation in the process.

- **Find friends who share your value of healthy living.** When people share a value or appreciation for something, they find joy in the process of doing it together.

- **Stick with positive self-talk.** Avoid cutting yourself down or punishing yourself if you don't succeed at a goal. Remind yourself that you can and will do better the next time you try.

ACADEMIC CONNECTION: The Metric System

In the United States we typically express measurements in what are called U.S. customary units. However, most of the rest of the world and much of the scientific community use the metric system. Metric is a system of measurement that has three main units: the meter (m) for length, the gram (g) for weight, and the second (s) for time. Each of these main measures is then expressed as larger or smaller units based on a standard prefix (see table). For example, a kilogram is the same as 1,000 grams, and a centimeter is the same as one hundredth (1/100) of a meter. If a man's height is 200 centimeters, how many meters tall is he? If a woman's weight is 60,000 grams, how many kilograms does she weigh?

Common Big and Small Numbers

Name	Number	Prefix	Symbol
trillion	1,000,000,000,000	tera	T
billion	1,000,000,000	giga	G
million	1,000,000	mega	M
thousand	1,000	kilo	k
hundred	100	hecto	h
ten	10	deka	da
Unit	1		
tenth	0.1	deci	d
hundredth	0.01	centi	c
thousandth	0.001	milli	m
millionth	0.000 001	micro	µ
billionth	0.000 000 001	nano	n
trillionth	0.000 000 000 001	pico	p

Does a High-Carbohydrate Diet Contribute to Mild Cognitive Impairment?

Most adults have considered the possibility of dying from heart disease or cancer. We're all familiar with the fact that these diseases are among the most common causes of death. At the same time, Alzheimer's disease is contributing to more deaths each year (see figure 14.6). In fact, Alzheimer's affects 5.2 million adults in the United States, and that number is expected to triple by 2050. While we know that eating a diet lower in saturated fat may help us hold off heart disease or cancer, what do we know about how diet affects the risk of Alzheimer's?

Seeking to answer this question, Mayo Clinic researchers tracked the eating habits of 1,230 people between the ages of 70 and 89 for one year. Next, the 940 people who showed no sign of cognitive impairment were asked to return for a 15-month follow-up. By the study's fourth year, 200 of those 940 people were beginning to show mild cognitive impairment (MCI), which can include problems with memory, language, thinking, and judgment.

People with the highest carbohydrate intake were nearly twice as likely to develop MCI as people who ate a balanced diet.

"Not everyone with MCI goes on to develop Alzheimer's disease, but many do," says Professor Rosebud Roberts, a researcher in Mayo's epidemiology division in Rochester, Minnesota. "A high-carbohydrate intake could be bad for you because carbohydrates impact your glucose and insulin metabolism."

Since sugar fuels the brain, a moderate amount is essential. However, high levels of sugar may actually interfere with the brain's ability to use the sugar for fuel. Roberts says high glucose levels might affect the brain's blood vessels and also play a role in the development of plaques in the brain that interfere with normal neural functioning. "Those proteins are toxic to brain health and are found in the brains of people with Alzheimer's," states Roberts.

The study found that people whose diets had the highest intake of protein (e.g., from chicken, meat, or fish) reduced their risk of cognitive impairment by 21 percent. Those whose diets were highest in fat (e.g., from nuts or healthy oils) were 42 percent less likely to have cognitive impairment. However, Janet DeMarzo, a medical doctor with the American Cancer Society, warns that "while these results show the benefits of a high-fat diet for the prevention of cognitive impairment, the same diet proves to increase the risk of cancer and heart disease."

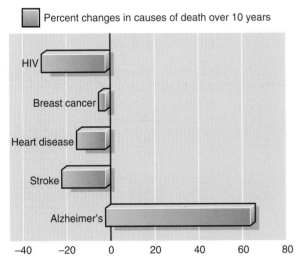

Figure 14.6 Recent changes in death rates. Alzheimer's has greatly increased while the others have decreased.

For Discussion

Do you think older adults at risk for Alzheimer's disease should eat a high-fat diet, which might reduce the chance of cognitive impairment but increase the risk of cancer and cardiovascular disease? Why or why not?

Reviewing Concepts and Vocabulary

As directed by your teacher, answer items 1 through 5 by correctly completing each sentence with a word or phrase.

1. Changes in motor skills, perception, and hearing are a normal part of _____ development.

2. The acquisition and development of skills such as language, problem solving, and reasoning are part of _____ development.

3. Periods of relatively rapid growth called _____ _____ can cause aches and pains as well as muscle cramps.

4. Bathing, preparing food, eating, and dressing are examples of _____ _____ _____ _____.

5. Regular exercise has been shown to play a role in reducing the risk of _____, which is the leading cause of disability among people over the age of 80.

For items 6 through 10, as directed by your teacher, match each term in column 1 with the appropriate phrase in column 2.

6. abstract thinking
7. reasoning skills
8. socioemotional development
9. chronological age
10. physiological age

a. the way you solve problems and make decisions
b. the number of years you have been alive
c. includes self-esteem, empathy, and friendships
d. how well your body systems are aging
e. the ability to consider things that are not visible, immediate, or concrete

For items 11 through 15, as directed by your teacher, respond to each statement or question.

11. What is socioemotional development?
12. What are two things you should never do when caring for an infant?
13. Describe two health careers that might interest you.
14. Why might young adulthood be a stressful time? Provide two reasons.
15. Define *intrinsic motivation* and give an example.

Thinking Critically

Write a response to the following prompt.

List and discuss the major physical and mental changes that occur with aging. Which ones can you affect through your own choices? What changes can you begin to make now to help you age well? Write a letter to yourself as you are now, and another letter to yourself at age 65, to remind yourself of these changes and motivate yourself to make healthy choices.

Take It Home

Think of a person you know and respect who is older than 65—for example, a parent, grandparent, neighbor, or family friend. Interview the person about his or her life. Find out what challenges the person faces and what steps he or she takes to try to overcome them. Ask the person what advice he or she has for you about staying healthy as you age. Write a brief report about what you learn.

Joggie Botma/fotolia.com

UNIT V

Avoiding Destructive Habits

● ● ● ● ● ● ● ● ● ● ● ● ● ● ●

Healthy People 2020 Goals

- Reduce tobacco use by adolescents.
- Reduce the initiation of tobacco use among children, adolescents, and young adults.
- Reduce exposure to secondhand smoke.
- Increase tobacco-free environments in schools.
- Reduce the proportion of adolescents and young adults (in grades 6 through 12) exposed to tobacco advertising and promotion.
- Reduce the sale of tobacco to minors.
- Reduce the proportion of adolescents who ride with a driver who has been drinking alcohol.
- Increase the number of states with ignition interlock laws for impaired driving offenders.
- Reduce binge drinking of alcohol.
- Reduce average annual alcohol consumption.
- Reduce fatalities related to alcohol-impaired driving (0.08 blood alcohol content or higher).
- Increase the proportion of adolescents who never engage in substance abuse.
- Increase the proportion of adolescents who disapprove of substance abuse.
- Increase the proportion of adolescents who perceive great risk associated with substance abuse.
- Reduce drug-induced deaths.
- Reduce steroid use among adolescents.
- Reduce nonmedical use of prescription drugs.
- Reduce the proportion of adolescents who use inhalants.
- Reduce the proportion of adolescents who have been offered, sold, or given an illegal drug on school property.

Self-Assessment Features in This Unit

- My Tobacco Knowledge
- My Alcohol Knowledge
- My Drug Knowledge

Making Healthy Decisions and Skills for Healthy Living Features in This Unit

- Preventing Relapse
- Finding Social Support
- Building Refusal Skills

Special Features in This Unit

- Advocacy in Action: Tackling Tobacco Ads
- Diverse Perspectives: Alcoholism
- Consumer Corner: Selecting and Using Over-the-Counter Drugs

Living Well News Features in This Unit

- What's in That Cigarette You're Smoking?
- Are Americans Set Up to Become Alcoholics?
- Is Aspirin a Miracle Drug?

15

Tobacco

In This Chapter

 Student Web Resources
www.healthforlifetextbook.org/student

PhotoDisc

Lesson 15.1
• • • • • • • • • •
Health Hazards of Tobacco Use

Lesson Objectives

After reading this lesson, you should be able to

1. explain how using tobacco or smoking began,
2. list at least three reasons that people use tobacco or smoke, and
3. list at least three diseases or disorders caused by tobacco.

Lesson Vocabulary

neurotransmitter, secondhand smoke, smokeless tobacco, sudden infant death syndrome (SIDS)

What do the U.S. Centers for Disease Control and Prevention (CDC), the American Cancer Society, the American Heart Association, the American Lung Association, and the American Medical Association have in common? They all recognize that tobacco use is the number one cause of preventable disease in the United States.

Most Americans who smoke started doing so before the age of 18, and according to the CDC about 70 percent of current smokers want to quit. This chapter explores the reasons that people smoke, the health risks of using tobacco, trends of smoking and smokeless tobacco use in the United States, ways to stop smoking, U.S. laws affecting tobacco use, and how tobacco use in the United States compares with use in other countries.

History

Some experts trace the tobacco plant more than 8,000 years into the past. You may already know that Native Americans have historically used tobacco in religious ceremonies and as medicine. You may also know that tobacco was, and still is, a common and important crop in certain parts of the United States. Of course, people were not aware of the health risks associated with tobacco use until extensive research was conducted in relatively recent times. Even before science produced strong research, however, cigarettes were referred to as "coffin nails," thus linking them to premature death. Still, many people believed that tobacco had healing powers.

This was not the first (or the last) time that a product or procedure intended for healing caused more harm than good. For example, over a period of centuries, bloodletting (intentional bleeding using leeches) was the treatment of choice for many diseases and disorders; in this practice, blood was removed from the body in the belief that doing so would remove toxins or poisons. Neither bloodletting nor tobacco use are included in modern medical practice. To the contrary, tobacco use is responsible for about 400,000 to 450,000 premature deaths per year.

Perhaps someday there will be so few smokers that ash trays will be valued as collector's items. That's what happened in the case of spittoons, which were common when many more people used **smokeless tobacco**. These people needed to spit frequently, rather than swallow the tobacco juice that mixed with their saliva. As a result, spittoons were as common as trash cans in bars, restaurants, and even private homes. Over time, spitting came to be viewed as unsanitary and offensive; laws were passed against spitting, and spittoons became a thing of the past. Unfortunately, as smokeless tobacco became less popular, smoking became more popular.

Types of Tobacco

Tobacco is legally available to adults in the U.S. in many different forms. Manufactured cigarettes are the most commonly used forms followed by cigars (large cigars, cigarillos, and little cigars), smokeless tobacco (chewing tobacco and snuff), pipe smoking, and small pockets of hookahs (water pipes). Other forms include bidis cigarettes (hand rolled in special leaves) mostly from India and kreteks (cigarettes containing cloves and tobacco). These modes of tobacco use are not considered to be safe with long-term use.

The Health Risks of Tobacco Use

Tobacco use poses many health risks. Figure 15.1 provides a partial list of diseases and disorders associated with or made worse by smoking.

Figure 15.2 shows the number of deaths attributed to smoking and **secondhand smoke**, as well as the major causes of death. The two major killers are respiratory disease and heart disease. Many of the health problems associated with smoking, such as cancer and heart and lung disease, do not occur until a person has smoked regularly for many years. As a result, people in their teens sometimes find it hard to feel concerned about something that might happen to them in 20 or 30 years. Either they can't imagine being that much older, or they believe that they'll be able to stop smoking before it's too late. However, as discussed later in this chapter, it can be very difficult to quit smoking. In addition, some of the negative effects can arise much sooner than others—for example, bad breath, yellowing of the fingernails, and asthma. Thirdhand smoke is when the smoke clings to clothes, walls, furniture, and so on. It can remain even if smoking has ceased and it may be associated with some increased risk of cancers.

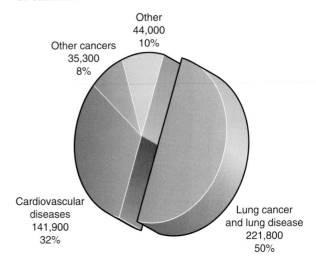

FIGURE 15.2 Deaths attributed to smoking.

Data is from www.cdc.gov/tobacco/data_statistics/tables/health/attrdeaths/.

◀)) HEALTHY COMMUNICATION

If teenage smokers could see 20 years into their future and knew for certain that smoking would cause them to develop cancer in their 40s, do you think this knowledge would be enough to make them kick the habit? Why or why not? Debate your perspectives with a peer who has different views from yours. Listen to each other's opinions and determine where you agree and disagree.

Smoking and Pregnancy

According to the March of Dimes (a U.S. nonprofit organization that advocates for infant health), exposure to tobacco during and after pregnancy (including secondhand smoke) puts embryos and babies at risk for developing many health problems including **sudden infant death syndrome (SIDS)** (see figure 15.3).

Why Do People Smoke?

People smoke for many reasons. Some people think smoking is necessary in order to fit in with their

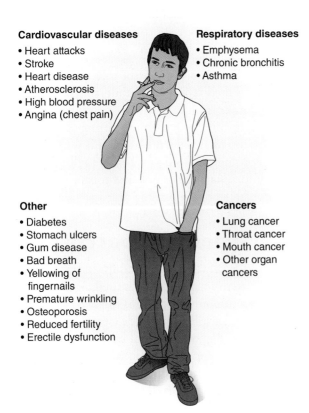

Cardiovascular diseases
• Heart attacks
• Stroke
• Heart disease
• Atherosclerosis
• High blood pressure
• Angina (chest pain)

Respiratory diseases
• Emphysema
• Chronic bronchitis
• Asthma

Other
• Diabetes
• Stomach ulcers
• Gum disease
• Bad breath
• Yellowing of fingernails
• Premature wrinkling
• Osteoporosis
• Reduced fertility
• Erectile dysfunction

Cancers
• Lung cancer
• Throat cancer
• Mouth cancer
• Other organ cancers

FIGURE 15.1 A partial list of diseases and disorders associated with or made worse by smoking.

Women who smoke during pregnancy are more likely to have vaginal bleeding or problems with the placenta.

Babies born to women who smoke during pregnancy are more likely to be born with birth defects such as cleft lip or palate or be underweight or still-born.

Babies exposed to secondhand smoke are more likely to die from SIDS (sudden infant death syndrome); be at greater risk for asthma, bronchitis, pneumonia, ear infections, and respiratory symptoms; or experience slow lung growth.

FIGURE 15.3 Effects of smoking on infant health.

friends who smoke, although peer pressure is not the top reason that people smoke. Some people who smoke want to imitate their favorite actor or singer. In addition, if a parent smokes, you're more likely to smoke. Some people also try smoking out of simple curiosity, others smoke as an act of rebellion, and some think it will help them lose weight. And then of course there's advertising.

Overall, men use tobacco products more than women, but the gap between males and females has been narrowing. Most people think they're not very affected by advertising, but research tells a different story. And think about it: Tobacco manufacturers wouldn't spend hundreds of millions of dollars each year in advertising and promotion if it didn't work.

⊕ CONNECT

Do members of your immediate family smoke? Do you think their choices regarding smoking have influenced (or will influence) your likelihood of smoking? Why or why not?

When you ask people who've tried smoking if their first experience of it was pleasant, most say no. Some people get dizzy or light headed, some cough, some feel nauseous, and others simply don't like the taste or the overall experience. If most people's first impression of smoking is bad, why do some people try it again and again? Smoking is an acquired taste. As with food, you sometimes come to like something only after trying it many times. With smoking, this process is encouraged by the addictive element of nicotine and even chemicals or additives—such as menthol—that tobacco companies add to cigarettes. People may grow to like the taste and the feeling of smoking that is made more intense by their dependence on nicotine.

In fact, if you count each puff of a cigarette as a dose, or hit, no other drug is used as frequently as nicotine. According to the National Institute on Drug Abuse (NIDA) (a research group of the U.S. government), cigarettes and other forms of tobacco (including cigars, pipe tobacco, snuff, and chewing tobacco) contain not only nicotine but also hundreds of other chemicals and substances (see figure 15.4). Nicotine is the addictive ingredient, and it is readily absorbed into the bloodstream whenever a tobacco product is chewed or inhaled. In fact, nicotine reaches the brain within 10 seconds of inhalation. For each cigarette, a typical smoker takes 10 puffs over a period of five minutes. Thus, a person who smokes about 1 1/2 packs (30 cigarettes) daily gets 300 hits of nicotine in his or her brain every day.

Sometimes people can be tricked into believing that light cigarettes are safer than regular cigarettes. This is not true. In fact, there is no established safe level of tobacco smoking. Sidestream smoke, or secondhand smoke, can be more dangerous than smoke that is directly inhaled from a cigarette, cigar, or pipe because the particles in the secondhand smoke are smaller. Most people are not exposed to secondhand smoke as often as smokers are exposed to direct smoke, though. Of course, smokers breathe in both direct and secondhand smoke.

When nicotine enters a person's bloodstream, it immediately stimulates his or her adrenal glands to release the hormone epinephrine (adrenaline). Epinephrine, in turn, stimulates the person's central nervous system and increases his or her blood pressure, respiration, and heart rate. In addition,

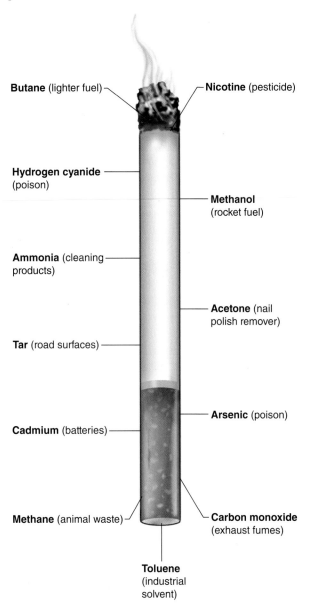

Butane (lighter fuel)

Nicotine (pesticide)

Hydrogen cyanide
(poison)

Methanol
(rocket fuel)

Ammonia (cleaning
products)

Acetone (nail
polish remover)

Tar (road surfaces)

Arsenic (poison)

Cadmium (batteries)

Methane (animal waste)

Carbon monoxide
(exhaust fumes)

Toluene
(industrial
solvent)

FIGURE 15.4 Cigarettes contain many harmful substances that are used in many other ways in addition to nicotine.

glucose is released into the person's blood, and insulin output from his or her pancreas is suppressed. These effects result in chronically higher blood sugar among nicotine users. Nicotine in cigarettes and in smokeless tobacco are both harmful. Nicotine from smoking may enter the body faster than nicotine absorbed through the mouth or gums. If the same amount of nicotine enters the body, regardless of the source, they are equally harmful, though. Because people tend to use tobacco products at a level that satisfies them, the blood levels of nicotine in smokeless and smoked tobacco users tend to be very similar over the period of a day.

Like cocaine, heroin, and marijuana, nicotine increases a person's level of the **neurotransmitter** dopamine, which affects the brain pathways that control reward and pleasure. For many tobacco users, long-term brain changes induced by continued nicotine exposure result in addiction—a condition of compulsive drug seeking and use, even in the face of negative consequences. Nicotine is actually more addictive than drugs like cocaine, but cocaine has a much greater potential for causing immediate harm than nicotine.

Comprehension Check

1. Give a historical reason why people used tobacco before there were tobacco companies.
2. What are two influences in society that increase the chance that a person will use tobacco?
3. How can using tobacco products during pregnancy be harmful to the embryo or fetus?

Take the following quiz to see how much you know about the dangers of smoking and tobacco use.

1. Chemicals are added to tobacco when cigarettes are made.
   a. true
   b. false
2. Nicotine is classified as a drug.
   a. true
   b. false
3. The average smoker begins to smoke at age 22.
   a. true
   b. false
4. Peers influence teens to begin smoking more than any other influence.
   a. true
   b. false
5. Light cigarettes are healthier than regular cigarettes.
   a. true
   b. false
6. There are such things as safe cigarettes.
   a. true
   b. false
7. Nicotine is more addictive than cocaine.
   a. true
   b. false
8. The nicotine in chewing tobacco is less harmful than the nicotine in cigarettes.
   a. true
   b. false
9. Smoke inhaled directly from a cigarette is more dangerous than secondhand smoke.
   a. true
   b. false
10. Men are more likely to smoke than women.
    a. true
    b. false

Here are the correct answers: question 1 a, 2 a, 3 b, 4 b, 5 b, 6 b, 7 a, 8 b, 9 b, and 10 a. If you got nine or ten answers right, you really know your stuff. If you got seven or eight right, you're ahead of most people but still have some things to learn. If you got five or six right, you could stand to brush up on the facts. If you got four or fewer right, seek out more information.

✔ Planning for Healthy Living

Use the Healthy Living Plan worksheet to help you quit smoking (if you smoke) or to continue being smoke free throughout your life. If relevant, consider whether you would use modern technology to help you.

Lesson 15.2
· · · · · · · · · · ·
Marketing, Policies, Cessation, and Advocacy

Lesson Objectives

After reading this lesson, you should be able to

1. describe current trends in tobacco smoking among young people,
2. name two policies that discourage people from smoking, and
3. describe at least three methods of smoking cessation.

Lesson Vocabulary

countermarketing, media literacy, product placement, social marketing

In the United States, about 20 percent of people smoke, and a little more than 3 percent use smokeless tobacco. Turned around, these numbers mean that 80 percent of Americans do *not* smoke, and 97 percent don't use smokeless tobacco. Among U.S. high school students in 2010, according to the CDC, about 17 percent smoked, and 6 percent used smokeless tobacco. Clearly, the overwhelming majority of high school students do not use any kind of tobacco product.

The graph presented in figure 15.5 shows U.S. smoking trends from 1965 to 2009. As you can see, the rate of tobacco use has been going down among both adults and teens. A short-term rise did occur in teen smoking in the 1990s, due in part to

a drop in cigarette prices at the time. In fact, it is estimated that every 10 percent reduction in the cost of cigarettes increases cigarette use among teenagers by 7 percent.

There are many reasons that fewer people in the United States smoke today than in years past. In a health textbook such as this one, you might expect to be presented with only facts about how harmful tobacco is to your health, but years of experience show that facts alone are not enough to decrease the number of smokers or to stop people from starting to smoke. Fortunately, several tactics *have* helped decrease tobacco use in the U.S.—increased price, policy and law changes, **countermarketing**, **social marketing**, and education.

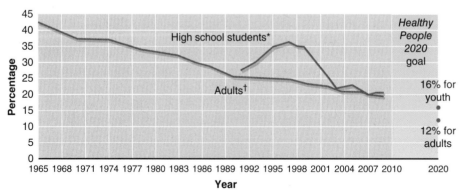

* Percentage of high school students who smoked cigarettes on 1 or more of the 30 days preceding the survey (Youth Risk Behavior Survey, 1991-2009). Data first collected in 1991.
† Percentage of adults who are current cigarette smokers (National Health Interview Survey, 1965-2009).

FIGURE 15.5 Trends in smoking among high school students and adults from 1965 to 2009.

From www.cdc.gov/chronicdisease/resources/publications/AAG/osh.htm.

Price

Price is important because the more expensive tobacco products are—whether due to price increases set by manufacturers or to increased taxes levied on tobacco products—the more likely it is that some smokers will either cut back or quit. Part of the reason is that people who earn less money tend to use tobacco products at a higher rate than people who earn more money. In addition, there comes a point with any product at which people feel that enough is enough and decide to cut back, stop, or switch to a cheaper alternative. For example, when the movie rental service Netflix raised its prices in 2011, it lost more than 800,000 customers; the company responded by lowering its prices. In the marketing of any product, price matters, and tobacco products are no exception.

With this in mind, many public health professionals have advocated for higher taxes on tobacco products, which would raise their overall price, thus meaning that fewer people would smoke. In addition, the money raised through the higher taxes could be used to help fund programs to help people quit using tobacco. Unfortunately, very few states have used tobacco taxes for tobacco prevention or cessation programs because these funds tend to go into general accounts and are spent on things like roads, bridges, and other needed products and services.

In another strategy, the state attorney generals of 46 U.S. states sued the largest four tobacco companies in 1998 for the medical costs of tobacco-related diseases and disorders that were paid by taxpayers. In the resulting Tobacco Master Settlement Agreement, the tobacco companies agreed to pay billions of dollars to the states in exchange for an agreement that the tobacco companies could not be held legally responsible for harm caused by tobacco products. Tobacco companies also agreed to cut back or eliminate advertising to youth.

Where there are fewer places for people to smoke, more people quit smoking.

Policies and Laws

In recent years, many policies and laws have dramatically changed how people view smoking in the United States. It is now hard to believe that at one time people could smoke on airplanes, in movie theaters, in school teachers' lounges, and even in hospitals. Smoke-free laws have been implemented in the majority of U.S. states, as well as the District of Columbia, Puerto Rico, the U.S. Virgin Islands, and hundreds of U.S. cities and counties that don't have statewide bans.

Many workplaces have created their own smoke-free policies—for example, banning smoking in company vehicles or even anywhere on the organization's property. Not surprisingly, more than 3,500 U.S. hospitals have also banned smoking on their property—inside or outside. In addition, nearly 800 college campuses have enacted total smoking bans.

Smoking bans have been passed for several reasons. Probably the most important one is to protect others from secondhand smoke. Just as construction companies require their workers to wear helmets to protect them from injury, policies and laws have been passed to protect workers from the dangers of secondhand smoke. The CDC estimates that exposure to secondhand smoke causes 46,000 deaths per year in the United States alone.

When children are exposed to secondhand smoke at home, they are more likely to suffer severe asthma attacks and other respiratory conditions, such as bronchitis, coughing, and sneezing. For these and

Photodisc

other reasons, 34 states have passed laws prohibiting smoking in commercial day care centers, and 33 prohibit smoking in home-based child care centers. Smoking bans reduce the risks of heart attack in both smokers and nonsmokers and thus are considered an effective mechanism for creating a healthier society.

Another reason for laws and policies against tobacco use is the fact that nonsmokers greatly outnumber smokers. The greater the gap grows between nonsmokers and smokers, the more likely communities are to enact policies and laws restricting smoking. Nonsmokers find it unfair to have to inhale secondhand smoke at work or in restaurants and other public places.

As you might expect, where there are fewer places for people to smoke, more people quit smoking. With the passage of more and more smoking bans—along with other factors such as the prohibition of cigarette lighters on airplanes—the habit of smoking is becoming increasingly difficult for people to maintain.

Legal Age for Buying Tobacco Products

In most U.S. states, it is illegal for a person under the age of 18 to purchase tobacco products (in a few states, the legal age is 19). New York City passed a law restricting the purchase of tobacco until the age of 21. Many communities conduct compliance checks by having people under the legal age try to buy tobacco in order to see if the business operator properly checks identification rather than selling the product to the minor. Businesses that sell to minors

are often fined, and many times the employee who sold to the minor is fired. If a business repeatedly sells tobacco to minors, it may lose its license to sell tobacco products. It is also illegal for adults to purchase tobacco for minors.

Depending on state law, minors who try to purchase tobacco products could also be fined or assigned to perform community service. Purchasing tobacco (or alcohol) with a fake ID is a much more serious offense, and it is also illegal to make, manufacture, or sell fake IDs; doing so can result in a felony conviction and a large fine.

CONNECT

Oddly, although it's illegal for minors to purchase tobacco products, it's not always against the law for them to use these products depending on what state they live in. Do you think it should be illegal for minors to smoke at all? Debate your perspective with your peers. Support your position with facts and be respectful of each other's opinions.

Smoking, Fires, and Housing Policies

According to the U.S. Fire Administration, almost a thousand people are killed by smoking-related fires each year in the United States, and 25 percent of those who die are family members, friends, or neighbors of the smokers who cause the fires. One-third of those who die in these fires are the children of the smokers.

Why Are the Rules Different for Young People?

Laws are often enacted for the purpose of protecting young people. The belief is that youths have not fully matured and therefore may not be able to make effective decisions about certain issues that carry high stakes. That's part of the reason we have separate juvenile and adult courts.

Even the tobacco industry now takes an official stand against young people smoking. Industry representatives say that opting to smoke or not to smoke is an adult decision. Of course, this stance leads some young people to think that smoking makes them more grown up. The fact is that almost 80 percent of adult smokers started smoking before the age of 18—and the younger people are when they start smoking, the greater their health risks later in life.

These grim statistics have led some communities to make laws requiring landlords to disclose whether or not they prohibit smoking. Such laws do not require landlords to have smoke-free buildings, but they do require landlords to disclose their smoking policy to prospective tenants. Do they allow smoking anywhere? Do they allow smoking in designated areas? Do they have smoke-free units? Do they mandate how far away from windows and doors a smoker must be while smoking?

This information allows prospective tenants to evaluate whether they and their family will be exposed to secondhand smoke and whether the apartment complex may have a greater fire risk due to smoking. When landlords do offer nonsmoking rental complexes, they make all units safer for everyone.

Marketing and Countermarketing

As a result of the Tobacco Master Settlement Agreement's restrictions on tobacco advertising, billboard advertisements for tobacco products disappeared, as did tobacco advertising at sport events. Big tobacco companies hire clever marketers, however, and they have managed to keep their message in front of young people. One common strategy they use is **product placement**—arranging for a product to appear prominently in a television show, movie, or other media production. The idea is that if people see a famous actor, musician, or athlete using a product, they will be encouraged to use the product themselves. It is illegal for tobacco companies to pay to have their product displayed, but they can promote product placement.

This technique often works. For example, a tobacco company can encourage the makers of a movie to show an actor smoking its brand of cigarette, and audience members may not even think about the fact that they're seeing an advertisement. According to the nonprofit organization Breathe California of Sacramento-Emigrant Trails, there were far fewer incidences of smoking in movies in 2009 than in 2003—but still many. Of the films nominated for Academy Awards in 2013, 61 percent showed people smoking usually without mentioning any consequences.

Although athletes today are more likely to talk publicly about tobacco prevention than to advertise tobacco products, they can of course be seen *using*

Be aware of marketing tactics in magazines and other media.

ADVOCACY IN ACTION: Tackling Tobacco Ads

tobacco products off the field if they do so. Mindful of athletes' status as role models, the Campaign for Tobacco-Free Kids launched a project called Knock Tobacco Out of the Park that succeeded in getting Major League Baseball to ban tobacco use by players, coaches, and managers at games (see figure 15.6). This was no small feat, given that smokeless tobacco had been part of the game of baseball for many years. In fact, the area where relief pitchers warm up is called the bullpen, which some think was named after ads for the Bull Durham brand of tobacco that used to appear near the area. The Campaign for Tobacco-Free Kids also gives awards every year to outstanding youth anti-tobacco advocates.

As a result of the Knock Tobacco Out of the Park campaign, major league players, managers, and coaches are no longer allowed to carry a tobacco tin or package in their uniforms at any time when fans are in the ballpark. They are also prohibited from using smokeless tobacco during televised interviews, autograph signings, team-sponsored appearances, and other events where they interact with fans.

Of course, the concern for smokeless or spit tobacco is because of the health hazards related to

FIGURE 15.6 The Knock Tobacco Out of the Park campaign persuaded Major League Baseball to prohibit tobacco use before, during, and after games.

Courtesy of The Campaign for Tobacco-Free Kids.

their use. Even using it for a short time can cause bad breath and yellowish stains on your teeth. Almost three-quarters of people that use spit tobacco get mouth sores. The more often people use smokeless tobacco on a daily basis and over longer periods of time, the more serious the consequences can be. The gums may recede and can cause dental problems. The nicotine—like in smoked tobacco—causes increased heart rate, high blood pressure, and sometimes irregular heartbeats. These can all contribute to cardiovascular disease. Oral cancers are greatly increased in smokeless tobacco users. These include cancers of the tongue, lips, gums, and cheeks. In some cases cancer-causing aspects of smokeless tobacco can reach the esophagus, stomach, and even the bladder. There are not nearly as many treatment programs for smokeless tobacco users as there are for smokers, but the quitline (1-800-QUIT-NOW) helps both smokers and smokeless tobacco users (often in English or Spanish and other languages in some communities). Since the nicotine levels in smokeless tobacco users often reach higher levels than in smokers, the treatment is very likely to use medical nicotine replacement products.

In 2009, the U.S. Food and Drug Administration (FDA) was given authority to regulate tobacco, including the ability to ban certain tobacco additives (e.g., menthol), though it has yet to do so. The FDA also has the authority to stop the use of terms such as "light" and "low tar" and other marketing tactics.

In recent years, young people themselves have taken the lead on some countermarketing (anti-tobacco marketing) initiatives. Students have learned to increase their **media literacy** through efforts such as the Media Literacy Project, which, along with other organizations, helps them

- develop critical thinking skills;
- understand how media messages shape culture and society;
- identify target marketing strategies such as sports that traditionally have been associated with tobacco use;
- recognize what the media maker wants them to believe or do;
- name the techniques of persuasion used;
- recognize bias, spin, misinformation, and lies;

- discover the parts of the story that are not being told;
- evaluate media messages based on their own experiences, skills, beliefs, and values;
- create and distribute their own media messages; and
- advocate for a changed media system.

One of the most successful counter-tobacco advertising initiatives is TheTruth.com campaign. This campaign started in Florida and included young people in all aspects of the marketing plan. It does not demonize smokers; instead, it counters the tobacco industry's marketing campaigns. This type of social marketing, applying commercial marketing to noncommerical purposes, is used by many anti-tobacco campaigns. You can learn more about smoking cessation by visiting the student section of the Health for Life website.

Smoking Cessation

It's hard to stop smoking or using smokeless tobacco. People who smoke get more out of it than just an addiction that causes diseases and disorders. Any habit that is repeated so frequently for such a long time is hard to change. Add to that the addictive nature of nicotine, and you have quite a challenge for behavior change. Of course, millions of people have been able to stop smoking. How did they do it? The answer varies.

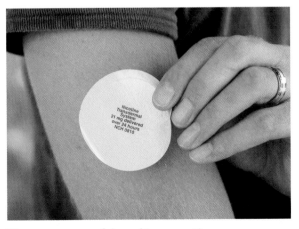

The most successful smoking cessation programs use counseling and social support, along with an alternative nicotine delivery option, such as nicotine patches.

HEALTH TECHNOLOGY

A relatively new product has been introduced to the market—electronic cigarettes, or e-cigarettes. These products liquefy and vaporize nicotine into an aerosol mist. Users puff (sometimes called "vape") on the e-cigarette to get the nicotine that they crave. It looks like a cigarette and has the approximate feel of a cigarette, but the vapor is not smelly to the user or to those nearby. E-cigarettes have helped many people cut back on traditional cigarettes, but because there is not enough research about the possible harmful effects of e-cigarettes, there has been considerable debate among experts about what to do about these new nicotine delivery systems. Some experts want to ban or regulate e-cigarettes until more is known about the possible harmful effects. Others believe that e-cigarettes are valuable in harm reduction. This means they believe that e-cigarettes are safer than traditional cigarettes. Regardless of the possible levels of harm that may be found, there are no health or medical experts who recommend the use of e-cigarettes by people who do not currently use nicotine products.

 ## CONNECT

Would you consider trying an e-cigarette? Why or why not?

For one thing, all U.S. states have a quitline (1-800-QUIT-NOW) that enables you to talk with a trained counselor. The smoking cessation programs that are most successful use counseling and social support, along with an alternative nicotine delivery option, such as nicotine gum, patches, inhalers, tablets, or lozenges. Some smoking cessation aids are available over the counter, and others require a prescription. Smokers can also use various other tactics to stop smoking, such as substituting a lollipop for a cigarette or placing a rubber band on the wrist and snapping it each time they crave a cigarette.

There are many organizations such as the American Cancer Society, the American Heart Association, and the American Lung Association that offer tobacco cessation programs either in person or online. Your health care professional can also recommend effective programs to you. Programs offer many ways to help tobacco users to quit—counseling, support groups, quitlines, smartphone apps, nicotine replacement products, and other techniques. To be successful, most people need to be motivated to quit. They need to believe that they can succeed and they need to identify the triggers associated with tobacco use (e.g., smoking after a meal). Some tobacco cessations programs are designed especially for teens.

As with most behavior change strategies, no single program works for everyone. There are enough options, however, that one is bound to work for you. It may take several tries, but persistence pays off. Just as you can't become a great athlete or musician (or anything) without making lots of mistakes, you can't stop smoking without facing some setbacks. But each setback you overcome makes it more likely that you'll eventually succeed.

 Quitting smoking is easy. I've done it a thousand times.

—Mark Twain, author and humorist

Comprehension Check

1. Are smoking rates in the U.S. higher now than they were 10 years ago? Why or why not?
2. Give two examples of policies that help reduce smoking.
3. Describe one method of smoking cessation.

Nikko is a high school student who moved to the United States from Greece, where he spent his early years around an extended family of smokers and where smoking seemed to be allowed most everywhere. Now, his parents both still smoke, and Nikko has been smoking since he was 13, but he doesn't know as many smokers as he used to. Most of his friends don't smoke, and they even make comments to him about how gross it is. His best friend James won't let him smoke in his car or house, and the campus where Nikko goes to school just became a tobacco-free zone.

When Nikko told his parents that he wanted to quit smoking and that he wanted both of them to quit, they were not receptive: "Everyone in the family smokes, and Uncle Leo lived to be 92, so it can't be that bad. Besides, we've tried quitting, and it's no use." Nikko feels frustrated because he knows how unhealthy it is, but he has a hard time quitting when cigarettes and smoke are all around the house. He has quit three times but always ended up smoking again after a few weeks; the longest he's managed to quit was for three months last summer. He also wants James to come to the house sometimes to play video games, but James complains about the smoke and won't come over.

For Discussion

What are some strategies Nikko could use to help himself stop smoking? What options might help him avoid another relapse? What are some strategies Nikko might use to help his parents quit smoking? To help you organize your thoughts, refer to the Skills for Healthy Living feature.

Relapse occurs when you stop implementing a healthy decision or return to an unhealthy habit. One example of relapse would be a smoker who quits for a month, then starts smoking again when facing a stressful situation. Once you stop a negative behavior, or begin a positive behavior, take the following steps to help prevent relapse.

- **Do a self-assessment.** Understand what might trigger your change in behavior.
- **Set goals.** You can use goals to maintain a behavior and to avoid relapse in the same way you can use them to start or stop a behavior in the first place. Use a series of short-term goals to keep you on track and motivated to stick with the behavior change.
- **Monitor your behavior.** Keep a journal or log that tracks your behavior. Doing so allows you to see patterns that might help you prevent a relapse such as recognizing that you automatically reach for a cigarette after a meal.
- **Tell other people what you're trying to accomplish.** When friends and family members know your goals, they can support you and help you stay accountable.
- **Don't let a small failure do you in.** If you have a setback, don't use it as an excuse. For example, if you try to quit smoking but take a puff of a friend's cigarette, don't use that as an excuse to give up on your efforts altogether. Acknowledge the mistake and get back on track right away.
- **Find a healthy distraction.** When you feel tempted to do something that could start a relapse, find a better activity. For example, instead of grabbing a cigarette, get a stick of gum or a piece of candy. Instead of drinking a can of soda, drink a glass of water to quench your thirst and fend off the urge.

What's in That Cigarette You're Smoking?

The main ingredient in cigarettes is tobacco—a leafy plant grown in warm climates. But that isn't the only thing. If you smoke, you're also ingesting more than four thousand chemicals, fifty-one of which are known to be carcinogenic (cancer causing). These chemicals also contribute to other serious health problems, such as emphysema, asthma, and heart disease. In fact, many of them are actually poisonous. See table 15.1 for a partial listing of chemicals found in cigarettes.

Three of the most widely known chemicals in cigarettes are nicotine, tar, and carbon monoxide. Nicotine is a strong poisonous drug that has been used in insecticides. In its pure form, just one drop on a person's tongue can be deadly. Tar is the oily material that remains after tobacco passes through a cigarette filter. When a smoker inhales, a lot of the tar sticks to and blackens his or her lungs. Carbon monoxide is a poisonous gas also found in car exhaust. When a smoker inhales carbon monoxide, it interferes with his or her respiratory and circulatory systems. It also gets into the smoker's bloodstream, where it reduces the amount of oxygen going to the person's heart. In addition, chemicals in cigarette smoke narrow the walls of the smoker's arteries, which means the person's heart must work harder and his or her blood pressure goes up.

"Choosing to smoke cigarettes is like choosing to stand in the middle of a toxic chemical plant, inhaling car exhaust and tar, while gradually suffocating to death," says anti-smoking advocate and public health official Madison Montgomery.

For Discussion

Do you think most smokers are fully aware of what is in their cigarettes? Do you think it would affect their smoking habit if they were fully aware? Why or why not? If you had the opportunity to educate the public about the chemicals in cigarettes, what would you tell them?

TABLE 15.1 Chemicals Found in Cigarettes

Chemical	Found in
Acetone	Nail polish remover
Ammonia	Cleaning products
Arsenic	Rat poison
Butane	Cigarette lighter fluid
Carbon monoxide	Car exhaust
Cyanide	Deadly poisons
DDT	Insecticides
Formaldehyde	Embalming fluids
Hydrogen cyanide	Gas chamber poison
Methoprene	Pesticides
Nicotine	Bug sprays
Sulfuric acid	Car batteries
Tar	Material similar to that used to make roads

Reviewing Concepts and Vocabulary

As directed by your teacher, answer items 1 through 5 by correctly completing each sentence with a word or phrase.

1. _____ _____ is the practice of showing a product in use by a TV or movie character to help promote the use of the product without direct advertising.
2. Two diseases that can be caused by smoking are _____ _____ and _____ _____.
3. The addictive component of tobacco is called _____.
4. Cigarette smoke inhaled by a nonsmoker is called _____ _____.
5. Smokeless tobacco has been regulated in the sport of _____.

For items 6 through 10, as directed by your teacher, match each term in column 1 with the appropriate phrase in column 2.

6. compliance check
7. 46,000
8. relapse
9. dopamine
10. more than 400,000

a. when you discontinue implementing a healthy decision or return to a negative habit
b. deaths each year by cigarette smoking
c. neurotransmitter released when the brain is exposed to nicotine
d. enforcing laws related to age and cigarette sales
e. deaths each year by secondhand smoke

For items 11 through 15, as directed by your teacher, respond to each statement or question.

11. What was the result of the Knock Tobacco Out of the Park campaign?
12. Why are laws related to purchasing tobacco products different for young people than for adults?
13. Why is quitting smoking so difficult for many people?
14. Name two types of institutions leading the way in banning smoking.
15. What is the federal agency that regulates tobacco in the United States?

Thinking Critically

Write a paragraph in response to the following question.

The legal age for purchasing alcohol in the U.S. is 21, whereas the legal age for purchasing tobacco products is 18 in most states. Tobacco kills more people than alcohol, and there is a movement to raise the legal age for purchasing tobacco products to 21 as they did in New York City. Opponents believe that if a person is old enough to vote, serve in the military, and sign a contract without a parent's or guardian's permission, then he or she should be able to make a decision—such as buying tobacco or alcohol. If you had the opportunity to vote on raising the age of tobacco purchase to 21, how would you vote? Explain your decision.

Take It Home

Share your response to the Thinking Critically question above with a parent or guardian. Ask for his or her opinion and compare it with your own. Does hearing this person's perspective change your thinking about the issue? Why or why not?

PhotoDisc

16

Alcohol

In This Chapter

 Student Web Resources
www.healthforlifetextbook.org/student

Fotosearch

Lesson 16.1

Alcohol Use, Misuse, and Health

Lesson Objectives

After reading this lesson, you should be able to
1. list two health problems associated with drinking alcohol,
2. explain the differences in how alcohol affects males and females, and
3. define *binge drinking*.

Lesson Vocabulary

acute alcohol poisoning, alcohol dehydrogenase, alcoholism, alcohol tolerance, binge drinking, ethyl alcohol (ethanol), heavy drinking, Prohibition

Alcohol has been part of human culture for thousands of years. Yet many societies still have a difficult time walking the tightrope between the positive and the negative aspects of its use. This lesson explains what alcohol is, discusses healthy and unhealthy levels of alcohol consumption, and addresses the short- and long-term health risks of alcohol consumption.

> " Always do sober what you said you'd do drunk. "
>
> —Ernest Hemingway

History

Given the use of alcohol throughout history, many people feel an attraction to it despite the negative consequences associated with drinking it. Alcohol has been viewed as a medicine, a stress reducer, a social lubricant, an evil, a killer, and a destroyer of families. Behavior associated with alcohol consumption is also connected with many types of crime, and alcohol misuse has been referred to as sinful, criminal, immoral, and sick.

Despite the millions of adults who regularly use alcohol with no adverse effect, a sizable portion of drinkers have mild, severe, or even deadly effects. As a result, most countries in modern society have restricted alcohol access only to adults. In the United States, the current legal age for drinking or purchasing alcoholic beverages is 21. U.S. laws regulating the drinking age have changed several times. In recent history, for example, the legal age has been

Some people view alcohol as a tool to reduce stress.
Photodisc

18, 19, and 21. At one time, the legal age was even reduced from 21 to 18, but alcohol-related deaths then greatly increased, and the age was reset at 21.

◀)) HEALTHY COMMUNICATION

Do you think 21 is an appropriate legal age for alcohol use? Do you think that teenagers can be responsible consumers of alcohol? Debate the issue with a classmate who sees it differently. Support your position with facts and be respectful of each other's opinions.

In your history classes, you've probably learned about **Prohibition**, which, through an amendment to the U.S. Constitution in 1920, made the sale and distribution of alcohol illegal. Many people ignored the laws, and criminal activity and corruption increased. In 1933, the amendment was repealed, and alcohol manufacturing and sales were once again legal. Several other countries, however, currently prohibit the sale and consumption of alcohol; in some other countries, the legal age for buying alcohol is 18.

Sound confusing? Well, it is. Why are there different legal ages for driving a car, buying tobacco, consuming alcohol, and getting married without a parent's or guardian's consent? The short answer is that the risks for these different behaviors are considered to be different. Of course, other cultural explanations go beyond the scope of this chapter. For our purpose here, it is enough to say that recent research reveals that drinking alcohol when you're young—when your brain is still developing—can hamper your ability to learn life skills. At least there is consistency in laws: A blood alcohol content (BAC) of 0.08 percent is the legal level of intoxication in all states (see lesson 2 for more information on BAC). Many of the health risks, policies, and laws associated with drinking alcohol (and a few possible benefits for adults) are summarized later in this chapter.

Alcohol and Alcohol Use

Ethyl alcohol (ethanol), the type of alcohol that people drink, is poisonous. Alcohol is also a depressant drug. Specifically, it depresses the parts of the brain that allow people to exercise good judgment. If consumed rapidly and in large amounts, it can also depress the part of the brain that controls breathing and heartbeat, which can result in coma or death. For example, people who drink a large amount of alcohol in a short time—as in a drinking contest or game—can suffer potentially fatal **acute alcohol poisoning**.

Fortunately, in most circumstances, the body automatically reacts to too much alcohol by causing the drinker to vomit or pass out. Vomiting protects the body by getting rid of some of the alcohol. However, if a person is somewhat conscious or passed out, he should not be induced to vomit because he could choke on his own vomit. It is never a good idea to leave someone alone who has passed out from drinking too much. Passing out, of course, stops a person from drinking more. However, if people drink too much too fast, they can bypass these safeguards of vomiting or passing out and the alcohol can kill them. A common misperception is that drinking coffee will speed up the sobering process. The body metabolizes alcohol at its own pace regardless of other drugs—like caffeine—that might be consumed.

Contrary to popular belief, being able to drink more than other people is not a good sign, because people who can drink a lot often do exactly that in the mistaken belief that alcohol can do them no harm. Furthermore, as people become more experienced drinkers, they develop an **alcohol tolerance**, which means that it takes more and more of the substance to feel the desired effects that they used to get by drinking less. This process can lead to a cycle of drinking more and more, thus increasing the likelihood of alcohol poisoning and many other health risks associated with **heavy drinking**.

Alcohol tolerance means that it takes more and more of the substance for drinkers to feel the desired effects that they used to get by drinking less.

Photodisc

A beverage's alcohol content depends on its alcohol concentration, or percent alcohol. A standard drink of wine contains 5 ounces (148 milliliters), whereas a standard drink of hard liquor contains 1.5 ounces (44 milliliters). This means that the glass of wine and the shot of liquor, in their respective standard amounts, contain about the same amount of alcohol (see figure 16.1 for more examples).

Problematic drinking has several categories. **Binge drinking** involves consuming a lot of drinks on a single occasion, typically five or more drinks within two hours for males and four or more drinks within two hours for females. Heavy drinking refers to the average number of drinks a person has on a daily basis over a long time ranging from months to years. More specifically, heavy drinking refers to consuming two or more drinks per day for men and one or more per day for women. *Excessive drinking* is a more general term that can refer to binge drinking, heavy drinking, or both. **Alcoholism** is a disease in which a person is dependent on alcohol. Symptoms include strong cravings for alcohol, loss of control over how much alcohol is consumed, high tolerance for alcohol, and physical dependence on alcohol.

Differences in Alcohol Tolerance Between Males and Females

For several scientific reasons, males and females tolerate alcohol differently. The most obvious reason is that the average adult female is smaller than the average adult male. The smaller a person's body is (whether male or female), the less alcohol it takes to raise blood alcohol content. Of course, this is not the only reason, especially since many females are larger than many males.

The second reason is that the average female has a higher percent of body fat than the average male. Body fat contains little water, so most females have less body water than most males. Alcohol is not absorbed into body fat; therefore, BAC is increased in those with more body fat. Of course, there are many males who have more body fat than females.

There are also two more reasons. First, women have less **alcohol dehydrogenase** (an enzyme) than men, which allows more of what women drink to enter the bloodstream as pure alcohol. Finally, the level of the hormone estrogen varies with the female menstrual cycle (and in women who take birth control pills), and increased estrogen can result in a higher level of blood alcohol.

Immediate Health Risks of Alcohol Use

Excessive drinking has immediate effects that increase your risk of many harmful health conditions. These immediate effects, which result most often from binge drinking, include the following:

- Unintentional injuries increase, including traffic-related injuries, falls, drownings, burns, and firearm injuries.
- Violent acts increase, including intimate partner violence and maltreatment of children. In fact, alcohol use is associated

12 oz. regular beer   5 oz. wine   1.5 oz. spirits

Each of these types of alcohol contains .6 oz. of alcohol.

FIGURE 16.1 Examples of what constitutes a standard drink for different beverages.

with two out of three incidents of intimate partner violence.

- Risky sexual behavior increases, including unprotected sex, sex with multiple partners, and risk of sexual assault. These behaviors can also result in unintended pregnancy and sexually transmitted infection.

- Miscarriage and stillbirth increase among pregnant women, along with the risk of physical and mental birth defects in their children.

- The risk increases for acute alcohol poisoning—a medical emergency resulting from a high blood alcohol level that suppresses the central nervous system and can cause loss of consciousness, low blood pressure, low body temperature, coma, respiratory depression, and death.

Excessive alcohol use accounts for about 79,000 deaths each year in the United States, making it the third-leading cause of death related to lifestyle. In 2005 alone, for example, more than 1.6 million hospitalizations and 4 million emergency room visits resulted from alcohol-related conditions, according to the U.S. Centers for Disease Control and Prevention.

Although a large percentage of people who smoke also drink, there are important differences between those who commonly drink and those who regularly smoke. For example, smoking too many cigarettes in a short time span will not kill you, but binge drinking can. Heavy smokers, unlike heavy drinkers, are not likely to have impaired judgment. Males are more likely than females to be drinkers, and whites are more likely than blacks and Latinos to be drinkers.

Tobacco and alcohol use are similar in that many of the diseases and disorders related to both of them occur later in life among regular, lifelong users. As a result, many young people are not concerned about what might happen to them in 20 or 30 years, because they haven't even been alive for that long. Unlike tobacco use, however, alcohol use also poses many health risks in the short term.

Long-Term Health Risks of Heavy Alcohol Use

Those who drink heavily over an extended period (months or years) can develop a range of chronic health problems (see table 16.1). In addition to increasing the risk of heart disease, cancer, and high blood pressure, heavy drinkers can experience disruptions in their social structure and livelihood. Common results of chronic drinking include family problems, broken relationships, job and career difficulties, and an increased risk of unintentional injury (e.g., in firearm and automobile crashes).

Alcohol and Calories

Since overweight and obesity are on the increase in the United States, people need to know that alcoholic beverages are high in calories and low in nutrients. For example, alcohol contains 7 calories per gram (a gram is the weight of an average paper clip), whereas carbohydrate and protein each contain only 4 calories per gram (fat contains the most, at 9 calories per gram). If a person drinks sweetened drinks (e.g., wine coolers) or mixes alcohol with sweetened soda, then the number of calories

Smoking too many cigarettes in a short time span will not kill you, but binge drinking can.

TABLE 16.1 Health Problems Resulting From Long-Term Heavy Alcohol Use

Anemia—drinking lowers the number of oxygen-carrying red blood cells.	Gout—this painful condition occurs when uric acid builds up in the joints; it is made worse by alcohol use.
Cancer—alcohol can raise the level of carcinogens (cancer-causing agents) in the body.	High blood pressure—drinking more than three drinks within an hour can temporarily raise blood pressure; repeated binge drinking can result in long-term high blood pressure.
Cardiovascular disease—heavy drinking causes blood platelets to clump together, thus increasing the risk of blood clots.	Infectious disease—drinking suppresses the immune system, thus leaving you more susceptible to illness and infectious disease.
Cirrhosis—heavy drinking commonly damages the liver by scarring.	Nerve damage—alcohol-related nerve damage can result in numbness and a pins-and-needles sensation.
Dementia—heavy drinking causes the brain to shrink at a faster rate than normal, which can contribute to the development of dementia.	Seizures—heavy alcohol use can cause seizures even in people without a history of epilepsy.
Depression—drinking and depression go hand in hand, often creating a vicious cycle.	

is further increased. People who are trying to lose weight or maintain their current weight are often advised not to consume the "empty calories" that come from alcoholic beverages.

Alcohol Use and Pregnancy

According to the CDC, there is no known safe amount of alcohol consumption during pregnancy. This doesn't mean that drinking during pregnancy will definitely cause problems in a newborn. It does mean that drinking increases the chance of something going wrong—and the more the mother drinks, the greater the risk.

Potential problems include miscarriage, stillbirth, and increased risk of fetal alcohol spectrum disorders (FASD). Figure 16.2 lists problems that can be caused by drinking alcohol during pregnancy. Of course, many women don't immediately know that they're pregnant, and most women quit drinking once they do know. However, a woman who is a drinker and is not yet aware of being pregnant will

When a woman drinks alcohol during pregnancy, her baby may suffer the consequences. Here are some of the major complications of drinking during pregnancy.

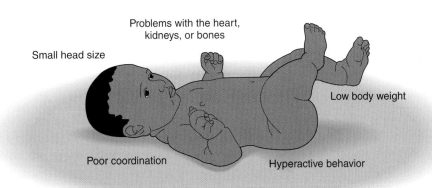

FIGURE 16.2 Problems related to drinking alcohol during pregnancy.

continue drinking, thus increasing health risks for the embryo. Therefore, a woman who is sexually active and not using reliable birth control should not drink alcohol.

Health Benefits of Drinking Among Adults

Some recent studies have shown that moderate drinkers (no more than two drinks per day if male, one if female) have less risk of developing heart disease than either people who don't drink at all or people who drink more than one or two drinks per day. However, although these studies show that alcohol consumption is not always bad for one's health, they are studies of adults—not young people. Recall that the younger a person starts drinking alcohol, the greater the risk of having alcohol-related health problems later in life. In addition, even if moderate drinking can improve some aspects of health, no medical or scientific organization recommends that you start drinking if you don't already drink. That's because of the many serious health risks associated with alcohol consumption. By way of emphasis, Utah, the U.S. state with the lowest alcohol consumption, also has the lowest rate of alcohol-related traffic deaths. Other factors may be involved, but the main reason is likely to be low alcohol consumption.

Even when alcohol is used responsibly, it can contribute excess empty calories to the diet.

© 1999 PhotoDisc, Inc.

Comprehension Check

1. What are two health problems associated with drinking alcohol?
2. How does alcohol affect males and females differently?
3. Explain the meaning of binge drinking.

SELF-ASSESSMENT: My Alcohol Knowledge

Answer *true* or *false* for the following questions. For a variation, compare your answers with those of a few friends or fellow students. See if you can all agree on the right answers.

1. Alcohol is a mood-altering stimulant.
   a. true
   b. false

2. Drinking coffee or taking a cold shower will sober a person up.
   a. true
   b. false

3. Alcohol's effects on the body vary according to the individual.
   a. true
   b. false

4. The most serious consequence of consuming alcohol is a hangover in the morning.
   a. true
   b. false

5. Blood alcohol charts that help you estimate your BAC based on your weight and the number of drinks that you had provide a safe and accurate means of determining how much alcohol is circulating in your bloodstream.
   a. true
   b. false

6. If an intoxicated person is semiconscious, you should encourage vomiting.
   a. true
   b. false

7. Women and men respond differently to alcohol.
   a. true
   b. false

8. Alcohol increases your sexual functioning.
   a. true
   b. false

9. If a person is passed out from drinking, he or she should be put in bed to "sleep it off."
   a. true
   b. false

10. The legal blood alcohol limit for driving for people under age 21 is 0.08 percent.
    a. true
    b. false

Here are the correct answers: 1 b, 2 b, 3 a, 4 b, 5 b, 6 b, 7 a, 8 b, 9 b, and 10 b. If you got nine or ten answers right, you're very knowledgeable about alcohol. If you got seven or eight right, you're above average in your knowledge. If you got six or fewer right, spend some time learning about alcohol to protect yourself and your family and friends.

✔ Planning for Healthy Living

Use the Healthy Living Plan worksheet to help you avoid engaging in underage drinking or to stop drinking alcohol if you already do.

Lesson 16.2

Culture, Advertising, and the Law

Lesson Objectives

After reading this lesson, you should be able to

1. describe how alcohol is marketed and advertised to young people,
2. define *BAC* and *DUI* and explain the relationship between them, and
3. explain what an alcohol diversion program is.

 Lesson Vocabulary

addiction, alcopop, blood alcohol content (BAC), diversion program, DriveCam, driving under the influence (DUI), ignition interlock

In this lesson, you'll learn about alcohol advertising and how individual students and student groups have been and continue to be involved in alcohol issues. You'll also be introduced to programs that treat people who have alcohol problems, and you'll learn how modern technologies are used to help people with alcohol problems.

> " Water is the only drink for a wise man. "
>
> —Henry David Thoreau

Alcohol and Popular Culture

For some reason, a culture has developed in the United States and other countries wherein many people believe that drinking is the best and perhaps only way to have fun. The fact is that most teens do not drink to excess, but the ones who do tend to be the most vocal. In addition, movies and TV shows often glorify drinking. It's a telling commentary that, according to Guinness World Records, the word *drunk* has more synonyms than any other word in the English language—more than 2,200! Clearly, then, the word is important in U.S. culture.

How many synonyms for *drunk* do you know? Since many of these terms strike many people as funny, they can suggest that being drunk has no negative consequences. As you've already learned, that is far from true. Even so, our slang has developed a bias toward a social, fun, and partying view

of alcohol—much like alcohol advertising itself. What does it say about a culture when it spends so much time talking about drinking? American humorist Fran Lebowitz once said, "Great people talk about ideas, average people talk about things, and small people talk about wine." She made the statement in jest, but it does make one wonder about the overemphasis on alcohol in conversation, on television, in movies, and in advertising.

 **CONNECT**

Do you think getting drunk is glamorized? Why or why not? What effect do you think social expectations have on your decision to drink alcohol or not? What other influences may play a role in your decision? Does advertising have much of an influence on you?

Advertising to Youth

For many years, alcohol advertising has been monitored by the Center on Alcohol Marketing and Youth (CAMY) at the Johns Hopkins Bloomberg School of Public Health. CAMY found that in 10 years, "youth exposure to alcohol advertising on U.S. television increased 71 percent . . . more than the exposure of either adults ages 21 and above or young adults ages 21 to 34." The center also noted that during the same time frame, alcohol advertising in magazines dropped dramatically. This is probably because young people have gravitated more to the Internet and less to magazines. Alcohol is also advertised on the radio through ads promoting **alcopops** (sweetened alcoholic beverages), distilled spirits, and wine. These ads are more likely to be heard by girls between the ages of 12 and 20 than by boys of the same age.

What about ads and public service announcements (PSAs) that deliver messages to counter underage alcohol use and alcohol abuse? It's true that messages such as "don't drink and drive" sometimes appear in alcohol advertising. But young people are 22 times more likely to see an ad promoting an alcohol product than one with a message like "drink responsibly." Furthermore, no definition of responsible drinking is given. As much as we don't like to admit it, advertising works—not just on others, but also on us—and alcohol advertising is all around us. It's not just in magazines, on the radio, on TV, on billboards, and in the in-store ads in grocery stores, convenience stores, and gas stations; it's also online and in product placement in movies.

The alcohol ads that have proven most effective at influencing young people use pitches aimed specifically at them. For example, they feature animals as lead characters and portray alcohol as providing instant gratification, thrills, and social status. In fact, according to most alcohol advertising, alcohol makes people more pleasing—to both themselves and others. Clearly, however, this is not true. In fact, people who binge-drink are more likely to damage property, get into arguments and fights, sexually assault someone, interrupt someone's sleep (as in a college dorm room), miss class, and do any number of other problematic things.

In addition to conventional advertising, alcohol is marketed to youth through products designed to appeal to young people. Consumer advocacy groups argue that companies use these products to intentionally—and illegally—target underage people and promote underage drinking. Of particular concern are sweet-flavored alcopop drinks such as hard lemon malt beverages and hard cola. These drinks often come in brightly colored packages that are attractive to young people. The combination of advertising and products designed to appeal to youth creates a powerful influence on underage drinking.

Alcohol Laws

Alcohol laws govern the sale, distribution, advertisement, and use of alcohol. Federal alcohol laws apply to everyone across the country; other alcohol laws vary by jurisdiction (city, county, or state). All of these laws govern where and when alcohol can be sold and when it can be consumed in public. For example, some states and local governments prohibit alcohol consumption in parks or on beaches. Others make it illegal for bars to sell alcohol after a given time (often 2 a.m.). Still others restrict or prohibit the sale of alcohol on Sundays. Open container laws make it illegal, as the name indicates, to have an open container of alcohol in certain areas, even if you're not actively drinking.

The consequences of breaking these laws vary by jurisdiction but can include fines, jail time, probation, suspension of driver's license, and the loss of a liquor license (e.g., in the case of stores and bars). In addition, schools and workplaces can enforce their own penalties for violation of their policies governing alcohol use.

Dangers of Caffeinated Alcoholic Beverages

When caffeine or another stimulant is mixed with alcohol, the combination can mask the depressant effects of alcohol, thus leading people to drink more. This is particularly dangerous because the stimulant does not reduce the underlying physiological effects of alcohol on the body. For a while, caffeinated alcoholic beverages (CABs) grew in popularity and were heavily marketed to teens and young adults. However, the risks associated with these drinks led the U.S. Food and Drug Administration to ban them. Teens and others who skirt this ban by combining energy drinks with alcohol put themselves at high risk of impaired judgment, alcohol poisoning, and other risks associated with excessive alcohol consumption.

Minimum Drinking Age Act

Despite the cultural influences and advertisements that promote drinking among teens, the National Minimum Drinking Age Act of 1984 makes it illegal to drink under the age of 21 anywhere in the United States (with the exception of parents being allowed to serve alcohol to their children in their own home). This law also makes it illegal to sell alcohol to minors or purchase alcohol for minors. In addition, laws in many states are getting stricter regarding adults who purchase alcohol for minors and for people who use fake identification cards to purchase alcohol. Punishment can include a large fine, probation, or jail time. If an adult purchases alcohol for a minor who is then seriously injured or dies due to an alcohol-related cause, the adult may receive a long jail sentence.

Alcohol and Driving

Laws also regulate the use of alcohol while driving for people of all ages. Currently, most states use a **blood alcohol content (BAC)** of 0.08 percent as the legal limit when driving for people ages 21 and over. For those under the age of 21, the BAC level is 0.02 percent in most places. It is not zero percent to allow for the use of some medications that contain alcohol. Blood alcohol content is the percentage of alcohol in the bloodstream. A BAC of 0.08 percent indicates that a person has 0.8 part alcohol per 1,000 parts of blood in the body. Because alcohol is absorbed directly through the walls of the stomach and small intestine, blood alcohol can be measured 30 to 70 minutes after a person has had a drink.

Table 16.2 summarizes the physiological and psychological effects of selected BAC levels. The table shows the BAC level at which each effect is usually first observed. Getting behind the wheel with a BAC above the legal limit is known as **driving under the influence (DUI)** or driving while intoxicated (DWI). Most deaths and injuries related to alcohol consumption result from vehicle crashes. According to the U.S. National Highway Traffic Safety Administration, more than 10,000 people died in alcohol-related crashes in 2009. Each year, one-third to one-half of these deaths occur in teens and young adults (under the age of 21).

Fortunately, recent years have brought decreases in both the total number of traffic deaths per mile driven and the number of alcohol-related crash deaths. Organizations such as Mothers Against Drunk Driving (MADD) have helped raise awareness and increase penalties for drinking and driving. In addition, roads and vehicles have become safer, and more people wear seat belts and use child safety

Mothers Against Drunk Driving is an organization that works to stop drunk driving.
Photodisc

seats. Despite these improvements, far too many alcohol-related traffic deaths still occur.

School Policies and Youth Courts

Schools have their own policies governing students who consume alcohol before coming to school, during school, or at school events. These policies, and the associated punishments, vary from school to school and from school system to school system. Most schools maintain a student code of conduct that explains the behaviors expected of students.

TABLE 16.2   Psychological and Physical Effects of Selected Blood Alcohol Content (BAC) Levels

BAC	Typical effects	Predictable effects on driving
0.02	• Some loss of judgment • Relaxation • Slight body warmth • Altered mood	• Decline in visual functions (e.g., rapid tracking of a moving target) • Decline in ability to perform two tasks at the same time (divided attention)
0.05	• Exaggerated behavior • Possible loss of small muscle control (e.g., focusing the eyes) • Impaired judgment • Lowered alertness • Release of inhibition	• Reduced coordination • Reduced ability to track moving objects • Difficulty steering • Reduced response to emergency driving situations
0.08	• Poor muscle coordination (e.g., for balance, speech, vision, reaction time, hearing) • Impaired detection of danger • Impaired judgment, self-control, reasoning, and memory	• Reduced concentration • Short-term memory loss • Greatly reduced coordination • Reduced information-processing capability (e.g., signal detection, visual search) • Impaired perception
0.10	• Clear deterioration of reaction time and control • Slurred speech, poor coordination, and slowed thinking	• Reduced ability to maintain lane position and brake appropriately
0.15	• Far less muscle control than normal • Vomiting (unless this level is reached slowly or the person has developed a tolerance for alcohol) • Major loss of balance	• Substantial impairment in vehicle control, attention to driving task, and visual and auditory information processing

Reprinted, by permission, from Human Kinetics, 2009, *Health and wellness for life* (Champaign, IL: Human Kinetics), 398.

PhotoDisc/Barbara Penoyar

DIVERSE PERSPECTIVES: Alcoholism

Hi. My name is Brenda, and I have always enjoyed alcohol. When I was single and in my early 20s, I would stay out late with my friends and would often drink until I passed out. Later on, after I was married and had a child of my own, I began to question my drinking habits. I noticed that I couldn't stop after just one glass of wine with dinner. I got to the point where I was having two drinks before my husband got home, then wine with dinner, and then I was sneaking into the kitchen after dinner for another round. One night, I drank so much that I passed out and cracked my head open. It was then that I realized I had to stop.

During the first year, learning how to live my life and get through big events like weddings and holidays without drinking was tough. I realized that life is hard, and getting and staying sober aren't easy. It was, and still is, a struggle. But my life is so much more interesting and adventurous now without drinking. I felt for years that I was anesthetized—numb. Today, I'm living in the moment. I feel my emotions, and I'm aware of everything with much more clarity. It's not boring—which is what you think life without alcohol must be when you're an alcoholic. I've learned the hard way that the opposite is actually true—it's exciting.

HEALTH TECHNOLOGY

Technological developments related to alcohol consumption include smartphone apps that can help people with various needs. Some, for example, help adult drinkers count their calories (people are often unaware of how many calories alcoholic beverages contain). Other apps can estimate an adult drinker's blood alcohol level based on height, weight, and what drinks he or she has consumed.

In addition, some auto insurance companies are offering driver cameras (one brand, for example, is called **DriveCam**) for use in cars driven by teenagers. These cameras monitor for erratic driving and send notifications to a parent's or guardian's computer. Some insurance companies even monitor the cameras themselves and raise the insurance rate if a teen driver often drives dangerously or erratically. Other companies leave it to parents and guardians to decide how to deal with bad driving.

Another form of technology that is growing in popularity is the **ignition interlock**, which tests the driver's BAC before allowing him or her to drive. This technology can be court-ordered for people who are found guilty of alcohol-related driving offenses. The device is installed in the vehicle at the offender's expense (usually about US$70 to US$100 per month, plus an installation fee of US$100 to US$200). Before the person can start the vehicle, he or she must breathe into the device, which determines the person's blood alcohol level. If it is above the legal limit, the car will not start. Some of the more sophisticated ignition locks include a camera to ensure that the proper person is blowing into the device. The intent, of course, is to keep people from driving under the influence of alcohol.

 CONNECT

Do you think advanced technologies (e.g., apps or online calculators that estimate BAC) help prevent drinking and driving? Why or why not? Share your perspective with your peers. Identify the specific points where you agree and disagree.

Some schools also use student courts, in which students serve as judge, jury, prosecutor, and defense counsel under the supervision of adults. Students also decide on the punishment when a student is found guilty. For example, a student court might address a case in which a student is accused of bringing alcohol to school or providing it to other students. Student court systems are not, however, appropriate for dealing with very serious offenses such as an alcohol-related car crash or a fight that resulted in an injury. The most common forms of restitution ordered by student courts are community service, oral and written apologies, and written essays reflecting on one's behavior and discussing how one plans to change it. Student courts do not take the place of formal legal actions that may also be pursued against the offender.

Diversion Programs

In some U.S. jurisdictions, youth and sometimes other first-time offenders in alcohol-related cases have the option of attending classes (often led by a specially trained counselor) instead of receiving a large fine, being placed on probation, or spending time in jail. The offender has to pay for the classes, and young people may be required to attend the classes with a parent or guardian. In some programs targeting DUI offenses, an offender who successfully completes the course may be able to have the offense removed from his or her police record. If so, the person's car insurance costs may stay the same, whereas offenders who do not complete a **diversion program** usually face a substantial cost increase for their vehicle insurance.

Alcohol Dependence and Treatment

Some people who drink alcohol develop a physical dependence (**addiction**). They crave alcohol and don't feel right unless they drink it. What this means is that for some people, drinking gets out of control. They are alcoholics. Many programs are available to help people stop drinking. They include treatment centers, counseling, behavior modification, medication, an Alcoholics Anonymous (AA) group or other support group, and even technology (e.g., smartphone apps and text messages). Groups also exist to help family members and friends of problem drinkers; examples include Al-Anon and Alateen. These groups are self-help groups or support groups, in which people with similar problems work together to help each other. Group support offers help for people with alcohol addiction. People who have taken control of their own alcohol problems help others who are trying to quit. In AA, a person who helps another person is called a sponsor. Since the sponsor has experienced similar problems and challenges, he or she serves as a guide for the person who is trying to stop drinking. It is difficult to change addictive behavior. Whenever possible, problem drinkers should seek help from others and know their options. Your school counselor or school nurse can inform you about local groups that help people with alcohol problems as well as their family members and friends. Make no mistake about it, quitting drinking for an alcoholic is very difficult, but with the right treatment, people can and do overcome their addiction. Most alcohol treatment programs believe that alcoholics should completely refrain from drinking because if the person starts to drink even small amounts, the drinking is likely to escalate to out-of-control again.

Comprehension Check

1. Give one example of how alcohol is marketed and advertised to young people.
2. How are BAC and DUI related?
3. How does a diversion program work?

Social support happens when people close to you, along with members of your community, support your positive health choices and encourage you to stick with them. You're more likely to stay on track when the people around you are supportive and encouraging.

Kerri has never had a drink of alcohol. Next week, she turns 21, and all of her friends are planning a big party for her at a local bar. Kerri is excited about celebrating her birthday with friends but doesn't want things to get out of control. She's curious about alcohol but also knows that she may be easily affected by it. Her mom struggled with alcoholism for years, and Kerri sees how hard it is for her to stay sober. Most of Kerri's friends have already turned 21, and many of them drink on a regular basis. One of the girls in the group drinks only once in a while because she doesn't want the extra calories in her diet. Kerri respects her friends' choice to drink but still isn't sure she wants to start down that road.

Ted is a popular guy at school, and as a student-athlete he attracts a lot of like-minded people. However, while almost all of his friends are physically active and eat well, they like to celebrate their victories on the field by drinking. Neither Ted nor any of his friends are of legal age to drink. Ted's older brother Matt is a pretty heavy drinker, and he has no problem supplying Ted and his buddies with alcohol when their parents are out of the house. At the last celebration, things got a little out of hand, and one of Ted's buddies passed out. Though this caused Ted a lot of anxiety and stress, his brother said it was no big deal, and his buddies blamed it on not eating enough while they were drinking. Ted is pretty worried about how much everyone is drinking now, but no one else seems to share his concern.

Kerri and Ted both need social support but for different reasons. Kerri needs to be supported in making a decision that might differ from the decision most of her friends make. Ted needs to be supported in his wish to keep his own and his buddies' behavior under control.

For Discussion

How might Kerri approach getting the support she needs? Who in her life might give her the best social support? Why? What should Ted do to build up his social support structure so that he can change his behavior and maybe help others as well? What are some long-term consequences for Kerri and Ted if they fail to get the social support they need in life? To guide your thinking about these questions, use the Skills for Healthy Living feature.

The ability to find and use a strong social support system helps you engage in healthy behaviors and avoid unhealthy ones. Social support has been shown to increase positive behaviors (e.g., physical activity, healthy eating) and prevent negative behaviors (e.g., smoking, alcohol abuse). Use the following guidelines to help you find and make use of strong social support.

- **Assess your current level of social support.** A key first step is to become aware of your existing social support structure. Make a list of your closest friends and relatives and the groups you belong to. Rate each person or group on your list as

either a positive or a negative influence on your health.

- **Set goals.** If you don't already have strong social support, set some goals to help you improve it. For example, do some research or clubs or other groups that include people who engage in the healthy behavior you're trying to adopt, then attend a meeting or gathering.

- **Find friends with similar interests and values.** People with common interests can help make positive lifestyle choices easier and more enjoyable. For example, if you want to quit drinking, spend more time with your nondrinking friends while you're working to quit. If you want to become more active, find friends who enjoy the same physical activities that you do and make plans to do the activities together.

- **Start your own club or team.** If you can't find a club or group that supports your needs, consider creating your own. Chances are good that others share your interest and can provide you with new forms of social support.

- **Talk about your interests.** Letting others know what you like can help you attract like-minded friends. Speak up when you're given a chance to share about yourself. If you like working out or eating a healthy diet, share that information during class discussions or activities, or make it a clear part of your social media communications.

- **Encourage others to join you.** If you want to make a change and stick with it, create a group challenge related to the activity. For example, set a healthy goal and see who can reach it first. Friendly competition can go a long way toward giving you the social support you need.

 ACADEMIC CONNECTION: Mathematical Conversions

The metric system is most often used as the system of measurement in scientific research, including health and fitness research. To understand measures in the metric system or to compare data expressed using the metric system to data expressed using U.S. customary units (pounds, inches), you need to be able to calculate conversions. A conversion is a change or transformation. When converting measures, you will multiply the original value by a known factor to get the desired value. For example, if 1 kilogram is equivalent to 2.2 pounds, you would need to multiply the weight in kilograms by a factor of 2.2 to get the equivalent weight in pounds. Following are some commonly used factors for

Multiply	By factor of	To find
Milliliters	.0353	fluid ounces
Kilograms	2.2046	pounds
Meters	3.2808	feet
Meters	39.37	inches

metric to U.S. customary units. If a research study suggested that a person who weighs 65 kilograms suffered a decrease in motor function after consuming 200 milliliters of wine, would you be able to convert that finding to pounds and ounces?

Are Americans Set Up to Become Alcoholics?

Different societies not only have different beliefs and rules about drinking, but they also show very different outcomes when people do drink (see table 16.3). For example, societies where daily drinking is the norm may have a higher rate of cirrhosis and other medical problems but fewer accidents, fights, homicides, or other violent alcohol-associated traumas. This may be because drinking itself is socially acceptable but drunkenness is not. Similarly, a culture that views drinking as a ritually significant act is not likely to develop many alcohol-related problems.

"One striking feature of drinking . . . is that it is essentially a social act," says Professor Kaufman, a social anthropologist specializing in the societal aspects of alcohol use. "The solitary drinker, so dominant an image in relation to alcohol in the United States, is virtually unknown in other countries. The same is true among tribal and peasant societies everywhere. In Italy, in contrast to America, drinking is institutionalized as part of family life and dietary and religious custom; alcohol (wine) is introduced early in life, within the context of the family, and as a traditional accompaniment to meals and a healthful way of enhancing the diet." Alcohol consumption is determined by many factors, such as social rules and expectations, customs and traditions, family history and beliefs, and religious beliefs.

"Such an approach to the socialization of alcohol use makes it less likely that drinking will be learned as a way of trying to solve personal problems or of coping with inadequacy and failure," says Randall Jessep, a social psychologist at a leading U.S. university.

For Discussion

What factors do you think contribute most to how a young person in America learns to use, abuse, or not use alcohol? Do you think our society promotes the responsible use of alcohol? Why or why not?

TABLE 16.3 Deaths From Alcohol Consumption per 100,000 People in Selected Countries

Rank	Country	Deaths per 100,000	Rank	Country	Deaths per 100,000
1	Turkey	0.0	6	Somalia	1.4
2	Italy	0.2	7	United States	1.6
3	Costa Rica	0.5	8	Kazakhstan	3.0
4	Kenya	0.7	9	Germany	3.8
5	United Kingdom	1.1	10	France	4.0

CHAPTER REVIEW

Reviewing Concepts and Vocabulary

As directed by your teacher, answer items 1 through 5 by correctly completing each sentence with a word or phrase.

1. Two natural physiological responses to drinking that protect people from acute alcohol poisoning are _____ and _____ _____.
2. A device that lets others monitor your driving is called a(n) _____.
3. When a person who drinks alcohol regularly over a long time no longer gets the same effect from drinking the same amount, she or he has developed a _____.
4. Alcohol has a _____ effect on the brain.
5. The English word with the most synonyms is _____.

For items 6 through 10, as directed by your teacher, match each term in column 1 with the appropriate phrase in column 2.

6. BAC
7. DUI
8. binge drinking
9. heavy drinking
10. alcoholic

a. driving with too much alcohol in the blood
b. consuming a large amount of alcohol in a short time
c. a person with an addiction to alcohol
d. the concentration of alcohol in the blood
e. consuming more than one drink (females) or two drinks (males) each day

For items 11 through 15, as directed by your teacher, respond to each statement or question.

11. Identify two things that make underage drinking unhealthy or dangerous.
12. What are two possible complications of drinking while pregnant?
13. How is drinking related to obesity in adults?
14. Name two treatments for alcohol dependence.
15. How is a diversion program for teen alcohol offenders different than going through the court system?

Thinking Critically

Write a paragraph in response to the following questions.

Alcohol use has some known health benefits among adults and is part of many social experiences. It also poses significant risks to individuals and society. Do you think society does a good job of balancing the benefits and risks of alcohol use? If you could change one thing about society's treatment of alcohol, what would it be? Why?

Take It Home

Have a discussion with your parents or guardians about their perspectives on drinking alcohol. What rules or expectations do they apply to themselves in regard to drinking? What expectations do they have for you, both now and as you approach the legal drinking age? Do their own experiences influence their thinking on this topic? Write a summary of what you learn; include your own response to their perspectives.

17

Drugs and Medicine

 Student Web Resources
www.healthforlifetextbook.org/student

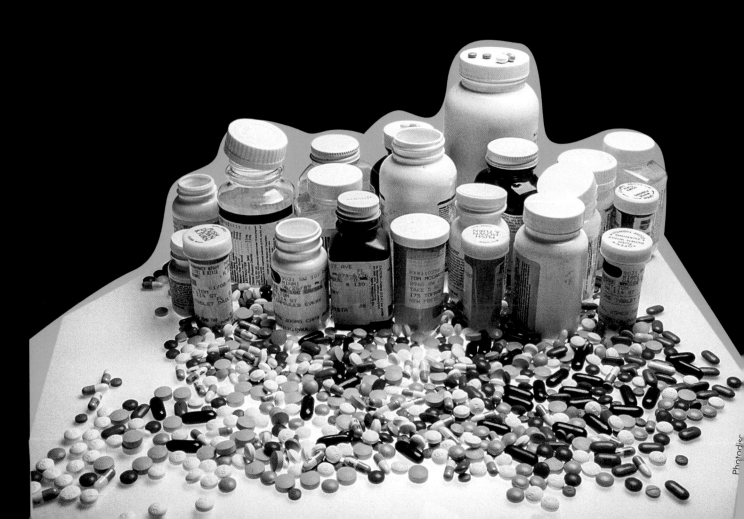

Photodisc

Lesson 17.1

Drug Classifications and Illicit Drugs

Lesson Objectives

After reading this lesson, you should be able to

1. explain what drug schedules are and what information they provide,
2. understand factors that contribute to illicit drug use, and
3. name examples of illicit drugs and identify the risks associated with each one.

Lesson Vocabulary

drug addiction, drug dependence, drug tolerance, illicit drug, licit drug, opiates, patent medicine, psychoactive drugs, withdrawal

In this chapter, you'll explore the roles that **licit** (legal) and **illicit** (illegal) **drugs** play in society. This first lesson focuses on the history of drug use in the United States and how drugs are classified based on their safety and effectiveness. It includes information about illegal drugs.

> " Let food be thy medicine and medicine be thy food. "
>
> —Hippocrates

History

As with alcohol and tobacco, drug use and abuse have been around almost as long as people have existed. Aztec priests, for example, used drugs for various ceremonies, and Incas used coca plant extracts in their religious ceremonies to build group togetherness. You may have read about Native American tribes passing the "peace pipe" or calumet, which contained tobacco. However, even though some people had religious or spiritual experiences under the influence of certain drugs, they did not use these drugs recreationally, meaning just for fun, as many people do now in the United States.

In the early days of the United States, drugs were not regulated by law. As a result, companies and so-called snake oil salesmen freely and openly sold **opiates** and cocaine products as cure-alls. The product's claims were, of course, too good to be true. Like a gambler who talks only about winnings and never about losses, snake oil salesmen talked only about the supposed positive effects of their products—not the possible addictive properties. They also didn't mention side effects or the fact that flawed self-treatment could delay proven treatments of the diseases or disorders from which their customers suffered.

As shown in figure 17.1, even something as common as Coca-Cola was originally sold as both a beverage and a tonic for "nervous affections." In fact, the first part of the name (Coca) refers to the coca plant—the same one that produces cocaine. The second part (Cola) refers to the kola nut, an extract of which is still an ingredient in Coca-Cola today.

The reality is that, in those bygone days, there was no effective treatment for many conditions. Even today, modern medicine cannot cure all ailments. Nevertheless, in the late 1800s, it became

FIGURE 17.1 An early advertisement for Coca-Cola.

obvious that some of the **patent medicines** (i.e., nonprescription proprietary drugs) just described were worse than the conditions they were promoted as treating. As a result, the Pure Food and Drug Act was passed in the United States in 1906. The intent of this law was to protect the public from tainted or otherwise unsafe food and drug products. In 1930, these protections were expanded with the creation of the U.S. Food and Drug Administration (FDA).

Drug Classifications

To regulate drugs, the FDA, along with the U.S. Drug Enforcement Administration (DEA), assigns each drug to one of five categories or schedules (see table 17.1). The higher the schedule number, the less dangerous the drug is considered to be. For example, drugs included in schedule I are considered very dangerous and not suited for medical use. Schedule V drugs, on the other hand, have little potential for abuse but may be useful in treating certain medical conditions. Drug schedules are used to determine which drugs should require a prescription, which should be available over the counter, and which are illegal.

As with many other aspects of drug use and regulation, the schedule system is the subject of some controversy. For example, marijuana is listed in schedule I, which means that the DEA and FDA view it as having no medical value. Nevertheless, many states and the District of Columbia have enacted laws to make medical marijuana legal by prescription. Adding to the confusion, these differences pit state laws against federal laws.

Illicit Drugs

Illegal drugs are generally referred to as illicit drugs. These are the drugs that you are most likely to see depicted on TV shows and in movies—for example, heroin, cocaine, and methamphetamine (meth). In the United States, some laws governing illicit drugs

TABLE 17.1 Definitions of Controlled Substance Schedules

Schedule and definition	Examples
Schedule I Substances in this schedule have no currently accepted medical use in the United States, a lack of accepted safety for use under medical supervision, and a high potential for abuse.	Heroin, LSD, marijuana, Ecstasy
Schedule II Substances in this schedule have a high potential for abuse which may lead to severe psychological or physical dependence (addiction).	Oxycodone (OxyContin, Percocet), morphine, opium, codeine, amphetamines, methylphenidate (Ritalin)
Schedule III Substances in this schedule have a potential for abuse less than substances in schedules I or II. Abuse may lead to moderate or low physical dependence (addiction) or high psychological dependence.	Combination products containing less than 15 mg of hydrocodone per dosage unit (Vicodin) and products containing not more than 90 mg of codeine per dosage unit (Tylenol with Codeine)
Schedule IV Substances in this schedule have a low potential for abuse relative to substances in schedule III.	Alprazolam (Xanax), clorazepate (Tranxene), diazepam (Valium), lorazepam (Ativan), midazolam (Versed)
Schedule V Substances in this schedule have a low potential for abuse relative to substances listed in schedule IV and consist primarily of preparations containing limited quantities of certain narcotics.	Cough preparations containing not more than 200 mg of codeine per 100 ml or per 100 g (Robitussin AC, Phenergan with Codeine)

In the United States, drugs and other controlled substances are categorized into five schedules under the Controlled Substances Act (CSA).

From www.deadiversion.usdoj.gov/schedules/#define.

are federal (national), whereas others vary from state to state. These laws make it illegal not only to use certain drugs but also to give illegal drugs (or your own prescription drugs) to another person, to manufacture or grow illegal drugs, to sell or buy illegal drugs, or to possess illegal drugs.

Using or distributing illicit drugs not only poses potential legal and health problems; there is also a good chance that an illegal, or "street," drug does not contain what the buyer intends to obtain. Studies have found that street drugs are often "cut" with dangerous substances or replaced by other drugs. For example, cocaine has been found to be cut with substances such as flour, powdered milk, ground drywall, rat poison, and battery acid. As a result, if a user has an adverse reaction (bad experience) with the drug, emergency room staff will not know how to treat the person properly because they don't know what drug, or poison, the person has ingested.

Risks of Illicit Drugs

Illicit drug use poses many other dangers. For one thing, loss of inhibition can lead a person to take risks that he or she normally wouldn't take—for example, engaging in risky sexual behavior (which might result in pregnancy or a sexually transmitted infection), driving while impaired, getting in a car with someone who is impaired, taking other drugs, and sharing infected needles. Illicit drugs also carry other physical and emotional health risks; for some examples, see table 17.2. Teens who use illegal drugs have most likely obtained them from friends or siblings.

TABLE 17.2   Some Illicit Drugs and Their Risks

Drug	Short-term risks	Long-term risks
Cocaine	Euphoria; increased energy; chatty; anxiety; tremors; mentally alert to sights, sounds, and touch; irregular heartbeats	Headaches; irregular heartbeats; chest pains; heart attack; stomach pain; nausea; stroke; seizures
Ecstasy	Euphoria; increased energy; alertness and tactile sensitivity; anxiety; increased or irregular heartbeat; dehydration; chills; sweating; impaired cognition and motor function; reduced appetite; muscle cramping; teeth grinding; muscle breakdown; death	High risk for people with cardiovascular disease; dehydration leading to liver and kidney failure; disturbing emotional reactions, confusion, depression, sleep problems, anxiety, and heart palpitations; toxic to the brain; impairs memory; possibly brain damage
Heroin	Euphoria; warm flushing of skin; dry mouth; heavy feeling in extremities; clouded thinking; alternating wakeful and drowsy states; itching; nausea; depressed respiration	Addiction; physical dependence; collapsed veins and abscesses from injecting; infection of heart lining and valves; arthritis and other rheumatologic problems; HIV; hepatitis C
LSD	Elation; depression; arousal; paranoia; panic; impulsive behavior; rapid shifts in emotion; distortions in perception; increased body temperature, heart rate, and blood pressure; nausea; loss of appetite; sweating; dry mouth; jaw clenching; numbness; sleeplessness; dizziness; weakness; tremors	Frightening flashbacks; hallucinogens; addiction (low potential); tolerance
Methamphetamine	Enhanced mood; stimulant effect of increased heart rate, blood pressure, body temperature, energy, and activity; decreased appetite; dry mouth; increased sexuality; jaw clenching	Addiction; memory loss; weight loss; impaired cognition; insomnia; anxiety, irritability; confusion; paranoia; aggression; mood disturbances; hallucinations; violent behavior; liver, kidney, and lung damage; severe dental problems; cardiac and neurological damage; HIV; hepatitis

From drugabuse.gov.

Drug use can also result in **drug dependence**, which means a person needs a drug in order to function. A person with drug dependence typically exhibits signs and behavior changes such as withdrawing from school activities, being easily aggravated, and being physically sloppy and unclean (see figure 17.2). **Drug addiction**, on the other hand, is the compulsive use of a substance despite negative or dangerous effects. A person can be physically dependent on a substance without being addicted to it.

Addiction often includes **drug tolerance**—needing an increasingly high dose to attain the same

effect. And, of course, once a person is addicted to a drug, he or she must also deal with emotional and physical **withdrawal** symptoms when quitting the drug (see figure 17.3).

Despite all of the possible dangers of using illicit drugs, millions of Americans do use them, including a significant proportion of teens (see figure 17.4). For some reason, people often believe they will experience only the positive aspects of drug use—that the negative aspects will happen only to other people. However, just as many people don't know they have an allergy until they use a certain substance or eat a certain food, there is no way to know how any

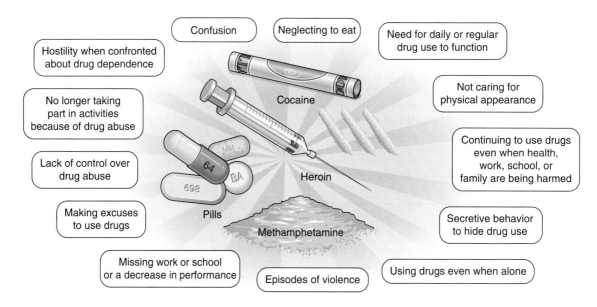

FIGURE 17.2 Symptoms and behaviors of drug dependence.

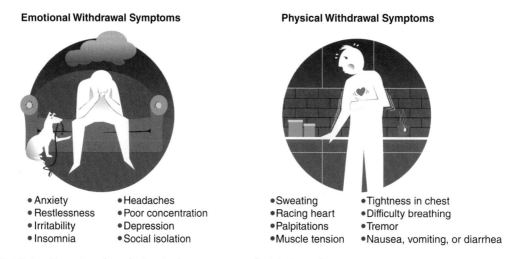

FIGURE 17.3 Emotional and physical symptoms of withdrawal.

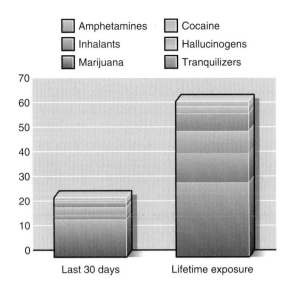

FIGURE 17.4 Percentage of teens reporting illicit drug use.

given person will respond to a specific drug, dosage, or mixture of drugs and alcohol until it happens. As you'll see in the next lesson, this is also true of prescription and over-the-counter drugs.

Marijuana

For marijuana, laws are changing so fast in many states that it is difficult to say what the legal status of marijuana is for adults. There are no states or organizations—even the National Organization for the Reform of Marijuana Laws (NORML)—that advocate for marijuana use by young people not suffering from disease. Of course, the marijuana

laws are changing because there are disagreements, even among experts, about the medical value of marijuana. Some people believe that the possible harms from marijuana use are less than already legal drugs (e.g., tobacco and alcohol for adults). Numerous states have legalized marijuana for certain medical conditions like treating the symptoms of cancer and for the nausea that chemotherapy might cause. Some people believe the use of marijuana should be a personal choice for adults. Others argue that marijuana has not been subjected to the rigorous testing that is required by other drugs to be approved by the FDA. The American Medical Association is against the legalization of marijuana.

As you read earlier in this chapter, marijuana is still classified as a schedule I drug, meaning that the FDA and the DEA haven't taken it out of the category that is considered *not for medical use*. Colorado was the first state to legalize the recreational use of marijuana by adults. This law comes with provisions about taxation and who can be licensed to sell marijuana. Since this law started on January 1, 2014, it is hard to see what the advantages and disadvantages will be, both short term and long term. The inhalation of smoke on a regular basis and over a long period of time is not good for the lungs and the rest of the respiratory system. The chapter on tobacco pointed out the hazards of tobacco smoke. Less is known about the long-term effects of ingesting marijuana.

Suffice it to say that marijuana is not suitable for use by young people. Their bodies are still growing and developing and should not be exposed to any known or unknown harms that marijuana use can cause.

Drug Use to Enhance Performance

As discussed in this book's chapter on emotional health and wellness, muscle dysmorphia is a condition in which a person sees one's own body very differently from its actual appearance. As a result, the person may resort to using steroids or other substances to gain muscle mass. Bulking up in this way to look more muscular or gain a performance advantage is tempting to many athletes, but it is also dangerous, illegal, and unethical. Most people agree that taking performance-enhancing drugs violates the spirit of good sporting behavior—sort of like having a secret motor in a sailboat race. It's just not fair, and it's not right. The Olympics and most sport organizations have strict rules against the use of performance-enhancing drugs such as steroids.

◆)) HEALTHY COMMUNICATION

Do you think marijuana use is more or less dangerous than cigarette smoking? Write a summary (one paragraph to one page long) of your answer; support your position with facts.

Why Do People Use Illicit Drugs?

Drugs occurring in nature (e.g., in plants or animals) were probably originally consumed by accident a long time ago. Someone ate the bark of a tree; accidentally ingested mold in a food item; or picked up a frog, thus getting a certain substance on his or her hand, and later put the hand in his or her mouth—and as a result experienced an altered state of consciousness. Many people in various cultures viewed such experiences as supernatural, allowing them to talk to the gods (many ancient people believed in many gods).

We now know that most **psychoactive drugs** distort people's judgment. These are generally the drugs that people take for thrill seeking, consciousness raising (i.e., people believe they have special insights into the meaning of life), or mood elevation. People who take psychoactive drugs may think they are stronger, braver, or more intelligent, but to outside observers this is not so. Still, some people are attracted to the prospect of an altered state of consciousness, and drugs offer a relatively easy—but often unsafe—way to experience it.

Many factors are known to influence a person's likelihood of using illicit drugs. For example, there is a strong connection between drug use and mental illness, especially for people with depression, bipolar disorder, anxiety disorder, and schizophrenia.

Young people often feel invincible and believe that bad things happen to other people but not to them. These types of beliefs may contribute to risky behavior. In addition, young people may be tempted to take "dares" thinking that they will be perceived as weak if they don't do something dangerous for the benefit of impressing their friends. People are also more likely to use drugs if they have easy access to drugs, their parents use drugs, they have low self-esteem, they are in stressful economic or emotional circumstances, or they live in a culture with high acceptance of drug use. The main reason that teens in the United States try illegal drugs is to help them deal with the pressures of school. The second reason is related to low self-esteem or to enhance social acceptance, according to a study by Partnership for a Drug-Free America.

Some people think that the attraction of drugs is similar to the lure of magic potions described in fairy tales. People may believe that a substance can make them happier, more beautiful, stronger, more likable, thinner, or more lovable. Drugs are also sometimes used to provide a temporary sense of escape or for producing the sensations and feelings they bring. In other words, people often look for external solutions to their problems rather than working to solve problems internally. This book's stress management chapter discusses the fact that people can learn to alter their consciousness without drugs—for example, through mindfulness techniques or yoga. Although it may take longer to solve problems internally, the resulting solutions

Instead of taking drugs to deal with the pressures of stress and school or to enhance social acceptance, try getting involved in a school activity.

Getty Images/DAJ

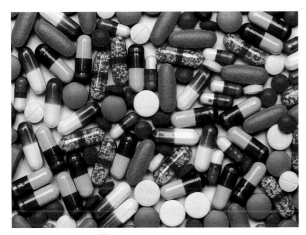

There are no magic potions to solve all of our problems.

Photodisc

their art over and over. Alcohol and drugs didn't make Amy Winehouse or Whitney Houston great singers or make Michael Jackson a great singer and dancer. In fact, drugs made it harder for them to perform and ultimately contributed to their deaths. Unfortunately, people who are dependent on drugs may deceive themselves into thinking that the drugs are essential to their performance. Add to this the addictive nature of drugs, and it's easy to explain why some people keep taking more and more drugs despite the risk of disease, injury, and death.

are more likely to be more permanent, and they are certainly healthier.

You may have heard of famous artists who used drugs and even attributed some of their creativity to their drug use. But drugs do not teach people how to play a musical instrument, write a book, or be a good actor or dancer. Talented people practice

⊕ CONNECT

Do you think famous people (e.g., singers, actors) are more likely to use and abuse drugs than the rest of us? Why or why not? What aspects of society might contribute to drug use and abuse? Are these factors more prevalent among famous people? Discuss your perspective with your peers. Support your perspective with facts and respect each other's opinions.

Comprehension Check

1. Explain what the different levels of drug schedules represent.
2. Give two reasons why people use illegal drugs.
3. Aside from the toxic effect of illegal drugs, name another safety concern about street drugs.

Your knowledge about drugs and medicine can help you make informed decisions and stay safe. Use the following self-assessment to help you get a sense of your drug knowledge. Answer each question with the best choice.

1. Using cocaine can result in which of the following?
   a. anxiety and tremors
   b. irregular heartbeat
   c. high energy
   d. all of these

2. The Aztecs used drugs in religious ceremonies.
   a. true
   b. false

3. It is illegal in the U.S. to take a prescription drug prescribed for someone else.
   a. true
   b. false

4. A person is at greater risk of abusing drugs if a parent has abused drugs.
   a. true
   b. false

5. What is the number one reason why U.S. teens say they *begin* using alcohol or drugs?
   a. pressured by their peers
   b. influenced by the media
   c. the pressures and stress of school
   d. anxious, depressed, or stressed

6. The original Coca-Cola product contained extracts from which of the following?
   a. coca leaves
   b. the opium poppy
   c. malt and barley
   d. none of these

7. Which of the following best defines a psychoactive drug?
   a. a drug used to treat infections
   b. a drug that only comes from natural sources
   c. a drug that causes mood elevation
   d. a drug that has no active ingredient
   e. none of these

8. What does it mean when a person has developed a tolerance to a drug?
   a. she is addicted
   b. the drug makes her sick
   c. over time she requires more of the drug to produce the original effect
   d. her habit has been broken

9. Which of the following is not a common reason why people use illegal drugs?

   a. living in a culture where drug use is common

   b. curiosity

   c. social pressure

   d. its category on the DEA and FDA drug schedule

   e. none of these

10. More than half of sports governing organizations approve of performance enhancing drugs.

   a. true

   b. false

Here are the correct answers: 1 d, 2 a, 3 a, 4 a, 5 c, 6 a, 7 c, 8 c, 9 d, and 10 b. If you got nine or ten questions right, you're very knowledgeable about drug issues. If you got seven or eight right, you're above average in your knowledge. If you got six or fewer right, spend some time learning about drugs to help protect yourself and your family and friends.

✔ Planning for Healthy Living

Use the Healthy Living Plan worksheet to help you prevent drug use now and in your future or to help you stop or gain control over existing drug use.

Lesson 17.2

Prescription and Over-the-Counter Drugs

Lesson Objectives

After reading this lesson, you should be able to

1. identify the three types of prescription drugs that are most commonly abused,
2. explain the risks associated with misuse of over-the-counter drugs, and
3. explain what the acronym SAFER stands for.

 ## Lesson Vocabulary

depressants, over-the-counter (OTC) drug, prescription drug, stimulants

Drug abuse doesn't occur only with illicit drugs. In fact, the misuse and abuse of both prescription and over-the-counter medications is a growing concern in the United States. This lesson gives you information about prescription and over-the-counter medications, including guidelines for safe use and the risks associated with misuse.

> " Always laugh when you can, it is cheap medicine. "
>
> —George Gordon Byron

Prescription Drugs

The purpose of **prescription drugs** is to help people treat illnesses or symptoms, such as pain and discomfort. The differences between prescription drugs and over-the-counter drugs are summarized in table 17.3. Prescription drugs have helped millions of people suffering from a wide range of diseases and disorders, and they have saved millions of lives, but no drug is free of potentially harmful side effects. A prescription should always do more good than harm; if it doesn't, it should be discontinued or replaced by a different one.

Prescription drugs can also be abused, particularly when they are used for nonmedical purposes. According to the U.S. National Institute on Drug Abuse (NIDA), about 12 million Americans used prescription drugs for nonmedical (i.e., recreational) reasons in 2010. The most commonly misused and abused prescription drugs are called opiates (used for pain relief), central nervous system **depressants** (used to treat anxiety disorders and depression), and **stimulants** (used most often to treat ADHD).

Another issue is overdose from prescription drugs. It is estimated that 2 people die each day in the United States from a prescription drug overdose, and another 40 are admitted to emergency rooms

TABLE 17.3 Prescription Versus Over-the-Counter Drugs

Prescription	Over-the-counter
• Prescribed by a doctor • Bought at a pharmacy • Prescribed for and intended to be used by one person • Regulated by the U.S. Food and Drug Administration (FDA) through an application process requiring research data, analysis of the drug's behavior in the body, and information about how the drug is manufactured	• Doctor's prescription not needed • Bought off the shelf in stores • Regulated by the FDA through monographs (in effect, recipe books that cover acceptable ingredients, doses, formulations, and labeling and that are updated when ingredients change)

Drug Controversies

If you do even a little research, you'll find considerable disagreement about many drug-related issues in the United States—for example, current laws, drug classifications, punishment for drug offenders, whether FDA regulations are too strict or too lenient, whether certain drugs should be legalized, whether the "war on drugs" has been successful, and why there is so much demand for illegal drugs. One prime example is the ongoing debate over the legalization of marijuana; see the earlier section about marijuana. Despite these debates, there is widespread agreement that drugs can be harmful and that we need to be careful to ensure the health and safety of all people.

with life-threatening conditions. Both of these problems may be made worse by the increasing availability of prescription drugs. NIDA notes that enough painkillers were prescribed in the United States to medicate every American adult around the clock for a month and that prescriptions for opiates and stimulants have increased steadily since 1991.

Blame for prescription abuse can be assigned to many factors: consumers themselves, ineffective tracking systems, illegal sources, and improper prescribing, to name a few. Experts are beginning to pay more attention to the misuse and abuse of

prescription drugs. More studies are being done, and more conferences held, to address the problem.

Although experts are far from solving the problem of prescription drug use, people can follow certain good practices to help prevent problems associated with prescription drugs. First, remember that prescription drugs are intended to help people who have medical problems. Prescription drugs should not make people feel worse or be used for recreational purposes. The sidebar titled Guidelines for Taking Prescription Medicines presents some of the most important practices you can follow to prevent problems with prescription medicines.

To help prevent problems with prescription drugs, always follow your doctor's instructions, and don't share your prescription or improvise on your dosage.

© Wavebreakmedia Ltd | Dreamstime.com

Over-the-Counter Drugs

Over-the-counter (OTC) drugs are available on the shelf in stores, rather than by prescription, because they are less likely to cause harm and less likely to need close monitoring (see table 17.3). OTC drugs can be helpful in treating minor disorders, aches, and pains. They are generally indicated for short-term use, but that doesn't mean they can't be harmful. Any drug can be harmful if not taken for the intended purpose, according to the instructions provided, and in the recommended dosage.

Abuse of over-the-counter drugs is most common among teens between the ages of 13 and 16. Young people may experiment with OTC medicines to which they have access in the medicine cabinet at home. This type of experimentation may seem less harmful than abusing prescription drugs or using illicit drugs, but it carries real risks. It also often leads to the use and abuse of more addictive drugs. Table 17.4 identifies some of the most commonly abused OTC drugs and their risks.

Guidelines for Taking Prescription Medicines

1. Make sure you understand why your medicine has been prescribed.

2. Make sure you get complete instructions about how and when to take the medication. If you don't understand the instructions, ask your doctor or pharmacist to explain them in simpler terms.

3. Know the common side effects of your medicine. Ask your doctor or pharmacist to explain them. If you don't understand the wording on the package insert, ask the doctor or pharmacist to give you a printout in language that is easier to understand.

4. Always tell your doctor and pharmacist about any other medications (prescription or otherwise) that you take so they can account for any possible drug interactions.

5. Don't improvise on your dosage—if you start to feel better, don't stop taking the medication without consulting your doctor or pharmacist.

6. Don't share your prescription with anyone else. Doing so is dangerous and against the law.

7. Make sure the medication is current. Don't save old medications after they have expired. Many communities have prescription drug take-back events where you can drop off unused or expired drugs and they will be disposed of properly.

8. If you have to take more than one medication, develop a system for keeping track of them.

9. Find out whether your medication requires you to avoid or limit certain foods or beverages. If so, there will often be a warning on the bottle or package insert. That's not always the case, so you should ask your doctor or pharmacist to be sure.

10. Alcohol reacts badly with many of the most commonly prescribed drugs. Not only is it illegal for minors to consume alcohol (except in states where it is legal to consume it in your own home under the supervision of a parent or guardian), but it is also dangerous when consumed with many prescription drugs.

Fads and Fantasies

Drug use tends to go in social cycles, and the rise of social media (e.g., YouTube, Vimeo, Twitter, Facebook) enables fads to catch on faster and spread further than ever before. Fads range from drinking cough medicine to using newer, more exotic-sounding substances, such as bath salts, K2, and Spice. Some people even post online videos of drug use, such as taking "eyeball shots" of vodka, which does not get a person drunk but can permanently damage the eye. All of these practices can be very dangerous, but since people see them online or on TV shows, they tend to think of them as safe and even funny.

In fact, there seems to be no end to the various substances that some people will try to sell or convince others to use with the promise of happiness, bliss, enlightenment, or just plain fun. It would take several books to describe all of the fads and fantasies associated with the latest drug, but the usual pattern involves big promises, followed by experimentation, followed by disappointment (including adverse side effects), followed by the next fad that comes along.

Perhaps some people will always believe that a magic potion somewhere out there will make them live happily ever after. In reality, no substance can live up to this expectation in the long run, and experimenting with fad drugs often leads to use of even harder and more dangerous drugs—and to addiction.

As discussed in this book's stress management chapter, you can learn to safely alter your consciousness through practices such as mindfulness

TABLE 17.4 Commonly Misused Over-the-Counter (OTC) Drugs and Their Risks

Drug	Risks from heavy dosing or long-term use
Dextromethorphan This is the active ingredient in more than 100 cough and cold medicines (e.g., Robitussin, NyQuil). Ten percent of teens report abusing cough medicine to get high.	Impaired judgment, vomiting, loss of muscle movement, seizure, blurred vision, drowsiness, shallow breathing, fast heart rate, death (from large dose combined with alcohol or other drugs)
Pain relievers These medications (e.g., acetaminophen, ibuprofen) are sometimes taken in doses higher than recommended to try making them work faster.	Liver failure, stomach bleeding, kidney failure, cardiac risks
Caffeine medicines and energy drinks OTC caffeine pills (e.g., NoDoz), energy drinks (e.g., 5-hour Energy), and pain relievers with caffeine have all been abused for the buzz or jolt of energy they seem to impart.	Serious dehydration, gastric reflux, panic attacks, heart irregularities, accidental death (particularly in people with an underlying heart condition)
Diet pills In large doses, diet pills can create a mild buzz. Misuse of diet pills can also signal a serious eating disorder. Abuse of diet pills often starts with trying just a few in order to lose weight, but some OTC medicines and herbal preparations can be addictive.	Nervousness, tremor, digestive problems, hair loss, insomnia, anxiety, irritability, extreme paranoia, blurred vision, kidney problems, dehydration, rapid and irregular heartbeat, high blood pressure, stroke, heart failure, death
Laxatives and herbal diuretics (water pills) As with diet pills, some teens and young adults abuse these drugs in an attempt to lose weight. Examples include uva-ursi, goldenseal, dandelion root, and rose hip.	Serious dehydration; life-threatening loss of important minerals and salts that regulate the amount of water in the body, the acidity of the blood, and muscle function; physical dependence from long-term use of laxatives
Pseudoephedrine This substance is sought out to make the illegal drug methamphetamine. It has also been taken as a stimulant to cause an excitable, hyperactive feeling.	Heart palpitations, irregular heartbeat, heart attack, episodes of paranoid psychosis (when combined with other drugs, e.g., narcotics)
Herbal ecstasy This combination of inexpensive herbs is sold legally in pill form. It is swallowed, snorted, or smoked to produce euphoria, increased awareness, and enhanced sexual sensation.	Muscle spasm, increased blood pressure, seizure, heart attack, stroke, death

techniques. And as corny as it may sound, people *can* get high on life. The key is to focus on finding internal solutions to problems. People often ask the wrong questions. For example, if a person gets frequent headaches, she may ask herself, "What drug can I take to make the pain go away?" It's natural to want to relieve pain, but it's also necessary to get to the real cause of the problem. A good question to ask in this situation is "Why do I have so many headaches?" Depending on the cause, the person might find relief by exercising, practicing a stress management technique, or eliminating a certain food from the diet. Self-treating when you don't know the cause is unlikely to work.

Drug Treatment

Just as different drugs can affect different people in different ways, some treatments work for some people but not for others. As discussed in the chapters on tobacco and alcohol, it is difficult to overcome dependence or addiction. Drug addiction

👥 CONSUMER CORNER: Selecting and Using Over-the-Counter Drugs

Over-the-counter drugs include a range of familiar medicines, such as aspirin, decongestants, antacids, NSAIDs (e.g., ibuprofen), sleep aids, and antihistamines. When purchasing OTC medications, you need to be a wise consumer. All OTC medications should be used only for their intended purpose, according to the directions provided, and in the recommended dosage. When buying and using OTC drugs, use the FDA's SAFER guidelines.

- **S**peak up (if the drug doesn't work or may be producing bad side effects).
- **A**sk questions (about what the drug can be expected to do).
- **F**ind the facts (ask your doctor or health care professional if he or she recommends this drug).
- **E**valuate your choices. (Is the OTC drug you want to buy the best way to treat your condition?)
- **R**ead the label (make sure this drug is appropriate for you and that it won't interact with any other drug you're taking).

Consumer Challenge

What are the main differences between prescription drugs and over-the-counter drugs? To help you research your answer, visit the student section of the Health for Life website.

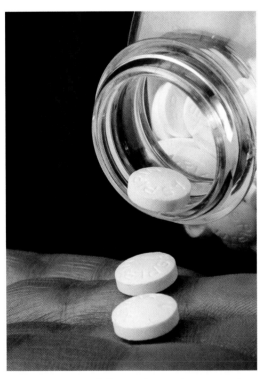

Use the SAFER guidelines when selecting and using OTC drugs.

Photodisc

is often recognized on the basis of the drug user developing a drug tolerance and thus craving more and more of the drug to get the same feeling. If the user is deprived of the drug, he or she goes through withdrawal, which (as discussed in this chapter's first lesson) can be emotional and physical. These are difficult problems to solve. Even if a person is not drug dependent or addicted, it can still be difficult to change or reverse a drug habit.

For people who are physically dependent or addicted, treatment can involve a range of responses, including counseling, medical intervention, behavior therapy, support groups (e.g., Narcotics Anonymous), and participation in a rehabilitation program. Some communities have drug courts in which minor drug offenders go through a program to help them stop using drugs instead of going to jail. Treatment can be complicated by dependence on more than one substance and by other medical problems. Despite these various challenges, hundreds of thousands of people in the United States have been able to return to a life free of drug dependence, misuse, and abuse. Of course, it is better to prevent drug problems than to have to treat them.

HEALTH TECHNOLOGY

Recovery from drug addiction is a challenging and continuing process. It is not uncommon for people to relapse during treatment or after active treatment ends. Could text messages help people who are recovering from drug dependence? Some researchers are experimenting with sending short messages to clients during and after their initial recovery. The messages are intended to encourage and motivate clients to continue their new, healthier behaviors.

Initial evaluations indicate that such text messaging may be helpful. In one study, Frederick Muench of the psychiatry department at Columbia University surveyed people in an addiction treatment program to find out what they wanted. He discovered that most of them wanted to receive text messages that, for example, recognized them for achieving milestones, such as a certain number of days clean. In addition, 96 percent wanted a friend to be notified (and 78 percent wanted a therapist to be notified) if they felt they were going to relapse. Overall, text messaging may help people who are recovering from drug addiction.

 CONNECT

How might text messaging be a tool for helping people maintain positive behavior changes when recovering from drug or alcohol abuse? For promoting other healthy behaviors, such as exercise and healthy eating? Do you think you would ever subscribe to such a service? Why or why not?

Comprehension Check

1. What are two reasons why people misuse prescription drugs?
2. How can OTC drugs be harmful?
3. What government agency created the acronym SAFER to help people safely take OTC drugs and what does the S represent?

Everyone says no to something at least once in a while, but sometimes it's more important than others. Being able to say no—that is, having strong refusal skills—helps you navigate risky or complicated situations with better results. Saying no may seem like a simple skill, but doing it effectively and comfortably requires confidence and practice. It's important to be able to say no without feeling guilty or self-conscious.

Emily was invited to her new friend Amelia's house after school. She liked Amelia and was excited to go, but when they got to the house she quickly realized that things weren't right. Amelia's parents weren't home, and her older brother was drinking beer and seemed to be on some sort of drug. When she asked Amelia about it, she said, "Yeah, my brother scores marijuana from a guy at work, and we light up out back when no one else is home." Emily immediately felt nervous because she doesn't agree with using drugs for recreation. Her stomach was in knots, and she felt really uncomfortable when she saw Amelia get a small package out of her brother's bag.

Charles was working hard to lose a few pounds and get in better shape. So far, he had lost 6 pounds (2.7 kilograms) in just under three weeks. Then a few of his buddies invited him over to watch the Super Bowl, and they were all bringing food with empty calories. He knew that they'd be eating a lot and that food would be a big part of the event. As part of his diet, however, Charles was eating only lean meats, fruits, vegetables, and whole grains, and he was drinking only water and tea. Last time the guys had watched a game together, they had all gotten sick on chicken wings, nachos, chili, and soda. Charles knew his friends would pressure him to join the party and tell him he could just take some diet pills the next day.

For Discussion

Both Emily and Charles need to use refusal skills. Emily is in a dangerous situation and is feeling uncomfortable. Charles isn't in danger, but he doesn't want to wreck his hard work or feel bad about his choices the next day. What strategies can Emily use to say no? What strategies can Charles use? What might some of the long-term consequences be if Emily can't develop effective refusal skills? What about Charles? To help you develop your answers, review the Skills for Healthy Living feature.

SKILLS FOR HEALTHY LIVING: Building Refusal Skills

Being able to say no is a key part of building refusal skills. Throughout your life, you'll be presented with opportunities and choices that may require you to say no in order to be true to your beliefs and values and maintain your health and safety. Use the following tips to help you say no when necessary.

- **Know what you believe and stick to it.** Having a strong and clear sense of your personal values goes a long way in helping you say no when you need to.
- **Be assertive.** When you say no, do it with conviction. You don't need to be mean or aggressive. Instead, stand tall, make eye contact with the person or people you're talking to, and simply say, "No, thank you" or "No, that is not something I am willing to do."
- **Don't apologize for saying no.** If you feel strongly about a choice you're making, don't apologize for it. Apologizing makes it easier for others to talk you out of your decision. Rather than saying, "I'm sorry, guys, but I don't want to do that," say, "I understand that you want to do this, but I don't want to, and I am saying no."
- **Offer alternatives.** If someone pressures you to do something you don't want to do, say no and also consider offering an alternative choice. If you don't want to smoke, suggest going for coffee instead.

If you don't want to be alone with someone else, suggest meeting in a public place like a park.

- **Support others when they say no.** If you offer your support when a friend or family member refuses something, that person will likely support you when you do so. You often get the same treatment from others that you give them.

- **Have a plan.** If you're going out with friends, know what your plan is and stick to it. Making spontaneous decisions may seem fun, but it often leads to situations where you feel pressured or uncomfortable. Having a plan for healthy living also makes it easier to say no to unhealthy food choices and to choose an active pursuit rather than a sedentary one.

 ## ACADEMIC CONNECTION: Understanding Risk (Probability)

In general terms, risk is the probability that an event will happen. Many things, like diseases, can't be predicted with certainty. The best you can do is estimate the likelihood that the disease will occur based on the information available to you. To understand how probabilities work, consider what happens when a coin is tossed. There are two possible outcomes: heads or tails. Given that reality, we say that the probability of the coin landing on heads is one in two, or 1/2, or 50%. The probability of the coin landing on tails is also one in two, or 1/2, or 50%. Similarly, when rolling a single die, there are six possible outcomes: 1, 2, 3, 4, 5, or 6. So, the probability of any one of those numbers occurring is one in six, or 1/6. When talking about a disease, such as in this chapter's Living Well News feature, risk is used to describe the chance that a person will develop the disease or have a recurrence of the disease. This risk, or probability, is based on research findings that look at the possible outcomes of a situation and determine the likelihood of each possible outcome based on all of the factors involved.

Is Aspirin a Miracle Drug?

"Taking a low dose of aspirin every day can prevent and possibly even treat cancer," BBC News reported in 2012. The painkiller is already taken by millions in order to cut the risk of heart attack and stroke (see table 17.5), but widely reported recent research suggests that it may play a role in fighting cancer as well.

In three research papers published simultaneously, doctors and researchers looked at cancer data recorded during dozens of trials that tested aspirin use for heart and circulatory health. They found that daily use of aspirin was linked to a drop in the short-term risk of developing cancer and could reduce both the risk of cancer spreading through the body and the risk of death due to cancer.

The reason for the potential beneficial effects is a particular chemical found in the drug that influences cell growth and development. Overall, a person's risk of cancer may drop 20 percent after 20 years of aspirin use. "The physiological reactions in the cells are similar to those seen from a dose of exercise," says medical researcher Patricia Rothchild of Oxford University.

It isn't all good news, however. Aspirin can cause painful stomach irritation, and there is a small but serious risk of bleeding associated with its use. Because of these risks, physician David Danielson says, "It is too soon to recommend that people should start taking daily aspirin simply for cancer prevention unless it has been specifically recommended to them by their doctor." There is certainly no reason for people under 18 to start on a daily low-dose aspirin.

However, Dr. Rothchild points out, "Studies suggest that 769 people would need to be treated with low-dose aspirin for one extra person to be harmed with major bleeding as a result, so it seems the known benefits might already outweigh the risks." For now, it appears the verdict is still out.

For Discussion

Based on the information in the table, who are the most likely people to use aspirin daily or every other day? Why do you think this is the case? Explain your answer.

TABLE 17.5 Aspirin Use By Adults Ages 18 to 65 in the United States

Characteristic	Aspirin use daily or every other day (%)	
Aspirin use by gender	Males	61.3%
	Females	47.4%
Aspirin use by age	18-44	4.6%
	45-65	27.0%
	Over 65	48.5%
Aspirin use by ethnicity	White non-Hispanic	22.3%
	Black non-Hispanic	15.1%
	Asian non-Hispanic	11.5%
	Hispanic	10.0%

Source: Agency for Health Care Research and Quality, Statistical Brief #179 (2007).

Reviewing Concepts and Vocabulary

As directed by your teacher, answer items 1 through 5 by correctly completing each sentence with a word or phrase.

1. The federal drug schedule for drugs considered to be the most dangerous is schedule _____.
2. The acronym SAFER can help you remember how to safely use what kind of drugs? _____
3. A drug requiring a physician's approval is called a _____ drug.
4. _____ drugs are generally the ones that some people take for thrill seeking, consciousness raising, and mood elevation.
5. Methamphetamine is an example of a(n) _____ drug.

For items 6 through 10, as directed by your teacher, match each term in column 1 with the appropriate phrase in column 2.

6. dependence
7. drug addiction
8. withdrawal
9. drug tolerance
10. licit drug

a. legal drug
b. physical and emotional condition that occurs when a drug is stopped
c. needing more of a drug because the body has adjusted to its effects
d. needing a drug to prevent feeling sick
e. compulsive use of a substance

For items 11 through 15, as directed by your teacher, respond to each statement or question.

11. Compare prescription and over-the-counter drugs.
12. Identify two guidelines for properly obtaining and using prescription drugs.
13. What does the acronym SAFER stand for, and what does it help you understand?
14. What are two ways to alter consciousness without using drugs?
15. What are some signs and behaviors associated with drug dependence?

Thinking Critically

Write a paragraph in response to the following questions.

Do you think that people who break the law while under the influence should be required to go to jail or to treatment? Explain your answers and use specific facts to support your positions.

Take It Home

Talk with your family members about safe use of over-the-counter medications. Take a written inventory of all OTC medications in your home and indicate where they are located. Make a list of tips or guidelines to help your family members be good consumers when buying, using, and storing medicines.

Photodisc

UNIT VI

Creating Healthy and Safe Communities

● ● ● ● ● ● ● ● ● ● ● ● ● ● ● ● ● ●

Healthy People 2020 Goals

- Reduce total injury rates in the population.
- Reduce rates of traumatic brain injury and traumatic spinal cord injury.
- Reduce rates of poisonings.
- Reduce rates of fatal and nonfatal unintentional injuries from fire, motor vehicle crashes, falls, suffocations, drowning, and sport and recreation accidents.
- Reduce the proportion of teens who report that they rode with a driver who was drinking alcohol.
- Decrease the rate of alcohol-impaired driving.
- Increase safety belt use.
- Increase bicycle helmet laws and motorcycle helmet use.
- Reduce homicides and firearm-related deaths and injuries.
- Reduce nonfatal physical assault injuries and physical assaults.
- Reduce fighting and bullying among teens.
- Reduce weapon carrying by adolescents on school property.
- Reduce child maltreatment.
- Reduce intimate partner and sexual violence.
- Reduce air toxic emissions to decrease the risk of adverse health effects.
- Reduce the amount of toxic pollutants.
- Increase recycling of municipal solid waste.
- Reduce indoor allergen levels.
- Increase the proportion of schools that engage in practices that promote a healthy and safe physical school environment.
- Reduce exposure to selected environmental chemicals in the population.
- Improve quality, utility, awareness, and use of information systems for environmental health.

Self-Assessment Features in This Unit

- My Injury Prevention and Emergency Preparedness
- How Green Are You?
- How Healthy Is My School Community?

Making Healthy Decisions and Skills for Healthy Living Features In This Unit

- Skill Building
- Overcoming Barriers
- Positive Attitudes

Special Features in This Unit

- Consumer Corner: Buying a First Aid Kit
- Advocacy in Action: Promoting Recycling
- Consumer Corner: Donating to Charities

Living Well News Features in This Unit

- Personal Watercraft Safety
- Can Earbuds Damage Hearing?
- Are We Failing at Community Health?

339

18

Safety and First Aid

In This Chapter

 Student Web Resources
www.healthforlifetextbook.org/student

Lisa F. Young/fotolia.com

Lesson 18.1

Safety

Lesson Objectives

After reading this lesson, you should be able to

1. identify the major causes of unintentional injury in youth,
2. explain four ways to reduce the risk of being in an automobile crash, and
3. identify the major types of intentional injury and explain the steps you can take to avoid becoming a victim.

Lesson Vocabulary

assault, battery, distracted driving, homicide, inattention blindness, intentional injury, road rage, traumatic brain injury, unintentional injury

While your teenage years are a critical time for developing healthy habits and setting the stage for living a healthy adult life, accidents and violence pose the greatest immediate threats to your life as a teen. Accidents, or **unintentional injuries**, are caused by unplanned events, such as automobile crashes, poisonings, fires, and drownings. Unintentional injury is the leading cause of death among teenagers, and motor vehicle accidents alone account for 73 percent of all accidental deaths. The leading causes of unintentional death among teenagers can be seen in figure 18.1. **Intentional injury** includes violence, suicide, self-injury, and homicide. Homicides are the second leading cause of death among teens in the United States and the majority of these homicides involve a firearm. Understanding gun safety is an important aspect of overall safety.

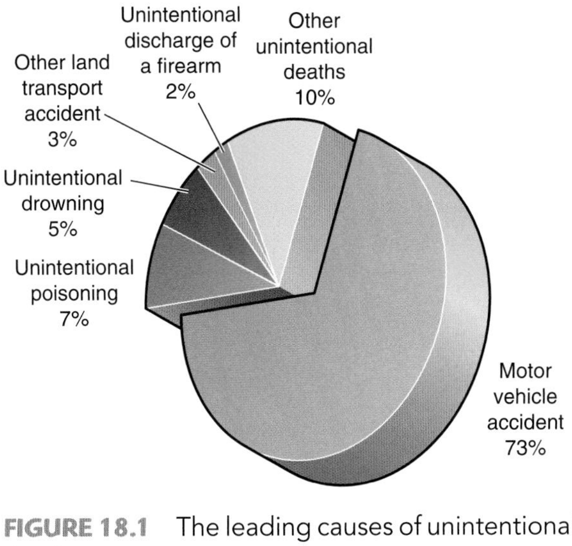

Staying Safe on the Road

Streets and highways can be dangerous places. The odds are that you will be in three or four traffic accidents in your lifetime, and about 30 percent of us willon be in a serious accident at some point. According to the National Highway Traffic Safety Administration, 20,000 people die from motor vehicle accidents each year. Motor vehicle accidents are the leading cause of death among teenagers. Fortunately, there are many safety precautions you can take to help you avoid accidents and limit your chances of being seriously hurt or killed if you are in an accident.

Seat Belts and Airbags

An average of eight teens between the ages of 16 and 19 die every day from motor vehicle injuries. In fact, one in every three teenage deaths results from an accident related to a motor vehicle. Teen drivers (age 16 to 19) are four times more likely than older drivers to crash, and teenage males are at the highest risk for accidents. To help keep yourself safe while driving or riding in a vehicle, always use your seat belt properly. Research shows that seat belt use reduces the severity of injuries by 60 percent and decreases the likelihood of death by 45 percent. American males aged 19 to 29 are the least likely to wear seat belts, and it is estimated that two-thirds

FIGURE 18.1 The leading causes of unintentional death among teenagers.

From USDHHS NCHS Data Brief, May 2010.

of people killed by automobile accidents were not wearing a seat belt at the time.

Drivers are not the only ones who can be saved by regular seat belt use. When everyone in the car buckles up, one out of every six deaths is avoided. Passengers who are not wearing a seat belt can be thrown from the vehicle or thrown into other passengers, thus causing additional injuries or deaths. Airbags further reduce the risk of death and serious injury from automobile accidents. However, they can be dangerous to children due to a child's small size, and most states require that children ride in the backseat.

Distracted Driving

According to the U.S. National Highway Traffic Safety Administration, driving while distracted increases your risk of an accident by 20 percent to 30 percent. **Distracted driving** includes driving while talking on the phone, texting, eating, drinking, applying makeup, or engaging in other activities that take your attention away from the road.

The number one cause of distracted driving is cell phone use, even when hands-free devices are used. Cell phone conversations result in what is called **inattention blindness** because the conversation leads the driver's attention away from the visual environment, distracting both the brain and the eyes. In fact, it is estimated that the distraction effect from talking on a cell phone while driving lasts for up to two minutes after the phone conversation is over. Talking to a passenger in the car is less distracting because one's attention remains focused within the vehicle. Your passenger can also alert you to any dangers.

Texting while driving is even more distracting and more dangerous, since it takes your focus and attention completely off of the road and other drivers. Texting while driving dramatically increases your risk of an accident; some estimates show the risk to be 23 times greater. Most states have passed laws prohibiting the use of cell phones while driving, and the concern over distracted driving is so great that a U.S. government website has been developed specifically to address the issue (www.distraction.gov). Florida and some other states have a law prohibiting texting while driving as well.

🔊 HEALTHY COMMUNICATION

Have you ever engaged in texting while driving? Have you seen others engage in this behavior? What are some specific things you could do to keep yourself and your friends and family members from texting while driving? Share your perspectives and ideas with your classmates.

Safe Driving Checklist

- Always wear a seat belt when driving or riding in a vehicle.
- Pay attention to the actions of other drivers.
- Keep your eyes on the road.
- Never text or use a handheld device while driving.
- Pull over or exit the road to take a phone call.
- Follow all rules of the road.
- Stay calm and do not react to aggressive or impatient drivers.
- Never drive under the influence of alcohol or drugs.
- Avoid driving when drowsy or sleepy.
- Keep passengers from becoming rowdy or distracting.
- Limit the number of passengers in your car (some state laws set limits) especially for new drivers.

Driving Under the Influence

Alcohol plays a role in 25 percent of all fatal car crashes. Across all age groups, men are significantly more likely than women to engage in driving under the influence (DUI). And although young men between the ages of 21 and 34 make up only 11 percent of the adult U.S. population, they account for 32 percent of all instances of drinking and driving.

Alcohol has also been shown to be a factor in many car crashes involving people under the legal drinking age of 21. In fact, 25 percent of young men (aged 15 to 20) killed in crashes were under the influence of alcohol at the time of their death. Alcohol impairs both judgment and coordination, thus making it hard to control reactions, speed, steering, and braking (see figure 18.2). Impairment begins after only one or two drinks; thus mixing *any* amount of alcohol with driving is dangerous.

Road Rage

Many people become impatient while driving, and some engage in emotional outbursts known as **road rage**. These outbursts can involve extremely aggressive driving, in which the car itself is treated as a weapon; they can also involve the use of guns or other weapons. Road rage is thought to play a part in as many as two-thirds of all fatal car crashes and one-third of nonfatal crashes.

People who display road rage may be experiencing frustration in other parts of life. That frustration can spill over when traffic is heavy or when another driver does something they think is stupid or annoying. The truth is that people often see other vehicles on the road merely as things; we may fail to remember that there is a living, breathing, feeling person behind the wheel. Road rage is also more common among individuals who are involved in an argument or difficult conversation on a cell phone while driving. The emotions stirred up in the conversation can spill over into aggressive driving behaviors. Alcohol use also contributes to road rage. Some psychologists have also suggested that individuals prone to road rage may have witnessed road rage and aggressive driving by their parents when they were younger and are now repeating these behaviors.

Regardless of the root cause, road rage poses a danger to the angry driver, any passengers, and fellow motorists. One way to reduce the chance of being a victim of road rage is to practice defensive driving. This approach to driving involves paying

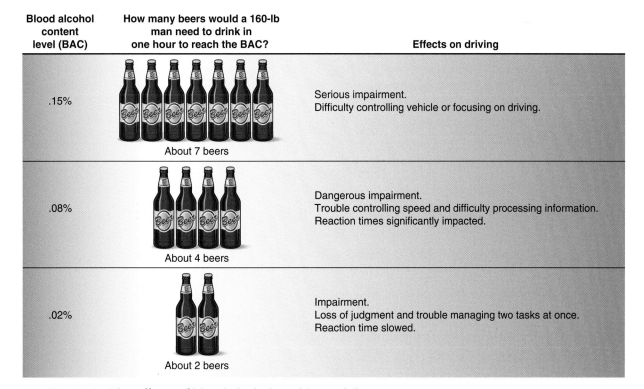

Blood alcohol content level (BAC)	How many beers would a 160-lb man need to drink in one hour to reach the BAC?	Effects on driving
.15%	About 7 beers	Serious impairment. Difficulty controlling vehicle or focusing on driving.
.08%	About 4 beers	Dangerous impairment. Trouble controlling speed and difficulty processing information. Reaction times significantly impacted.
.02%	About 2 beers	Impairment. Loss of judgment and trouble managing two tasks at once. Reaction time slowed.

FIGURE 18.2 The effects of blood alcohol on driving ability.

close attention to other drivers but not expecting them to always do what you think they should. Other useful tactics include taking deep breaths to remain calm and talking with yourself rationally about how to respond if you're confronted by an enraged driver. Even if you feel the other driver is at fault, keeping your cool and letting the situation go could save your life.

Staying Safe at Home

Home accidents are among the leading causes of death among young children and injury among adults. People often feel secure at home and forget that real and serious risks are present. The most common categories of home injury include falling, fire, and poisoning; another home safety issue involves heavy computer use. Each is discussed here.

Falling

Falls are the second-leading cause of death from unintentional injury, following motor vehicle crashes. The risk of falling is increased by poor lighting, uneven surfaces, high-heeled shoes, objects on the ground, and even distracted walking. Tips for preventing falls are provided in the accompanying text box.

Fire

In 2010, there were 384,000 home fires in the United States, resulting in 2,640 deaths (not including firefighter deaths) and 13,350 injuries. Home fires account for about 85 percent of all U.S. fires.

The number one cause of these fires is cooking, but smoking causes the most fire-related deaths.

The majority of deaths involving fire result not from burns but from smoke inhalation. Smoke from any type of fire contains a mixture of heated particles and gases. The particular type of smoke is influenced by what is burning, the fire's temperature, and the amount of available oxygen. However, any type of fire smoke is potentially deadly. Death from smoke inhalation can occur when oxygen is absent (simple asphyxia), when inhaled chemicals damage respiratory tissues and cause swelling or airway collapse (chemical irritation), or when chemicals interfere with oxygen use at a cellular level (chemical asphyxia). The leading cause of death related to smoke inhalation is carbon monoxide—an odorless, colorless, tasteless gas that causes chemical asphyxia.

Poisoning

Poisoning occurs when any substance interferes with normal body function after it is swallowed, inhaled, injected, or absorbed. Every day, 87 people die from unintentional poisoning in the United States. Those most likely to suffer illness or death from accidental poisoning are children under the age of five. Each year, half a million children swallow poisonous material, including medication not intended for them as well as cleaning supplies.

Adults are most likely to suffer accidental poisoning when they take someone else's prescription drug or when they consume a combination of drugs (whether over-the-counter or prescription) without medical clearance. The leading cause of medication-

---

Tips for Preventing Falls

- Get regular exercise, which the Centers for Disease Control and Prevention (CDC) identifies as the number one way to prevent falls.
- Put nonslip treads or carpeting on stairways.
- Equip stairways with a secure rail.
- Clear floors of small objects.
- Firmly secure rugs and carpets.
- Equip bathtubs with nonskid rubber mats and grab bars.
- Keep outdoor walkways and steps in good repair. Regularly clear snow, ice, and debris. Be aware of pets that may be in the way.

⚛ HEALTH SCIENCE

Different types of fire require different types of fire extinguisher. For example, a grease fire and an electrical fire require the application of different types and concentrations of chemicals. Extinguishing agents are separated into five major types, and fire extinguishers are labeled to indicate which types of fire they will safely put out. Class A extinguishers are used for ordinary combustible materials, such as wood, clothing, and paper; class B extinguishers are for putting out fires involving flammable liquids, such as grease and gasoline; class C extinguishers are suitable for use on fires involving appliances and other electrical equipment; class D extinguishers cover flammable metals; and class K extinguishers are typically used in industrial kitchens with large amounts of flammable cooking oil.

zimmytws/fotolia.com

Most homes benefit from a multipurpose class A/B/C fire extinguisher. Extinguishers can be heavy, and they require regular maintenance because of the chemicals and pressures involved.

related unintentional poisoning among adults is prescription painkiller medication. You should never take any medication prescribed for someone else. Medications are prescribed with specific consideration for the person's body weight, metabolic conditions, and other medications or supplements in use. Taking a medication not intended specifically for your needs is dangerous and potentially deadly. Keep all medications carefully labeled and stored out of the reach of both children and any adults for whom addiction or drug abuse is a problem.

Computer Use and Injury

Repetitive strain injury (RSI) occurs when too much stress is placed on a part of the body, resulting in inflammation (pain and swelling), at playmuscle strain, or tissue damage. This stress generally occurs from repeating the same movements over and over again. RSI is common in sport- and work-related settings, and is especially common among people who spend a lot of time using a computer keyboard.

Though most common in adults, RSI is becoming more prevalent among teens because they spend more time than ever playing video games and using computers, smartphones, and tablets for both school-work and social communication. Common signs and symptoms of RSI include tingling, numbness,

The leading cause of medication-related unintentional poisoning among adults is prescription painkiller medication. You should never take any medication prescribed for someone else.

Bill Crump/Brand X Pictures

General Care for Poisoning

- Remove the person from the source of the poison.
- Check for consciousness, breathing, and signs of life.
- Care for any life-threatening conditions such as lack of breathing or pulse.
- If possible, ask questions of the victim to get more information (e.g., What substance was ingested? How much was ingested? When was it ingested?).
- Look for any nearby containers, and take them with you to the telephone.
- Call a poison control center—in the United States, the American Association of Poison Control Centers (1-800-222-1222)—or 911.
- Follow the directions provided to you by the poison control center or emergency services call taker.

Take regular breaks when texting or playing video games.

AVAVA/fotolia.com

or pain in the affected area; stiffness or soreness in the neck or back; feelings of weakness or fatigue in the hands or arms; and popping or clicking sensations in the joints. To help prevent RSI, take regular breaks every 30 minutes or so when you are engaged in any repetitive task. If you experience symptoms, see a physician.

Staying Safe at Play

Recreational activity is an important and necessary part of living a healthy life. However, many recreational activities carry some risk of injury or even death. Therefore, whenever you're engaged in a recreational activity, consider your safety first. Guidelines vary by the activity, but it's always a good

idea to carry a cell phone and a small first aid kit and to participate in the activity with at least one other person. Whether you're with others or alone, always inform someone else of your plans. If your plans take you outside, know the weather forecast and dress appropriately (the next lesson provides more information about weather-related risks).

Drowning

About ten people die from unintentional drowning each day in the United States, and half of drowning

Making sure your life jacket fits properly is the first step before being on open water.

Human Kinetics/Mark Anderman/The Wild Studio

deaths occur in children under the age of 14. A majority of drowning deaths occur in swimming pools. Contributing factors include lack of swimming ability, absence of protective barriers (e.g., fences) around pools, and lack of supervision. The risk of drowning in open water settings is increased by alcohol use and failure to use a life jacket. Drowning can also occur in a bathtub, especially if a seizure disorder is involved. The most effective way to protect yourself from drowning is to learn basic swimming skills.

Bicycling and Skateboarding

Bicycle accidents account for nearly 2 percent of transportation-related deaths in the U.S. In 2010, 618 people died from bicycle-related accidents. The most effective way to reduce serious injury while bicycling is to wear a helmet, and many states require helmet use, especially among youth. Other good safety practices include wearing bright colors, avoiding night riding, and staying clear of road hazards and construction zones. You should also keep your bike in good repair, remain alert while riding, and follow all rules of the road.

Skateboarding remains a popular recreational activity, as well as a mode of transportation for some young people. When boarding, wear a helmet, knee and elbow pads, and wrist guards. Stay away from roads with heavy traffic, do not skate in areas with blind hills or turns, and practice stunt skateboarding only in designated skate parks.

High-Risk Recreational Activities

Not surprisingly, the risk of unintentional injury can be high when doing risky or thrill-seeking activities such as bungee jumping, ski or snowboard jumping, and parachuting. Young people often feel full of life and have a sense of being invincible and therefore may place themselves in risky situations more often than others do. Thus it's critical for you to recognize the risks in any activity you choose to do and protect yourself against unnecessary risk. Always maintain and use appropriate protective equipment and exercise reasonable judgment about your skills and abilities and the environment you're in.

Concussions

Traumatic brain injury (TBI) is a serious public health problem in the United States. A TBI is

CONNECT

How do you think society views high-risk recreational activity, such as skydiving, bungee jumping, and base jumping? Do you think risk takers are viewed as more courageous or heroic than the average person? How might social norms about high-risk behavior influence your choices now or in the future? Under what circumstances might you be more likely to engage in a high-risk recreational activity? Discuss your answers with your peers.

Properly fitting protective equipment such as helmets can help reduce the risk of getting a concussion.

caused by a bump, blow, or jolt to the head and is a penetrating (or open) head injury that disrupts the normal function of the brain. Most traumatic brain injuries are concussions. The severity of these injuries may range from mild (limited interruption in cognitive function) to severe (causing a prolonged period of unconsciousness). Some contact sports such as football have come under increased scrutiny because of the relatively high risk of players getting concussions. Properly fitting protective equipment such as helmets can help reduce the risk of getting a concussion. Any bump, blow, or jolt to the head should be checked by a physician.

Staying Safe at Work

Most Americans spend a significant amount of their time on the job and at the workplace. Injury risks in the workplace can include a wide range of things such as falling objects and debris, tripping hazards, lifting heavy or awkward items, performing repetitive tasks, and being exposed to hazardous chemicals, substances, and materials, to name a few. All workers in the U.S. have the right to a safe workplace; the rates of workplace injury, illness, and death have declined by 67 percent since 1970. These improvements are partly due to the passage of the Occupational Safety and Health Act of 1970. The law requires employers to provide their employees with working conditions that are free of known dangers and that follow all Occupational Health and Safety Administration (OSHA) standards. Employers must work to eliminate hazards as a first line of defense against illness and injury rather than simply relying on the use of masks, gloves, ear plugs, or other protective equipment.

Young workers (under the age of 18) are also protected under OSHA guidelines. In addition, the Fair Labor Standards Act (FLSA) sets limits on the number of hours youth under the age of 18 may work and on the occupations for such young workers. Following general health and safety guidelines, exercising caution in job tasks, following all job-specific rules and regulations, and reporting hazardous working environments are important steps for preventing worksite injury and illness. You can learn more about occupational health and safety by visiting the student section of the Health for Life website.

Intentional Injuries

Intentional injuries include any injury that has been purposely inflicted, either by oneself or another person. Examples are assaults, homicides, self-inflicted injuries, and suicides. Self-inflicted injuries and suicide are covered in the chapter on emotional health and wellness. Bullying and relationship vio-

---

Avoiding Risky Situations

- Keep doors and windows at your home locked. Never let a stranger into your home and never let a stranger know that you are or will be home alone.
- If you are meeting someone you do not know or who you met on the Internet, agree only to meet in a public place and take a friend with you.
- Don't hide keys to your home in obvious places, like under a doormat.
- Always be alert when walking, especially if you are alone. Avoid being distracted with electronic devices (e.g., phone, tablet). Take headphones off or keep the volume down so that you can hear what is happening around you. Walk confidently and briskly if you are feeling uneasy. Attackers often prey on people they think are confused, scared, or uncertain.
- Avoid dark and deserted places. If you must go to a dark or isolated area, make sure you have at least one other person with you. Also make sure someone else knows where you are going and when you expect to be back.
- Park your car in well-lit areas and always do a quick scan under the car and in the backseat before getting in the vehicle.
- When driving, keep car doors locked. If your car breaks down, stop and call the police, turn on the hazard lights, pop the hood, and remain in the locked vehicle. If someone stops to offer help, remain in your car until police arrive. If you do not have a phone, ask the person to call for you.
- Do not give rides to strangers or hitchhikers.
- If someone tries to rob you, give up your possessions and get away as quickly as possible.
- Call the police immediately if you witness a crime in progress.

lence are addressed in the chapter on family living and healthy relationships.

Assault, Battery, and Homicide

According to the CDC, almost one-third of U.S. high school students reported being in a physical fight in 2011, and almost 8 percent reported having been threatened with a weapon. **Assault** is an act of immediate harmful or offensive contact that creates fear for a person. **Battery** is harmfully or offensively touching another person. Both assault and battery should be reported to legal authorities.

Homicide refers to taking the life of another person. In 2010, 4,828 young people aged 10 to 24 were victims of homicide in the U.S. This is an average of 13 deaths each day. Over 80 percent of these homicides involved a firearm.

Gun Safety

In addition to being used in homicides, guns can be a cause of intentional and unintentional injury. Basic gun safety can help reduce the risks associated with firearms. Gun safety includes the following basic rules.

- Treat every gun as if it were loaded.
- Never treat a gun as a harmless toy or prop.
- Always store guns unloaded.
- Lock guns in a rack or safe and hide the keys or combination.
- Store ammunition away from guns and keep it locked.
- Don't keep guns in your home if someone in your family has a mental illness, severe depression, or potential for violence.

Recognizing and Preventing Violence

There is no way to guarantee that you will not be the victim of a violent act. However, there are general steps you can take to avoid risky situations and to help minimize the chances that you or others will become the victim of a violent crime. In addition, people who commit violent acts may display certain warning signs (see Warning Signs of Violent Behavior sidebar). If you see these signs in someone, it is important to tell a trusted adult. Individuals who commit acts of violence may suffer from mental illness (e.g., depression and suicidal tendencies) or may have issues with substance abuse, although most people with mental illness are not violent. Reporting observations and concerns will help save the lives of innocent victims.

Warning Signs of Violent Behavior

- Sudden lack of interest in school and regular activities
- Obsessions with violent games and movies
- Depression and mood swings
- Writing that shows despair and isolation or is extremely angry or violent
- Lack of anger management skills (i.e., losing one's temper often or is easily made angry)
- Talking about death or suicide
- Bringing weapons to school or work
- Violence toward animals

Comprehension Check

1. Identify two causes of unintentional injury in youth.
2. Explain one way to reduce the risk of being in an automobile crash.
3. Explain three specific actions to limit your risk of becoming a victim of violent crime.

Answer each question yes or no, then add up the total number of yes responses and evaluate your score according to the guide at the end of the assessment.

There is a fire extinguisher in my home, and I know where it is.	Yes	No
There are smoke detectors installed in my home.	Yes	No
There are first aid kits or first aid supplies in my home, and I know where they are.	Yes	No
I always wear a seat belt when I am in a motor vehicle.	Yes	No
There is a first aid kit in my car.	Yes	No
I always follow safety guidelines when riding my bike or skateboard.	Yes	No
I am confident in my ability to administer CPR to an adult.	Yes	No
I know what to do if a person chokes and becomes unconscious.	Yes	No
I know how to treat injuries such as sprains and strains.	Yes	No
I know what to do if someone shows signs of becoming suddenly ill.	Yes	No
I have successfully treated minor scrapes and bruises in the past.	Yes	No
I have practiced my first aid skills in a variety of situations.	Yes	No
I am confident in my ability to stay calm in an emergency situation.	Yes	No
I keep emergency numbers stored in my phone or another handy location.	Yes	No
I know how to use an AED for victims of sudden cardiac arrest.	Yes	No

My score for Injury Prevention and Emergency Preparedness = _____ (total number of yes answers)

If you gave 13 to 15 yes responses, you're well prepared to both avoid and deal with a variety of emergency situations. If you gave 10 to 12 yes responses, you're somewhat prepared to avoid and deal with a variety of emergency situations. If you gave 9 or fewer yes responses, you may be putting yourself at risk and may not be ready to deal with an emergency situation.

✔ Planning for Healthy Living

Use the Healthy Living Plan worksheet to improve your emergency readiness.

Lesson 18.2

First Aid and CPR

Lesson Objectives

After reading this lesson, you should be able to
1. describe the three basic emergency action steps for administering CPR,
2. explain basic first aid procedures for common emergency scenarios, and
3. identify the signs of sudden illness that might require medical attention.

Lesson Vocabulary

closed fracture, closed wound, dislocation, heatstroke, Heimlich maneuver, hypothermia, open fracture, open wound, sprain, strain

We can find ourselves in the midst of an emergency at any time. You can help keep yourself and others safe in an emergency by learning basic steps for cardiopulmonary resuscitation (CPR) and first aid.

Emergency Action Steps

At some point, we will all face an emergency, and that emergency is more likely to involve a loved one than someone we don't know. As a result, emergencies are often particularly stressful and emotional. Remaining calm and thinking quickly can make the difference between saving and losing a life. Regardless of the type of emergency, you should always follow three basic steps: check, call, and care (the three Cs).

Check

Emergency scenes can be unsafe both for those involved in an accident and for those wanting to help. Always check the scene for safety. Use your senses—hearing, sight, and smell—to check for anything out of the ordinary that could signal danger, such as smoke, spilled chemicals, strange odors, screaming or crying sounds, downed electrical wires, and confused or disoriented people. If a scene is clearly dangerous, do not go near it. Instead, call 911 and wait for professionals to arrive.

If the scene does not appear dangerous, look for clues about what happened. Check for fallen items, such as a ladder or step stool, a spilled medicine bottle, tire tread marks, broken glass, or anything else that might indicate what happened. Check carefully to see how many people are hurt and if anyone else is available to help. Your observations will be important when you communicate with emergency personnel in the next step.

Call

Most of the time, calling for help is the most important thing you can do to help an ill or injured

Calling 911

When you call 911, an emergency call taker, or dispatcher, will answer the phone. Call takers are specifically trained to deal with crises over the phone. The caller will ask for your phone number and address or location and will want to know the nature of the emergency. When using a wireless phone to make a 911 call, it is especially important to be able to provide your location since it will not be automatically indicated to the dispatcher. If you are in an unfamiliar location, look for street signs or major landmarks, such as buildings with specific business names or logos.

The call taker will likely ask you a lot of questions in order to determine the most appropriate action to be taken. Remain calm and focus on answering the questions without panicking or becoming frustrated. Call takers may also provide you with basic CPR or first aid information to assist you until help arrives.

person. When calling, remain calm and observant. Answer the questions that the call taker asks. Be prepared to provide information about the location and describe the emergency and each victim's condition.

In situations where a victim's breathing might be impaired, you may need to provide care before placing a call to emergency services. If other people are around, you can instruct someone else to call 911 while you provide immediate care. Care-first situations include the unwitnessed collapse of a person younger than about 12 years and any instance of drowning. In these cases, try to provide oxygen as quickly as possible. See sidebar titled Learn Cardiopulmonary Resuscitation (CPR). If you are alone with the victim in these situations, attempt to provide care before you call.

Care

You may need to provide care in an emergency situation. Fundamental first aid guidelines for several common conditions are provided in the remainder of this chapter.

Helping a Conscious Choking Victim

The **Heimlich maneuver** is used to dislodge a piece of food or other object from a conscious person who is choking. The maneuver is safe for children over one year old and adults. A separate technique is used for infants. You can also perform the Heimlich maneuver on yourself. In any case, you may need to repeat the procedure several times before the object is dislodged. Each technique is described below.

When performing the Heimlich maneuver on a child over one year old or an adult, complete the following steps.

1. For a conscious person who is sitting or standing, position yourself behind the person and reach your arms around his or her waist (figure 18.3).

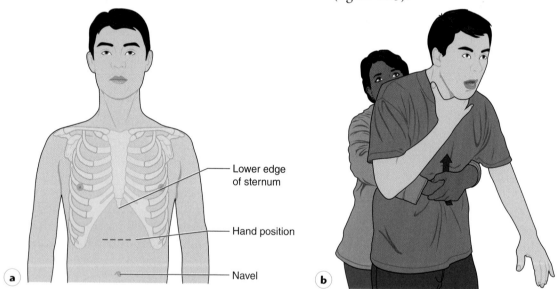

FIGURE 18.3 (a) Locating hand position, and (b) performing the Heimlich maneuver.

Basic Care Guidelines

- Do no harm.
- Monitor the person's breathing and consciousness.
- Keep the person from getting chilled or overheated.
- Help the person rest in the most comfortable position possible. If the person may have a spinal injury, do not move him or her unless there is immediate danger.
- Reassure the person and help him or her stay calm but alert.
- Give any specific care needed.

2. Place your fist, thumb side in, just above the person's navel and grab the fist tightly with your other hand.

3. Pull your fist abruptly upward and inward to increase airway pressure behind the obstructed object and force it from the windpipe.

4. If the person is conscious and lying on his or her back, straddle the person facing the head. Push your fist upward and inward in a maneuver similar to the one above.

5. If the person becomes unconscious, call 911 and begin CPR.

If you are alone and choking, you can perform the Heimlich maneuver on yourself with the following steps.

1. Make a fist. Place the thumb below your rib cage and above your navel.

2. Grasp your fist with your other hand. Press it into the area with a quick upward movement.

3. You can also lean over a table edge, chair, or railing. Quickly thrust your upper abdomen against the edge of the surface.

If an infant is choking (i.e., unable to cough or cry forcefully, demonstrating difficulty breathing and turning a bluish color), follow these steps.

1. Lay the infant facedown along your forearm. Use your thigh or lap for support. Hold the infant's chest in your hand and jaw with your fingers and firmly support the head. Point the infant's head downward, lower than the body.

2. Give up to five quick and forceful blows between the infant's shoulder blades using the palm of your free hand.

Follow these steps if the object does not come out of the airway after five blows.

1. Turn the infant faceup. Use your thigh or lap for support. Support the head.

2. Place two fingers on the middle of the infant's breastbone just below the nipples.

3. Give up to five quick thrusts down, compressing the chest 1/3 to 1/2 the depth of the chest.

4. Continue with five back blows followed by five chest thrusts until the object is dislodged

or the infant loses alertness (i.e., becomes unconscious).

5. If the infant becomes unconscious, call 911 and begin CPR.

Basic First Aid

If you've ever cleaned a cut or scrape, then applied antibiotic ointment and covered the area with a bandage, you've performed first aid. Being skilled in first aid includes knowing how to recognize injuries and illnesses and how to manage or treat them. Using proper first aid procedures can prevent infection, slow bleeding, aid healing, and even save a life.

> " Take some time to learn first aid and CPR. It saves lives. "
>
> —Bobby Sherman, actor and singer

Minor Burns

Burns are soft tissue injuries that can affect the skin and the layers of fat, muscle, and bone beneath the skin. Burns are classified by their source (heat, chemical, electricity, or radiation) and their depth. The deeper the burn, the more severe it is. First-degree burns affect only the top layer of skin and generally heal within a week without permanent scarring. Second-degree burns, or partial-thickness burns, affect several layers of skin and often include blistering. Healing is slower, and scarring may occur. Third-degree burns, or full-thickness burns, destroy all layers of the skin and some of the underlying tissue. Treatment will likely include skin grafting (surgery) and painful rehabilitation. All types of burn can be serious and can require medical care; even a first-degree burn can be considered critical if it affects a large area of the body or affects a particularly sensitive area.

Small thermal (heat) burns are common and can be treated by running cool water over the affected area, then covering it loosely with a sterile dressing to prevent infection. Chemical burns from a liquid source can be treated in the same manner. Chemical burns from dry powders should first be gently brushed off to remove the burning substance before applying running water. To reduce the risk of burns, follow safety practices around heat, chemicals, and electricity. Also follow all manufacturer

Learn Cardiopulmonary Resuscitation (CPR)

When a person's breathing and heart stop, time is critical. Brain damage can begin after 4 minutes without oxygen, and it becomes likely after 6 to 10 minutes. A person's chances of survival are directly affected by early recognition of symptoms, followed by early CPR and defibrillation (restoration of normal heart rhythm) and early access to advanced medical care. This sequence is known as the chain of survival, and it often depends on the initial steps taken by the person who is present when a cardiac event occurs.

Cardiopulmonary resuscitation (CPR) is a first aid procedure that is performed when the heart or breathing has stopped, and it saves many lives each year. The procedure uses chest compressions to keep blood flowing, preventing brain damage and death until expert medical help arrives. CPR training is strongly recommended, and many schools and several national organizations offer CPR classes and certification. According to the National Institutes of Health, "Even if you haven't had training you can do 'hands-only' CPR for a teen or an adult whose heart has stopped." Hands-only CPR is *not* recommended for use with children.

The American Heart Association recommends "two steps to staying alive": First, call 911 or direct someone else to call 911. Second, start chest compressions—push hard and fast at the center of the chest. The technique for chest compression is shown in the figure.

CPR techniques and procedures are often revised based on new research and findings. For this reason, a regular check of the National Institutes of Health website for the latest information is recommended.

Using an Automated External Defibrillator

If an automated external defibrillator (AED) is immediately available, use it as soon as you have determined that the individual in need is unresponsive and without a pulse. All AED devices will include written or verbal instructions as part of the device. Follow these general guidelines when using an AED.

1. Turn on the AED.
2. Wipe the person's bare chest dry and apply the pads. Place one pad on the person's upper right chest and the other pad on the person's lower left side of the chest.

---

guidelines and wear appropriate clothing and safety gear when dealing with chemicals or working in an environment where burns might occur.

Any major burn requires immediate medical attention. Call 911 immediately if you come across a person with large burns, suspected lung burns, or burns of the head, neck, hands, feet, or genitals. Immediate medical care is also required for any burn where the skin is clearly charred and underlying tissues look exposed or damaged, as well as any burn suffered by a person under age 5 or over age 60.

Wounds

Any injury to the body's soft tissue is commonly referred to as a wound. **Closed wounds** occur when the skin's surface is not broken but damage occurs below the surface. **Open wounds** involve damage to the skin's surface and typically include some bleeding. Most small closed wounds, such as bruises, do not require special care; they generally heal themselves. Larger bruises can be treated with light pressure, to control the internal bleeding. Ice should be applied for 20 minutes at a time, and you

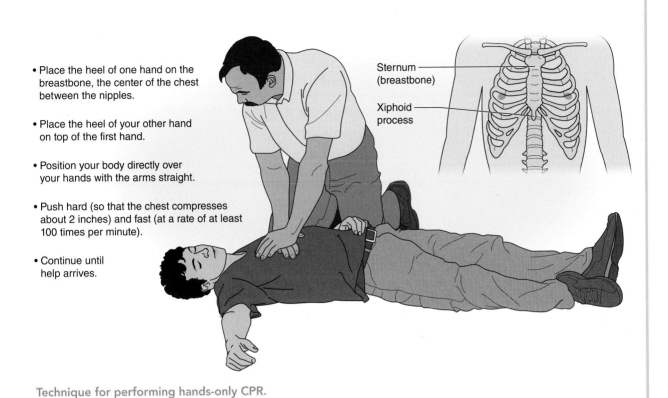

- Place the heel of one hand on the breastbone, the center of the chest between the nipples.

- Place the heel of your other hand on top of the first hand.

- Position your body directly over your hands with the arms straight.

- Push hard (so that the chest compresses about 2 inches) and fast (at a rate of at least 100 times per minute).

- Continue until help arrives.

Sternum (breastbone)

Xiphoid process

Technique for performing hands-only CPR.

3. Plug the connector into the AED.

4. Allow the AED to analyze the heart rhythm. Advise all bystanders to "stand clear" and do not touch the person.

5. Deliver a shock by pushing the button if indicated and prompted to do so by the AED. Be sure that no one is touching the AED and that there are no hazards present (e.g., water, wires) when delivering the shock.

should use a barrier such as a towel between the ice bag and the skin. A closed wound may be very serious if the individual cannot move the affected body part or is in obvious pain. Serious internal damage may also be indicated if an injured extremity is blue or extremely pale. In such cases, call 911 for assistance.

Open wounds include abrasions (scrapes), lacerations (cuts), avulsions (tearing), and punctures (holes). All open wounds require some sort of dressing, or covering, to control bleeding and prevent infection. For minor open wounds,

apply direct pressure using a clean hand or sterile dressing (e.g., gauze) to control bleeding. Once the bleeding has stopped, wash the wound with warm water and soap. An open wound needs to be cleaned thoroughly. Any wound with dirt present should be rinsed in warm water for at least five minutes.

Finally, apply antibiotic ointment to the wound and cover it with a sterile bandage. Any major open wound that is bleeding profusely must be treated immediately with direct pressure to control the bleeding, and you should call 911. Never remove

CONSUMER CORNER: Buying a First Aid Kit

First aid kits are recommended for all homes and automobiles. You may also need one in other settings, such as a workshop, with camping or hiking supplies, or in a workout bag. Most first aid kits contain all of the basic supplies you need for treating minor injuries, including bandages, antiseptic and antibiotic ointment, and medical tape. Some kits are much larger and contain special items. When selecting or preparing a first aid kit, ask yourself the following questions.

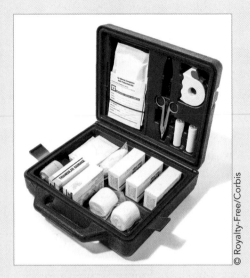

© Royalty-Free/Corbis

- **Where will I use the kit?** For home or automobile use, a basic kit is sufficient. If you'll be in a remote wilderness location or other high-risk situation (e.g., a workshop), you need a larger, more comprehensive kit.

- **What sort of container is best for my needs?** A home kit will do fine in a soft-sided bag. However, a kit for use outdoors is best kept in a hard-shelled container. The size of the container is also important. If you want the kit to be handy, make sure it fits in the space you have available.

- **How much do I want to spend?** If money is an issue, start with a basic kit. You can always add items to the kit over time.

- **What unique needs do I have?** If you have allergies, asthma, diabetes, or another condition that requires you to carry medication or supplies, buy a kit with enough room to add those items. If you live in a cold climate where you might be without power or get stranded in poor weather, choose a kit designed for outdoor use that includes emergency blankets and food. Consider any other particular needs you have.

Regardless of what kind of kit you buy or create, check it regularly to ensure that any medications and ointments are not outdated and that the supplies remain intact.

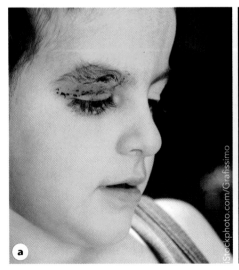

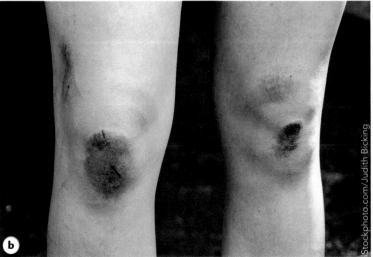

Open wounds can include *(a)* lacerations (cuts) and *(b)* abrasions (scrapes).

blood-soaked dressings from a serious open wound; instead, continue to add clean dressings to absorb the blood. Removing bloody dressings can increase bleeding or bring germs into the site. Once the bleeding is under control, use a sterile bandage (wrap) to provide compression.

Muscle, Bone, and Joint Injuries

Injuries to muscles, bones, and joints happen often and to people of all ages. These injuries can happen at school, home, work, or play. They can be painful and often have long recovery periods that can make life difficult. Fortunately, they are rarely life threatening, but if left untreated they can cause serious problems, including disability. The general care appropriate for most muscle, bone, and joint injuries is to follow the RICE formula (see the accompanying text box). Serious bone or joint injuries such as a broken bone require immediate medical care.

Fractures

The term *fracture* refers to a break, chip, or crack in a bone. The most common kind is a **closed fracture**, which does not break through the skin. If the affected bone tears through the skin, the injury is an **open fracture**. Another type of bone injury is **dislocation**, in which the bone moves away from its normal position near a joint; as a result, motion at that joint is lost or severely impaired. All suspected fractures and dislocations must be treated by a physician.

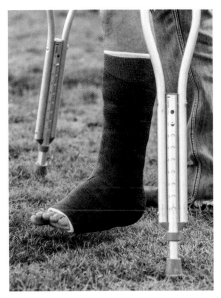

Broken bones require immobilization by a cast to allow them to heal.

Sprains and Strains

Sprains and **strains** are relatively common. A sprain involves the tearing of a ligament, whereas a strain involves the stretching or tearing of a muscle or tendon. Severe sprains and strains often cause extreme pain, swelling, bruising, unusual appearance in the injured area, and a temporary loss of functioning. Once the initial swelling has been treated with the RICE formula, severe strains and sprains may require immobilization by a cast, brace, or splint and surgery to repair the tissue may be needed.

The RICE Formula for Treating Injury

R is for rest. After first aid has been given for the injury, the body part should be immobilized for two to three days to prevent further injury.

I is for ice. A sprain or strain should be immersed in cold water or covered with ice in a towel or plastic bag. Ice the area for 20 minutes, starting immediately after the injury occurs, to reduce swelling and pain. Ice or cold should be applied several times a day for one to three days.

C is for compression. Use an elastic bandage to limit swelling. For a sprained ankle, keep the shoe laced and the sock on the foot until compression can be applied with a bandage (the shoe and sock compress the injured area in the meantime). The compression should not be too tight, and it should be taken off periodically so as not to restrict blood flow.

E is for elevation. Raise the body part above the heart to reduce swelling.

Note: Many people use the PRICE system where the P stands for protection.

Sudden Illness

It's usually easy to tell when an accident has occurred, but it can be more challenging to know what to do if someone becomes suddenly ill. Many chronic health conditions (e.g., diabetes, cardiovascular disease) can result in the onset of a sudden and serious situation, such as a stroke, diabetic reaction, or seizure. If a person demonstrates signs of a sudden and serious injury, call 911 and be prepared to describe the signs you're seeing. Don't be afraid to speak directly to the individual to help you determine what might be causing the signs. People with a chronic disease may understand what they are experiencing and may have medications available.

Weather-Related Emergencies

Weather conditions affect how our bodies function. Extremely hot and extremely cold conditions can quickly become life threatening. Even when weather conditions don't seem extreme, you can face weather-related risks depending on what you're wearing, what you're doing, and how well you're fed and hydrated.

Heat-Related Emergencies

Common heat-related emergencies include heat cramps, heat exhaustion, and **heatstroke**. Heat cramps (muscle spasms) can be an early sign of a more serious heat-related emergency. If a person experiences heat cramps, especially in the legs or abdomen, help him or her rest in a cool place and if possible provide cool water or a commercial sport drink.

In heat exhaustion, body temperature rises, and the person becomes nauseous, dizzy, exhausted, or weak and may have skin that is cool, moist, pale, or flushed. The most severe form of heat emergency is heatstroke, which is a serious medical emergency because body systems begin to shut down. Clear signs of heatstroke include changes in consciousness, along with rapid, shallow breathing and a weak pulse. For both heatstroke and heat exhaustion, seek medical assistance and have the person rest in a cool place and loosen any tight clothing. Apply loose, cool, wet clothing. Give water slowly, about 4 ounces (118 milliliters) every 15 minutes. Physical activity should be stopped for the remainder of the day, and 911 should be called if any changes occur in consciousness.

Cold-Related Emergencies

Two types of emergencies related to cold weather are frostbite and **hypothermia**. You can reduce your risk for both by wearing proper attire when engaged in outdoor activities in cold weather. Symptoms of frostbite include a lack of feeling in the affected area and skin that appears waxy, is cold to the touch, or is discolored. Avoid rubbing the frostbitten area and do not attempt to rewarm the area if there is any chance of refreezing. Call 911 or get the person to a hospital for proper care. Hypothermia results when the entire body cools below normal temperature; if untreated, it causes death. Hypothermia can be signaled by shivering, numbness, a glassy stare, indifference, or loss of consciousness. Keep the person warm and dry and seek immediate medical or emergency care.

Signs of Sudden Illness

- Changes in consciousness (e.g., severe dizziness, light-headedness, unconsciousness)
- Nausea or vomiting
- Difficulty speaking or slurred speech
- Numbness or weakness
- Changes in breathing or difficulty breathing
- Blurred vision or loss of vision
- Changes in skin color
- Profuse sweating

HEALTH TECHNOLOGY

Automated external defibrillators (AEDs) are portable, battery-operated devices that can deliver an electric shock to the heart. An AED is an essential tool for treating cardiac arrest and ventricular fibrillation, in which the heart contracts in an uncontrolled way and is therefore unable to deliver adequate blood to the body. The practice of delivering an electric shock to the heart dates back to 1899, when two French physiologists delivered an electric shock to a dog in ventricular defibrillation and successfully restored normal heart rhythm. With the AED, modern technology has made defibrillation possible in an affordable, self-contained device that is now found in many public places and buildings.

AEDs are simple and safe to use. Sticky pads with sensors (called electrodes) are attached to the chest of the person who is having a cardiac event, and the device itself provides step-by-step verbal and visual instructions. The electrodes can detect the person's heart rhythm and determine whether normal heart functioning has been restored by the delivery of the electric shock. Prompt use of an external defibrillator can save up to 60 percent of treated victims.

CONNECT

Do you know how to use an external defibrillator? What types of facility might benefit from having a defibrillator on site? What circumstances might make it important for a family to consider purchasing a defibrillator? To research your responses, visit the website of the American Heart Association (www. heart.org).

Emergency Preparedness

Everything discussed in this chapter should be taken into consideration when creating an emergency preparedness plan. An emergency preparedness plan involves taking actions to keep yourself and your loved ones safe before an emergency occurs so that you can remain safe during the emergency. You may need to activate your emergency preparedness plan in the event of natural disasters, pandemic emergencies (rapidly spreading disease), technological emergencies (e.g., a blackout or nuclear power plant disaster), or terrorist attacks. Each type of emergency requires specific consideration, but all emergencies share some common considerations. First, consider your physical safety. Many emergencies will require either sheltering in place or evacuating. Determine the safest place to be in each type of emergency you may face and make

sure every member of the family knows the plan. Develop a family communication plan so that you know how you will get and stay in contact during an emergency. It is also important to make an emergency supply kit that will prepare you for any type of disaster. Nonperishable food, water, sanitation needs, light sources, blankets, first aid supplies, and other items unique to your circumstances need to be part of your disaster kit. You should also learn about the emergency alert systems in place at your school, workplace, and community. Getting early warning about dangers is one of the most effective tools for staying safe in all types of situations. It is also important to be familiar with local emergency plans. Many communities have designated shelter facilities where aid, medical help, and food are available during emergencies. You can learn more about emergency preparedness in the student section of the Health for Life website.

Comprehension Check

1. What are the three emergency action steps that should be followed for administering CPR?

2. What are the basic first aid procedures for common emergency scenarios such as treating an open wound?

3. How do you know if a person has a sudden illness that might need medical attention?

MAKING HEALTHY DECISIONS: Skill Building

David is a high school sophomore who was in a serious car crash during middle school. His dad had often been impatient on the road and had driven aggressively. David suffered only minor injuries in the crash, but his dad was more severely injured (abrasions and broken bones). At the scene, David felt helpless and didn't know what to do to help himself or his dad. Ever since that night, David has been studying first aid almost obsessively. He never wants to feel unprepared again. When his school has emergency preparedness days, David is very particular and criticizes others who are learning and practicing their skills. He obsesses over the details of the scenario and argues with others about the right thing to do.

Jennifer, also a sophomore, doesn't understand David's obsession with being prepared for emergencies. She figures nothing will really happen to her, and if it does she can just look up the answers online or rely on someone nearby to help. On emergency preparedness days at school, Jennifer goofs off, and she thinks that learning CPR and first aid is a waste of time.

For Discussion

Neither David nor Jennifer is building skills in the right way. What would you tell David about his approach to skill building? How might you encourage Jennifer to take her skill building seriously? Which of the two do you most resemble when it comes to developing your CPR and first aid skills? See the Skills for Healthy Living feature to help you address these questions.

SKILLS FOR HEALTHY LIVING: Skill Building

Emergency situations can be stressful and cause a sense of panic and fear. In order to help yourself and others during an emergency, keep your CPR and first aid skills fresh.

- **Get good training.** High-quality CPR and first aid instruction is readily available in most communities. Seek out training opportunities, for example, at your local Red Cross chapter, community center, fire or police station, safety council, or school. Some communities offer free training for community members at CPR events.

- **Revisit your training as often as needed.** Most CPR cards are good for 12 months, and most first aid cards for 3 years, but research shows that much of what is learned is forgotten within 3 months. Don't be shy about attending training more often than required or reviewing resource materials regularly.

- **Practice responding to emergency situations before they occur.** As with sport, music, and other skills, the more you practice your CPR and first aid skills, the more likely you are to use them effectively during a real emergency. To prepare yourself to respond in a variety of situations, think about realistic emergency scenarios and rehearse your responses in your mind. Don't, however, try to imagine every possible scenario; focus on general situations and the skills they might require.

- **Don't wait for an emergency to occur to learn how to respond.** Learn a variety of first aid and CPR skills, even if they don't seem to apply to you or your current life. For example, a person may not think to learn how to provide CPR for an infant if he or she doesn't have children, and someone living in a tropical climate might not think to learn how to treat cold-related emergencies. However, emergencies occur in all sorts of unexpected situations, and being prepared before the fact is the only way to ensure that you can be effective in helping.

- **Communicate about emergency plans with others.** Talking about emergency plans and skills can help you remember what you need to do in a given situation and can enable a sense of calm when an emergency occurs. For example, you can help reduce the risks associated with emergencies by reviewing fire exits, locations of fire extinguishers, and basic fire safety with family members and reminding teammates to dress properly to prevent heat- or cold-related injuries.

- **Remain focused and calm.** The better your skills—and the more regularly you practice them—the more likely you are to remain calm and focused during an emergency. When facing an emergency, take deep breaths, focus on the situation, and think one step at a time. If you have trouble remembering all of the specifics, calmly think through the situation and do the best you can.

 ACADEMIC CONNECTION: Causation and Correlation

One of the most common causes of confusion when reading scientific and health-related studies is the difference between causation and correlation. Causation means that one thing results in a specific change in another. The first is the reason why the second happens. For example, we now have enough evidence to know that smoking (the first thing) causes lung cancer (the second thing). Correlation means that two things are related to one another. For example, smoking is correlated to alcoholism, but smoking does not cause alcoholism. If one thing causes another, then the two things are also most certainly correlated. But just because two things occur together does not mean that one caused the other, even if it seems to make sense. For example, as stated in this chapter, mental illness is correlated (related) to incidences of violence. This means that these two factors have been shown to occur together more often than chance alone would predict. However, just because this correlation exists, it doesn't mean that mental illness directly causes violent acts. As a consumer of health information, you need to distinguish correlation from causation in order to accurately interpret and apply the information you learn.

Personal Watercraft Safety

In 2008, Michigan passed a law setting the minimum age for operating a personal watercraft at 14. Personal watercraft are vehicles that are propelled by machinery and are designed to be operated by a person sitting, standing, or kneeling on the vessel. Like many states, Michigan had previously allowed children as young as 12 to operate personal watercraft if they had a boater safety certificate and a parent on board. The new law bans anyone under 14 from operating a personal watercraft under any circumstances and allows only those over age 16 to do so without a supervisor on board. Supporters of the law believe that young teens do not have the maturity to maneuver what is essentially a motorcycle on water, and they support their position by citing accident statistics—personal watercraft make up only about 10 percent of water traffic but are involved in 30 percent of water traffic accidents.

Opponents of the law note that personal watercraft are no more dangerous than other forms of boating and that evidence is lacking against younger operators. U.S. Coast Guard data show fatal drownings while using a personal watercraft are quite low when compared with those associated with paddle boats, open motorboats, and cabin motorboats. This difference results primarily from the fact that most states require personal watercraft operators and passengers to wear life jackets. Studies show that only 9 percent of people who drown while using a personal watercraft are wearing a life jacket.

More generally, the most common injury sustained by personal watercraft users is blunt force trauma (trauma caused by injury, impact, or attack). Overall, the top five causes of boating accidents are operator inattention, operator inexperience, excessive speed, improper lookout, and alcohol (see table 18.1 for details). Of these factors, alcohol is the leading secondary factor in fatal personal watercraft accidents. It contributes to excessive speed, improper lookout, and operator inattention.

For Discussion

Have you ever been in a risky situation involving swimming or a personal watercraft? If so, what happened, and what did you do to minimize your risk? If you haven't been in this situation, what steps could you take to minimize the chances that you will experience such an incident?

TABLE 18.1   Top Five Contributing Factors in Personal Watercraft Accidents

Contributing factor	Accidents	Deaths	Injuries requiring medical attention
Operator inattention	624	58	426
Operator inexperience	553	49	321
Excessive speed	407	53	297
Improper lookout	398	37	305
Alcohol use	365	94	248

Source: United States Coast Guard Boating Safety Division, *2012 Boating Statistics.*

Reviewing Concepts and Vocabulary

As directed by your teacher, answer items 1 through 5 by correctly completing each sentence with a word or phrase.

1. Prescription _____ are the leading cause of death from unintentional poisonings among adults.
2. _____ is the harmful or offensive contact of another person.
3. When performing adult CPR, give _____ compressions per minute.
4. Wearing a _____ helps reduce the risk of injury while bicycling or skateboarding.
5. The term _____ refers to a break, chip, or crack in a bone.

For items 6 through 10, as directed by your teacher, match each term in column 1 with the appropriate phrase in column 2.

6. alcohol
7. distracted driving
8. males aged 19 to 29
9. eight
10. teens aged 16 to 19

a. number of teens (aged 16 to 19) who die each day in a motor vehicle crash
b. least likely to wear a seat belt
c. four times more likely to crash
d. plays a role in 25 percent of all fatal car crashes
e. increases accident risk by 20 to 30 percent

For items 11 through 15, as directed by your teacher, respond to each statement or question.

11. Describe the three emergency action steps.
12. What does the acronym RICE stand for?
13. What is the difference between a sprain and a strain?
14. Provide two examples of intentional injuries.
15. What are three warning signs that a person might become violent against others?

Thinking Critically

Write a paragraph in response to the following questions.

You're walking home from work one day when you notice an older gentleman lying on the sidewalk. He is moaning, and his dog is standing near him on a leash. It's a sunny day, and you don't see any notable objects or blood on the sidewalk. What are some possible reasons that the man is on the ground? What are your next steps?

Take It Home

With the help of a parent or guardian, develop an emergency preparedness plan for your family. Identify potential emergencies. Address the following in your plan.

1. Determine your evacuation and communication plans.
2. Create an emergency supply kit.
3. Determine the local evacuation and emergency plans and services.

Then, write down your emergency plan and share it with family members.

363

19

A Healthy Environment

In This Chapter

www Student Web Resources
www.healthforlifetextbook.org/student

Alexey Stiop/fotolia.com

Lesson 19.1
Our Changing Environment

Lesson Objectives

After reading this lesson, you should be able to

1. list Barry Commoner's laws of ecology,
2. explain the importance of the four Rs, and
3. explain what is meant by the term *climate change*.

Lesson Vocabulary

biodegradable, climate change, ecology, global warming, sanitary landfill

Four basic laws of ecology have been formulated to help us better understand how our choices affect the environment. These laws, developed by American biologist Dr. Barry Commoner and others, are described in this lesson.

Human Impact on the Environment

The study of the interaction between people and the environment is known as **ecology**. Of course, humans have interacted with the environment as long as they have existed. However, as the human population has grown and technologies have evolved, our environmental impact has increased, and ecology has become an increasingly important area of study. The earth is home to seven billion people, all of whom eat, travel, go to the bathroom, and use various products. We throw things away and use energy in various forms and for various reasons. In addition, we have developed farming practices and advanced industry in ways that are not always friendly to the environment. Over time, we've discovered that we have to be careful about how much we consume, how we dispose of our waste, and how we affect the environment through our farming, industry, and technology.

Four Laws of Ecology

Barry Commoner (1917–2012) was an American biologist who once ran for U.S. president and who formulated four laws of ecology. These laws help us better understand how our choices affect the environment.

1. Everything is connected to everything else (what affects one organism affects us all). The earth is very complex, and all living things are in some way dependent on, or affected by, other living things. For example, honeybees pollinate many of the plants that humans rely on for food. In fact, one in every three bites of human food depends on the work of honeybees. However, when we humans use pesticides to control other insects, they can also hurt honeybees, thus dramatically affecting our own food supply.

2. Everything must go somewhere (when we throw something away, we have to realize there is no "away"). Our globe is a closed system. When we burn firewood, the fire produces smoke, which can fall back to earth as sediment when the embers cool or can be absorbed by plants, bacteria, and algae, in which it is broken down and used for energy or other processes. Unused gases from the smoke can also linger in the atmosphere and form pollution. In other words, the wood, like everything we use, never simply disappears.

3. Nature knows best (humans learn from nature and depend on nature to live; it is difficult to improve on nature and natural laws). In essence, this law suggests that the whole is greater than the sum of its parts. The earth is always changing, and the delicate balance of each part of nature plays a role in that change. For example, new forests are formed over thousands of years when seeds from briars, shrubs, vines, and trees are blown or carried by animals or water into a new area. Eventually, the seeds take root, and trees and shrubs start to grow and eventually dominate the grasses and herbs. Over time, the animal life also changes,

A fire ring represents the second law of ecology that says everything must go somewhere.

as field mice and rabbits who thrived on grasses make way for the animals of the forest, such as deer, squirrels, and owls. If humans clear a field and then plant a forest, our quick actions can devastate the naturally occurring habitats of animals and plants, displacing animals and upsetting the area's natural food supply.

4. There is no such thing as a free lunch (everything has a cost, which can come, for example, in the form of pollution-related health problems or the money we pay to light and heat our homes, businesses, and schools). Every action we take carries consequences—sometimes positive, sometimes negative. For example, if we overfish a particular body of water, we might increase the number of fish available for sale as food, which might reduce the cost to the consumer in the short term. However, we would also reduce the number of fish alive to reproduce and sustain the species, perhaps ultimately leaving it endangered or extinct.

" I believe that you shouldn't have to leave your neighborhood to live in a better one. "

—Majora Carter, activist

The Four Rs

The four Rs refer to actions we can take to support a healthy environment (see figure 19.1):

- Refuse
- Reduce
- Reuse
- Recycle

Originally there were only three Rs, but many people saw an important distinction between reducing the use of something (e.g., a plastic bag), which means you'll continue to use it, and simply refusing to use it at all. Some people suggest that in order to really reduce, we have to refuse at least some of the time.

Whether you prefer four Rs or three Rs, the message should be clear: Don't use things that you don't need. Do avoid single-use items. Most plastic bags, for example, are used only once, usually for a short time, and then thrown away. Reuse means using the bag again—for example, on your next shopping trip, to carry a wet bathing suit, or to store things in. Recycling, in turn, means making sure that the plastic bag gets to a recycling center where it can be turned into another product. Not only are most plastic bags not taken to recycling centers, but even when they are, they are difficult to convert into new products, since that involves a costly and difficult process.

A cloth bag, on the other hand, addresses all four Rs. If you have a cloth bag (the key is to remember

A cloth bag addresses all four Rs.

© Cvandyke | Dreamstime.com

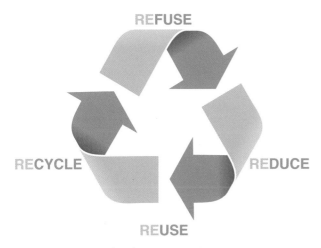

FIGURE 19.1 The four Rs.

to take it with you when you shop!), you can *refuse* to use a plastic or paper bag. Thus you have *reduced* the need for plastic bags, and you can also *reuse* your cloth bag over and over. When it finally does get torn or worn out, you can *recycle* it or, depending on the type of cloth, perhaps even compost it.

The four Rs are listed in the order of their importance. If you refuse a product, you don't need to worry about the next three Rs. If you reduce the amount of the product, you have fewer products to reuse. And if you reuse a product, you don't need to recycle it, at least not yet.

CONNECT

How do your peers affect your adoption of the four Rs? Do you experience peer pressure related to these practices? What could you do to encourage yourself and your friends to adopt the four Rs? Do you belong to any groups or organizations that help protect the environment?

Conspicuous Consumption

On average, each person in the United States generates 4.6 pounds (2.1 kilograms) of waste material every day—up from 2.7 pounds (1.2 kilograms) in 1960. As a result, some people refer to the nation as a "throwaway society" in which products either don't last very long or get discarded quickly in favor of a newer model. This way of life is becoming more

and more problematic, in part because much of the stuff we throw away neither gets recycled nor goes to a sanitary landfill. So where does it go?

Captain Charles Moore has an answer. He has spent many years studying the items that end up in ocean waters. In his book *Plastic Ocean,* he describes the largest garbage dump in the world—an area twice the size of Texas in the Pacific Ocean that is strewn with plastic debris. Dubbed the Great Pacific Garbage Patch, this massive area serves as a stark warning about human consumption. Recycling efforts have not kept pace with our production of trash.

Captain Moore believes that plastic producers should be held responsible for making products that can be more easily recycled, that last longer, and that are not toxic to animals (including people). Of course, it is also everyone's responsibility to do a better job of recycling and making sure that our discarded products are disposed of appropriately. With this need in mind, it's always good to remind yourself of the four Rs as you go through your daily life: refuse products you don't need, reduce the number and amount of products you use, reuse any product that you can, and, if you can't do any of the first three Rs, recycle the product.

Sanitary Landfills

Plastics of all sorts have also become problematic for the environment beyond the Great Pacific Garbage Patch. Most plastics are petroleum based, which means they require fossil fuels to be manufactured. Fossil fuels contribute to air, land, and water pollution. Plastics also disturb or endanger animals that accidentally eat them or get entangled in them. And they are not **biodegradable**—that is, they do not break down or decompose. As a result, they take up space in **sanitary landfills**—sites where waste (the stuff we throw away) is taken to keep it separated from the rest of the environment.

Despite these issues, plastics keep increasing in availability. In fact, a large number of the goods we buy are either made of plastic or packaged in plastic. The more things we throw away (not just plastics), the more trips have to be made to the landfill, and the more energy is consumed in doing so.

In sanitary landfills, each day's waste is covered by dirt to prevent attracting birds or rodents. Sanitary landfills are located in places that minimize the

⬤ ADVOCACY IN ACTION: Promoting Recycling

Not surprisingly, people are more likely to recycle when appropriate recycling bins are readily available. Evaluate your school to determine whether an *effective* recycling program is in place.

If your school doesn't provide recycling bins or lacks some needed options (e.g., paper, plastic, refuse, glass), determine what bins the school should add and what company or community organization will recycle the materials. You can even create a map showing where recycling bins should be located. Then write a one-page letter to the school board advocating for the purchase and appropriate placement of the needed recycling bins. Include information about the four Rs and explain why recycling is important for both environmental and personal health.

If your school already has adequate recycling bins, create posters to place above the bins that explain their importance and encourage students, teachers, and staff members to use them regularly.

likelihood of contaminating water sources and they have liners to prevent contaminants from leaching into water systems. When full, they can be turned into parks or recreation areas. In some landfills, the methane gas that is given off by the biological action of the buried materials can help to produce electrical power (see Health Science sidebar in this chapter). Poorly managed sanitary landfills can contaminate bodies of water and wells. Even in well-managed landfills, there is a concern about how effective they will contain contaminants 50 or more years into the future.

Climate Change

The term **climate change** is often used interchangeably with the term **global warming**, but, according to the U.S. Environmental Protection Agency (EPA), "Global warming is causing climate patterns to change. However, global warming itself represents only one aspect of climate change. *Climate change* refers to any significant change in the measures of climate lasting for an extended period of time." Some of these changes are shown in figure 19.2.

Climate change can result from

- natural factors such as changes in the sun's intensity;
- natural processes within the climate system, such as changes in ocean circulation; and
- human activities that change the atmosphere's composition (e.g., through the burning of fossil fuels) or the land surface (e.g., deforestation, reforestation, urbanization, desertification).

Global warming refers to an average increase in the temperature of the atmosphere near the earth's surface and in the troposphere (i.e., the layer of the atmosphere from the earth's surface to about six miles above the earth), which can contribute to changes in global climate patterns. The warming can result from a variety of causes, both natural and human induced. In common usage, the term often refers to the warming that can occur as a result of greenhouse gas emissions related to human activity.

Most climate scientists have concluded that climate change is placing great stress on the environment and that we must make major environmental changes. We can't depend on fossil fuels forever. Experts agree that we need to diversify our energy usage by increasing our use of renewable energy sources, such as wind, solar power, and biomass (animal waste and mostly plant material). We can also make houses and businesses more energy efficient. If we work together to create a more energy efficient society, we will be able to affect climate change for the better.

🔊 HEALTHY COMMUNICATION

Is your community a leader in addressing climate change? Should individuals be primarily responsible for changing their behaviors, or should society enact laws and regulations that require changes in how cars, houses, businesses, and manufacturing operations are powered? Debate your position with your peers. Support your position with facts and be respectful of others' opinions.

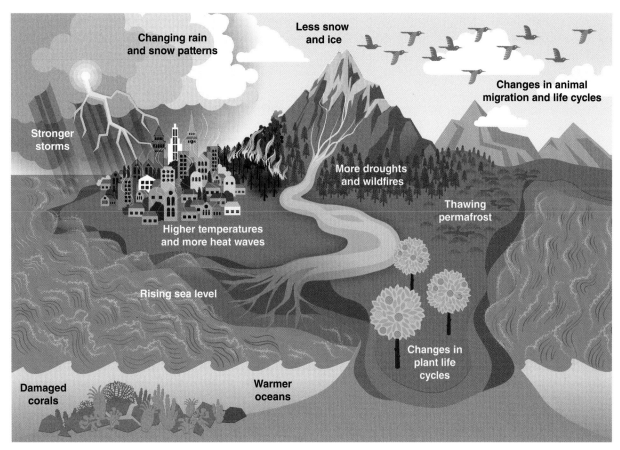

FIGURE 19.2 Effects of climate change.

⚛ HEALTH SCIENCE

Landfills are large sources of U.S. methane gas emissions—a major contributor to the erosion of the ozone layer that helps protect us from the sun's ultraviolet radiation. Landfill methane is produced when organic materials (e.g., yard, household, and food wastes) are decomposed by bacteria under anaerobic conditions (i.e., in the absence of oxygen). Methane production varies greatly from landfill to landfill, depending on site-specific characteristics such as moisture content, landfill design, operating practices, and climate.

Methane generated by a landfill is emitted when it migrates through the landfill cover. During this process, the soil oxidizes approximately 10 percent of the generated methane, and the remaining 90 percent is emitted. Landfill methane can be captured and used as fuel to generate electricity through the development of well fields and collection systems at the landfill. Collected methane can be used for on-site power generation or piped to a nearby generating station.

Comprehension Check

1. Which of Barry Commoner's laws of ecology best relates to sanitary landfills?
2. Explain why the order of the four Rs is important.
3. What is the difference between global warming and climate change?

✔ SELF-ASSESSMENT: How Green Are You?

Indicate your level of agreement with each of the following statements. Total the points associated with your responses to figure your green score, then use the scale provided at the end of the assessment to interpret your score.

	Always	Sometimes	Never
1. I do not leave the water running when I am washing dishes or brushing my teeth (I turn it off and on as needed).	3	2	1
2. I use a cloth bag when I buy items at the store.	3	2	1
3. I walk, ride a bike, or use public transportation.	3	2	1
4. I participate in recycling programs.	3	2	1
5. I eat food from my own garden, a community or school garden, or a farmer's market.	3	2	1
6. I help conserve energy by keeping the thermostat at 68°F (20°C) or below in the winter and 78°F (26°C) or above in the summer.	3	2	1
7. I volunteer for projects, organizations, or school activities that help protect or clean up the environment.	3	2	1
8. I refuse to buy products that I don't really need.	3	2	1

Add up your points. My green score is _____.

A score of 19 to 24 suggests that you have habits and behaviors that help protect the environment and your health.

A score of 16 to 18 suggests that you have some green habits and behaviors but also have room for improvement. Try to change at least one behavior to make your lifestyle more green.

A score of 15 or lower suggests that you have habits and behaviors that are not very green. It's time to make some changes. Try to change at least two behaviors to make your lifestyle more green.

✔ Planning for Healthy Living

Use the Healthy Living Plan worksheet to help you change your environmental health habits.

Lesson 19.2

Green Schools and Communities

Lesson Objectives

After reading this lesson, you should be able to

1. explain two steps that individuals can take to reduce water pollution,
2. list at least two air pollutants and identify two actions that individuals can take to reduce their contribution to air pollution, and
3. define the term *conservation* and identify two types of conservation.

Lesson Vocabulary

built environment, complete streets, conservation, farm-to-school, green school, LEED certified

Water, air, soil, and noise pollution affect the health of both people and the environment. For example, more than a billion people in the world lack access to safe drinking water, and five thousand people die each day from drinking unsafe water. In the United States, almost half of all lakes, rivers, and streams are too polluted for safe fishing or swimming. Similarly, individuals who live in areas with heavy air pollution are 20 percent more likely to die from lung cancer than those who live in environments with clean air. And though the United States contains only 5 percent of the world's population, it consumes 25 percent of the world's resources.

As a result, improving our use and conservation of resources can improve both individual and environmental health. This lesson focuses on air pollution, water pollution, and conservation. In addition, the Living Well News feature addresses the effect of noise pollution on personal health.

Water Pollution

Water is one of our most important resources; in fact, we literally can't live without it. Therefore, we must conserve our clean water supply and keep it clean and free of chemicals and other pollutants.

Water pollution is not new. With the advent of the Industrial Revolution, factories began releasing large amounts of pollutants directly into rivers and streams. People were also dumping raw sewage into rivers and lakes, and over the years more and more chemicals were handled in the same way. In 1969, chemical pollution caused a fire on the Cuyahoga River that drew national attention, and the burning river became a symbol of how industrial water pol-

Some people drink from water bottles because they think public drinking water is unsafe. This is untrue for the majority of public water systems, and water bottles contribute to the problem of plastic waste.

lution was destroying America's natural resources. In response, the public demanded better pollution controls, and science supported the demand to clean up water supplies in the interest of public health.

As you may recall, microorganisms can cause illness and many of these microorganisms can live in water. That's why we have to treat water in order to make it safe. Fortunately, the overwhelming majority of public water systems in the United States provide safe drinking water. This is due in part to the work of the U.S. Environmental Protection Agency (EPA), which helps regulate the quality of water, air, and soil.

The general safety of public drinking water in the United States makes it unnecessary to drink bottled water. In fact, drinking water from plastic bottles contributes to the problem of plastic waste. Not only do most plastic bottles not get recycled, but also the bottling and transporting of water uses a lot of energy. In addition, certain types of plastic bottles may leach toxins into the liquid in the bottles.

Since water is all around us in streams, rivers, wells, lakes, and oceans, we need to actively protect it from contamination. Contaminated water can contribute not only to infections but also to some types of cancer, kidney damage, skin irritations, nervous system problems, and fertility problems. We can all do our part to help keep water safe (see table 19.1).

Air Pollution

Like water pollution, air pollution poses many risks to human health, including lung and heart disease. Also like water pollution, air pollution is not new. The main cause of air pollution is the burning of fuel that releases chemicals into the air—for example, at power plants and other industrial operations, as well as in the combustion engines that power cars, trucks, and airplanes.

The United States, like many countries, has enacted laws to protect the quality of the air we breathe, most notably the Clean Air Act Extension of 1970. This comprehensive federal law (since updated) regulates air emissions from stationary and mobile sources. Among other things, it authorizes the EPA to establish the National Ambient Air Quality Standards to protect the public's health and welfare and specifically to regulate the emission of air pollutants.

Throughout history, people have debated what pollutant levels are safe and to what extent governments should control businesses' and individual's activities related to air pollution. It is not always easy to decide, for example, where to draw the line and when there is a conflict between earning a living and protecting the environment. For example, some people think the EPA's rules are too strict and that they make it too difficult or expensive to do business. Others see the rules as too lenient and think they should regulate even more substances to protect people from harm. Scientific research can help people decide which substances should be regulated and to what extent. Table 19.2 summarizes four of the main air pollutants, their origins, and the health problems associated with them. In 2013, the World Health Organization added air pollution to its list of known carcinogens (i.e., something that causes cancer).

The EPA offers many suggestions for reducing air pollution (see the student section of the Health for Life website). Examples include deciding not to buy things you don't need, recycling as many things as you can, turning off (or better yet, unplugging) appliances and lights you aren't using, and choosing rechargeable batteries to power devices that you use frequently.

TABLE 19.1   How to Keep the Water Supply Safe

Action item	Notes
Don't put anything except water down storm drains.	Contaminants (e.g., motor oil, detergent, fertilizer, pesticide) get carried by storm water to local waterways and cause unnecessary harm.
Whenever possible, avoid using pesticides and chemical fertilizers.	They pose a serious threat to your health and safety and pollute both ground and surface water, which can harm fish, other animals, and humans.
Choose nontoxic household products whenever possible.	Dangerous fumes from toxic products can contaminate the air, and toxins can enter the water supply. The best way to avoid polluting is to use products that are not dangerous to the environment in the first place.
Don't flush unwanted or out-of-date medicine down the toilet or put it down the drain.	Find out if your county or city has a program for collecting unwanted pharmaceuticals. If not, remove all labels and wrap the product up before putting it in the garbage. If possible, pour water or vinegar into the bottle to destroy pills and make them inaccessible to children.

TABLE 19.2   Selected Major Air Pollutants

Pollutant	Source(s)	Human health effects
Particles (often referred to as particulate matter or PM)	• Internal combustion engines (e.g., cars, trucks) • Industry (e.g., factories) • Burning wood and coal • Cigarette smoke • Bush and forest fires	Long-term exposure is linked to health problems, such as lung disease (including cancer), heart disease, and asthma attacks.
Ozone (O_3)	Ozone is formed by complex chemical reactions involving oxides of nitrogen and some hydrocarbons. It is the main ingredient of smog in summer and early autumn.	Ozone affects the lining of the lungs and respiratory tract and causes eye irritation. It also damages plants, buildings, and other materials.
Carbon monoxide (CO)	• Motor vehicle exhaust • Burning of various materials (e.g., coal, oil, wood) • Industrial processes (e.g., waste incineration)	Inhaled carbon monoxide enters the bloodstream and disrupts the supply of oxygen to the body's tissues. Health effects depend on the extent of exposure. Depending on which organizational guidelines you choose, the permissible exposure amount ranges from 25 parts per million to 50 parts per million.
Carbon dioxide (CO_2)	Burning of fossil fuels in, for example, coal and natural gas energy plants, motor vehicles, and airplanes	Carbon dioxide is the main greenhouse gas that contributes to global warming, which in turn contributes to increases in asthma, respiratory disease, heart and lung disease, and cancer. It also contributes indirectly to increases in malaria, Lyme disease, encephalitis, hantavirus, cholera, cryptosporidiosis, and salmonella.

Adapted, by permission, from EPA Victoria. Available: www.epa.vic.gov.au/air/aq4kids/main_pollutants.asp.

You can also help prevent pollution when you travel by using public transportation, walking, or riding a bike whenever possible. If you do drive, plan thoughtfully so that you can get several things done in one trip instead of going back and forth to the same area. You can also keep your tires properly inflated and aligned to improve gas mileage. Avoid spilling gas (don't "top off" the tank; do replace the gas cap tightly) and have your car tuned up regularly for better gas mileage and to reduce emissions. You can also carpool or ride the bus to school.

If you have a respiratory condition (e.g., asthma) or want to prevent a respiratory problem, check the daily air quality forecast online. If you have a smartphone, try one of the free apps available to keep you updated about the air quality where you live.

Conservation

Conservation involves the preservation, protection, and restoration of natural ecosystems (see table 19.3). It is closely related to sustainability, which involves using a resource in such a way that it is not permanently damaged or depleted. Water and energy conservation are two types of conservation that you can practice every day.

For example, if we let a faucet run, we not only waste water but also add to the water that must be treated (it goes down the drain just like the water we actually use). Fortunately, there are lots of actions we can take to conserve water on a daily basis; for some examples, see figure 19.3. Similarly, if you walk, bike, or take public transportation, you help

TABLE 19.3　Types of Conservation

Type	Significance
Water	Only 1% of the earth's water is freshwater. Therefore, gathering, cleaning, storing, and distributing freshwater is critical to human survival and global health.
Soil	Topsoil holds most of the nutrients needed to support plant life. It is eroded, however, by deforestation, poor farming practices, and other human actions.
Wetland	Wetlands provide valuable flood protection, as well as habitat for plants and wildlife. The U.S. Environmental Protection Agency estimates that one-third of the nation's threatened and endangered species depend strictly on wetlands, making wetland conservation necessary if we are to prevent further environmental losses.
Prairie	Prairies are some of the most endangered ecosystems in the world, and they have experienced losses of more than 90% in some states (e.g., Iowa, Illinois). Like wetlands, prairies provide valuable habitat for plants and wildlife. They can also play a role in conserving other natural resources, such as soil.
Energy	The rising cost of fossil fuels and growing environmental concerns have made energy conservation a priority for many governments and individuals. The goal of energy conservation is to properly balance the need for energy with the environmental impact of fulfilling that need.

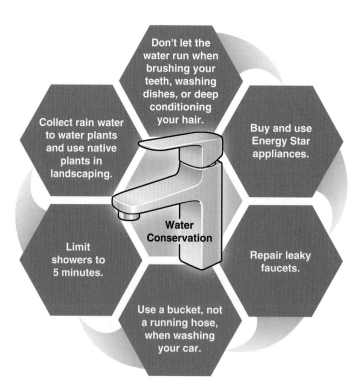

FIGURE 19.3　Ways to conserve water.

conserve energy (and you're reducing the air pollution emitted by car engines). Other daily choices you can make to conserve energy are shown in figure 19.4. Conserving water, energy, and other resources is an excellent way to reduce pollution that can adversely affect health.

Complete Streets

Conserving energy doesn't just mean reducing energy use or advocating for renewable fuel sources. It can also be incorporated into building and urban design (see the Health Technology feature for more information). For example, many organizations

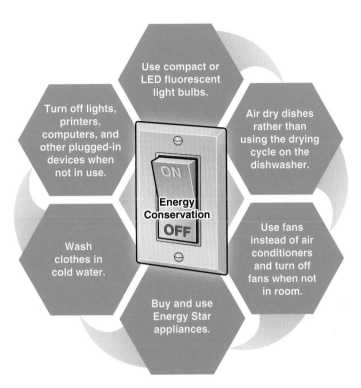

FIGURE 19.4 Ways to conserve energy.

in the United States and around the world now advocate for **complete streets**—that is, streets designed and operated to enable safe access for all users, including pedestrians, bicyclists, motorists, and transit riders of all ages and abilities. Complete streets make it easy to cross the street, walk to shops, and bicycle to work. They allow buses to run on time and make it safe for people to walk to and from train stations. This initiative is an example of how energy conservation can be integrated even into a modern endeavor such as urban (city) design. The value of complete streets is summarized in figure 19.5.

Green Schools

The movement for creating **green schools** is growing. The Green Schools Initiative advocates for schools to address what it calls the four pillars (see figure 19.6). The first pillar involves striving to be free of toxic substances, which means re-evaluating the chemicals used in cleaning supplies, in chemistry classes, and as pesticides. Pillar two involves using resources in a sustainable way—for example, using recycled paper whenever possible and recycling as many materials as possible. Pillar three calls for each school to have or be involved with healthy,

green spaces. This might mean growing food in a school garden or having a local farm deliver fresh food to the school cafeteria. This is called **farm-to-school**, where farms deliver fresh foods directly to the schools. The fourth pillar involves teaching students about the environment and encouraging them to get involved in organizations and in the community to help maintain or improve the environment. An overarching theme of green schools is they observe the precautionary principle, which can best be summarized by the phrase *better safe than sorry*. If you are not sure if an action or behavior is safe or not, you should not do it. At the very least, do more research before you act.

School Gardens

School gardens are becoming increasingly popular, and they can meet many needs. Food grown in a school garden can be served in the cafeteria, thus providing fresher food that doesn't have to be transported, which saves energy. Gardens also help students and teachers learn about nature and where food comes from. In addition, gardening is a good form of exercise and a good way to socialize and build community. Many organizations support school gardens and provide resources that can

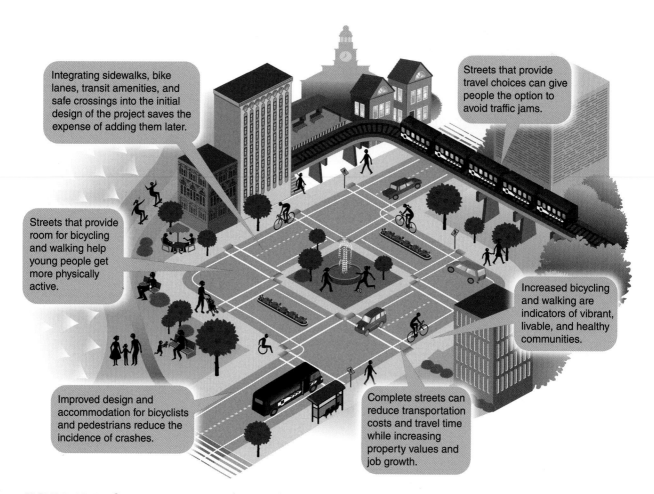

FIGURE 19.5 Streets are not complete until they are safe and convenient for travel by foot and bicycle, as well as for transit users, people with disabilities, and people in automobiles.

Facts are adapted from The National Complete Streets Coalition *Benefits fact sheet, and the Bicycle Coalition of Maine*, April 2009. www.bikewalklee.org/BWL_PDFs/BWL_facts/051109completeStreets.pdf.

help you start, operate, and maintain a garden at your school. To find them, just do a web search for information about school gardens.

Other Ways to Help Solve Environmental Health Problems

Numerous groups and organizations are dedicated to protecting the environment and improving human health, and many of them are led by young people. These organizations take a variety of focuses—for example, policy change, community cleanup, and community togetherness.

Some schools follow their own environmental checklists through cooperation among students, teachers, and staff. One example is the Georgia School Environmental Checklist, which includes questions such as the following: Are cleaning products and science and art supplies free of toxic substances? Does the school control pests and unwanted weeds without the use of pesticides?

In addition, groups such as Youth Service America and Do Something organize youth service and youth involvement projects, some of which provide opportunities for which groups can receive funding. Not all the projects are related to the environment, but many are. As the saying goes, "if you're not part of the solution, you're part of the problem."

♥ HEALTH TECHNOLOGY

The environment created by people is referred to as the **built environment**, and it can include elements such as green (environmentally friendly) buildings; bicycle lanes and bike racks; complete streets; sidewalk cafes; playgrounds; water parks, fitness parks, and traditional parks; fountains and public art; and community and school gardens. When people—planners, architects, politicians, public health professionals, and everyday citizens—work together thoughtfully on the built environment, they can create healthier communities.

For example, designers can use new computer technology to test their designs and see which type of home is most energy efficient or which type of street is safest. If, for example, a building meets the standards required to become **LEED certified**, it will use less energy and water. If a building has solar panels, the occupants can use their personal computers to track, in real time, how much solar energy is being produced. They can also view an estimate of the money they're saving and the carbon they're preventing from being released into the atmosphere. They can even use a smartphone to monitor how much solar energy they are producing in the building where they work or live.

⊖ CONNECT

How important do you think it is for new buildings to be built to green standards? If you were renting an apartment or buying a home, how important would it be to you that it meet green standards? Explain your perspective.

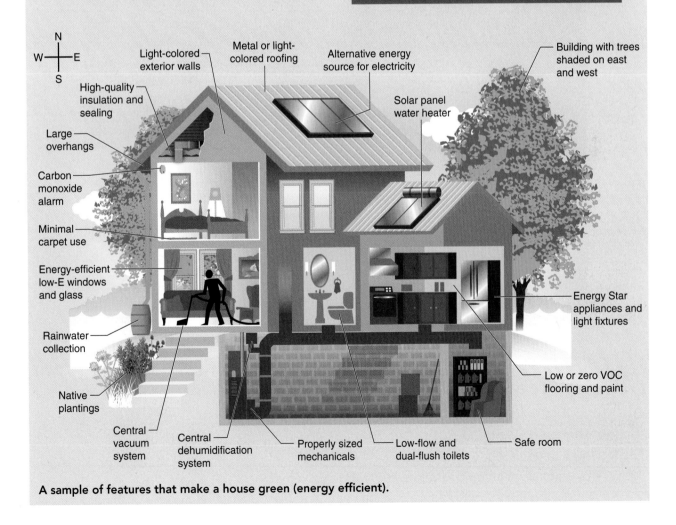

A sample of features that make a house green (energy efficient).

Pillar one	Pillar two	Pillar three	Pillar four
Strive to be free of toxic substances	**Use resources sustainably**	**Create a green, healthy space**	**Teach, learn, engage**
• Children's environmental health	• Energy efficiency and alternatives	• Green schoolyards and gardens	• Environmental education
• No pesticides, lead, or mold	• Green building design	• Rethink school lunch	• Hands-on, place-based learning
• Green building and cleaning materials	• Environmentally sound school supplies	• No junk food, fast food, or soda	• Involve children in greening their schools
	• Reduce, reuse, and recycle	• Farm-to-school organic produce	

FIGURE 19.6 The four pillars of a green school.

Rooftops make school gardens possible in urban areas.

nickos - Fotolia

Comprehension Check

1. How can you reduce water pollution?
2. How can air pollution contribute to health problems?
3. What is the relationship between conservation and reducing the amount of things you buy?

Jerry wanted to eat a healthier diet but found it easier to eat at the convenience store beside his workplace. Their hot dogs and nachos were regularly on special, he could get plenty to eat for very little money, and there were no other convenient places within walking distance (he didn't have a car). As for dinner, he was often too tired to care.

One of Jerry's co-workers with a car usually drove to a sandwich shop a few miles away for lunch, but Jerry didn't feel comfortable asking for a ride. Besides, their lunch hours didn't always line up. In addition, Jerry sometimes had only a couple of dollars and wouldn't be able to buy a sandwich anyway. True, his parents usually kept carrots and apples in the house, but he always seemed to forget about them. When his friend Samson asked why he didn't just bring a healthy lunch to work, he said, "A guy can't live on carrots and apples anyway, so I'd still be buying this other stuff, so it really doesn't matter."

For Discussion

What barriers does Jerry have to overcome in order to change his eating habits? What is one strategy Jerry might use to overcome his barriers? What are three specific action steps Jerry could take? In answering these questions, consider the guidelines presented in the Skills for Healthy Living feature.

SKILLS FOR HEALTHY LIVING: Overcoming Barriers

People can face many barriers when trying to make healthy behavior changes. Some barriers involve the environment (e.g., access to food choices, exercise facilities, health care, and support groups), some involve personal characteristics (e.g., existing health conditions), and some are psychological (e.g., low self-confidence, lack of time management skills). Overcoming such barriers is a necessary skill for successfully adopting any healthy behavior—or quitting any unhealthy behavior. Here are some helpful strategies.

- **Identify and evaluate your barriers.** The first step in overcoming a barrier to behavior change is recognizing the barrier in the first place.
- **Set goals.** Set both short- and long-term goals to give you direction and purpose.

- **Take small steps.** Use small, manageable action steps that help you progress toward your goals.
- **Develop a new way of thinking.** Avoid negative self-talk. Do use positive self-talk to improve your self-perceptions and self-confidence. Focus on things you can do and use phrases like "I can" and "I will" in place of "I can't" or "I won't."
- **Get active.** Join a community or school group that provides social support.
- **Don't quit.** If a barrier seems too big to overcome and you begin to feel discouraged, don't quit. Stick to your action steps.

Can Earbuds Damage Hearing?

A stunning number of teens—nearly one in five—have lost some of their hearing, and the problem has increased substantially in recent years, according to a new study based on data from the U.S. Centers for Disease Control and Prevention. The researchers compared hearing loss in about three thousand teenagers tested between 1988 and 1994 with hearing loss in nearly two thousand students tested in 2005 and 2006. They found that hearing loss was more common in the more recently tested group (20 percent versus 15 percent).

In most cases, the loss was mild, affecting only the ability to hear sounds at 16 to 24 decibels (e.g., a whisper or dripping water; see table 19.4 for decibel levels for various sounds). However, that loss can have an effect in daily life. Students with slight hearing loss "will hear all of the vowel sounds clearly, but might miss some of the consonant sounds," such as t, k, and s, says Dr. Gary Curhan. "Although speech will be detectable, it might not be fully intelligible."

Although the researchers didn't single out ear phones or earbuds or any other listening device for blame, they did find a significant increase in high-frequency hearing loss, which they said may indicate that noise caused the problems. And they cited a 2010 Australian study that linked the use of personal listening devices with a 70 percent increase in the risk of hearing loss among children. In fact, some young people turn their digital players up to 85 decibels (about as loud as a hair dryer or vacuum cleaner)—a level that approaches U.S. workplace exposure limits (see table 19.5). Habitual listening at such a level can turn microscopic hair cells in the inner ear into scar tissue.

For Discussion

Do you think earbuds have affected your hearing or the hearing of someone you know? Will the information presented in this article change how you listen to your personal entertainment? Why or why not?

TABLE 19.4 Environmental Noise

Sound	Decibel level
Threshold of hearing	0
Whisper-quiet library at 6 ft. (about 2 m)	30
Normal conversation at 3 ft. (about 1 m)	60–65
City traffic (inside car)	85
Train whistle at 500 ft. (about 150 m), truck traffic	90
Subway train at 200 ft. (about 60 m)	95
Sustained exposure at this level may result in hearing loss.	*90–95*
Hand drill	98
Snowmobile, motorcycle	100
Sandblasting, loud rock concert	115
Pain begins.	*125*
Even short-term exposure can cause permanent damage (this is the loudest recommended exposure when hearing protection is used).	*140*
Jet engine at 100 ft. (30 m)	140
12-gauge shotgun blast	165
Death of hearing tissue	*180*
Loudest sound possible	*194*

Reprinted, by permission, from Galen Carol Audio. Available: www.gcaudio.com/resources/howtos/loudness.html.

TABLE 19.5 Noise Safety Levels

OSHA* daily permissible noise level exposure	
Hours	Sound level (decibels)
8	90
4	95
2	100
0.5	110
0.25 or less	115

*U.S. Occupational Safety and Health Administration.

Reprinted, by permission, from Galen Carol Audio. Available: www.gcaudio.com/resources/howtos/loudness.html.

Reviewing Concepts and Vocabulary

As directed by your teacher, answer items 1 through 5 by correctly completing each sentence with a word or phrase.

1. The four Rs stand for _____, reduce, reuse, and recycle.
2. The precautionary principle is the saying "better _____ than sorry."
3. The U.S. governmental unit charged with looking out for the environment is the Environmental _____ Agency.
4. One of Barry Commoner's laws of ecology is that _____ knows best.
5. One disease or disorder that can be caused by air pollution is _____.

For items 6 through 10, as directed by your teacher, match each term in column 1 with the appropriate phrase in column 2.

6. climate change
7. complete street
8. conspicuous consumption
9. biodegradable

10. built environment

a. made by humans
b. buying products that you don't really need
c. can be broken down by microorganisms
d. accommodates all types of transportation for people of all ages and abilities
e. long-term change in temperature, precipitation, or wind

For items 11 through 15, as directed by your teacher, respond to each statement or question.

11. Explain one of the four laws of ecology.
12. What is a sanitary landfill?
13. Which international organization formally recognized the connection between air pollution and cancer?
14. What is one of the four pillars of a green school?
15. Identify one major air pollutant and one of its main sources.

Thinking Critically

Write a paragraph in response to the following question.

What type of conservation (from table 19.3) do you think is most important for the world today? Support your opinion with fact and reason.

Take It Home

Save all of the plastic items that your family uses in a one-week period. Include wrappers, bottles, caps, lids, straws, and everything else you use that is plastic. At the end of the week, take a picture of your plastic and compare it with a picture from a friend who has a family of similar size. After you photographed the plastic, did you recycle all of it that could be recycled?

Alexey Stiop/Fotolia.com

mmunity and blic Health

 **Student Web Resources**
www.healthforlifetextbook.org/student

iStockphoto/Lisa F.

Lesson 20.1
Public Health

Lesson Objectives

After reading this lesson, you should be able to

1. define *public health* and identify types of public health providers;
2. understand the difference between primary, secondary, and tertiary prevention efforts; and
3. explain the difference between the prevalence and the incidence of a disease.

Lesson Vocabulary

developing nations, epidemiologist, health disparities, incidence, prevalence, primary prevention, public health, secondary prevention, tertiary prevention

Have you ever wondered who inspects restaurants for cleanliness? Who writes the public service announcements you see on television? Who tracks illness and outbreaks in communities? Or who decides which vaccinations are required for attending school? These issues and many others are part of the general activity of **public health**—the art and science of protecting and improving the health of individuals and groups of people.

Public health officials carry out educational campaigns, such as public service announcements, and deliver a range of programming designed to inform the public about health issues. They also seek to affect the health behaviors of large groups of people. Other aspects of the public health system are research and policy making. Overall, public health efforts are made by local and state health departments, federal agencies, private organizations, and international agencies. See figure 20.1 for the 10 essential public health services.

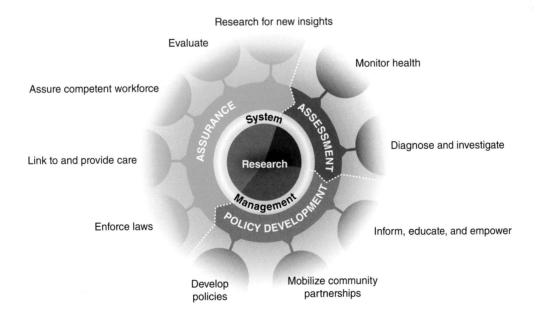

FIGURE 20.1 The public health wheel illustrates the relationship among core functions, specific responsibilities, and the 10 essential public health services.

Local and State Health Departments

In most U.S. states, public health services are provided by county, city, and state health departments. Many public health department services are provided free of charge to the consumer, whereas others are priced on the basis of the individual's socioeconomic status. One major charge for all health departments is to help limit the effect of **health disparities**. These disparities are defined by the Centers for Disease Control and Prevention (CDC) as the preventable differences in the burden of disease, injury, violence, or opportunity for optimal health that people in socially disadvantaged populations experience. These populations may be characterized by certain race or ethnicity identifications, gender, education, income, disability, geographic location, or sexual orientation. Providing essential services to people disadvantaged by these disparities ensures the health and productivity of the nation.

Federal Agencies

The federal agency with the widest reach and biggest effect on public health in the United States is the Department of Health and Human Services (HHS). This agency includes many operating divisions, such as CDC and the National Institutes of Health (see table 20.1 for a complete listing). HHS establishes most U.S. health and safety standards, compiles and analyzes health information, supports state and county health departments, and supports research and education efforts. The websites maintained by the HHS operating divisions are excellent sources of public health information.

Other U.S. agencies involved in public health include the Occupational Safety and Health Administration (often referred to by its acronym OSHA), which regulates worksite health and safety; the Department of Agriculture, which is responsible for the inspection of meat and agricultural products; and the Environmental Protection Agency, which oversees areas related to environmental health.

TABLE 20.1   Divisions of the U.S. Department of Health and Human Services (HHS)

Division	Responsibilities
Administration for Children and Families	Programs that improve the lives of children from low-income families, as well as individuals with disabilities
Administration for Community Living	Promotes the economic and social well-being of families, children, individuals, and communities through a range of educational and supportive programs in partnership with states, tribes, and community organizations
Agency for Healthcare Research and Quality	Access to health care and improved quality of health care
Agency for Toxic Substances and Disease Registry	Monitoring and investigation of risks to human health from toxins
Centers for Disease Control and Prevention	Research, data collection, and information distribution on almost all diseases and disorders
Centers for Medicare and Medicaid Services	Medicare and Medicaid programs
Food and Drug Administration	Food and medicine safety
Health Resources and Services Administration	Assistance for underserved groups such as homeless people
Indian Health Services	Health care for Native American populations
National Institutes of Health	Biomedical research
Substance Abuse and Mental Health Services Administration	Prevention and treatment of substance abuse and mental illness

Nongovernmental Organizations

Many private organizations are also invested in public health. They include charitable and religious organizations and private for-profit organizations. Well-known examples are the American Heart Association, the American Cancer Society, and the American Diabetes Association. Smaller organizations—such as community centers, churches, and local nonprofit agencies—are also involved in public health efforts. For example, they operate food banks and shelters for people who have low income or are homeless. Hospitals also serve public health needs by providing free clinics, screenings, and vaccination services.

 CONNECT

Is there a food bank in your community? Is there a homeless shelter? What are two ways that a food bank or homeless shelter can help the community it serves? What is one thing you could do to support a food bank or shelter this year?

Public Health and Prevention

Public health efforts fall into three categories based on the type of prevention they seek: primary, secondary, and tertiary (see figure 20.2). **Primary prevention** includes actions and services that reduce risk and avoid health problems—for example, efforts to keep underage people from drinking. **Secondary prevention** involves recognizing risks for (or beginnings of) problems and intervening before serious illness or effects arise. One example is an educational program aimed at college students who engage in social drinking; the goal is to help young people understand the risks of drinking and avoid becoming alcoholics.

CONSUMER CORNER: Donating to Charities

One great way to support a community and develop an altruistic (giving) attitude is to make a financial donation to a charity that supports a cause you find meaningful. Unfortunately, we live in a world where some people take advantage of others' generous hearts by organizing scams and committing fraud. Use the following guidelines to help you determine whether a charity is legitimate and worthy of your donation. Be suspicious of any charity that

- fails to provide detailed information about its identity, mission, costs, and planned use of your donation;
- refuses to provide proof that a contribution is tax deductible;
- uses a name closely resembling the name of a better-known, reputable organization (this could be a sign that someone is trying to trick you);
- thanks you for a pledge you don't recall making, then asks you to consider giving more;

- uses high-pressure tactics, such as trying to get you to donate immediately;
- asks for donations in cash or asks you to wire money (all reputable charities accept multiple forms of payment, such as check, credit card, and direct pay options);
- offers to come collect the donation immediately; or
- guarantees sweepstakes winnings in exchange for a contribution (by law, you never have to give a donation to be eligible to win a sweepstakes).

Consumer Challenge

Identify three charities of your choosing and visit their websites. Look for information about mission, costs, planned uses of the donations, tax status, and donation methods. Evaluate the charities using the information you gather and determine your willingness to contribute to each cause based on what you learn.

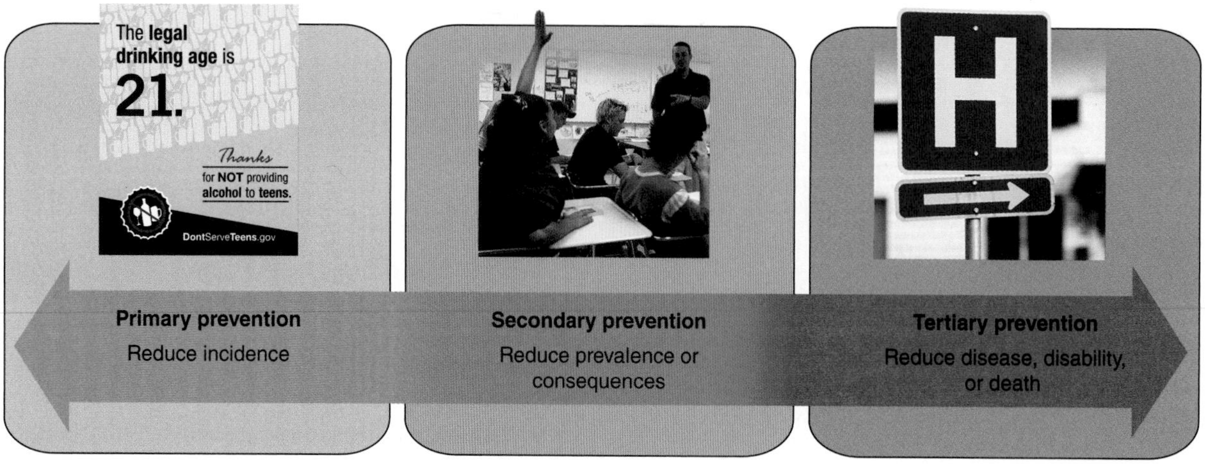

FIGURE 20.2 Levels of prevention in public health.

Finally, **tertiary prevention** is best thought of as the prevention of death. It involves treatment and rehabilitation of a person who is already sick, such as a person being treated for liver damage due to a lifetime of alcohol abuse. As you might expect, public health efforts are most effective at the primary and secondary levels of prevention.

One major public health goal is to reduce both the incidence and the prevalence of disease and disability. **Incidence** refers to the number of new cases that occur in a year. **Prevalence** refers to the number of existing cases. Both the incidence and the prevalence of diseases, disabilities, and related health behaviors are tracked and studied by public health workers called **epidemiologists**. Tracking the incidence rate of a communicable disease, for example, can help public health officials determine whether there is an epidemic—a widespread occurrence of an infectious disease in a community at a particular time.

Following the prevalence of a disease over time can also help officials determine how effective public health interventions are. For example, studying how positive health behaviors (e.g., healthy eating and regular physical activity) affect disease rates and quality of life can help us better understand and promote the benefits associated with these behaviors. You can learn more about the study of epidemiology by visiting the student section of the Health for Life website.

Global Public Health Organizations and Issues

Public health is a concern not only in the United States; all developed countries maintain public health services. In addition, global organizations provide public health guidance, programming, and support. Examples include the World Health Organization, the United Nations Children's Fund (UNICEF), and the Peace Corps. While prosperous countries such as the United States must address issues such as excessive food consumption and lack

Healthy People 2020

This book's introductory chapter discusses the *Healthy People 2020* report, which plays a significant role in guiding public health efforts in the United States. The goals established by the report help public health departments and private agencies prioritize their efforts. For example, one public health goal established in *Healthy People 2020* is to reduce by 10 percent the number of schools that have a serious violent incident. This goal encourages schools and local health departments to work together to create anti-bullying and anti-violence education, policies, and programs. A web link to the *Healthy People 2020* report is included in the student section of the Health for Life website, and relevant *Healthy People 2020* goals are listed at the start of each unit in this book.

⚛ HEALTH SCIENCE

Malaria was eliminated in the United States by a concerted effort made from 1947 to 1951, yet somewhere in the world a child dies from malaria every 30 seconds. In Africa, one in every five childhood deaths is attributed to malaria. Poorer individuals are at highest risk because their homes and dwellings provide little protection from infected mosquitoes. They can't afford preventive medication or, if symptoms arise, medical care. The elimination of malaria in the United States was aided by spraying homes with mosquito-killing insecticides, spraying insecticides over large land areas, and removing mosquito nesting sites. In addition, U.S. residents have access to medicine that helps prevent and treat malaria.

iStockphoto.com/Viktor Kitaykin

The advances in chemical and medical science that contributed to effective insecticides and medications are certainly not new, yet malaria remains a global threat. This disparity illustrates the fact that even when science can solve a particular health problem, challenges may still exist in distributing the solution to those most in need. In addition, many developing countries have little in the way of organized public health services, and citizens often have no education or awareness of options that might exist. Therefore, humanitarians and scientists must often work together to make the greatest gains in global public health.

of exercise, much of the world faces very different public health issues, and the biggest challenge in global public health is poverty.

Countries with a poor economy and low standards of living are sometimes referred to as **developing nations**, and these are the places where the majority of the world's people live. These countries often face particularly intense public health problems, including malnutrition and widespread disease (e.g., malaria, AIDS). As a result, major global health initiatives are focused on bringing vaccinations, antibiotics, safe water, and sustainable farming techniques to developing countries.

Another key effort focuses on creating educational opportunities for more children around the world. Access to education is considered a primary way to end the cycle of poverty and improve global public health. It opens doors for employment, which can bring individual freedom as well as opportunities for acquiring healthier food, safer living conditions, and higher-quality health care.

🔊 HEALTHY COMMUNICATION

If you had US$1,000 to donate to a group addressing a serious health problem, what would it be? Why? Would you choose to support a cause in the United States or donate to a group addressing a global health issue? Why? Share your response with a group of classmates or peers.

❝ Of all the forms of inequality, injustice in health care is the most shocking and inhumane. ❞

—Martin Luther King, Jr.

Comprehension Check

1. What types of organization serve the public health in the United States? Provide three specific examples.
2. What are the three levels of prevention addressed by public health services? Which are the most effective in improving public health?
3. What is the difference between the prevalence and the incidence of a disease?

Your school is an important community to which you belong. This assessment asks you to think about aspects of a healthy school community and consider your connection to your school. Answer each question by circling the proper response, then add up the total number of points as directed in the assessment. You may need to ask a teacher or school staff member for help in answering some of the questions in parts 1 and 2.

	Yes (2 points)	No (0 points)
Part 1: Health and safety		
My school . . .		
has a no tolerance policy for harassment or bullying.	2	0
has emergency plans, like evacuation routes, in place.	2	0
has active supervision in place to ensure safety and reduce violence.	2	0
is a safe physical environment.	2	0
does not allow smoking on campus.	2	0
is kept clean and bright.	2	0
provides help to those who want to quit smoking.	2	0
has at least one full-time nurse on campus.	2	0
provides counseling and mental health services.	2	0
Part 2: Nutrition and physical activity services		
My school . . .		
requires students to take physical education.	2	0
provides physical activities after school.	2	0
requires students to take health education.	2	0
promotes healthy food and beverage choices.	2	0
provides healthy and low-fat food.	2	0
has a clean and pleasant cafeteria.	2	0

Total points from parts 1 and 2: _____
The higher the score, the healthier and safer the school community.

Part 3: My school engagement		
As a member of my school, I . . .		
am involved in at least one club or organization at school.	2	0
feel comfortable at my school.	2	0
feel connected to my school and have school pride.	2	0
feel safe from violence or bullying.	2	0
know how to get help if I feel stressed, am depressed, or have anxiety.	2	0
am physically active almost every day.	2	0
make healthy food choices most of the time.	2	0

Total points from part 3: _____
The higher the score, the more your school community is helping you be a healthier person.

✔ Planning for Healthy Living

Use the Healthy Living Plan worksheet to address an aspect of community or public health—for example, getting more involved in your neighborhood or advocating for ways to meet a specific community health need.

Lesson 20.2

Community Health and Advocacy

Lesson Objectives

After reading this lesson, you should be able to

1. explain the various meanings of *community* and identify ways in which communities affect personal health,
2. understand the steps for developing healthy communities, and
3. define *advocacy* and explain the keys to being an effective advocate.

Lesson Vocabulary

advocacy, community, community health, stakeholder

One part of public health is **community health**, which is concerned with issues affecting the health of a specific community of people, usually defined by a specific geographic area. Community health efforts take into account the unique features of the community and its environment; they also use input from community members when generating programs and services. Community health efforts address public health issues identified as most important at the local level—for example, sanitation, safe water, public safety, and laws and policies that promote good health. They may also include services and programs targeting groups of people at risk for particular health problems. This lesson will help you understand the types of community around you and how to advocate for positive change related to health issues in those communities.

Communities

What communities do you belong to? Are you part of a neighborhood or school? Are you a member of a club or team? Do you have a religious or cultural community? All of us belong to multiple communities. A **community** is any group of people who share common characteristics or interests. Examples include your city or town, your neighborhood, your school, your family, and your cultural groups. Each of these communities can affect your health.

Your Neighborhood and Your Town or City

Where you live can dramatically influence your health. Each city, town, and state has its own characteristics, people, laws, opportunities, and basic health services (e.g., emergency medical services and access to community health centers). Some communities also have laws that affect health, such as bans on smoking in public areas. Others promote healthy living in their design itself—for example, by including lots of parks, bicycle lanes, and sidewalks to facilitate active living. Local crime patterns can also affect both individual health behaviors and the overall community's health. With this reality in mind, some neighborhoods organize watch programs so that children can safely play outside and travel to and from school. Some schools make their gyms, playgrounds, and tracks accessible to the public when they aren't being used for school activities. Some schools also have afterschool programs that have physical activity components.

Your School

Your school is a strong community that influences your health in many ways—for example, breakfast and lunch choices, mental health counseling, nursing services, and vaccination clinics. Your school environment, if clean and well lit, can also enhance your mental health. In contrast, schools that are dirty, moldy, dark, run-down, or unsafe increase the risk of injury and illness. Schools can also implement policies to protect health, as in anti-bullying and anti-smoking programs. In addition, schools can provide opportunities to engage in health-enhancing behaviors, such as physical activity, through physical education and afterschool programs.

The bottom line is that all schools should establish services, environments, policies, and programs that promote the health and well-being of their students, faculty, and staff. One strategy is provided by the CDC in its coordinated school health model (see figure 20.3). You can learn about other tools used to promote healthy schools in the student section of the Health for Life website.

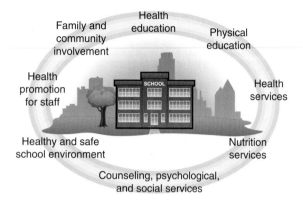

FIGURE 20.3 The coordinated school health model.

Your Cultural Community

The word *culture* can refer to many things. For example, you may belong to an ethnic cultural group with a strong tradition of gathering, supporting each other, and celebrating life together. You may also have a culture defined by your religion, your politics, or your sexual orientation. Regardless of its basis, a cultural community can provide you with strong social support and increase your sense of belonging through its rituals and traditions. In fact, a cultural community can influence many aspects of your life, such as your diet, your attitude toward exercise, and the choices you make about smoking and drinking.

Developing Healthy Communities

Healthy communities don't just happen. People in a community must work together to make it healthy. To do so, they must feel a sense of belonging and care about the outcome of community health efforts. When people feel interested or concerned—particularly when they are affected by the outcome of an

action—they are referred to as **stakeholders**. An invested group of stakeholders and advocates is crucial to the success of any community project. Do you care about the health of your community? Are you involved in it? To make a difference in your community's health, you must do three things: get informed, get involved, and become an advocate.

Getting Informed

If you want to make a positive difference, you must understand the issues that people in your community care about. You can learn about local issues in various ways, such as reading local newspapers or blogs, listening to news radio shows, watching informative shows on local and public television stations, and attending community meetings. Social media outlets also provide forums where people express their concerns about their communities. Using social media to follow public leaders or local organizations can give you a sense of important issues and the types of actions the community tends to support. Other strategies include interviewing local officials and leaders and surveying peers and community members about key topics.

Getting Involved

Once you're aware of the issues facing your community, you should get involved with one

© MM Productions/Corbis

or more causes that you care about. You can get involved by joining an organization, voicing your opinion at community and civic meetings, or taking on a leadership role in a school organization. Another great way to engage with your community is to volunteer your time and energy. Select a cause that you're passionate about and ask around about ways to help.

For example, if you care about literacy, you might choose to volunteer your time tutoring children. If you're passionate about the environment, you might participate in local cleanup days or even organize your own cleanup club. You can also choose volunteer opportunities that allow you to help someone while also building your own skills and exploring an area of interest. Examples include volunteering in a hospital, senior center, youth club, or afterschool program. Whatever you choose to do, volunteering can be rewarding for both you and your community.

Becoming an Advocate

Advocacy is a critical skill. It involves speaking, writing, or organizing in support of an individual or cause. To be an effective health advocate, you must first know and believe in the positive and health-enhancing nature of what you're advocating. A good health advocacy effort educates other people about the particular behavior or issue, provides strategies and solutions to influence others' health behaviors, and provides support to encourage the necessary behavior changes or other actions. Advocacy can be focused at the individual level (benefitting a friend or peer), the classroom level (supporting policies and practices that promote healthy behavior), the school level (involving the entire school community in policies, actions, or improvements), or the societal level (writing to government representatives or taking other actions to influence change on a larger scale).

Becoming an advocate takes courage, and it is rarely done without facing some opposition. People are passionate about issues they care about, and their opinions often differ from yours. When advocating on any issue or cause, you need to respect the views of others while working calmly and rationally to share your own perspectives and ideas.

How to Advocate Effectively

Step 1: Understand and define the issue. Learn what issues matter to the community you're involved in. Ask a lot of questions, conduct a survey, read, and listen. Clearly define the issue you're working on and seek to understand it from as many perspectives as you can. Share your knowledge with others.

Step 2: Create solutions. Identify realistic solutions to the problem. Start by brainstorming as many solutions as you can. Be specific and offer concrete suggestions for how the community might improve. Check community resources and policies to ensure that your solutions can be supported and the actions you take do not violate any existing laws or regulations.

Step 3: Gather support. Your strategy for gathering support will vary depending on the issue you're addressing and the goal you're working toward. In some cases, you might need to gather the support of community leaders and officials by writing thoughtful letters or circulating a petition. In other instances, you might need to gather the support of peers to implement a change. Examples of strategies for gathering support are social media, web pages, flyers, and public speaking (e.g., at club or organizational meetings). If you're trying to influence a group of people with whom you do not usually interact, approach their leaders and influential members of the group. In all cases, be thoughtful about whom you want to reach with your message, then use appropriate means to gather their support.

Step 4: Implement your plan. Take action, be persistent, and expect to face challenges along the way. Stay positive in your message and be respectful of others.

HEALTH TECHNOLOGY

Social media has emerged as a major force for change in community health and advocacy because it makes it easier than ever before to communicate with large numbers of people in a community or even across the globe. The most common social media outlets for advocating community change are the electronic newsletters of agencies and nonprofit organizations, Facebook, Twitter, YouTube, and blogs.

Social media also allows people to stay updated on issues in a community and to follow community leaders. For example, more than 80 percent of government officials, including members of the U.S. Congress, use Twitter at least once a week, allowing constituents to follow their actions and decisions. During the 2008 U.S. presidential election, social media was used strategically for the first time to motivate a large youth vote that significantly affected the results. When used appropriately, social media can also help bring about positive community changes that promote good health and wellness.

CONNECT

Using your favorite forms of social media, find a way to connect to a public health service or official. Share your chosen connection with your classmates. Consider making a directory of social media sites that students can use to become informed and stay updated about important health issues in your community.

Accessing Community and Public Health Resources

Most communities provide a range of health resources for members of the public. Knowing the community resources available to you and others when in need is an important part of being a healthy citizen. If you're in need of a resource, or aren't sure of what's available, begin by asking a trusted adult. Adults often know of resources because they've used them; they may also have advice about where to look. Another good source is your local phonebook. Check the government listings under titles such as "Community Health Services" and "Human Health and Safety."

You can also conduct a web search to find a good list of resources. Begin your web search with established organizations, such as those mentioned in table 20.1 or elsewhere in this chapter. Also consider looking at the website of your local city or county government or health department and the local chapters of aid organizations such as the American Red Cross. Once you've located a few resources, make calls or inquiries to see which organization provides the services you need. If a particular group doesn't meet your need, ask someone there for a reference to other resources that might be of help to you.

Comprehension Check

1. How does your neighborhood, city, or another community influence your health?
2. How can becoming informed and involved in a community help you to make the community healthier?
3. What are the four steps involved in effective advocacy?

Malcolm is one of only a dozen African Americans in his high school; most of his school community consists of Latinos and Asian Americans. His school is in an area of the city that has a long history of serving immigrants and their families, and many of the students come from lower socioeconomic conditions. Malcolm's immediate family is small, including just his parents and himself, and they are financially comfortable. He also has a large extended family, but all of them live in a different state.

Malcolm is a good student and wants to go to college to study business. Some of the kids at school harass him for being too studious and others just ignore him altogether. Lately, Malcolm has been feeling isolated and discouraged about life. Going to school is becoming more stressful, and he recently started smoking cigarettes to help him cope and try to fit in better at school. His grades have slipped a little, and he's starting to question his own ambition. Everything seems less interesting, and his attitude is increasingly negative.

For Discussion

Do you understand Malcolm's attitude toward his situation? What things would you advise him to do to improve his attitude? How has his community affected his attitude and health behaviors? What community resources might be available to help Malcolm improve his situation? In answering these questions, refer to the Skills for Healthy Living feature for guidance.

SKILLS FOR HEALTHY LIVING: Positive Attitudes

Maintaining positive attitudes is an important part of having good mental and physical health. For some people, positive attitudes seem to come easily; for others, it requires conscious effort and practice. Everyone, however, can develop and maintain a positive mental outlook and a positive attitude. Here are some suggestions to help you build and maintain a positive attitude.

- **Use positive language.** Avoid using negative words and phrases, such as "I can't," "never," "I don't," "always," and "I won't." Instead, practice framing your sentences with positive phrases, such as "I choose," "I can," "I will," or, when referring to something you feel less confident about, "I might."

- **Surround yourself with positive friends.** You and your friends influence each other. When someone in a group is negative, others in the group also tend to act and feel negative more often. Similarly, when members of a group are positive and hopeful, others in the group will more often be hopeful and positive as well.

- **Smile.** Though it may sound funny, it's been proven that smiling or laughing intentionally for 30 seconds can help you feel happier. Try smiling at strangers in public or when you are alone. Do things that make you laugh. When you feel happy, you tend to be more optimistic and positive in your attitudes.

- **Pay attention to your emotions.** When you do feel angry, frustrated, hopeless, or negative, attend to how you feel and what caused your feelings. Don't avoid these feelings. Instead, acknowledge that you have them, explore why you have them, and address them with positive thoughts and actions. You can't always control what happens to you or around you, but you can control how you react to it.

- **Limit your screen time.** Unrealistic media images and messages can lead people to feel inadequate and unattractive. Pay attention to what you watch and how it makes you feel. Avoid shows, magazines, and other media sources that leave you feeling bad about yourself.

- **Keep a gratitude journal.** Write down three things each day that you feel thankful for. Do this every day for a week and see how it affects your attitude.

- **Keep a success journal.** Write down three things each day that you achieved or did well. Periodically, read through your successes and remind yourself how capable you are.

- **Share your feelings.** Share how you're feeling with someone you trust to be supportive. Keeping negative emotions tied up inside can hurt your physical and emotional health, and it can get worse over time. Share how you feel and talk about ways in which you might handle a challenging situation and improve your attitude toward it.

- **Take time to play.** Do things you love. Play a sport or make music. Draw, write, or cook. Spend time following your passions and doing things you love.

- **Give to others.** Do things to help others and serve your community. Helping others in need can remind you of what's most important and help you feel proud of who you are.

 ## ACADEMIC CONNECTION: Making Sense of Concentrations

Mercury, often found in fish, is considered toxic to humans at concentration levels of one part per million. Just how much is that? Concentrations are mathematical measures often used in health science to help researchers and consumers understand how much of a substance is present in a particular liquid or solid. For example, visualize an object 1 inch (2.5 cm) long in a space that is 16 miles (26 km) long. That's the equivalent of one part per million. Another example is to think of a 55-gallon (208 L) barrel of water. It would take only four drops of mercury in the barrel to reach a concentration of one part per million. A single minute over the course of two years is also equivalent to one part per million.

Concentrations can be expressed in other ways. One is milligrams per liter (mg/L). Another is milligrams per deciliter (mg/dL). Concentrations such as mg/dL are used in laboratory reports that show how much of a particular element is found in the blood. For example, a healthy total blood cholesterol reading is considered to be less than 200 mg/dL (milligrams per deciliter). Since a deciliter is equal to 1/10 of a liter, this is equivalent to 2,000 mg of cholesterol per liter of blood, or 2,000 parts per million.

Are We Failing at Community Health?

More than 20 million Americans sought care at community health centers in 2011. These centers provide much-needed services, such as prenatal care, diabetes prevention and care, and childhood immunization. Unfortunately, a recent analysis of federal data by Kaiser Health News (a nonprofit, nonpartisan health policy research and communication group) found that many community health centers are failing Americans in diabetes care, childhood immunization, and cervical cancer screening for women, among other areas (see table 20.2).

"We feel good about quality overall, but there is clearly room to improve," says Mary Wakefield, who oversees community health centers for the U.S. Health Resources and Services Administration. She points out that some community health centers do perform better than private health service facilities in certain areas. For instance, 75 percent of centers performed significantly better in helping individuals with high blood pressure manage their condition, and more than 40 percent do significantly better than the national average in making sure women get timely prenatal care.

Elizabeth Rayes, 38, of Warner Robins, Georgia, credits a nurse at her local community health center for counseling her on how to control her diabetes even though she can't afford a blood glucose meter to test herself. "They do a great job," she says.

Compared with the clientele at a typical doctor's office, community center patients are nearly six times as likely to be poor, more than twice as likely to be uninsured, and nearly three times as likely to be on Medicaid, the combined state and federal health insurance program for people who are poor. "Given the complex nature of diseases and the many factors that contribute to them, it might be unreasonable to expect centers that serve the poor to perform above the average when compared to the well-staffed and financially sound medical centers and hospitals," says Dr. Jonathon Starkovich, who runs a community center outside of Athens, Georgia.

For Discussion

What do community health centers do, and who do they serve? What did this article teach you about how income level can affect the quality of health care that a person receives?

TABLE 20.2 Sampling of Community Health Centers: Performance on Key Measures

Center	State	Diabetes control*	Hypertension control**	Childhood immunization***
Yakima Valley Farm Workers Clinic	Washington	64	77	80
Shackelford County Community Resource Center	Texas	60	Not available	58
Family Health of Darke County	Ohio	83	96	70
Camillus Health Concern, Inc.	Florida	49	Not available	100
National average (all health service providers)	—	88	68	67

*Diabetes control: Percentage of adults, aged 18 to 75, with diabetes whose blood sugar is under control.

**Hypertension control: Percentage of adults, aged 18 to 85, with hypertension whose blood pressure is under control.

***Childhood immunization: Percentage of children who receive all seven federally recommended vaccines by age two.

Source: 2010 Health Center Data, Department of Health and Human Services.

Reviewing Concepts and Vocabulary

As directed by your teacher, answer items 1 through 5 by correctly completing each sentence with a word or phrase.

1. _____ involves taking action in support of an individual or cause.
2. In order to help develop a healthy community, you need to get informed, get _____, and become an advocate.
3. _____ _____ is the art and science of protecting and improving the health of individuals and the nation.
4. _____ _____ refer to differences in health status between people that are related to social or demographic factors.
5. Countries with a poor economy and low standards of living are sometimes referred to as _____ nations.

For items 6 through 10, as directed by your teacher, match each term in column 1 with the appropriate phrase in column 2.

6. primary prevention
7. secondary prevention
8. tertiary prevention
9. incidence
10. prevalence

a. intervening before serious illness or effects occur
b. the number of new cases of disease in a year
c. prevention of death
d. the number of existing cases of disease
e. actions and services designed to reduce risk and avoid health problems

For items 11 through 15, as directed by your teacher, respond to each statement or question.

11. Name two divisions of the U.S. Department of Health and Human Services.
12. Which government agency oversees worksite health conditions?
13. Explain the difference between the incidence and the prevalence of a disease.
14. List the four steps of effective advocacy.
15. What are two things a person can do to develop a more positive attitude?

Thinking Critically

Write a paragraph in response to the following prompt.

Think about all the services and policies at your school that are designed to positively affect your health. Write down as many as you can think of. For each service or policy on the list, identify what purpose it has and what health behavior or disease it is meant to affect.

Take It Home

Make a list of the communities to which you and your family belong. How do you think your family's health is positively or negatively influenced by each community? Write down as many influences as you can for each community and share your list with a family member.

Glossary

This glossary contains definitions of all the boldfaced terms throughout the book. You can also find all the vocabulary terms grouped by lesson on the student web resource.

abstract thinking—Ability to consider ideas that are not visible, immediate, or concrete.

accelerometer—Device that measures movement; frequently used to measure steps, intensity of movement, and duration of physical activity.

accountability—Following through with the commitments you make to yourself and others.

acquired immune deficiency syndrome (AIDS)—Infectious disease caused by the human immunodeficiency virus (HIV).

action steps—Things you can do immediately to begin progressing toward your goal.

activities of daily living—Tasks one does on a regular basis, such as bathing, eating, dressing, and grooming.

acute alcohol poisoning—Potentially fatal overdose of alcohol or a medical emergency resulting from binge drinking.

addiction—Physical dependency on a chemical substance such as alcohol, nicotine, or heroin.

adolescents—People transitioning through puberty.

advocacy—Taking action in support of an individual or cause.

agility—Ability to change body position quickly and control your body's movements.

air quality index—Scale used to rate pollution levels ranging from good air quality to very unhealthful.

alcohol dehydrogenase—The *de–* prefix means "to remove." When a word ends in *–ase* it means that it is an enzyme. The *hydrogen* means just that, hydrogen. Dehydrogenase is an enzyme that removes hydrogen atoms. Alcohol dehydrogenase is an enzyme that removes hydrogen atoms from the alcohol molecule; it breaks down the majority of the alcohol that enters the human body.

alcoholism—Disease in which a person is dependent on alcohol.

alcohol tolerance—After continued drinking of alcohol over a long time, the consumption of the same amount of alcohol creates less effect.

alcopop—Flavored alcoholic beverage to which various fruit juices or other flavorings have been added, such as wine coolers and some malt beverages.

alveoli—Small air sacs in the lungs that exchange gases with the blood through capillary beds.

Americans with Disabilities Act—Ensures the civil rights of all Americans who have mental or physical disabilities.

anaerobic activity—Activity so intense that your body cannot supply adequate oxygen to sustain it for a long time.

anorexia nervosa—Eating disorder characterized by starvation, weight loss, and intense feelings of being fat or overweight.

antibiotic—Prescription drug that kills or inhibits bacteria that cause disease.

anxiety disorder—When feelings of anxiety occur regularly or interfere with a person's ability to function normally.

appetite—Psychological need for food.

arteriosclerosis—Hardening of the arteries.

asanas—Postures or positions in yoga.

assault—An act of immediate harmful or offensive contact that creates fear for a person.

assertive behavior—Behavior that involves making a firm verbal statement letting another person know how you feel.

assertiveness—Act of being honest and direct in communication.

atherosclerosis—Clogging of the arteries.

athlete's foot—Fungal infection of the feet that results from a warm, moist environment.

attention-deficit/hyperactivity disorder (ADHD)—Most common mental disorder diagnosed in children and young adults. Factors include hyperactivity, inattention, and problems with impulse control.

attitude—Your feelings about something.

bacteria—Simple single-cell organisms that are commonly found in air, soil, and food and on the bodies of plants and animals and that can produce toxins and cause illness.

balance—Ability to maintain an upright posture while standing still or moving.

battery—Harmfully or offensively touching another person.

binge drinking—When men consume 5 or more drinks and when women consume 4 or more drinks in about a 2-hour span.

biodegradable—Capable of breaking down (decomposing) by bacteria or other micro-organisms.

biofeedback—Technique, often using special equipment, that enables a person to gain some element of voluntary control over what people often believe are involuntary body functions.

blended family—Formed when a parent remarries.

blood alcohol content (BAC)—Percentage of alcohol in the bloodstream. A BAC of 0.08 percent is the legal level of intoxication in all states.

body composition—The proportional amounts of body tissues, including muscle, bone, body fat, and other tissues that make up your body.

body image—Thoughts, feelings, and actions in response to your body shape, size, or appearance.

body mass index (BMI)—Measure of body weight in relation to body height that is associated with certain health risks.

built environment—Any human-made structure or system such as buildings, parks, roads, or bicycle paths.

bulimia—Eating disorder characterized by overeating and purging (vomiting, engaging in excessive exercise, using laxatives) in order to rid the body of unwanted calories.

bullying—The act of repeatedly doing or saying something to intimidate or dominate another person.

calorie—Unit of energy or heat that describes the amount of energy in a food (the true term is *kilocalorie*).

cancer—Uncontrolled growth of abnormal cells in the body.

carbohydrate—One of the six major classes of nutrients composed of sugar, starch, and fiber.

cardiac muscle—Heart muscle.

cardiorespiratory endurance—Ability to exercise your entire body for a long time without stopping.

cardiovascular disease (CVD)—A physical illness that affects the heart, blood vessels, or blood. Examples include heart attack and stroke. It's the leading cause of death in the United States.

casual friendship—A friendship between individuals who share some commonalities (e.g., classmates or co-workers) that is not characterized by the formation of a deep bond.

cholesterol—Waxy, fatlike substance found in meat, dairy products, and egg yolk; a high amount in the blood is implicated in various types of heart disease.

chronic disease—Disease that lasts a lifetime.

chronological age—Number of years a person has been alive.

climate change—Any significant change in measures of climate (such as temperature, precipitation, or wind) lasting for decades or longer.

closed fracture—Break in a bone where the damage has occurred below the surface and has not punctured through the skin.

closed wound—When the skin's surface is not broken and damage and has occurred below the surface.

close friendship—A friendship with emotional ties and the sharing of intimate personal information. Close friends provide support and guidance.

cognitive development—Acquisition and development of skills such as language use, problem solving, and reasoning.

cognitive theory—Theory that addresses a person's ability to use information to make reasonable decisions and create reasonable solutions to problems.

complete streets—Streets that provide for safe, convenient, efficient, and accessible use by all users: motor vehicles, pedestrians of all ages and abilities, people with disabilities, bicyclists, and people who use public transportation.

community—Any group of people who share common characteristics or interests.

community health—Concerned with issues affecting the health and wellness of a specific community of people.

compulsive behavior—Unreasonable behavior done in an attempt to prevent a feared outcome.

conservation—Involves the preservation, protection, and restoration of natural ecosystems.

controllable risk factor—Risk factor that you can act on to change.

coordination—Ability to use your senses together with your body parts or to use two or more body parts together.

coronary circulation—Process of providing the heart tissue with necessary blood and nutrients.

coronary heart disease—When the arteries that send blood to the heart become clogged or hardened.

countermarketing—Methods to reduce demand for a product (like tobacco) by revealing the products' unhealthy aspects or bad effects on society.

criterion-referenced health standards—Fitness ratings used to determine how much fitness is needed to prevent health problems and to achieve wellness.

culturally and linguistically appropriate services (CLAS)—Standards primarily directed at health care organizations, but they are recommended to be used by any health care provider to ensure that a patient understands the treatment within the bounds of their cultural practices.

culture—A set of rules governing behavior in a society. It is influenced by morals, values, and religious beliefs.

cyberbullying—Bullying that takes place through electronic technology, such as cell phones, computers, tablets, and social media sites.

cystic fibrosis—Genetic disorder caused by inheriting a particular defective gene from each parent.

date rape—Forced sex that occurs between two people who already know each other.

dating violence—Various kinds of physical, emotional, and sexual abuse that take place in a dating relationship.

dementia—Loss of brain function over time; affects memory, judgment, behavior, thinking, and language.

depressants—Prescription drugs used to treat anxiety disorders and depression.

depression—Mood disorder characterized by extreme sadness and hopelessness that interferes with normal functioning.

determinant—Factor affecting fitness, health, and wellness.

developmental milestones—Major physical and behavioral signs one expects to see in a normally developing infant or child during a particular period or at a particular age.

developing nations—Countries with poor economies and low standards of living.

diabetes—Disease in which a person's body is unable to regulate sugar levels, leading to an excessively high blood sugar level.

disability—Restriction or impairment that makes a person unable to perform activities or actions in a way that they would normally be performed.

dislocation—When the bone moves away from its normal position near a joint and motion at the joint is lost or severely impaired.

distracted driving—Driving while talking on the phone or texting or while eating, drinking, applying makeup, or engaging in similar activities.

distress—Bad or unhealthy stress that contributes to anxiety and a feeling of being overwhelmed.

diversion program—Program that substitutes classes or training instead of fines or punishments, usually for minor or first-time offenses.

divorce—Legal termination of marriage.

DriveCam—Cameras typically installed in a teenager's car to monitor for erratic driving and send notifications to a parent's or guardian's computer.

driving under the influence (DUI)—Driving while under the influence of alcohol or drugs.

drug addiction—Compulsive use of a substance despite negative or dangerous effects.

drug dependence—When a person needs a drug in order to function.

drug tolerance—Condition that occurs when a person who is a regular and excessive user of an addictive drug needs more of that drug to get the same effect that they used to get with a smaller amount of that same drug.

ecology—Study of living organisms and how they interact with the environment.

electronic medical records (EMR)—Medical records that are stored electronically or digitally to make the exchanging of medical records faster. An EMR system may be part of a stand-alone health information system that allows the secure storage, retrieval, and modification of medical records. The records might include X rays and other diagnostic tests, medical histories, and any other information that may enable the health care provider to help the patient.

emotional wellness—How you feel and how you react to situations as a result of how you feel.

empty calories—Non-nutritional calories in foods that come from solid fat or added sugar.

empty nest—In child-rearing families when the last child leaves home and parents find themselves at home alone.

enabler—People who make it easier (enable you) to engage in a certain habit. Negative enablers make it easier to engage in a destructive habit or make it harder to stay on track with your positive behavior changes.

energy balance—Balance between caloric intake and caloric expenditure.

epidemiologist—Public health worker who tracks, monitors, and studies the incidence and prevalence of diseases and disabilities.

essential amino acid—One of the nine amino acids that must be eaten in the diet for normal protein metabolism to occur.

essential body fat—The minimum amount of body fat that a person needs to maintain health.

ethyl alcohol (ethanol)—Name of the alcohol in beer and liquor.

eustress—Good or healthy stress that motivates a person or provides fulfillment.

extended family—Grandparents, aunts, and uncles.

family role—The role that a person plays in a family including financial duties, household chores, and child rearing. Roles vary from family to family.

farm-to-school—Program that connects schools and local farms with the intention of serving healthy meals at school, improving student nutrition, providing education about growing food and the connections between health and nutrition, and supporting local farmers.

fight-or-flight response—Body's response to stress, which includes an increase in heart rate and blood pressure and elevation of blood sugar level. This prepares the body to either fight or flee from a perceived threat.

FITT formula—Prescription (based on frequency, intensity, time, and type) for appropriate physical activity.

flexibility—Ability to use joints fully through a wide range of motion without injury.

frequency—How often a task is performed; in the FITT formula, it refers to how often physical activity is performed.

frostbite—Condition that results when body tissues become frozen.

functional fitness—Capacity to function effectively when performing normal daily tasks.

fungi—Single-cell or multi-cell plantlike organisms that thrive in warm, humid environments and can infect the skin or other body systems.

gender—The social and cultural roles of people (masculine or feminine).

gene—Basic unit capable of transmitting characteristics from one generation to the next.

generalized anxiety disorder—Class of mental illness that includes intense feelings of worry, fear, or severe uneasiness that do not stem from a specific source or cause.

global health—Health of everyone on our planet.

global warming—Average increase in the temperature of the atmosphere near and above the earth's surface, which can contribute to changes in global climate patterns.

green school—Four main areas, or pillars: strive to be free of toxic or poisonous materials, use sustainable products like recycled paper and promote the 4Rs, promote green spaces around the school, and teach the students about the environment as part of a planned curriculum.

growth spurts—Rapid period of growth when the bones get longer and may ache or cause pain.

harassment—Includes name calling, teasing, or bullying.

health—Freedom from disease and a state of optimal physical, mental, social, intellectual, and spiritual well-being (wellness).

health behavior—Behavior taken by a person to maintain or gain good health.

health behavior contract—Agreement you make with yourself to change a specific health behavior.

health claim—Regulated statement about a food product that relates directly to a health condition or disease such as "heart healthy" or "helps prevent osteoporosis."

health disparities—Differences in health status between people that are related to social or demographic factors such as race, gender, income, or geographic region.

health literacy—Degree to which individuals have the capacity to obtain, process, and understand basic health information and services needed to make appropriate health decisions.

health psychology—Study of human health behaviors.

health-related physical fitness—Parts of physical fitness that help a person stay healthy; includes cardiorespiratory endurance, flexibility, muscular endurance, strength, power, and body composition (fatness).

healthy lifestyle—Way of living and making healthy choices such as eating well and doing regular physical activity that help you prevent illness and enhance your wellness.

Healthy People 2020—Document that identifies health goals to be accomplished by the year 2020.

heat index—Scale that rates the safety of the environment for exercise based on temperature and humidity.

heatstroke—Condition caused by excessive exposure to heat and resulting in a high body temperature and dry skin.

heavy drinking—Consuming two or more drinks per day for men and one or more per day for women over a long period ranging from months to years.

Heimlich maneuver—Used to dislodge a piece of food or other object from a conscious person who is choking.

homicide—Taking the life of another person.

hormones—Also called chemical messengers; they communicate information from one cell to another and coordinate functions throughout the body.

human immunodeficiency virus (HIV)—Virus in bodily fluids of infected people and can be transmitted to others through sexual contact and in blood.

humidity—Relative amount of moisture in the air.

hunger—Physiological drive to eat.

hypertension—Condition in which blood pressure is consistently higher than normal.

hyperthermia—Exceptionally high body temperature often associated with exposure to hot or humid environments.

hypokinetic disease—Health problem caused partly by lack of physical activity.

hypothermia—Abnormally low body temperature often associated with exposure to cold and windy environments.

ignition interlock—Device installed in a motor vehicle that is designed to keep people from driving if they have been drinking. The driver has to blow into a monitor that determines if the driver has been drinking. If so, the vehicle will not start.

illicit drug—Drug that is illegal to use, such as heroin or alcohol, which is illegal for people under age 21.

immune system—Body system that protects against infections.

impulse control—Ability to resist making rapid decisions without fully considering the consequences.

inattention blindness—When a distraction disrupts the driver's attention to the visual environment, distracting both the brain and the eyes.

incidence—Refers to the number of new cases of a disease that occur in a year.

influenza—Common viral infection that attacks the upper respiratory system.

insoluble fiber—Fiber that cannot be broken down by the digestive system.

intensity—Magnitude or vigorousness of a task; in the FITT formula, it refers to how hard you perform a physical activity.

intentional injury—Includes violence, suicide, self-injury, and homicide.

kidney dialysis—Process of filtering the blood through a machine when the kidneys are damaged.

LEED certified—Stands for leadership in energy and environmental design. To be LEED-certified buildings, homes or neighborhoods must meet certain standards for energy efficiency, green building materials, and indoor environmental quality.

licit drug—Drug that is legal to use, such as prescribed drugs or over-the-counter drugs.

localized infections—Infection that affects only one body part or organ.

lower body fat—Fat located in and around the hips and thighs that does not pose significant health risks and may have some protective benefits.

macronutrients—Nutrients needed in large quantities.

manic-depressive disorder—Episodes of depression that alternate with periods of extreme excitability and restlessness (also called bipolar disorder).

manipulation—Indirect pressure to get someone to do something inappropriate or harassing.

maturation—Process of becoming fully grown and developed.

media literacy—Having the skills to analyze, evaluate, and create messages in a variety of media, including knowing how to figure out if you are being manipulated.

medical history—Record of person's current state of health, which includes a list of past diseases, injuries, treatments, medications, and other health and medical information.

medical home—Having a personal physician who provides comprehensive, culturally appropriate care. Your physician also helps to coordinate care with other providers.

medical scientist—Expert who conducts research in hopes of improving overall human health.

mental disorder—Illness that affects the mind and reduces a person's ability to function.

micronutrients—Nutrients needed in smaller quantities (also called non-energy-yielding nutrients).

mindfulness—Purposefully paying attention to what you are doing by being present in the moment.

mineral—Essential nutrients that help regulate the activities of cells.

muscle dysmorphia—Disorder typically seen in males that involves an intense desire to become more muscular accompanied by excessive exercise, extreme dietary practices, or steroid abuse.

muscular endurance—Ability to use your muscles many times without tiring.

negative energy balance—State that the body is in when energy output is greater than energy input.

nephrons—Filtering units of the kidney that remove toxins from the bloodstream.

neurotransmitter—Chemical substance that is produced by a nerve cell that allows nerve cells to complete a circuit to send messages from nerve cells to nerve cells.

nuclear family—A father and mother with children, sometimes referred to as a traditional family.

nutrient claim—Regulated statement about a food product that relates to the nutrition content of the food, such as "low fat" or "fat free."

nutrient-dense food—Foods that contain a lot of vitamins and minerals and fewer calories.

nutritionist—Ungoverned term that anyone can use to claim that they have nutrition information.

obesity—Condition of being especially overweight or high in body fat.

obsession—Unwanted thought or image that takes control of the mind.

1-repetition maximum (1RM)—Test of muscle strength in which you determine how much weight you can lift (or how much resistance you can overcome) in one repetition.

online dating—The process of searching for a romantic partner on the Internet. It is also called Internet dating.

open fracture—Break in a bone where the bone has pushed through the skin's surface.

open wound—Involves damage to the skin's surface and typically involves some bleeding.

opiates—Natural or synthetic drug that has a depressant or calming effect on the central nervous system (originally opiates were only drugs that came from the opium poppy).

over-the-counter (OTC) drug—Drug that can be bought without a doctor's prescription.

overweight—Condition of weighing more than the healthy range.

patent medicine—Drug that is intended to prevent or alleviate the symptoms of a disease or disorder that is produced and owned by a company.

pathogen—Dangerous microorganism that causes a disease is known as a pathogen.

patient education—Planned learning experience that may use a variety of methods such as teaching, counseling, and behavior modification techniques to help patients deal more effectively with any disease, disorder, or health condition.

peer pressure—The pressure an individual can feel from peers. It can be positive where peers serve as role models encouraging us to try new things and be better in some way, or it can be negative by encouraging us to make poor decisions and behave badly, thus ultimately leading to negative consequences.

personal health—Choices and actions you take as an individual (related to health and wellness) that affect your health. Some of these include regularly brushing and flossing your teeth, washing your hands before meals and after using the bathroom, and getting enough sleep.

personality—Unique mixture of qualities and traits that distinguish you from others.

phenotype—Visible characteristics of an organism resulting from the interaction between its genetic makeup and the environment.

phobias—Intense fears and anxieties that relate to a specific situation or object.

Physical Activity Pyramid—Diagram or model that describes the various types of physical activity that produce good fitness, health, and wellness.

Physical Activity Readiness Questionnaire (PAR-Q)—Seven-question assessment of medical and physical readiness that should be taken before beginning a regular physical activity program for health and wellness.

physical development—Changes in weight, height, motor skills, and sensory perceptions as a person develops.

physical fitness—Capacity of your body systems to work together efficiently to allow you to be healthy and effectively perform activities of daily living.

physiological age—How well the body systems are aging relative to what is expected at a particular age.

platonic friendship—A relationship, often with a member of the opposite sex, in which there is no romantic involvement.

positive energy balance—State that the body is in when energy intake is greater than energy output.

post-traumatic stress disorder—A person who has experienced or witnessed a traumatic event, such as a war or terrorist attack, experiences intense flashbacks or nightmares that produce high anxiety and may interfere with sleep, concentration, and relationships.

power—Capacity to use strength quickly; involves both strength and speed.

prescription drug—Drug prescribed by a doctor to help treat illnesses or symptoms, such as pain and discomfort.

prevalence—Refers to the number of existing cases of disease and disability.

primary prevention—Actions and services designed to reduce risk and avoid health problems.

principle of overload—The most basic law of physical activity, which states that the only way to produce fitness and health benefits through physical activity is to require your body to do more than it normally does.

principle of progression—Principle stating that the amount and intensity of your exercise should be increased gradually.

principle of specificity—Principle stating that the type of exercise you perform determines the type of benefit you receive.

priority healthy lifestyle choice—One of the key lifestyle choices (regular physical activity, sound nutrition, and stress management) that help you prevent disease, get and stay fit, and enjoy a good quality of life.

product placement—Form of advertising where products are placed where they are not generally associated with advertising, such as movies, TV shows, music videos, or news programs.

progressive resistance exercise (PRE)—Exercise that increases resistance (overload) until you have the amount of muscle fitness you want; also called progressive resistance training (PRT).

Prohibition—The 18th amendment (1920), which made the sale and distribution of alcohol illegal until it was repealed by the 21st Amendment in 1933.

proprioceptive neuromuscular facilitation (PNF)—Flexibility exercise using proprioceptive neuromuscular facilitation; a variation of static stretching that involves contracting a muscle before stretching it.

protein—Provides the body with energy and builds, repairs, and maintains body cells. Protein is easily found in animal products.

protozoan—Large single-cell organism that can move through the body in search of food. It attacks the body by releasing enzymes or toxins that can destroy or damage cells.

psychoactive drugs—Drugs that change a person's perceptions or mood.

psychotherapy—Method of treating mental disorders that involve talking about your condition and related issues with a mental health provider.

puberty—Time when the pituitary gland triggers production of testosterone in boys and estrogen and progesterone in girls. Puberty typically begins between ages 9 and 12 for girls and between ages 11 and 14 for boys and includes such body changes as hair growth around the genitals, menstruation in girls, and sperm production in boys.

public health—Practice of preventing disease and protecting, improving, and promoting good health within groups of people using research, policies, and health communications. Public health is sometimes referred to as population health because it focuses on groups of people in a community, state, or country.

public health scientist—Expert who studies disease prevention and wellness promotion in communities.

pulmonary circulation—Process of moving blood from the heart to the lungs and back to the heart again.

reaction time—Amount of time it takes to move once you recognize the need to act.

reasoning skills—Ability to solve problems and make decisions. Changes allow you to think more critically and evaluate ideas more carefully.

reframing—Method of viewing a situation or event differently, such as instead of complaining about having to wait in a long line, view it as a time to listen to music or audiobooks or a time to tweet, text, e-mail, or phone a friend.

refusal skills—Techniques for saying no and sticking with it.

registered dietitian (RD)—Formally educated and licensed nutrition practitioner.

resting metabolic rate—Calories used each day to maintain normal physiological function.

risk factor—Any action or condition that increases your chances of developing a disease or health condition.

road rage—Emotional outbursts that occur while driving.

role model—A person who imparts values and information to others.

sanitary landfill—Site where waste is isolated from the rest of the environment. It is daily covered in layers of dirt to reduce attracting birds and rodents. When sanitary landfills are full, the land can be reclaimed as a park or recreation area and sometimes the methane gas that the landfill produces can be used to produce electricity.

satiety—Comfortable state between meals without feeling hungry or full.

saturated fat—Fat that is more dangerous to health and comes mostly from animal sources.

secondary prevention—Recognizing risks or the beginning of problems and intervening before serious illnesses or effects take over.

secondary sex characteristics—Physical changes that occur during puberty; the start of ovulation in girls and sperm production in boys.

secondhand smoke—Tobacco smoke that is inhaled involuntarily or passively by someone who is not smoking. Also referred to as sidestream smoke or environmental tobacco smoke.

self-assessment—Test that helps you figure out your current health status and set goals for good health.

self-care—A person's decisions and behaviors in coping with a health problem, or improving health, or preventing certain health problems. Self-care is in addition to medical care, not instead of medical care.

self-esteem—How a person perceives oneself.

self-management skill—Skill that helps you adopt a healthy lifestyle now and throughout your life.

self-regulation skills—Self-management skills.

separation—A test period for married couples to separate that is not legally recognized.

sex—Refers to the biological factors (male or female) that influence your fitness, health, and wellness.

sexual coercion—The use of force, manipulation, or intimidation to get someone to participate in unwanted sexual activity.

skeletal muscle—Muscle attached to bones that makes movement possible.

skill-related physical fitness—Parts of fitness that help a person perform well in sports and activities requiring certain skills; includes agility, balance, coordination, reaction time, and speed.

skills for healthy living—Skills that can help you accomplish a desired goal or keep doing a good thing that you already do.

sleep apnea—Disorder that results in poor sleep or inability to sleep, characterized by pauses in breathing or shallow breathing during sleep.

SMART goal—Goal that is specific, measurable, attainable, realistic, and timely.

smokeless tobacco—Tobacco that is not smoked, such as chewing tobacco and snuff.

smooth muscle—Involuntarily controlled tissue found in the walls of hollow organs.

social marketing—Applying commercial marketing concepts and techniques to noncommercial purposes.

socioemotional development—Emotional and social development; markers of growth are self-esteem, empathy, and friendship.

soluble fiber—Fiber that can be partially broken down by the digestive system.

speed—Ability to perform a movement or cover a distance in a short time.

spirituality—Person's sense of purpose and meaning in life, beyond material values.

sprain—Injury to a ligament.

stages of health behavior change—Precontemplation, contemplation, preparation, action, and maintenance.

stakeholder—Someone who has an interest or concern in something.

state of being—Overall condition of a person.

stimulants—Prescription drugs most often used to treat ADHD.

storage fat—Additional body fat. Up to a certain point, it does not appear to be harmful for health.

strain—Injury to a tendon or muscle.

strength—Amount of force your muscles can produce.

stressor—Anything that causes wear and tear on the body, whether physically or mentally.

stroke—Condition in which the supply of oxygen to the brain is severely reduced or cut off resulting in damage to the brain.

structure/function claim—Statement found on a food or supplement, such as vitamins, that relates to a function or specific structure in the body such as "improves eyesight" or "builds strong bones." These claims are not regulated by the FDA.

sudden infant death syndrome (SIDS)—Sudden and unexpected death of an apparently healthy infant.

suicide—Ending one's own life.

support group—People with common diagnoses and conditions who provide informational, emotional, and moral support for one another.

systemic circulation—Process of delivering blood to all areas of the body aside from the heart and lungs.

systemic infections—Infections that affect the entire body, not just a single organ or body part.

target ceiling—Your upper recommended limit of activity for optimally promoting fitness and achieving health and wellness.

target fitness zone—Correct range of physical activity; exercise above your threshold of training and below your target ceiling.

telemedicine—Medical information exchanged electronically from one site to another to improve a person's health status.

tertiary prevention—Treatment and rehabilitation after a person is sick to avoid further illness or death.

threshold of training—Minimum amount of overload you need in order to build physical fitness.

time—Length of a task; in the FITT formula (first *T*), it refers to the optimal length of an activity session designed to improve fitness and promote health and wellness.

toxic food environment—A place where high-calorie, high-fat food is abundant and inexpensive.

traditional family—A father and mother with children, sometimes referred to as a nuclear family.

traumatic brain injury—Caused by a bump, blow, or jolt to the head and is a penetrating head injury that disrupts the normal function of the brain. Most traumatic brain injuries (TBIs) are concussions.

type—Specific kind of task; in the FITT formula (second *T*), it refers to the specific kind of physical activity that is performed.

uncontrollable risk factor—Risk factor that you cannot change.

unintentional injury—Injury caused by unplanned events such as automobile crashes, poisonings, fires, and drowning.

unsaturated fat—Fats that is less dangerous to health and comes mostly from plant sources.

upper body fat—Fat located in and around the abdominal organs that is associated with high blood cholesterol and heart disease risk.

vitamins—Organic compounds essential for normal growth, functioning, and maintenance of the body.

viruses—Smallest of all pathogens; they take enter a cell and take over normal functioning.

warm-up—A series of activities that prepares the body for more vigorous exercise.

weekend warrior—Person who does no regular physical activity on most days of the week but then does a lot of activity on one day.

weight cycling—Repeated bouts of gaining and losing weight.

wellness—Positive component of health that involves having a good quality of life and a good sense of well-being as exhibited by a positive outlook.

wind-chill factor—Index used to determine when dangerously low temperatures and unsafe wind conditions exist.

withdrawal—Physical sickness that a person with a physical dependence (addiction) develops when he or she can't or isn't able to take the drug to which he or she is addicted.

World Health Organization (WHO)—Organization that focuses on public health. They issued a statement proclaiming that good health is not merely the absence of disease or illness; rather, it is a more complete state of being that includes wellness.

Index